THE THEORY OF THE
T

In this book, Robert Doran offers the first in-depth treatment of the major theories of the sublime, from the ancient Greek treatise *On the Sublime* (attributed to "Longinus"), and its reception in early modern literary theory, to the philosophical accounts of Burke and Kant. Doran explains how and why the sublime became a key concept of modern thought and shows how the various theories of sublimity are united by a common structure – the paradoxical experience of being at once overwhelmed and exalted – and a common concern: the preservation of a notion of transcendence in the face of the secularization of modern culture. Combining intellectual history with literary theory and philosophical analysis, his book provides a new, searching, and multilayered account of a concept that continues to stimulate thought about our responses to art, nature, and human events.

ROBERT DORAN is Associate Professor of French and Comparative Literature at the University of Rochester. He is the author of *The Ethics of Theory: Philosophy, History, Literature* (forthcoming) and the editor of three books: *Philosophy of History After Hayden White* (2013); Hayden White's *The Fiction of Narrative* (2010); and René Girard's *Mimesis and Theory* (2008).

THE THEORY OF THE SUBLIME
FROM LONGINUS TO KANT

ROBERT DORAN

University of Rochester

CAMBRIDGE
UNIVERSITY PRESS

CAMBRIDGE
UNIVERSITY PRESS

University Printing House, Cambridge CB2 8BS, United Kingdom

Cambridge University Press is part of the University of Cambridge.

It furthers the University's mission by disseminating knowledge in the pursuit of
education, learning and research at the highest international levels of excellence.

www.cambridge.org
Information on this title: www.cambridge.org/9781107499157

First published 2015

A catalogue record for this publication is available from the British Library

Library of Congress Cataloguing in Publication data
Doran, Robert, 1968–
The theory of the sublime from Longinus to Kant / Robert Doran, University of Rochester.
pages   cm
Includes bibliographical references and index.
ISBN 978-1-107-10153-1
1. Sublime, The.   I. Title.
BH301.S7D67   2015
111'.85–dc23
2014048652

ISBN 978-1-107-10153-1 Hardback
ISBN 978-1-107-49915-7 Paperback

For my father:

Francis Yates Doran (1918–2010)

Contents

Acknowledgments

This book would not have seen the light of day without the guidance, encouragement, and insights of Hayden White and Jean Bessière. Although it bears little resemblance to the doctoral thesis they supervised many years ago, this book is nevertheless a testament to their scholarly example and deep understanding of literary theory, philosophy, and intellectual history. I greatly appreciate their unwavering support and friendship over the years.

René Girard has been an important interlocutor for this project, as well as a great teacher and friend. My approach to philosophy was shaped in large part by Richard Rorty's seminars at Stanford University and discussions in his office. Jean-Pierre Dupuy's courses on philosophy at Stanford and his research group at the CREA, Ecole Polytechnique, were an inspiration. I greatly benefited from Jacques Derrida's seminars at the EHESS – part of what would become the Burke chapter was given as an oral presentation in his 1999–2000 seminar – as well as from a conversation with him about the sublime during a ride from the San Jose airport. Annual meetings in a Parisian café with Samuel Weber, whom I met as a participant in his Paris Program in Critical Theory, constantly challenged me to rethink my concepts and methods. Conversations with Karl Heinz Bohrer about "suddenness" helped me to understand the temporal dimension of sublimity. Numerous exchanges with Marcel Hénaff have broadened my knowledge of philosophy and anthropology.

Paul Crowther read the entire manuscript, offering copious comments and suggestions that helped me to clarify my overall conception and presentation. His scholarship on Kant, especially his pioneering *The Kantian Sublime: From Morality to Art*, has been a constant inspiration. I am especially indebted to Stephen Halliwell, whose thorough reading of the Longinus material led to vital improvements. Halliwell's magisterial *The Aesthetics of Mimesis: Ancient Texts and Modern Problems* was a model for this project; for it showed how an idea originating in ancient thought could be brought into fruitful dialogue with modern conceptions and how a diverse and contested concept like mimesis could be treated in a unified way. Marsh McCall and David Glidden also provided stimulating commentary on the Longinus material. I am very grateful to Allen Wood, who read an early version of the Kant chapters with a sharp critical eye. Many thanks to Pierre Keller, Samantha Matherne, Sandra Shapshay, and Ralf Meerbote, all of whom offered valuable advice on aspects of the Kant material. Larry F. Norman gave me crucial suggestions on the Boileau chapter. David Quint's comments on the Boileau and Dennis chapters were as meticulous as they were enlightening. John Briggs generously shared his thoughts on the chapters on Dennis and Burke.

I owe the idea for writing a book on the sublime to Massimo Lollini, who, knowing my philosophical interests, urged me to take a seminar he was teaching on "Vico and the Settecento." Lollini's wonderful book, *Le muse, le maschere e il sublime: G. B. Vico e la poesia nell'età della "Ragione spiegata,"* was an early inspiration.

I would like to thank the Office of the Provost at the University of Rochester for a subvention that covered the permissions for the image that appears on the cover. Many thanks to my colleagues at the University of Rochester for their support, encouragement, and friendship.

Hilary Gaskin, my editor at Cambridge University Press, has been wonderfully patient and supportive. I am grateful for her kind attention and guidance, as well as for the invaluable insights and suggestions provided by the two anonymous readers of the manuscript. I must also thank Beatrice Rehl, who showed initial interest in the project before she was promoted to Director of Humanities Publishing at Cambridge University Press.

Finally, I do not know how to express my gratitude to Sabine, the mother of our twin boys Max and Adrian, who made heroic efforts to keep the project on track amid the challenges of raising two very energetic *Jungs*.

My father, Francis Yates Doran (1918–2010), passed away during the writing of this book. Only when composing the eulogy for his funeral service did I realize how much he inspired this project. No one better understood the sublime in music, as when he entered an enraptured state while listening to Luciano Pavarotti's rendition of Puccini's "Nessun dorma" or Arthur Rubinstein's RCA recording of Chopin's *Ballade in g minor*. It is to his memory that this book is dedicated.

Key to abbreviations and translations

Except for works by Plato, Aristotle, and Longinus, citations from the texts listed below are indicated parenthetically and by abbreviation. Citations from Longinus's *On the Sublime* (*Peri hypsous*) are indicated by chapter and line number and are taken from the translation by D. A. Russell in *Ancient Literary Criticism: The Principal Texts in New Translations*, ed. D. A. Russell and M. Winterbottom (Oxford: Oxford University Press, 1972), 460–503. Citations from Plato and Aristotle are indicated by Bekker Number. Citations from Aristotle's *Poetics* are from the translation by Stephen Halliwell, in *Aristotle* Poetics, *Longinus* On the Sublime, *Demetrius* On Style (Cambridge, MA: Harvard University Press, 1995, Loeb Classical Library), 3–141. Citations from Aristotle's *Rhetoric* are from the translation by George A. Kennedy (Oxford: Oxford University Press, 1991). Citations of Plato are from *Complete Works*, edited by John M. Cooper (Indianapolis: Hackett Publishing Company, 1997). All quotations from the Bible are from the King James version.

APP   *Anthropology from a Pragmatic Point of View* (1798). In: Immanuel Kant, *Anthropology, History, Education*. Ed. Gunter Zoller and Robert B. Louden. Cambridge: Cambridge University Press, 2007.

CF   *The Conflict of the Faculties* (1798). Trans. Mary Gregor and Robert Anchor. In: Immanuel Kant, *Religion and Natural Theology*. Cambridge: Cambridge University Press, 1996.

CPaR   *Critique of Practical Reason* (1788). Trans. Mary Gregor. In: Immanuel Kant, *Practical Philosophy*. Ed. Mary J. Gregor. Intro. Allen Wood. Cambridge: Cambridge University Press, 1999.

CPuR   *Critique of Pure Reason* (1781/1787). Immanuel Kant, *Critique of Pure Reason*. Ed. and trans. Paul Guyer and Allen Wood. Cambridge: Cambridge University Press, 1998.

CPJ   *Critique of the Power of Judgment* (1790). Immanuel Kant, *Critique of the Power of Judgment*. Ed. Paul Guyer. Trans. Paul Guyer and Eric Matthews. Cambridge: Cambridge University Press, 2000.

CW   *The Critical Works of John Dennis*. 2 vols. Ed. Edward Niles Hooker. Baltimore: Johns Hopkins University Press, 1943.

E   *A Philosophical Enquiry into the Origin of Our Ideas of the Sublime and Beautiful* (1757/1759). Edmund Burke. Ed., intro., and notes J. T. Boulton. New York: Routledge, 1958/2008.

FI   *First Introduction*. In: Immanuel Kant, *Critique of the Power of Judgment* (1790). Ed. Paul Guyer. Trans. Paul Guyer and Eric Matthews. Cambridge: Cambridge University Press, 2000.

G   *Groundwork of the Metaphysics of Morals* (1785). Ed. and trans. Mary Gregor. In: Immanuel Kant, *Practical Philosophy*. Ed. Mary J. Gregor. Intro. Allen Wood. Cambridge: Cambridge University Press, 1999.

LA   *Lectures on Anthropology*. Immanuel Kant, *Lectures on Anthropology*. Ed. Robert B. Louden and Allen W. Wood. Cambridge: Cambridge University Press, 2013.

O   *Observations on the Feeling of the Beautiful and Sublime* (1764). Intro. and trans. Paul Guyer. In: Immanuel Kant, *Anthropology, History, Education*. Ed. Gunter Zoller and Robert B. Louden. Cambridge: Cambridge University Press, 2007.

NS   *The New Science of Giambattista Vico* (1725/1744). Trans. Thomas Goddard Bergin & Max Harold Fisch. Ithaca, NY: Cornell University Press, 1968. (References are to section numbers, rather than to page numbers.)

TS   *Traité du Sublime* (1674). In: Longinus, *Traité du sublime*. Trans. (1674) and Préface (1674–1701) Nicolas Boileau. Including Boileau, *Réflexions critiques* (selections). Ed., notes, and intro. Francis Goyet. Paris: Le Livre de Poche, 1995.

WB   *Works of Monsieur Boileau*. 2 vols. Ed. and trans. John Ozell and Pierre Desmaizeaux. London, 1712.

Introduction

We are reasserting man's natural desire for the exalted, for a concern with our relationship with absolute emotions.
— Barnett Newman, "The Sublime Is Now" (1948)[1]

We also speak of the beauty of Newton's unification of the movements of the planets and the movements of projectiles. We saw the discovery of DNA offers us a "beautiful" way to explain processes of biological evolution. The sublime, by contrast, neither integrates nor unifies. It transcends.
— Richard Rorty[2]

The sublime is one of the most important and often-discussed concepts in philosophical aesthetics, literary theory, and art history. Meaning "loftiness," "height," or "elevation" and typically associated with notions of ecstasy, grandeur, terror, awe, astonishment, wonder, and admiration, the sublime refers at once to a specific *discourse*, the *theory* of sublimity, and to an *experience*,[3] that of *transcendence*, which has its origins in religious belief and practice.[4] As this study will contend, it is the tension between a literary-aesthetic concept and an experience with mystical-religious resonances that motivates the critical concept of sublimity, creating multilayered nexuses between religion, art, nature, and society.

This study starts from the presupposition that the critical horizon and reception of the sublime is framed in large measure by three classic or

---

[1] Newman, *Barnett Newman: Selected Writings and Interviews*, 173.
[2] *Take Care of Freedom and Truth Will Take Care of Itself: Interviews with Richard Rorty*, ed. Eduardo Mendicta, 70.
[3] Of course, "experience" has its own discursive norms, which will be elucidated herein. However, unlike the mystic's experiences, which are esoteric, aesthetic experience is shared.
[4] As Baldine Saint Girons notes, "the 'first men' no doubt had no reason to distinguish aesthetic values from religious values" (*Fiat Lux: Une philosophie du sublime*, 25, my translation).

I

foundational theories, those of Longinus, Edmund Burke, and
Immanuel Kant,[5] and that a searching exploration of these and two
other key or pivotal theories, those of Nicolas Boileau and John Dennis,
will allow for a deeper understanding of a fundamental question: how
did a term discussed in an obscure Greek fragment become one of the
most important and consequential concepts in modern thought? The
historical approach to the topic, as exemplified in Samuel Holt Monk's
seminal 1935 monograph *The Sublime: A Study of Critical Theories in
XVIII-Century England*, has given us valuable insights.[6] The present
study contends, however, that such a question requires a systematic
treatment of the sublime as a unified discourse.

The twofold aim of this book is to provide a detailed and analytical
treatment of the key theories of sublimity, the first such comprehensive
account in a single volume,[7] while at the same time elucidating what it was
about this concept that allowed it to play an outsized role in modern
thought. Thus, although this book builds on the rich literature on the
topic, it also departs from the typological or more localized approach that
characterizes much of the scholarly engagement with the sublime, namely
the taking of a particular period, aesthetic movement, author, or theme
as a starting point (for example, the neoclassical sublime, the eighteenth-
century sublime, the Romantic sublime, the natural sublime, the religious
sublime, the rhetorical sublime, the aesthetic sublime, the Kantian

---

[5] Even a cursory look at how the subject is taught in university courses reveals that these theories are
considered essential.
[6] Although the title would appear to limit this book to English sources of the eighteenth-century,
Monk's inclusion of chapters on Longinus and Boileau and of a substantial summary of Kant's
theory of sublimity lent the work an aura of comprehensiveness and authority that has yet to be
surpassed. Defining "the sublime" as a distinct area of inquiry, with its own history and rationale, this
pioneering effort effectively shaped all subsequent attempts to characterize the concept's origins and
significance. Monk's legacy is, however, ambiguous: on the one hand, he endowed the discourse of
sublimity with a certain coherence; but, on the other, he endorsed or established the division that has
been the greatest obstacle to a unified conception of sublimity, namely that between the so-called
rhetorical sublime and the *aesthetic* sublime: between Longinus's treatise and the literary criticism
directly inspired by him, on one side, and, on the other, the philosophical aesthetics that developed
in the eighteenth century and that seized on the sublime as a counterpoint to the beautiful. I address
this in detail below. For more recent historical approaches to the topic, see Dietmar Till, *Das doppelte
Erhabene* (2006) and the forthcoming book by James Porter, *The Sublime in Antiquity* (I have seen
only the table of contents of this work, which indicates some areas of contact with the present study).
Historical theorists such as Hayden White (in *The Content of the Form: Narrative Discourse and
Historical Representation* [1986]) and F. R. Ankersmit (in *Sublime Historical Experience* [2005]) have
also contributed to the debate about the modern significance of the sublime.
[7] I am thus distinguishing my study from the survey accounts, which treat a wider range of theories,
but in a more disparate, less focused manner, and also from the monograph accounts of a single
author (such as Burke and Kant), which obviously have more scope for greater detail.

sublime, and so on).[8] Such an approach is partly a function of the interests and competencies of individual scholars and theorists; but it is also a reflection of the widely held view that the historical vicissitudes of the sublime, coupled with the sheer range and multiplicity of its uses, argue against the feasibility or even the possibility of an overarching or systematic account, as if coherence in more limited contexts was all that could be hoped for. One critic speaks, for example, of the "multifariousness of the concept of sublimity."[9] Indeed, over its long history, and particularly in more recent criticism, the sublime has often been seen as torn between mutually opposed categories: ancient/modern, classical/Romantic, rational/irrational, empirical/transcendental, material/metaphysical, ethical/aesthetic, textual/psychological. What commonality justifies the use of a single term across such divergent viewpoints and discursive contexts? But the question can also be reversed: what is it about the concept of the sublime that inspired some of Europe's most important and influential critics and philosophers to devote considerable effort to its elucidation and theorization?

This study also differs from efforts to introduce coherence into the discourse of sublimity via an extrinsic theory, namely psychoanalysis or poststructuralism.[10] Instead, it contends that the sublime possesses an intrinsic critical function, and that an argument for its unity can be launched from the perspective of the theory of sublimity itself. This approach has the advantage of permitting a broad appreciation of the multiple functions and dimensions of this concept, in particular as these relate to the "subjective turn" of modern thought.

---

[8] See, for example: T. R. Henn, *Longinus and English Criticism* (1934); Jules Brody, *Boileau and Longinus* (1958); Théodore Litman, *Le Sublime en France: 1660–1714* (1971); David B. Morris, *The Religious Sublime: Christian Poetry and the Critical Tradition* (1972); Thomas Weiskel, *The Romantic Sublime: Studies in the Structure and Psychology of Transcendence* (1976); Paul Crowther, *The Kantian Sublime: From Morality to Art* (1989); Suzanne Guerlac, *The Impersonal Sublime: Hugo, Baudelaire, Lautreamont* (1990); Frances Ferguson, *Solitude and the Sublime: Romanticism and the Aesthetics of Individuation* (1992); Dominique Peyrache-Leborgne, *La poétique du sublime: de la fin des Lumières au Romantisme* (1997); Robert R. Clewis, *The Kantian Sublime and the Revelation of Freedom* (2009).

[9] David Morris, *The Religious Sublime*, 8. Jean Bessière speaks of the "difficulté de la cohérence" of the discourse of sublimity ("Le Sublime aujourd'hui: D'un discours sur le pouvoir de l'art et de la littérature, et de sa possible réécriture," 420). Some have even wondered if a theory of the sublime is possible. See Jane Forsey, "Is a Theory of the Sublime Possible?" and Guy Sircello, "How Is a Theory of the Sublime Possible?"

[10] For a psychoanalytic account, see Thomas Weiskel, *The Romantic Sublime: Studies in the Structure and Psychology of Transcendence* (1976) and Harold Bloom, *The Anxiety of Influence: A Theory of Poetry* (1973); for a poststructuralist approach, see Peter de Bolla, *The Discourse of the Sublime: Readings in History, Aesthetics, and the Subject* (1989) and Frances Ferguson, *Solitude and the Sublime: Romanticism and the Aesthetics of Individuation* (1992). Ferguson describes her account as "sympathetic to deconstruction" (*Solitude and the Sublime*, 9).

Indeed, it is the relation between the sublime and modern subjectivity that is at the heart of this work. For I argue that what unites the key theories of sublimity, such as they were understood and articulated during the early modern period (1674–1790),[11] is a common structure – the paradoxical experience of being at once *overwhelmed* and *exalted* – and a common concern: the preservation of a notion of transcendence in the face of the secularization of modern culture. While it may be a commonplace that the sublime denotes a kind of transcendence (the literal translation of Longinus's term *hypsos* is "elevation"), what has not been adequately explored is the relation between transcendence and the power of the mind in the sublime. Indeed, it is this connection that allows the sublime to play a constitutive role in the development of modern subjectivity. Thus, by tracing in a systematic and focused manner the transcendence-structure of sublimity (defined in more detail below), following its developments, transformations, and dispersals across a variety of intellectual contexts, this study aims to bring out its multilayered significance – historical, religious, sociological, psychological, political, semantic, and anthropological – for modern thought.[12] While some of these aspects have formed the basis for various theses regarding the discourse of sublimity, this examination regards them as effects or extensions of a common transcendence-structure.

Due to space constraints, this study concentrates on the origins and establishing of the critical concept of sublimity, beginning with the ancient Greek fragment *On the Sublime*, attributed to "Longinus," and its reinterpretation in neoclassical and baroque poetics, to the seminal theories of Burke and Kant, the latter of whom is generally considered to be the most important and consequential theorist of the sublime. Although for a long time neglected by scholars and philosophers,[13] Kant's theory of sublimity has become, over the past forty years or so, the subject of a veritable avalanche of critical reexamination, both in Continental and

---

[11] That is, from the publication of Boileau's translation of Longinus in 1674 to the appearance of Kant's third *Critique* in 1790.

[12] Perhaps the closest analog to what I endeavor to do in this book is Stephen Halliwell's magisterial *The Aesthetics of Mimesis: Ancient Texts and Modern Problems* (2002), which discusses the Western tradition of mimesis in terms of an oscillation between the poles of "world-reflective" and "world-creating" mimeticism.

[13] Paul Guyer recounts: "In *Kant and the Claims of Taste* [1979], I argued that Kant's analysis of the sublime does not materially add to his argument for the intersubjective validity of aesthetic judgments, and, narrowing speaking, that may be true. But more broadly, I wrote that Kant's analysis of the sublime 'will not be of much interest to modern sensibilities, and thus ... most of what we can or will learn from Kant must come from his discussion of judgments of beauty.' No statement in that book has come in for more criticism than this remark, and justifiably so. By way of

Anglo-American thought. Indeed, recent reassessments of Kant's third *Critique* have led to a great revival of philosophical interest in the sublime, first in French thought, in works by Jacques Derrida and Jean-François Lyotard published in the 1970s and 1980s,[14] and then in Anglophone philosophy and intellectual history, beginning in 1989 with Paul Crowther's pioneering *The Kantian Sublime: From Morality to Art*, and followed, most notably, by John Zammito (1992), Paul Guyer (1993), and Henry Allison (2001).[15] This revival can be said to have reached a fever pitch in the late 1980s, with the almost simultaneous publication of several collective volumes in the United States, France, and Germany.[16] The stream of commentary on Kant's theory of sublimity has continued well into the first two decades of the 2000s and shows no signs of abating.[17]

The exploration of Kant's theory offered in Part III of this volume is informed by an integral reading of Kant's oeuvre, including his pre-Critical writings, his lectures on anthropology, his moral philosophy, and, of course, the third of his great *Critiques*, to which multiple chapters are devoted. Examining Kant's place in the discourse of sublimity and aesthetic thought more generally, this study highlights the specifically subjective meaning of Kant's account. For what both Anglophone and French writing on Kant's concept of sublimity have either ignored or not sufficiently emphasized, in my view, is the importance of the idea of

---

mitigating circumstances, I can only plead that my dismissal of the sublime accurately reflected, not its centrality in Kant's own thought, but at least the prevailing attitude in the analytical aesthetics of the preceding two decades" (*Kant and the Experience of Freedom*, 187). This antisublime sentiment seemed in fact to be the norm as late as the 1991 collection *Kant's Aesthetics*, edited by Ralf Meerbote and published by the North American Kant Society, in which there is no discussion of the sublime.

[14] See Jacques Derrida, *La vérité en peinture* (1978, translated as *The Truth in Painting*, 1987) and Jean-François Lyotard, *Leçons sur l'analytique du sublime* (1991, translated as *Lessons on the Analytic of the Sublime*, 1994). In this vein, see also, Paul de Man, *Aesthetic Ideology* (1996).

[15] See John Zammito, *The Genesis of Kant's* Critique of Judgment (1992); Paul Guyer, *Kant and the Experience of Freedom* (1993); Henry Allison, *Kant's Theory of Taste* (2001). Prior to Crowther's 1989 study, there are no monographs on the Kantian sublime in English. Thus Crowther's 1989 work, along with Lyotard's seminal 1991 study (tr. 1994), appeared to have opened the floodgates, as it were, for the reconsideration of Kant's theory of the sublime in English.

[16] See Jean-François Courtine, Michel Deguy, Eliane Escoubas, Philippe Lacoue-Labarthe, Jean-François Lyotard, Louis Marin, Jean-Luc Nancy, and Jacob Rogozinski, *Du Sublime* (1988) (English translation: *Of the Sublime: Presence in Question* [1993]); *New Literary History* (The Sublime and the Beautiful: Reconsiderations) 16.2 (1985); *Merkur* (Die Sprache des Erhabene. Das Bild des Erhabenen. Die erhabene Tat.) 487–488 (1989); and *Revue d'Histoire Littéraire de la France* (Le Sublime) 68.1 (1986).

[17] I could mention Kirk Pillow's *Sublime Understanding: Aesthetic Reflection in Kant and Hegel* (2000), Rodolphe Gasché's *The Idea of Form, Rethinking Kant's Aesthetics* (2003), F. R. Ankersmit's *Sublime Historical Experience* (2005), Robert Clewis's *The Kantian Sublime and the Revelation of Freedom* (2009), Sanford Budick's *Kant and Milton* (2010), and Emily Brady's *The Sublime in Modern Philosophy: Aesthetics, Ethics, and Nature* (2013).

sublimity of mind – aesthetic high-mindedness, heroic subjectivity – an idea inherited from Longinus (his concept of *megalophrosynê*). Kant notes that "it is the *disposition of the mind* [*Geistesstimmung*] resulting from a certain representation occupying the reflective judgment, but not the object, which is to be called sublime" (CPJ, 5:250, my emphasis).[18]

My choice of figures to include as the "key" theorists of sublimity (insofar as the emergence of this notion in modern thought is concerned) may strike some as arbitrary. While few readers will quarrel with the multi-chapter treatments of Longinus and Kant, or with the substantial chapter on Burke, the inclusion of chapters on Nicolas Boileau (1636–1711) and the somewhat obscure English writer and critic John Dennis (1657–1734) requires some justification. While Boileau is well known as the popularizer of Longinus as well as of the concept of the sublime, he is not generally seen as having contributed much of substance to the theory of sublimity – hence the slight attention accorded to him, even in the surveys or monographs on the sublime.[19] I argue, however, that Boileau's role in the development of the theory of sublimity has been vastly underappreciated by recent criticism and that the modern interpretation of sublimity owes a great deal to Boileau's efforts.[20]

John Dennis's role in the development of the theory of sublimity, while less public than Boileau's, is no less important. For it is Dennis's literary criticism – in particular his highlighting of the role of emotion in Longinus's theory of sublimity and formulation of a notion of complex pleasure ("delightful horror") more than twenty years before Joseph Addison[21] – that creates the conditions under which the transition to the "aesthetic" apprehension of sublimity in philosophical aesthetics becomes possible. As Monk observes, "the presence of emotion in art is the point of departure for the eighteenth-century sublime."[22] Breaking with

---

[18] It should also be noted that many see Kant's idea of sublimity as a term that exclusively applies to the mind and its products to be highly problematic. Most recently (2013), Brady has observed how "it might appear that the Kantian sublime is too humanistic, and perhaps too anthropocentric, to serve as a plausible theory for understanding aesthetic appreciation of nature" (*The Sublime in Modern Philosophy*, 92).

[19] For example, Philip Shaw's survey *The Sublime* refers to Boileau only once and in passing. Boileau is mentioned three times in a cursory manner in Weiskel (1976) and is completely absent from Ferguson (1992). Admittedly, these last two focus mostly on British Romanticism, but they also aspire to treat the "theory of the sublime" more generally.

[20] However, I simultaneously argue against those who see the Longinian sublime as an "invention of Boileau." Boileau is rather the first interpreter to truly understand Longinus's theory of sublimity.

[21] Addison simply repeats Dennis when he speaks of a "pleasing kind of horror" in his *Spectator* articles of 1712 (see Addison, *Critical Essays from the Spectator*, No. 419).

[22] Monk, *The Sublime*, 14. Monk does indeed devote a chapter to Dennis in his study, and Dennis plays an outsized role in Morris's *The Religious Sublime*. Most recently, Emily Brady's *The Sublime*

neoclassical aesthetics, Dennis's singular emphasis on violent emotion represents the beginning of a bifurcation in the theory of the sublime, with one strand orientated toward the *pathetic* (terror, the irrational, the sensational) and the other toward the *noetic* (the mental, the intellectual, the rational), Burke being the primary exponent of the first and Kant of the second.[23] Indeed, Burke's theory of sublimity would have been quite impossible without Dennis's emphasis on sacred terror, and Kant's association of sublimity with reason was in large part an effort to reclaim a viable idea of transcendence from irrationalism. Finally, Dennis's explicitly religious orientation helps to clarify how the sublime can mediate between secular and religious attitudes. Thus, while not a "major" theorist of sublimity, I nevertheless consider Dennis to be, like Boileau, "pivotal" with regard to the architectonics of this study.

Given that this is not a survey,[24] the limitations of a single volume, coupled with the structural unity this study endeavors to articulate, have made it impossible to include substantial discussions of less important theories or treatments, as interesting as these might be, and as a more properly historical approach might be inclined to include.[25] Thus Boileau's French contemporaries (Rapin, Bouhours, Saint-Evremond),[26] the pre-Burkean English critics (Addison, Shaftesbury, Baillie),[27] as well as the eighteenth-century German aestheticians (Baumgarten, Meier, Mendelssohn, Lessing, Herder)[28] receive only cursory mention. The rich post-Kantian tradition of sublimity – in the thought of Friedrich Schiller, Arthur Schopenhauer, Samuel Taylor Coleridge, G. W. F. Hegel, and to

---

in *Modern Philosophy* (2013) includes a short subsection entitled "Sublime Style: Longinus and Dennis" (12–15).

[23] Both can be found in Longinus, however, in his first two sources of sublimity: grand conceptions (*noêseis*) and strong emotion (*pathos*).

[24] Surveys include: Pierre Hartmann, *Du Sublime: Boileau à Schiller* (1997); Philip Shaw, *The Sublime* (The New Critical Idiom) (2005); James Kirwan, *Sublimity: The Non-Rational and the Rational in the History of Aesthetics* (2005); and Baldine Saint Girons, *Le sublime de l'antiquité à nos jours* (2005). Multiauthor anthologies include: *La littérature et le sublime*, ed. Partick Marot (2007) and *The Sublime: From Antiquity to the Present*, ed. Timothy M. Costelloe (2012). The latter includes a survey of the theories of the sublime (Part I); pages 11–49 treat the figures studied in this volume.

[25] Perhaps the most exhaustive study of the sublime is Baldine Saint Girons's magisterial *Fiat Lux: Une philosophie du sublime*. This work favors a synchronic perspective, dispersing the sublime over a number of thematic categories, according to various "risks": of "obscurity," "simplicity," "power," "testimony," "passion," and "virtue."

[26] See Théodore Litman, *Le Sublime en France (1660–1714)*.

[27] See Samuel Monk's *The Sublime* and the anthology *The Sublime: A Reader in British Eighteenth-Century Aesthetic Theory*, eds. Andrew Ashfield and Peter de Bolla.

[28] See Lewis White Beck's *Early German Philosophy: Kant and His Predecessors*.

some extent in Friedrich Nietzsche (in his concept of the Dionysian) –
would require a volume of its own.[29]

The experience of transcendence and the dual structure of sublimity

As mentioned above, the discourse of the sublime has its origins in a first- or
third-century Greek fragment entitled *Peri hypsous* (*On the Sublime*), attributed to "Longinus." Apparently unknown in antiquity – it is not referenced
in any extant sources, and its manuscript came to light only in 1554 – the
treatise aroused little critical interest until it was translated into French by
Boileau in 1674. Through the influence of Boileau's Preface to his edition,
the putative subject of the treatise, *hypsos*, subsequently translated by most
languages with the Latinate "sublime," following Boileau's lead, quickly
acquired a currency in the literary criticism of the late seventeenth and
early eighteenth centuries, achieving in a few years a European-wide fame.
As the eighteenth century progressed, the sublime was increasingly detached
from its reference to Longinus and Boileau, emerging as one of the leading
concepts in the new field of what is now called "aesthetics," where it was
often contrasted with the beautiful. The term was codified, most notably, in
Burke's *A Philosophical Enquiry into the Origin of Our Ideas of the Sublime
and the Beautiful* (1757/1759) and then, most remarkably, by Kant in the last
of his *Critiques*, which deals with aesthetic judgment (1790).

   As this brief aperçu suggests, it is difficult to imagine how the notion of
the sublime could have ever become a topic in literary criticism or aesthetics if Longinus's fragment had been lost or if Boileau had never drawn
attention to it. Unlike the concept of the beautiful – a perennial topic of
the philosophy of art and aesthetics, the "theory" of which is quite diffuse –
the very existence of the sublime as a critical notion is dependent on its
specific theorization in a few key texts. That is to say, if experiences of
overpowering awe, emotional transport, sacred terror, and so forth had
not been subsumed under a unifying term such as "the sublime," there
would have been no *discourse* for the theories of Burke and Kant to build
upon;[30] for despite their reputation for innovation, these accounts are in

---

[29] See the recent monographs by Brady, *The Sublime in Modern Philosophy* (2013), which treats the
post-Kantian sublime extensively, and Sophia Vasalou, *Schopenhauer and the Aesthetic Standpoint:
Philosophy as a Practice of the Sublime* (2013). See also the recent essays by Paul Guyer, "The German
Sublime After Kant" (2012) and Sandra Shapshay, "Schopenhauer's Transformation of the Kantian
Sublime" (2012).
[30] And if Longinus's *hypsos* had been translated systematically as "elevation" or "loftiness" rather than
as "the sublime," it might not have had the same impact in modern thought.

fact based on established conventions.[31] The seeming heterogeneity of the major theories of sublimity is thus restrained by, on the one hand, the term's conventionality, and, on the other, the assumption that these are attempting to describe *the same basic experience* – that of transcendence conceived aesthetically – even if the critical frameworks used to account for it are radically divergent.[32]

Certainly the largest hurdle to understanding the sublime as a coherent discourse is the gulf that supposedly separates the "rhetorical sublime" of Longinus and Boileau from the "aesthetic sublime" of Burke and Kant. This study is thus at odds with the widely accepted view that, while Longinus's treatise was instrumental in introducing the concept of sublimity into modern critical discourse (via Boileau), its importance is restricted to a generative function, with no lasting substantive or theoretical influence.[33] Instead, this study views Longinus's treatise as having a *structuring effect* on the modern discourse of sublimity insofar as it sets a basic pattern, which is then revised and developed by later writers, without ever truly escaping the basic Longinian insight (transcendence conceived aesthetically).[34]

This is most apparent in the characterization of the experience of sublimity, namely as overpowering astonishment and awe, and as an elevation of the mind above its normal state. As Longinus expresses it at the beginning of his treatise:

> Sublimity [*hypsos*] is the source of the distinction of the very greatest poets and prose writers and the means by which they have given eternal life to their own fame. For grandeur produces ecstasy (*ekstasis*) rather than

[31] Zammito notes that "in the *Third Critique*, Kant drew certain features and illustrations from the conventional wisdom. He accepted the association, starting with Longinus, of the sublime with the grand – indeed, even the infinite – and within that framework, with such ideas as formlessness and unboundedness. He also accepted the complex psychological account of the experience of the sublime, which had been articulated first for the eighteenth century by Addison" (*The Genesis of Kant's* Critique of Judgment, 277). However, I contend (in Chapter 5) that Dennis, not Addison, is responsible for the "complex psychological account of the experience of the sublime."

[32] Suzanne Guerlac perceptively notes that "the key texts on the sublime of Longinus (and Boileau), Burke, and Kant appear at turning points in the history of philosophy. They belong to different discursive horizons – a premetaphysical one with Longinus, a Cartesian one with Boileau, an empiricist one with Burke, and, of course, a critical or idealist one with Kant. The relative stability of the operations of the sublime throughout these various elaborations is impressive" (*The Impersonal Sublime*, 1). Indeed, it is this "stability" that this study seeks to elucidate.

[33] I thus argue against the widespread idea that, as D. A. Russell expresses it, "the main contentions of Burke's essay on 'The Sublime and the Beautiful' . . . owes little or nothing to L[onginus] or even to Boileau except the initial impetus to discussion" ("Introduction," in Russell, *"Longinus" On the Sublime*, xlv).

[34] Thus this book could not be characterized as an "influence study," since it involves the tracing of the structural elements of which later authors may or may not be consciously aware.

persuasion in the hearer; and the combination of wonder (*thaumasion*) and astonishment (*ekplêxis*) always proves superior to the merely persuasive and pleasant. This is because persuasion is on the whole something we can control, whereas amazement (*ekplêxis*) and wonder (*thaumasion*) exert invincible power and force and get the better of every hearer. (1.4)

Although Longinus is speaking here about the verbal arts, the *subjective* import of his characterization of the sublime experience is easily detachable from the medium of its cause. The fact that this feeling of ecstasy is produced more paradigmatically – but not exclusively – by nature in Burke's and Kant's theories does not thereby negate the real continuity between Longinus and modern aesthetics.[35] Longinus's description of an *intensity of effect/affect* allows eighteenth-century thinkers to account for experiences that do not comport with the category of the beautiful (or taste), but can nevertheless be considered aesthetic. Indeed, the specific language Longinus employs to describe the effect of sublimity – awe, astonishment, amazement, wonder, admiration, and so on – will be echoed by every major theory, whether from the vantage point of literary criticism (Boileau, Dennis), empirical psychology (Burke), or transcendental philosophy (Kant). Even more important, however, is the particular nature of this experience of affective intensity, the specific *structure of experience* that Longinus outlines in his treatise.[36] This structure is already apparent in the above-cited passage: that of a *dual* structure of being *overwhelmed* or *overawed* – as indicated by the Greek terms *thaumasion* (wonder, awe, admiration) and *ekplêxis* (astonishment, amazement, stupor) – coupled with the idea of being *exalted* or *elevated* – as expressed in the notion of *ekstasis* (literally: a going outside or beyond oneself, self-transcendence, rapture). Thus, according to Longinus, the sublime exerts an "invincible power and force" (1.4), "tears everything up like a whirlwind, and exhibits the orator's whole power [*dynamis*] at a single blow" (1.4), and holds "complete domination over our minds" (39.3); but also: "It is our nature to be elevated and exalted by true sublimity [*hypsos*]" (7.2). This dual structure of sublimity is also paradoxical: on the one hand, being overwhelmed/dominated by the encounter with the transcendent in art or nature induces a feeling of *inferiority* or *submission*; on the other, it is precisely by being overpowered that a high-minded feeling of *superiority* or *nobility of soul* (mental expansiveness, heroic sensibility) is attained. The

---

[35] See Chapter 12 for a discussion of Kant's view of sublimity in art.

[36] Weiskel claims to have found "a structure that is immanent in a vast and eclectic theory" (*The Romantic Sublime*, 5), but it is only via an extrinsic theory (psychoanalysis) that this putatively "immanent" structure becomes apparent.

tension between these two poles of a single experience – of being at once below and above, inferior and superior, humbled and exalted – produces the special dynamism of the sublime, creating nexuses with diverse areas of human reality (the religious, the political, the social, the anthropological).

This dual structure can be found in all the major theories of sublimity. Boileau writes that "the Sublime is a certain force of discourse, which elevates and ravishes the soul" (le Sublime est une certaine force de discours, propre à élever et à ravir l'âme [TS, 155, my translation]). The idea of being ravished (*ravi*) implies a certain violence (the encounter with a superior power), even in its metaphorical usage.[37] Burke conceives of the dual structure of sublimity in terms of an elevating terror, noting (following Longinus and Boileau) that the sublime "hurries us on by an irresistible force" (E, 57) and that "the mind always claim[s] to itself some part of the dignity and importance of the things which it contemplates" (E, 47).[38] Kant interprets the dual structure in terms of the humbling (or humiliation) of sensibility and the concomitant exaltation of reason, the revelation of our supersensible vocation: "What is excessive for the imagination . . . is as it were an abyss, in which it fears to lose itself, yet for reason's idea of the supersensible to produce such an effort of the imagination is not excessive but lawful, hence it is precisely as attractive as it was repulsive for mere sensibility" (CPJ, 5:258). The idea of complex pleasure (attraction/repulsion or pleasure/pain), considered to be the hallmark of sublimity in Burke and Kant, is therefore also a reflection of this dual structure: on the one hand, the pain in being overwhelmed/overpowered (imaginative overload, terror), the feeling of being *inferior* to nature; and, on the other, the pleasure in being elevated, the feeling of being, as Kant writes, "*superior* to nature within us, and thus also that outside us" (CPJ, 5:269, my emphasis). Moreover, Kant is paraphrasing Longinus and Burke when he writes in his *Anthropology from a Pragmatic Point of View* that sublimity "awakens in us a feeling of our own greatness and power" (APP, 7:243). As I argue in Chapter 8, the dual transcendence-structure of sublimity is also present in Kant's moral theory, specifically as expressed in his second *Critique*, where, invoking the concept of sublimity, Kant contends that "the moral law unavoidably *humiliates* every human being when he compares it with the sensible propensity of

[37] Following Boileau, John Dennis comments that the sublime "commits a pleasing Rape upon the very Soul of the reader" (CW I, 359). Boileau often uses the verb *ravir* (ravish/rape) along with *enlever*. In the Preface to his translation, Boileau writes that the sublime "uplifts, ravishes, and transports" (TS, 70).
[38] The latter statement is actually a paraphrase of *On the Sublime*, 7.2.

his nature" (CPaR, 5:74, my emphasis), but also that "one can in turn never get enough of contemplating the majesty of this law, and the soul believes itself *elevated* in proportion as it sees the holy elevated above itself and its frail nature" (CPaR, 5:77, my emphasis).

While the dual transcendence-structure of the sublime and its corresponding mental disposition of high-mindedness (nobility of mind) can be considered the main theme of this study, my focus on the specifically subjective dimension of sublimity allows several subthemes to become visible: (1) the idea of sublimity as a secular analog of religious transcendence; (2) the complex and dynamic interrelation between the literary-rhetorical and philosophical-aesthetic interpretations of sublimity (including their common anthropological basis); and (3) the idea of sublimity as cultural critique (the bourgeois appropriation of aristocratic nobility of mind, on the one hand, and the critique of bourgeois culture from the perspective of the sublime, on the other). I now elucidate these subthemes in turn.

Sublimity and the religious (sacred) origins of the aesthetic

In formulating the concept of sublimity as the experience of transcendence, specifically as domination-exaltation, Longinus effects both a demystification and a remystification: he transforms an experience rooted in the religious or the mystical realm, as evidenced by his use of *ekstasis* (a term with strong religious, even biblical, resonances),[39] into a protoaesthetic experience of *intensity*, as indicated by the use of such terms as "awe," "astonishment," "wonder," "ecstasy," "amazement" – terms that apply equally well to both secular-aesthetic and religious contexts. One can thus speak of the "religious origins of the aesthetic," to the extent that, from its inception, the sublime offers itself as an *aesthetic analogue* of religious experience.[40]

It is thus not surprising that the sublime lends itself to a Christian interpretation in the modern reception of this notion, and its suitability for such an interpretation was certainly part of its appeal. Adam Phillips is thus nominally correct in his observation that "in Burke's *Enquiry*, with its relatively cursory references to Christianity, we find the beginnings of a

---

[39] See Chapter 1, where I point out that the ecstatic experience was previously understood according to the Platonic idea of *enthousiasmos*, divine possession. *The American Heritage Dictionary of the English Language* (4th edition) defines "enthusiasm" as: "1. Ecstasy arising from supposed possession by a god; 2. Religious fanaticism."

[40] Thus in a purely religious context the concept of the sublime would be superfluous.

secular language for profound human experience."[41] However, this "secularizing" movement had already begun in Longinus's treatise, and "secularization" itself is a paradoxical concept when applied to the "sublime," a term that relies heavily on metaphorical equivocation: for, insofar as they are the source of an ecstatic feeling, art and nature are in some sense divinized or sacralized; whereas religion, to the extent that its monopoly over transcendence is contested by the aesthetic, is to some degree secularized. The sublime therefore lies at the ambiguous frontier of the literal-religious and figurative-aesthetic. Hence the significance of Pierre Daniel Huet's objection (first articulated in 1678) to the idea that the phrase from Genesis "Let there be light," found in Longinus and promoted by Boileau, should be considered sublime; according to the ecclesiastic Huet, it is a category mistake to employ a term of rhetorical and literary analysis to refer to the Bible.[42] Later theorists, however, will freely exploit parallels between an aesthetics of transcendence and properly religious experience and meaning: John Dennis claims that the sublimity of great poetry, paradigmatically Milton's *Paradise Lost*, is necessarily and essentially due to its deployment of "Religious Ideas"; Burke will speak about the sublime terror produced by the thought of God's almightiness; and Kant in his third *Critique* will connect "the sublimity of our own nature" to "the idea of the sublimity of religion and its object" (CPJ, 5:263). In his *Anthropology*, Kant observes that "such an affect [astonishment] is stimulated only by reason and is a kind of *sacred awe* at seeing the abyss of the supersensible opening before one's feet" (7:261, my emphasis), thereby highlighting the religious origins and resonances of the experience of sublimity.

Although Longinus sometimes employs religious language or references as a kind of hyperbole[43] and often plays with the tension between the mystical-religious and the secular-poetic,[44] he nevertheless seeks to emphasize a human or "humanist" perspective.[45] Jeffrey Barnouw offers an excellent description of the humanistic thrust of the Longinian sublime, which he compares to that of Petrarch and St. Augustine:

---

[41] Phillips, Introduction to Burke, *A Philosophical Enquiry into the Origin of Our Ideas of the Sublime and the Beautiful*, xi.

[42] This is extensively discussed in Chapter 4 of this study.

[43] "Other literary qualities prove their users to be human; sublimity [*hypsos*] raises us towards the spiritual greatness of god" [36.1]; "he [Demosthenes] concentrates [vehemence and power] all in himself – they are divine gifts, it is almost blasphemous to call them human" [34.4]).

[44] As in Longinus's reinterpretation of the concept of (divine) inspiration as emulation (*zêlôsis-mimêsis*). See Chapter 2.

[45] I thus could not disagree more with Thomas Weiskel, who proclaims that "a humanistic sublime is an oxymoron" (*The Romantic Sublime*, 3).

> The "image of greatness in the mind" in "Longinus" differs from that in Augustine and Petrarch in its psychological basis and ethical import, essentially – as will become clear – because of its openness to experience. There is no other-worldly orientation to the Longinian sublime, except for the positive concern with posterity in the form of pursuit of fame and glory.... The intuition of inner greatness does not turn the individual away from common and public experience in "Longinus"; indeed it remains rooted, in part, in political oratory and touches the concerns of reputation and interest in civic life.[46]

Longinus's concept of aesthetic transcendence thus connects an individual's "inner greatness" (*megalophrosynê*) to the social and historical realms. Far from being a merely "private" experience, sublimity is for Longinus firmly embedded in public life. In his massive study *L'Age de l'éloquence*, Marc Fumaroli notes that "the convergence between Longinus and St. Augustine offered a precious resource: profane eloquence ... could find in the aesthetics of Longinus a way of remaining itself, all while respecting a kind of consonance with religious eloquence and with the religious arts."[47] But of course Longinus could only play this role because of the religious resonances of the sublime (*hypsos*).

While the Longinian sublime contains no "other-worldly orientation," it clearly draws on its structural affinity with religious experience, an affinity that would become consequential in a modern intellectual attitude strongly influenced by Christianity. The dual structure of sublime experience reflects the Christian (and especially Protestant) relation to God or the divine: we are overwhelmed and overawed before God's greatness and power ("God-fearing"), but are also exalted and elevated by God's love. Thus Burke remarks that "false religions have generally nothing else but fear to support them" (E, 70). This sentiment is echoed by Kant, who uses the dual transcendence-structure of sublimity to distinguish enlightened from archaic religion: "In this way alone does religion internally distinguish itself from superstition, that latter not providing a basis in the mind for reverence [*Ehrfurcht*] for the sublime, but only for fear and anxiety before the being of superior power" (CPJ, 5:264).

---

[46] Barnouw, "The Morality of the Sublime: To John Dennis," 32.

[47] Fumaroli, *L'Age de l'éloquence*, 168, my translation. Fumaroli also observes that "by putting Cicero and profane eloquence under the aegis of Longinus, the Venetian humanist [Paul Mantius, a sixteenth-century editor of Longinus] created a secular pendant to St. Augustin, and made *On the Sublime* a counterweight to *On Christian Doctrine*" (*L'Age de l'éloquence*, 168, my translation).

Sublimity and the subjective turn: from rhetoric to aesthetics

As mentioned above, the conventional view of the Longinian sublime is that it is reducible to a merely rhetorical or stylistic meaning,[48] despite the fact that the modern career of this term would be launched on the basis of Boileau's defense of the Longinian sublime as an antistylistic and antirhetorical concept (in the 1674 Preface to his translation).[49] Boileau in fact cleaves closely to Longinus's treatise, which asserts that (1) sublimity "produces ecstasy [*ekstasis*] rather than persuasion in the hearer" (1.3), thus separating sublimity from rhetoric in the traditional Aristotelian sense; (2) treats *all* the verbal arts (philosophy, history, poetry, oratory) of which specifically oratorical examples constitute only a relatively small part;[50] and (3) deems the rhetorical-technical sources (*technê*) of sublimity to be the *least* important, the most important being the two "natural" or mental sources of grandeur of thought or conception (*noêsis*) and vehement emotion (*pathos*). One can thus distinguish between Longinus's transrhetorical *theory* of sublimity, namely his subjective and intersubjective account of literary practice (contained principally in chapters 1–15 of his treatise and in the digressions of chapters 33–36 and 44), which I elucidate in Part I of this volume, from Longinus's *illustration* of sublimity in terms of a specific technics of discourse.

This said, there is a deeper meaning of rhetoric – namely, its anthropological meaning – that can be said to be fundamental to Longinus's theory. Like the most consequential of ancient rhetorical treatises, such as Aristotle's *Rhetoric* and Quintilian's *Institutio Oratoria*, Longinus's *On the Sublime* is not merely concerned with eloquence per se, but treats a broad range of questions that concern the human being in general (even if, for Aristotle and Quintilian, the putative end is persuasion): namely, the effect of the arts on the reader/spectator, the psychology of the emotions, the nature of the imagination (*phantasia*), as well as the moral and spiritual development of the individual. In this sense, rhetoric can in fact be considered an early form of anthropology (in the philosophical not the

---

[48] Guerlac notes the "tendency to trivialize the Longinian sublime as merely rhetorical" (*The Impersonal Sublime*, 1).

[49] An exception would be David Morris, who writes: "The term *rhetorical sublime* is unsatisfactory because it implies that sublimity in literature is mainly a matter of stylistics . . . but few eighteenth-century writers believed that style alone created the sublime" (*The Religious Sublime*, 5).

[50] Longinus's treatise is, however, addressed to a young student, Terentianus, who is interested in acquiring skills in public speaking, for Longinus writes: "Let us then consider whether there is anything in my observations which may be thought useful to public men [*politikoi*]" (1.2). I address this seeming contradiction in Chapter 1.

ethnographic sense).[51] From the perspective of intellectual history, then, rhetoric and aesthetics are far from being antipodes: the kinds of questions that had previously been the province of rhetoric are, in the modern era, taken up by anthropology and aesthetics.[52] Kant's *Anthropology* (a compendium of his lecture courses), for example, contains many passages that are in effect a dry run for discussions of aesthetic matters in the *Critique of the Power of Judgment*.

Like "rhetoric," the meaning of the word "aesthetics" has also undergone major shifts and is constantly subject to misunderstanding. The term, which derives from the Greek *aisthetikos* ("sensitive, perceptive"), was first coined in 1735 by the German philosopher Alexander Baumgarten, who sought thereby to establish the philosophical ground for a "critique of taste." In his *Critique of Pure Reason* (1781/1787), Kant endeavors to "correct" Baumgarten's usage by returning "aesthetics" to its original meaning of "sense perception"; but by the time of his third *Critique*, having discovered an a priori basis for the critique of taste (reflective judgment), Kant reverses course, now using "aesthetics" to denote the appreciation of nature and fine art as a distinct mode of experience separate from the cognitive and the moral. Seizing on Kant's conception of aesthetics as justification for the idea of *l'art pour l'art*, nineteenth-century critics and writers (particularly in France and Great Britain) shift the meaning of "aesthetics" from a question of judgment to one of the autonomy of art and the artist.[53] However, it would be a mistake to attribute the idea of *l'art pour l'art* to Kant, whose aim in separating

[51] Martin Heidegger, whose *Being and Time* has been described as an exercise in philosophical anthropology (most notably by his teacher, Edmund Husserl), observes in this work that "contrary to the traditional orientation of the concept of rhetoric according to which it is some kind of 'discipline,' Aristotle's *Rhetoric* must be understood as the first systematic hermeneutic of everydayness of being-with-one-another" (*Being and Time*, 130). Nancy S. Struever remarks that an early commentary (1924) by Heidegger on Aristotle "remains, arguably, the best twentieth-century reading of Aristotle's *Rhetoric*" ("Alltäglichkeit, Timefulness, in the Heideggerian Program," 127).

[52] David L. Marshall notes that "rhetoric is crucial in the rise of German aesthetics, for instance. Thus *aisthetā* in Baumgarten, *phantasia* in Lessing, and *hypotyposis* in Kant all connote rhetoric" (*Vico and the Transformation of Rhetoric in Early Modern Europe*, 21).

[53] Hence Jacques Rancière's designation of an "aesthetic regime of art," which he describes as follows: "Even if histories of art begin their narratives with cave paintings at the dawn of time, Art as a notion designating a form of specific experience has only existed in the West since the end of the eighteenth century" (*Aisthesis: Scenes from the Aesthetic Regime of Art*, ix). Douglas Crimp makes a similar point from the perspective of museum history: "Art as we think about it only came into being in the nineteenth century, with the birth of the museum and the discipline of art history, for these share the same time span as modernism (and, not insignificantly, photography).... The idea of art as autonomous, as separate from everything else, as destined to take place in *art* history, is a development of modernism" ("The End of Painting," 81, original emphasis).

aesthetic from other types of judgments is precisely to show its moral significance as the experience of autonomy (freedom).[54]

The vicissitudes of the notion of "aesthetics" cannot be easily separated from the emergence of the sublime, given that the sublime played a fundamental role in the eighteenth-century turn toward a properly subjective perspective on art and nature. While oftentimes the term "aesthetics" is understood as encompassing or even as synonymous with the philosophy of art, the term precisely marks the shift from an objective to a subjective perspective on art and natural beauty, in conjunction with the rise of the concept of taste.[55] This subjective orientation divides into two aspects: (1) *reception aesthetics*, the psychological (or even physiological) response to artworks and nature, including questions of taste and judgment (Kant), but also of sensation (Burke); and (2) *creation aesthetics*, the theory of genius (most notably in Edward Young [1683–1765], Alexander Gerard [1728–1795], and Kant).[56] Longinus's theory of sublimity is in fact a model for both the creative and receptive aspects of aesthetics. In addition to codifying the idea of the *intensity of experience* (awe, astonishment, ecstasy), discussed above, Longinus's treatise is also the first theory of the creative process, of "genius" in the modern sense of the term, as Part I of this study argues. Kant will also treat both aspects in his *Critique of the Power of Judgment*, where nature and art are seen as analogous in terms of their effects and where the fine or beautiful arts (*schöne Künste*) are defined as arts of genius (as opposed to mere craft, *technê*).

With regard to creation aesthetics, the continuity between Longinus and modern theories of genius has been eloquently demonstrated in M. H. Abrams's classic *The Mirror and the Lamp: Romantic Theory and the Critical Tradition* (1953).[57] It is with respect to reception aesthetics that

---

[54] Guyer remarks that "Kant turns to aesthetics to make the moral motivation of reason more sensibly palpable to ourselves" (*Kant and the Experience of Freedom*, 21).

[55] Hence we often seek to subjectivize anachronistically. Hans-Georg Gadamer notes, for example, that the translation of Aristotle's *eleos* and *phobos* as "pity" and "fear" (in the *Poetics*) "gives them a far too subjective tinge.... The German word 'Jammer' (misery) is a good equivalent because it too refers not merely to an inner state but to its manifestation" (*Truth and Method*, 130).

[56] See Edward Young, *Conjectures on Original Composition* (1759) and Alexander Gerard, *An Essay on Genius* (1774).

[57] "Something approaching the nineteenth-century displacement of the audience by the author as the focal term of reference is to be found in one classical rhetorician, Longinus – the exemplar and source of many characteristic elements of Romantic theory" (Abrams, *The Mirror and the Lamp*, 72). Jean Bessière comments on the gulf that separates the Romantic author-subject from the authorial consciousness implied in realism and symbolism: "Romantisme: la littérature est pertinente par la subjectivité de l'écrivain, du poète, dépositaire du droit littéraire et du droit public de la littérature – l'expression et la liberté dans les arts, telles quelles sont données par un individu singulier, sont bonnes pour toute la société et pour chacune des classes de la société puisque cet individu reconnaît

commentators perceive a large rift between the "rhetorical" and the "aesthetic" approaches to sublimity. Indeed, the commonplace that eighteenth-century aesthetics is concerned more fundamentally with the experience of nature than with art has led many to view Longinus as a marginal figure at best in the modern history of sublimity. However, the gulf between nature and art in seventeenth- and eighteenth-century thought is not as wide as it is often made out to be. David Morris, for example, criticizes the tendency to see "sublimity in nature and sublimity in literature [as] essentially unrelated phenomena, developing along disconnected, if parallel, lines,"[58] contending that, "to the integrated vision of many eighteenth-century Englishmen, nature and art did not occupy separate realms but often appeared as aspects of a single object of consciousness."[59] Morris finds confirmation in a line from Alexander Pope's *Essay on Criticism* (1709): "*Nature* and *Homer* were, he [Virgil] found, the same."[60]

A consideration of the key theories of sublimity reveals a broad overlap between the aesthetics of nature and the literary criticism that developed in the seventeenth and eighteenth centuries. In fact, the impetus for discussions of sublimity in nature is Longinus's treatise itself:

> [Nature] implanted in our minds from the start an irresistible desire for anything which is great and in relation to ourselves, supernatural. . . . It is a natural inclination that leads us to admire not the little streams, however pellucid and however useful, but the Nile, the Danube, the Rhine, and above all the Ocean. Nor do we feel so much awe before the little flame we kindle, because it keeps its light clear and pure, as before the fires of heaven, though they are often obscured. (*On the Sublime*, 35.3–4)

Such reflections inspired British writers such as the theologian Thomas Burnet, whose seminal *Sacred Theory of the Earth* (1681/1684) comments

---

l'utopie de l'imaginaire et dit toute pertinence. Réalisme, symbolisme : il n'y a plus de détenteur prééminent du droit de la littérature" (*La littérature et sa rhétorique*, 27). In this vein, Longinus can certainly be considered a proto-Romantic.

[58] Morris, *The Religious Sublime*, 4.

[59] Morris, *The Religious Sublime*, 6. Barnouw identifies two widespread misunderstandings concerning Longinus and his interpreters: "(a) That 'Longinus' was concerned mainly with a 'rhetorical sublime' which is largely irrelevant to modern poetic sensibility and its characteristic 'natural sublime,' and (b) that 'pre-romantic' interest in the sublime was incompatible with the 'neo-classical' preoccupation with rules and regularities that led to its dissolution" ("The Morality of the Sublime," 33).

[60] Quoted in Morris, *The Religious Sublime*, 6, original emphasis. Somewhat analogously, one could also cite Spinoza's pronouncement that "the method of interpreting Scripture does not widely differ from the method of interpreting nature – in fact, it is almost the same" (Spinoza, *Theologico-Political Treatise*, Chapter 7).

directly on Longinus,[61] and John Milton, who, in *Paradise Lost* (1667/ 1674), was the "first English poet to practice the 'Aesthetics of the Infinite,' the transfer of vastness from God to interstellar space, then to terrestrial mountains."[62] Taking their inspiration from Longinus, Burnet and Milton thus create the conditions under which late seventeenth- and early eighteenth-century critics such as John Dennis and Joseph Addison could develop a notion of the sublimity of nature in terms of grandeur (infinity) and power (terror), a half century before Burke's *Enquiry*.

Even if Burke's and Kant's theories of sublimity appear prima facie to be more oriented toward nature, a closer examination reveals a great dependence on ideas of literature and art. The importance of Milton for Burke's theory is well known. However, the relation between Kant's theory of sublimity and literature (or art more generally) has rarely been considered a fruitful line of inquiry,[63] this despite, in the third *Critique*, the architectural examples in the section on the Mathematically Sublime, the footnote on the sublimity of the inscription over the temple of Isis, and, most important of all, the section on the "aesthetically sublime," which is directly concerned with issues of literary representation.

Sublimity as cultural theory

My effort to uncover some structural and thematic unity in the theory and discourse of sublimity challenges the notion that the sublime requires an appeal to an extrinsic theory (such as psychoanalysis) as an organizing principle. I see the theory of the sublime as possessing a critical function of its own, namely as an implicit theory of culture, a notion that goes back to Longinus's treatise, which extends beyond questions of verbal expression to the elucidation of a specific moral and cultural outlook.[64] This is particularly in evidence in the final chapter of the treatise, which links the dearth of literary greatness to cultural decline and decadence. This fusion of aesthetic reflection and cultural critique will become an important feature of the modern theory of sublimity.

---

[61] It was originally published in Latin in 1681 (*Telluris Theoria Sacra*) and then translated into English in 1684.

[62] Marjorie Hope Nicolson, *Mountain Gloom and Mountain Glory: The Development of the Aesthetics of the Infinite*, 273. Burnet was considered by contemporaries to be "an artist second only to Milton" (Nicolson, *Mountain Gloom and Mountain Glory*, 193).

[63] An exception would be Sanford Budick, whose *Kant and Milton* (2010) has shone a welcome light on a previously obscure relation.

[64] Namely, what one could call a "heroic subjectivity," an aesthetically realized high-mindedness that is at once a cultural, moral, and social ideal. On multiple occasions Longinus calls great writers "heroes" (*hêrôs*); in Greek *hêrôs* refers to a quasi-divine figure, intermediate between men and gods.

As the index of an affective state of high-mindedness – elevation/
nobility of soul – the transcendence-structure of the sublime becomes an
important factor in shaping attitudes toward the great social revolution of
modernity: the decline of the feudal nobility and the emergence of a
middle class, the shift from a culture based on an aristocratic-warrior
ethos to one reflecting bourgeois-mercantile values. By connecting aesthetic intensity and elevation to the idea of nobility of mind, by replacing
properly religious experience with an analogous, aesthetically inflected
structure, the sublime represents one of the pivot points on which the
transition from a traditional or hierarchical to a democratizing society is
thought. In effect, what thinkers such as Boileau, Burke, and Kant achieve
through the sublime is a bourgeois appropriation of aristocratic subjectivity (the heroic cast of mind). The extent to which the sublime is used to
exalt the bourgeois individual through the aesthetic is perhaps the least
understood aspect of the discourse of sublimity.

It is certainly no accident that the period during which this social
revolution occurs – from the Fronde of 1650–1653 (the French civil war
pitting the nobility against monarchical absolutism, paving the way for the
centralization of power in the nation-state and the concomitant destruction of the feudal order) to the French Revolution (1789–1799), which
consolidated the power of the bourgeoisie as the dominant social class –
overlaps almost exactly with the period of the most intense interest in
sublimity: from Boileau's translation of 1674 to Kant's third *Critique*,
published in 1790. Just twenty years after the Fronde, Boileau extolls the
heroic nature of the third-century philosopher and critic Cassius Longinus
(whom he took to be the author of *On the Sublime*),[65] associating his ideal
of mental elevation with the seventeenth-century figure of the *honnête
homme* (a man of high sensibility, refinement, and probity), a term that
identifies an emergent social category (generally associated with the middle
class, though not necessarily) with a mental disposition. Boileau thus sees
Longinus's concept of sublimity, exemplified in the heroic life of the
author himself, as a means of restoring the unity between a dispositional
and a social designation, a unity that had been torn asunder with the
conversion of the warrior aristocracy into courtiers under Cardinal
Richelieu and Louis XIV.[66] Thus, as I contend in Chapter 4, sublimity

[65] I address the question of the authorship of *Peri hypsous* in Chapter 1.
[66] "Nobility" had thereby become a mere class designation, detached from the noble mental disposition that had previously defined and legitimated it. René Girard remarks that from the perspective
of the nineteenth century: "Il y eut d'abord la noblesse; il y eut ensuite la classe noble; finalement il
n'y a plus qu'un parti" (*Mensonge romantique et vérité romanesque*, 150).

effectively captures for Boileau the ideal of mental elevation for the proto-bourgeois man of taste.[67]

In the chapter on Burke (Chapter 6), I explore the idea, suggested by Tom Furniss and Emma J. Clery,[68] that Burke's putatively aesthetic treatise is also a subtle commentary on class struggle. Burke's associations of the sublime with the bourgeois merchant class, specifically in his references to "labour" and "self-preservation," in effect treat aesthetic concepts as proxies for sociopolitical categories, surreptitiously claiming for the bourgeoisie the heroic values of the old nobility. In the words of Furniss, "Burke seeks to create an image of the upwardly mobile man of ability (the 'self-made man') as an heroic and virtuous laborer whose sublime aspirations are quite different from the beautiful but debilitating luxury of the aristocracy (and of women)."[69] Thus, for Burke, terror is both mentally and *socially* elevating; the sublime puts the bourgeois in touch with his heroic self, as expressed in his industry, ambition, and imaginative confrontation with terror.

Despite his emphasis on the transcendental conditions of aesthetic judgment, Kant also sees the sublime in terms of cultural critique. Kant's analysis of the transcendence-structure of the Dynamically Sublime clearly describes a heroic mental disposition – the resistance to a superior power, the transcendence of one's attachment to life (courage in the face of danger) – even if the experience of sublimity does not actually determine the will (as in morality). This aesthetically realized high-mindedness is, in principle, universally accessible, but in practice requires "culture," according to Kant, and is therefore more of a bourgeois concept.[70] Thus, in the Dynamically Sublime, the bourgeois aesthete feels his or her heroic resistance to nature both external (natural power) and internal (instinct of self-preservation), all while being in a position of safety. But, as I argue in Chapter 11, Kant also manifests a strong ambivalence toward the bourgeois class and its values. Referring to "the debate" concerning "whether it is the statesman or the general who deserves the greater respect in comparison to the other" (CPJ, 5:263), Kant claims that aesthetic judgment, that of

---

[67] To my knowledge only D. A. Russell among twentieth-century critics has perceived the importance of Boileau's exaltation of Cassius Longinus: "The eighteenth century saw in [Cassius Longinus's] brilliant career and heroic death an appropriate setting for the noble and liberty-loving mind revealed in *Peri hypsous*" ("Introduction," *"Longinus" On the Sublime*, xxiv).

[68] Tom Furniss, *Edmund Burke's Aesthetic Ideology: Language, Gender and Political Economy in Revolution*; Emma J. Clery, "The Pleasure of Terror: Paradox in Edmund Burke's Theory of the Sublime."

[69] Furniss, *Edmund Burke's Aesthetic Ideology*, 2.   [70] I discuss this in Chapter 12.

sublimity specifically, decides in favor of the general.[71] Thus, "war is sublime," due to the heroic mentality it supports. Kant contrasts the sublimity of war with "a long peace [that] causes the spirit of mere commerce to predominate, along with base selfishness, cowardice, and weakness, and usually debases the mentality of a populace" (CPJ, 5:263).[72] This opposition between the bourgeois "spirit of mere commerce" and the sublimity of the warrior mentality (the general) reveals that Kant is not altogether sanguine about the direction of modern society, despite the success of the Enlightenment and the revolution then underway in France as he was writing these words. As Jean-Jacques Rousseau saw, "individualism" can mean both rational autonomy and egotism.

That this cultural-critical aspect of the discourse of sublimity is not often perceived or commented on can be attributed in part to the antisubjectivist bent of much of contemporary thought. The sublime appears very differently from a posthumanist, postmodernist perspective, that is, from a perspective in which subjectivity no longer constitutes an essential or even a viable point of reference. Far from signifying an elevation of mind or heroic values, the sublime in contemporary critical theory has been assimilated into an antimodern or anti-Enlightenment discourse that is opposed to the values the sublime previously embodied.[73] According to this revaluation, contemporary critical writing on the sublime has tended to see it as undermining (*de*constructing) rather than forming (*con*structing) modern conceptions of subjectivity. The sublime is thus generally used to reinforce or embellish notions such as difference, negativity, ineffability, impossibility, heterogeneity, unrepresentability, and so forth.[74] Indeed, one of the principal reasons for the sublime's most recent success is its ability to assert, confirm, or otherwise further current critical

---

[71] I argue in Chapter 10 that the Mathematically Sublime also implies a heroic subjectivity.

[72] Interestingly, Kant is here aligning himself with the "time-honored aristocratic disdain for mercantile activities" (David Quint, *Epic and Empire*, 257). Quint further notes that "this prejudice was institutionalized by sixteenth-century statutes in Spain and France that forbade noblemen from practicing trade" (Quint, *Epic and Empire*, 257).

[73] Bessière speaks of an "abandonment of the notion of elevation" in these accounts of sublimity ("Le sublime aujourd'hui," 423, my translation).

[74] Crowther makes a similar point in his *The Kantian Sublime*, as he reflects on why the "sublime" has suddenly become "fashionable" in the late 1970s and 1980s: "It is precisely this fashionable dimension of contemporary relevance which introduces a worrying aspect to these appropriations of the sublime. Derrida's and de Man's discussions, for example, examine Kant fundamentally in the context of recent poststructuralist approaches to language; Weiskel reconstructs Kant's theory on the basis of clues provided by structural linguistics and psychoanalysis; Lyotard uses Kant in a way that centers on sublimity's possible relevance to avant-garde modernist and postmodern art. In all these cases, in other words, Kant's theory is put to the use on the base of, or in the service of, some broader set of theoretical interests" (3).

projects – a purpose for which it appears remarkably apt, much more so than the concept of beauty, which seems hopelessly outdated.[75]

***

A few words on the organization of the present study. Part I examines Longinus's *Peri hypsous*, focusing specifically on his subjective and inter-subjective *theory* of sublimity – sublimity as a critical concept – arguing against the narrow technical-rhetorical interpretation of the Longinian sublime as a kind of grand style. Part II explores the reception of Longinus's treatise and the development of the transcendence-structure of sublimity in tandem with the emergence of subjective aesthetics, beginning with Boileau's edition of Longinus (1674) and Dennis's *The Advancement and Reformation of Modern Poetry* (1701) and *The Grounds of Criticism in Poetry* (1704), and culminating in Burke's *A Philosophical Enquiry into the Origin of Our Ideas of the Sublime and Beautiful* (1757/1759). Part III traces the evolution of Kant's concept of sublimity, from his early *Observations on the Feeling of the Beautiful and Sublime* (1764) to his *Critique of Practical Reason* (1788) and *Critique of the Power of Judgment* (1790), insisting on the idea of sublimity of mind as the key to understanding Kant's evolving theory.

A note on the use of the term "sublime" itself. A variety of alternative translations have been proposed for Longinus's Greek word *hypsos*, of which "height," "elevation," and "loftiness" are the most often cited. The question of the propriety of the term "sublime" to render Longinus's central concept is a vexed one. To allow Longinus's meaning to show itself without the burden of the modern history of sublimity, I have elected to regularly employ *hypsos* in Part I, in addition to "sublimity" or "the sublime." Generally speaking, however, this book is a study of the *concept* of sublimity, whether expressed in the Greek *hypsos*, the Latinate *sublime*, or the German *das Erhabene*.[76]

---

[75] However, some critics, such as Rodolphe Gasché, have recently questioned the validity of using the sublime in this manner: "The current interest in the sublime, particularly among scholars of the postmodern, is no doubt largely the result of a continuing misinterpretation of Kant's idea of the beautiful" (*The Idea of Form*, 119). Gasché feels that when Kant's idea of "form" is properly understood the Kantian sublime will no longer be seen as a simple "alternative" to the beautiful (*The Idea of Form*, 119–154).

[76] While I follow all English translations of Kant's third *Critique* in using a form of "sublime" for *das Erhabene*, it should be noted that the German term is actually a closer approximation of Longinus's *hypsos* than "sublime" and might be better rendered in English as "elevation." The German verb *erheben* means "to raise up" or "to elevate." "Sublime," of course, has no verb form in English ("to sublimate" has a different meaning, even if it is etymologically related).

PART I

Longinus's theory of sublimity

Across two millenniums we breathe the breath of life, not the mold of schools and libraries. The appearance of this unknown Greek has something miraculous about it.

– Ernst Curtius[1]

---

[1] Curtius, *European Literature in the Latin Middle Ages*, 399.

CHAPTER I

Defining the Longinian sublime

The Greek fragment *Peri hypsous* (*On the Sublime*), attributed to "Longinus," is, among ancient treatises, second only to Aristotle's *Poetics* in terms of its influence on modern literary criticism, aesthetics, and the philosophy of art.[1] The extent and nature of this influence is, however, a matter of great debate. Is *Peri hypsous* simply a rhetorical treatise that offers an especially powerful account of the grand or high style? Or is it the source of the one of the most enduring and consequential of aesthetic concepts in modern thought, the *sublime*? This study argues that the intelligibility of the modern concept of sublimity depends on the latter view.[2] Part I thus seeks to elucidate how Longinus's *theory* of *hypsos* – of what *hypsos* is, of how it is produced, of why it is important – endows the concept of sublimity with certain structural features that motivate and shape the modern project of defining a secular concept of transcendence.[3] For what is distinctive and original about Longinus's approach is its specifically subjective import: its focus on the creative and receptive dimensions of the verbal arts, that is, on the *mind* of the writer and on the *effect* on the audience – hence the crucial role of Longinus's treatise in the "subjective turn" of modern aesthetics.

Given the larger aims of this study, I will not attempt, in these first three chapters devoted to Longinus, to offer a comprehensive reading of *Peri hypsous*. Rather I concentrate on those sections of the treatise that reveal the

---

[1] Plato's discussions of art and poetry are of course also very influential; however, save for the *Ion*, these are not concentrated in a treatise or dialogue, but rather appear as ancillary parts of larger discussions, as in the *Republic* and the *Symposium*.

[2] Narrowly construed, this point per se is not controversial. In a recent book on Kant (*Kant's Critique of Taste: A Reading of the* Critique of Judgment, 302), Henry Allison remarks that "largely as a result of [Longinus's] treatise, the topic of the sublime assumed central significance in the aesthetic reflections of the eighteenth century." However, what is not typically recognized is the extent to which the Longinian concept has a structuring effect on the modern interpretation of sublimity.

[3] In the sense of: "The state of excelling or surpassing or going beyond usual limits" (http://www.th efreedictionary.com/transcendence, accessed June 7, 2014).

coherent aesthetic and philosophical program that made the sublime one of the key concepts of modern thought. These sections, namely 1–15, 34–36, and 44, can be said to form Longinus's "theory of sublimity," his subjective and intersubjective account of literary practice.[4] Chapter 1 of this study explores how Longinus introduces and situates *hypsos* in the opening sections (1–7) of his treatise; Chapter 2 analyzes Longinus's five sources of *hypsos*, giving particular attention to the first two "natural" sources of grandeur of conception (*noêsis*) and strong emotion (*pathos*) (8–15); and Chapter 3 shows how the themes of natural grandeur (34–36) and cultural decline (44), though they may appear digressive, are in fact integral to Longinus's account. The remaining sections of *Peri hypsous* (16–33; 37–43) resemble a more conventional "rhetorical treatise": the enumeration of technical-stylistic devices and the illustration of good and bad usage through myriad examples. I briefly discuss these sections at the end of Chapter 2, with reference to the dichotomy between nature and artifice in Longinus's theory.

This chapter begins by addressing the vexed question of the authorship of *Peri hypsous*, which is especially important with regard to the modern reception of the treatise.[5] The second section traces Longinus's relation to ancient style, contending that his use of the term *logos* (discourse) in his brief definition of *hypsos* (1.3) has been mistakenly adduced in support of the rhetorical-stylistic interpretation of the treatise. I thus follow G. M. A. Grube in arguing for a more expansive interpretation of *logos* in Longinus, namely as the nexus of thought and expression, to better understand the author's admittedly ambiguous definition and how it fits within the basic subjective orientation of his theory. I conclude this section by noting that even if other rhetorical or stylistic treatises of the Roman period contain some philosophical elements, none approach Longinus's systematic effort to elucidate the idea of sublimity or grandeur in the verbal arts as the "echo of a noble mind" (9.1). The third section explains how Longinus defines *hypsos* as the dual experience of being at once overwhelmed and elevated, dominated and exalted. Through a careful examination of the key terms used to characterize this experience – *ekstasis* (ecstasy), *thaumasion* (awe), and *ekplêxis* (astonishment) – I show how Longinus combines religious and

---

[4] I thus largely agree with Mats Malm, who observes: "In *Peri Hupsous* chapter 16 and onwards consist mainly of a rather conventional presentation of figures and tropes. The first part of the treatise, through chapter 15, is what is usually regarded as the treatise on the sublime" ("On the Technique of the Sublime," 5).

[5] Throughout the seventeenth and eighteenth centuries the author was taken to be the heroic Cassius Longinus (213–273 AD).

poetic connotations to define an aesthetic concept of transcendence as an experience of *intensity*, an experience Longinus also characterizes temporally in terms of *kairos* (the moment). The fourth section explores how Longinus defines *hypsos* from the perspective of its *production*, contending that Longinus's theory of sublimity doubles as a theory of creativity, of *genius* – the first such theory in Western thought. I argue that Longinus's definition of genius as a combination of nature and *technê* (art) exposes a broader dialectic between nature and culture in the sublime. The fifth section studies Longinus's contrast between authentic sublimity and its simulacrum, in particular how the idea of the "true sublime" points to a universal and transhistorical conception of aesthetic experience and judgment, an idea that is somewhat at odds with the singular experience of ecstasy articulated at the beginning of the treatise.

1.1   In search of "Longinus"

The origins of *Peri hypsous* are obscure. Not mentioned in any ancient source, the treatise emerges only during the Italian Renaissance, with the circulation of several manuscript copies.[6] The *edito princeps* was published in 1554 by Francesco Robortello (1516–1567), an Italian humanist and philologist who had authored an influential commentary on Aristotle's *Poetics* a few years prior.[7] Robortello's Greek-only edition was quickly followed by three more Greek editions, those of Paulus Manutius (Venice, 1555), Franciscus Portus (Geneva, 1569), and Pietro Pagano (Venice, 1572), the last of which included a Latin translation.[8] At a time when the poetics of Horace and Aristotle were the dominant force in shaping critical attitudes, *Peri hypsous* made only a slight impression.[9] The fortunes of the treatise would change dramatically, however, with Nicolas Boileau's translation into French in 1674.[10] Boileau's edition became an

---

[6] There are twelve surviving manuscripts of the *Peri hypsous*: the oldest dates from the tenth century, the others from the fifteenth and sixteenth centuries. All appear to derive from the tenth-century manuscript (Parisinus [gr.] 2036).

[7] Francesco Robortello, *In Aristotelis poeticam explicationes* (1548).

[8] Jules Brody observes that Portus's edition served "as the basis for all subsequent editions until the eighteenth century. And from the point of view of effective influence, Portus, rather than Robortello, deserves credit for the *princeps*" (*Boileau and Longinus*, 10).

[9] Brody notes that there were "nine Greek texts, twenty-nine Latin and six vernacular versions of [Aristotle's] *Poetics*," in the seventeenth century (*Boileau and Longinus*, 11). See also Marvin T. Herrick, *The Fusion of Horatian and Aristotelian Literary Criticism, 1531–1555*.

[10] Boileau's French edition was preceded by two other translations into the vernacular: an Italian translation by Niccolò Pinelli (Padua, 1639); and an English version by John Hall (London, 1652). These translations had very little impact, however, on the reception of Longinus's treatise. Eva

instant sensation, transforming "Longinus" into a major European critic and introducing the term "sublime" into the critical lexicon.[11]

The first question that confronts the reader of *Peri hypsous* is that of the status of the text, namely the issues of dating, authorship, and incompleteness. Approximately one third (roughly 1000 lines) of the text is missing. The lacunae occur regularly throughout the text, and, with the exception of the discussion of emotion, *pathos*,[12] they do not disturb the author's main lines of thought. With respect to authorship and dating, the scholarly consensus over the past 150 years or so has, with a few notable exceptions,[13] come down on the side of an unknown "pseudo-Longinus," thought to have lived in the first century AD. The oldest manuscript we possess, from a volume of tenth-century manuscripts containing *The Problems of Aristotle*,[14] attributes the fragment to "Dionysius" or "Longinus," referring, presumably, to the rhetorician and historian Dionysius of Halicarnassus (60–c. 7 BC)[15] and the philosopher and political advisor Cassius Longinus (213–273 AD), respectively.[16] However, because the equivocation was not perceived until much later (the "or" appearing only in the table of contents of the tenth-century collection),[17] "Dionysius Longinus," the name inscribed

Madeleine Martin ("The 'Prehistory' of the Sublime," 82) speaks of an anonymous French translator who preceded Boileau.

[11] Boileau follows the practice of the early Greek editions, whose Latin subtitles used the adjective *sublimis*. See Chapter 4.

[12] See Chapter 2 of this study.

[13] At least two major critics, G. M. A. Grube and Malcolm Heath, have argued in support of Cassius Longinus (third century) as the author. See: Grube's introduction to Longinus, *On Great Writing (On the Sublime)*, trans. G. M. A. Grube, as well as Grube's *The Greek and Roman Critics*, chapter 21; and Malcolm Heath, "Longinus, *On Sublimity*." On the other hand, C. M. Mazzucchi, in his Italian edition of Longinus (*Del sublime*, 2010), allows for the possibility of an otherwise unknown "Dionysius Longinus."

[14] This manuscript, preserved at the Bibliothèque Nationale de France, in Paris, is labeled Parisinus (gr.) 2036.

[15] Dionysius of Halicarnassus came to Rome in 30 BC and remained for twenty-two years. Many of his works have survived. There are some superficial resemblances between the author of the *Peri hypsous* and Dionysius of Halicarnassus (notably, the comparison between Cicero and Demosthenes), but this attribution has been definitively ruled out. Dionysius of Halicarnassus's critique of Plato's style and praise for Lysias are diametrically opposed to the views expressed in *Peri hypsous*.

[16] The list of Cassius Longinus's works (none of which is extant) in the *Suda* includes *Homeric Questions*; *Whether Homer Is a Philosopher*; *Homeric Problems and Solutions*, and two treatises on Attic diction. A substantial fragment of Cassius Longinus's *On the Chief End* was preserved by his student Porphyry, who mentions Cassius Longinus in his biography of Plotinus.

[17] The first challenge to the authorship of the treatise was by the Italian scholar Girolamo Amati, who in 1808 came across a Vatican manuscript (V. 285), in which the author is referred to as Dionysius *or* Longinus, a finding confirmed, as mentioned above, by the table of contents of the tenth-century manuscript (Parisinus [gr.] 2036). Benjamin Weiske's edition of 1809 was the first to proclaim this fact and to cast doubt on the attribution to Cassius Longinus.

at the head of the manuscript, was taken to be Cassius Dionysius Longinus, that is, the third-century Cassius Longinus, an attribution that prevailed from the sixteenth to the early nineteenth centuries.[18]

To all appearances, the author of *Peri hypsous* was a Greek rhetorician living in Rome, where he worked as a tutor to noble Roman families (educated Romans were bilingual at this time, and Greek teachers were much sought after). Written in the form of an epistle to Postumius Terentianus, presumably a young Roman nobleman, Longinus endeavors to explain how to achieve *hypsos* – elevation, loftiness, sublimity – in writing and speaking. The author presents himself as a pedagogue of great breadth and experience; he refers to four other works he has authored (none of which has survived): a treatise on *pathos*, another on Xenophon, and two on the art of composition. Longinus's writing, particularly in the opening sections, is quite dense, suggesting that he is perhaps summarizing arguments rehearsed elsewhere. Following the Greek rhetorical tradition, Longinus's references and citations cover all the major genres of artistic writing: history, philosophy, poetry (lyric, epic, drama), and oratory.[19] Longinus reveals his cosmopolitism by comparing the Latin orator and theorist Cicero with the Greek orator Demosthenes (a rare foray into Latin literature by a Greek writer)[20] and by quoting from the Hebrew Bible ("Let there be light . . .").[21] Conspicuously absent from *Peri hypsous* is any discussion or even mention of style levels (high, middle, low), a virtual catechism of Latin but also Greek rhetorical works of early Rome (in Dionysius of Halicarnassus, for example). Most striking of all is the treatise's lively, pithy, and refreshingly unpedantic style, a stark contrast to the rhetorical manuals of the era.

---

[18] I discuss how the heroic death of Cassius Longinus influenced Boileau's conception of sublimity in Chapter 4.

[19] Dietmar Till observes that, during this period, "rhetoric no longer aims at oral communication, but expands into new fields like historiography, natural philosophy, and theology. All of these new fields are primarily literary, rather than oral. Rhetoric is transformed from the art of speaking to a textual theory" ("The Sublime and the Bible: Longinus, Protestant Dogmatics, and the 'Sublime Style,'" 58). "Textual theory" may be too modern a concept, but the idea that Longinus's notion of rhetoric is far more expansive than many give him credit for is crucial to my argument in Part I.

[20] Richard Macksey notes that *Peri hypsous* can be seen as "the first significant example of the comparative spirit at work" ("Longinus Reconsidered," 914). Scholars speculate that Longinus might not have had direct knowledge of Cicero, but he was rather influenced by Caecilius's comparison of Cicero and Demosthenes. See Heath, "Longinus, *On Sublimity*," 49.

[21] Some critics believe that this reference to the Bible might have been a later interpolation, but no conclusive case has been made. For a discussion of the controversy surrounding Boileau's use of this example, see Chapter 4.

1.2 Longinus and ancient rhetoric: sublimity (*hypsos*), discourse (*logos*), and the question of style

The opening sentence of Longinus's treatise reads: "My dear Postumius Terentianus, you will recall that when we were reading together Caecilius's monograph *Peri hypsous* we felt that it was inadequate to its high subject, and failed to touch on the essential points" (1.1). The immediate impetus for Longinus's treatise is another *Peri hypsous*, by the first-century critic and historian Caecilius of Calacte, a member of Dionysius of Halicarnassus's circle and thus a rough contemporary of Longinus,[22] if the first-century dating is accepted. Caecilius will in fact serve as Longinus's interlocutor and foil throughout the treatise. According to the Byzantine *Suda* lexicon, Caecilius was a Jew, and thus he may be Longinus's source for the citation from Genesis 1:3 ("Let there be light . . ."). Although only short fragments of this critic's works are extant,[23] we can surmise that Caecilius was a dry, technically oriented teacher who, together with Dionysius of Halicarnassus, played an important role in the revival and defense of Atticism, the restrained, classical style of fifth- and fourth-century Greece. This movement saw itself as a counterweight to the then fashionable Asiatic style – the florid or bombastic style – which the Atticists considered decadent. Although Longinus also uses the notion of *hypsos* to support an Atticist position,[24] he criticizes what he considers to be Caecilius's extreme form of Atticism, particularly Caecilius's preference for the Attic orator Lysias over Plato (see 32.8).[25] Indeed, the contrast Longinus draws between himself and Caecilius turns principally on their views of Plato.[26]

Within Greek rhetoric of the Roman period (146 BC to 330 AD), Caecilius, Dionysius of Halicarnassus, and Longinus (whether or not "Longinus" is their exact contemporary) form a subgroup. A word search of the extant texts reveals that, among ancient rhetoricians, only these

---

[22] Caecilius of Calacte and Dionysius of Halicarnassus are considered to be the two most important rhetorical theorists of the Augustan age. See Rhys Roberts, "The Literary Circle of Dionysius of Halicarnassus."

[23] Among the other works Caecilius is known to have authored include *On the Style of the Ten Orators, History of the Servile Wars, On Rhetoric and Rhetorical Figures*, and *Against the Phrygians*.

[24] George Kennedy notes that "[*Peri hypsous*] certainly belongs to the classicizing, Atticizing movement of this whole period" (*A New History of Classical Rhetoric*, 192). Looking forward, Ernst Curtius asserts that "Asianism is the first form of European Mannerism, Atticism that of European Classicism" (*European Literature in the Latin Middle Ages*, 67).

[25] Known for the simplicity of his style, Lysias became a rallying cry for supporters of Atticism; Dionysius of Halicarnassus wrote a treatise on Lysias.

[26] See D. C. Innes, "Longinus and Caecilius: Models of the Sublime."

three feature *hypsos* in their writings.[27] The fact that the use of *hypsos* is limited to such a small group of writers is evidence of a critical tradition that developed to some extent independently. Nevertheless, other rhetoricians do employ similar terms, such as "grandeur" (*megethos*), a term that Longinus uses as a virtual synonym for *hypsos*, or Demetrius's *deinotes* (forcefulness) in his treatise *On Style*. While these terms might be considered to have a family resemblance, what sets Longinus's term apart is its association with a quality of mind (*megalophrosynê*, high-mind-edness). Of course, Longinus does have a great deal to say about the technique (*technê*) of *hypsos*, its stylistic manifestation; however, as we will see in the next chapter, he subordinates this to what he calls the "natural" sources of grand conceptions (*noêseis*) and vehement emotion (*enthousiastikon pathos*). Thus while Longinus's treatise is certainly moti-vated and shaped by these discussions of the high style, his conception of *hypsos* reaches far beyond them.

Despite his theoretical ambitions, Longinus treats *hypsos* as if it were a well-established topic of discussion, too self-evident or well known to require extensive definition, telling his student, Terentianus, that "Caecilius tries at immense length to explain to us what sort of thing 'the sublime' is, as though we did not know" (1.1) and that "your education dispenses me from any long preliminary definition [of *hypsos*]" (1.3). *Hypsos* is thus not a new concept Longinus intended to invent, even if he proposes a new *theory*. That Longinus effectively creates the concept of "the sub-lime" is a function of the fact that no other ancient text on *hypsos* is extant, and the extant treatises that do discuss *hypsos* or *megethos* (grandeur) are, as noted above, stylistically oriented and do not possess the philosophical depth of Longinus's account.

Much of the controversy surrounding whether *hypsos* is primarily a philosophical (protoaesthetic) or a stylistic (technical-rhetorical) notion can be traced to Longinus's brief characterization of *hypsos* in the opening section of his treatise:[28] "Sublimity [*hypsos*] is a kind of eminence or excellence of discourse [*logoi*]. It is the source of the distinction of the very greatest poets [*poiêtai*] and prose writers [*suggrapheis*] and the means

---

[27] Dionysius of Halicarnassus uses *hypsêlos* to describe the elevated or grand style, which he contrasts with the plain (*ischnos*) style.

[28] Indeed, critics have long lamented that *Peri hypsous* lacks a comprehensive definition of its central term. John Baillie in his influential *An Essay on the Sublime* (1747) sums up the view of many when he writes: "Longinus has entirely passed over the inquiry of what the sublime is, as a thing perfectly well known" (http://www.earthworks.org/sublime/Baillie/index.html, accessed July 6, 2013).

by which they have given eternal life to their own fame" (1.3).[29] Longinus can be said to make three basic points in this dictum: (1) *hypsos* is intrinsically related to *logos*; (2) *hypsos* implies a transgeneric conception of literary value; and (3) *hypsos* is universal and transhistorical. Commentators generally fixate on the first point, though the others are equally important and will be developed in more depth in other parts of the treatise.

Prima facie the first point appears to support the technical-stylistic interpretation of *hypsos*, and it is no doubt what prompted the Renaissance editors of *Peri hypsous* to classify it as a contribution to the *genera dicendi* – a dissertation on the grand style.[30] This view was overturned only with Boileau's edition of 1674, which for the first time distinguished *le sublime* from *le style sublime*. Sans Boileau, *hypsos* would have no doubt remained a concept of style for a very long time, and the idea of aesthetic transcendence that coalesced around the term "sublime" would have never played the important role that it did in eighteenth-century thought.[31]

Given the significance of this definitional passage for the interpretation of Longinus's *hypsos* we must take care to analyze it properly. Of the greatest importance is the fact that Longinus uses the term *logoi* instead of *charaktêr* (style) or *lexis* (style, diction). *Logos* (*logoi* in the plural) is a notoriously difficult word to pin down, much less translate, given the plethora of meanings it possessed in ancient Greek. It can mean "speech," "discourse," or "language," but it can also be translated as "reason" or

---

[29] Grube, who refuses to use the term "sublime" in his edition of Longinus, translates this passage thus: "Great passages have a high distinction of thought and expression to which great writers owe their supremacy and their lasting renown" (*On Great Writing*, 4).

[30] The Latin titles given to the first editions are instructive: F. Robortello (Basel, 1554), *Dionysii Longini rhetoris praestantissimi liber, De grandi, sive sublimi orationis genere*; P. Manutius (Venice, 1555), *Dionysii Longini De sublimi genere dicendi*; F. Porto (1570), *Dionysii Longini De grandi, sive sublimi genere orationis*; G. de Petra (Geneva, 1612), *Dionysii Longini ... De grandi, sive sublimi genere orationis*; G. Langbaine (Oxford, 1636, Latin and Greek, Latin translation by de Petra), *Dionysiou Longinou rhêtoros Peri hypsous logou biblion: Dionysii Longini rhetoris præstantissimi liber De grandi loquentia sive sublimi dicendi genere Latine redditus hypothesesi synoptikais et ad oram notationibus aliquot illustrates*.

[31] It is thus no coincidence that in the introduction to his 1958 translation of *Peri hypsous*, which he entitles *On Great Writing*, Grube virtually paraphrases Boileau's Preface, writing that "Longinus is not concerned with the grand or any other kind of style. Many of the examples he gives have nothing grand about their *style* – e.g., in the ninth chapter, Ajax silently striding away, his prayer to Zeus, and the quotation from *Genesis*. What grandeur there is is of conception, not of expression.... For purposes of translation, we shall be much closer to the meaning of *hypsos* and its derivatives and synonyms throughout if we render them by a quite general word such as 'greatness' or 'great writing' and the like" (*On Great Writing*, xi). Grube's title may have been inspired by E. E. Sikes, who translates Longinus's title as "On Great Writing" in his *The Greek View of Poetry* (1931), 209. But if "great writing" were all that was at issue, then comedy could be considered sublime as well, which is definitely not the case for Longinus (despite 40.2).

"logic" in a more philosophical setting. Fyfe translates *logoi* in this passage as "language"; Rhys Roberts uses "expression"; while, as seen above, Russell has "discourse." In the notes to his translation, Roberts remarks that *logoi* (in the plural) is "probably the nearest Greek equivalent for literature, though more especially applied to prose writings."[32] Grube's translation of *logoi* as "thought and expression" is perhaps the most perceptive solution, given its introduction of a subjective element. In a footnote to this passage, Grube observes:

> The Greek word *logos*, either in the singular or the plural, can refer to the content of a passage (what is being said) or to the language in which it is said, or both. It is here usually translated as the second, i.e., "distinction of language" or the like. This I believe is mistaken, for we find later that diction or the choice of words is but one of the five sources of sublimity, and Longinus puts a great deal of emphasis on the mind of the writer throughout; indeed, the thought alone, without its expression, may be sufficient. *Logos* therefore refers here to both thought and expression.[33]

Grube understands that in Longinus's usage *logos* is not merely a function of *technê* (rhetorical art) but includes an element of *noêsis* (thought or conception), which, according to Longinus, is the most important source of *hypsos*.[34] Longinus himself remarks that "in discourse [*logos*], thought [*noêsis*] and diction [*phrasis*] are of course very much involved with each other" (30.1). Indeed, Grube's rendition has the advantage of being able to join the "technical" with the "natural" sources of sublimity, which Longinus takes care to distinguish without necessarily separating them.[35]

We might also consider the notion of *logos* put forth by Philo of Alexandria (c. 20 BC to c. 50 AD), a Hellenistic Jew thought to have influenced Longinus (some in fact believe he is the "Philosopher" referred to in the concluding section of the treatise). Philo identifies *logos* with the creative principle of the universe that mediates between man and God – a conception derived from Stoicism (also an influence on Longinus), which Philo attempts

---

[32] Roberts, *Longinus On the Sublime*, 203. "*Logoi* [in Longinus's treatise] may be rendered by such equivalents as diction, style, discourse, language, composition" (Roberts, *Longinus On the Sublime*, 203).

[33] Longinus, *On Great Writing*, 4, n. 2.

[34] James Arieti and John Crossett similarly observe that when reading Longinus "we may take the combination of thought or intention, and tongue or speech, to be *logos*" (*Longinus: On the Sublime*, 9).

[35] Malcolm Heath remarks that "it might, indeed, be objected against Longinus's argument that *technê* itself is a product of human rationality: humans are rational, and therefore also technical, by nature. But Longinus could reasonably maintain that *logos*, which is a direct expression of our rational nature, has precedence over any derivative manifestation of our rational nature" (*Ancient Philosophical Poetics*, 177).

to syncretize with Judaism. The most famous expression of this view of *logos* is found in the Gospel of John (first century AD), which opens with the iconic phrase: "In the beginning was the Word [*logos*] and the Word [*logos*] was with God, and the Word [*logos*] was God" (1.1). The divinization of (secular) literature (*logoi*) is also a hallmark of Longinian *hypsos*: "Sublimity [*hypsos*] raises us toward the spiritual greatness of god" (36.1).

Boileau's distinction between sublimity and the sublime style satisfied the vast majority of Longinus's readers from the sixteenth to the eighteenth centuries. However, with the advent of modern philology in the nineteenth century there has been a reconsideration of Longinus's place in ancient rhetoric. Twentieth- and twentieth-first-century critics are divided, even polarized, on the question of whether, or the extent to which, *Peri hypsous* should be considered a treatise on the grand style. In the first modern scholarly edition of the treatise in English (1899), Rhys Roberts asserts that "the object of the author is to indicate the essentials of a noble and impressive style."[36] The great romance philologist Erich Auerbach writes similarly in 1958: "The most important among the theorists of the Imperial Age, the unknown author of the Greek treatise *On the Sublime*, who probably lived in the first half of the first century AD, spoke impressively on the matter. The lofty style [*der hohe Stil*], he says in substance, is not, like the middle style, intended to please and persuade but to fire with enthusiasm and to carry away."[37] More recently (2000), Jeffrey Walker has stated that "'Longinus' has written a highly specialized rhetorical treatise focused wholly on the principles and techniques of a single type of persuasive style."[38]

On the other side of the argument are important classicists such as Grube and Russell. Grube opines that "Longinus especially differs from the analytical and rhetorical approach of his fellow critics. Not since Plato had this kind of emphasis been laid upon the writer's mind."[39] Russell concurs: "To say that *hypsos* is that which fills us with joy and pride, stays in the mind, and pleases universally, is to go much deeper into the essential qualities of greatness in literature than any stylistic description can do.... [H]igh thinking and strong passion ... are functions of qualities of character and mind in the writer."[40] Russell goes even further, remarking that "at no point in their history did *hypsos* and its cognates quite lose their moral and social connections; they are never quite at home in literary

---

[36] Roberts, *Longinus On the Sublime*, 23.
[37] Auerbach, *Literary Language and Its Public in Late Latin Antiquity and in the Middle Ages*, 194.
[38] Jeffrey Walker, *Rhetoric and Poetics in Antiquity*, 118.   [39] Grube, *On Great Writing*, xiii.
[40] Russell, "Introduction," in *"Longinus" On the Sublime*, xxxviii.

criticism."[41] On this view, *hypsos* can be considered a social-psychological metaphor that is never fully literalized by its stylistic manifestation.

Needless to say, this study sides with Russell's and Grube's nonstylistic, subjective interpretation of *hypsos*, considering it more of a philosophical than a strictly rhetorical concept.[42] In a recent book (2011), Stephen Halliwell stresses that *Peri hypsous* represents a "marriage of the traditions of Greek rhetoric ... with the mentality of Greek philosophy."[43] In a similar vein, Dimitrios Vardoulakis observes that the "concerns of *Peri hypsous (On the Sublime)* go far beyond criticism, engaged as it is on a number of perennial philosophical issues, such as human nature," and that there are thus "philosophical presuppositions which underpin *hypsos*."[44] Like Halliwell and Vardoulakis, I am inclined to see in Longinus's elaboration of *hypsos* a philosophical effort to understand the human being from the perspective of the verbal arts, without thereby denying the rhetorical-stylistic dimension of Longinus's text.

Inextricably tied to the question of Longinus's relation to ancient style is the question of his originality. Those who insist on a rhetorical-stylistic interpretation of *Peri hypsous* are more prone to see Longinus as conventional or traditional, whereas those who see Longinus's project in a more expansive and philosophical light are generally more inclined to perceive uniqueness and originality. Thus Grube writes of *Peri hypsous* that "its importance as a work of literary theory and criticism, its uniqueness among ancient critical texts, are obvious."[45] Ernst Curtius similarly asserts that "great criticism is extremely rare. Hence it is rarely recognized. If the whole of late Antiquity has not a word to say about 'Longinus,' that is one of the clearest symptoms of its debilitated intellectual energy."[46] Russell, on the other hand, retorts that "Ernst Curtius, in company of many, exaggerates. It is Longinus's eloquence, and the fact that no similar work survives, that have led people to think him more mysterious than he really is. In fact, he represents a tradition."[47] Russell sees Longinus as representing a

---

[41] Russell, "Introduction," in *"Longinus" On the Sublime*, xxx.

[42] More recently (1993), Baldine Saint Girons has remarked that "Longinus ... largely transcends the field of rhetoric" (*Fiat Lux: Une philosophie du sublime*, 31 [my trans.]).

[43] Stephen Halliwell, *Between Ecstasy and Truth: Interpretations of Greek Poetics from Homer to Longinus*, 328.

[44] Dimitrios Vardoulakis, "The Play of *Logos* and *Pathos*: Longinus' Philosophical Presuppositions," 47. In the earliest English translation of Longinus to circulate widely, that of William Smith (1739), the translator notes in his introduction: "Having traced our author thus far as a *Critic*, we must view him now in another light, I mean as a *Philosopher*. In Him these are not different, but mutually depending and co-existing parts of the same character" (*Dionysius Longinus on the Sublime*, xxvi).

[45] Grube, *On Great Writing*, vii.   [46] Curtius, *European Literature*, 400.

[47] Russell, *Aristotle/Longinus/Demetrius*, 152.

distinctively *Greek* tradition,[48] one associated with the move away from the tripartite division of styles – the *genera dicendi* – that typify Roman rhetoric, to notions of qualitative types of writing,[49] such as Dionysius of Halicarnassus's *epithetoi aretai* (additional virtues), discussed in the first century BC, and Hermogenes's *ideai* (tones or forms of speech), formulated in the second century AD.[50] Russell, however, notes that *Peri hypsous* "is sharply distinguished from anything Hermogenes wrote by its firm moral basis."[51] Indeed, Longinus's combination of moral philosophy and rhetoric in his use of *hypsos* to denote an affective state of high-mindedness (*megalophrosynê*) is quite unique, even if, as noted above, Longinus's use of the term *megethos* (grandeur) as a quasi-synonym for *hypsos* invites comparison with other rhetoricians of the Roman period.

One can also see Longinus as, in the words of one critic, the "culmination" of a Greek tradition that laid "increasing weight on force and passion, partly in reaction to Alexandrian refinement."[52] If we compare Longinus's treatise with Demetrius's *On Style*, for example, we find unmistakable parallels. A phrase from Demetrius such as "long clauses also produce grandeur [*megethos*]" (44) seems indistinguishable from a passage in Longinus such as "nothing is of greater service in giving grandeur [*megethos*] to what is said than the organization of the various members" (40.1). Demetrius also presents his project in terms that appear to mirror Longinus's sources of *hypsos* (thought/conception, emotion, figures, diction, composition): "I shall begin with grandeur, which men today identify with true eloquence. Grandeur has three aspects, thought [*dianoia*], diction [*lexis*], and composition in the appropriate way" (38). However, in Demetrius the concept of grandeur is presupposed and is subordinate to style, whereas in Longinus the elucidation of grandeur/ sublimity is the principal object of the treatise, and style (figures, diction,

---

[48] Francis Goyet, on the other hand, perceives a continuity between *Peri hypsous* and the Latin rhetorical tradition. Goyet sees Longinus's *hypsos* as merely a variant on the Latin concept of *movere*, the capacity of the verbal arts to have a strong emotional impact on the reader/spectator (to "move" or "stir" emotionally). Longinus is considered exceptional only because he is writing in Greek. See Goyet, "Introduction," TS, 7–18.

[49] The first systematic presentation of style levels appears in the unattributed *Ad Herennium* (first-century BC). However, the origins are likely Greek; some scholars believe that the tripartite scheme was invented by Theophrastus (c. 371–c. 287 BC).

[50] Hermogenes identifies seven *ideai*: Clarity, Grandeur (*megethos*), Beauty, Speed, Ethos, Verity, and Gravity or Decorum. "Grandeur," the term that most closely approximates sublimity, is subdivided into six categories: Magnificence, Asperity, Vehemence, Vigor, Splendor, and Circumlocution. One critic has observed that "one might see in the Greek proliferation of style-types an emerging notion of literary aesthetics" (anonymous reader of the manuscript for this book).

[51] Russell, *Aristotle/Longinus/Demetrius*, 154.

[52] Debora Shuger, "The Grand Style and the *genera dicendi* in Ancient Rhetoric," 32.

composition) an ancillary consideration. Moreover, what Demetrius understands by "thought," *dianoia*, in his treatise is really subject matter.[53] Similarly, Aristotle in *Poetics* 19 speaks of "diction [*lexis*] and thought [*dianoia*]" as parts of tragedy. *Dianoia* is thus not a psychical or subjective notion, as in Longinus's second source of sublimity, *noêsis* (thought/conception).[54]

Finally, we come to the vexed question of how to translate *hypsos*, a question whose importance is often underestimated. Despite the almost universal acceptance of "the sublime" or "sublimity" as a translation for Longinus's *hypsos* in English, as well as other Latin-based languages, there is really no satisfactory English equivalent. The most literal translations would be "height," "elevation," or "loftiness." The image of height allows *hypsos* to function as a metaphor for certain attributes of mind or expression, such as "elevated thoughts" or "a lofty passage," attributes also associated with a noble or high-minded disposition. As Longinus understands it, *hypsos* thus connotes a kind of outstripping of oneself in terms of one's mental capacity or state of mind, a going beyond normal human limits in the sense of being proximate to the divine. However, unlike the Latinate "sublime," *hypsos* loses its metaphoricity when applied to objects in the world, where it refers only to things that are *physically* high or elevated, such as mountains, platforms, buildings, clouds, and so on. Hence the absurdity of calling the ocean "elevated," though we might well call it "sublime."

As a metaphor for a human quality, *hypsos* (or, as an adjective, *hupsêlos*) and the Latinate "sublime" are virtually identical: "a sublime passage," "a sublime thought," or "a sublime mind" are the exact equivalent (in Longinian terms) of "an elevated passage," an "elevated thought," or "an elevated mind."[55] However, the term "sublime" functions *only* in a figurative sense – hence its ability to bring this sense to bear on objects in the world (the "sublimity of the ocean"). Using the term "elevation" (*hypsos*) to describe a mountain range (or a raised platform, for that matter) activates only the literal sense, whereas characterizing a mountain range as "sublime" introduces a host of metaphorical connotations (majesty, power, and so

---

[53] In the same vein, Aristotle's notion of *spoudaios* (elevation) refers to "the subject matter of serious in contradistinction to comic poetry (48b34, 49b10)" (Stephen Halliwell, Introduction to Aristotle's *Poetics*, in: *Aristotle/Longinus/Demetrius*, 13).

[54] I explore the concept of *noêsis* in more detail in Chapter 2.

[55] The etymology of "sublime" derives from a combination of *sub* (under) and *limen* (threshold or limit). The possibility of a different etymology has been discussed by E. Partridge, *Origins: An Etymological Dictionary of Modern English*, 358.

forth) that "elevation" does not, when applied to objects in the world. *Qua* metaphor, then, *hypsos* pertains *exclusively* to the human realm, analogizing human words, thoughts, or actions to the imposing aspect of physical height (and there is of course the ubiquitous association between divinity and height, epitomized in the Hebrew *'Ēl 'Elyōn*, "God Most High"). This is why Kant will complain that the German translation of *hypsos, das Erhabene* – which is actually much closer to *hypsos* and to the English word "elevation" than to "the sublime" – is generally used improperly. It should refer, he argues, not to great or overpowering objects in nature, but to the mental disposition activated by such experiences (sublimity of mind).[56] No doubt many of the interpretive problems associated with the use of the term "sublime" could be solved by replacing it with "elevation," though, to my knowledge, only one critic (the twentieth-century philosopher Monroe Beardsley) has advocated its use.[57]

1.3 The experience of sublimity (*hypsos*): ecstasy (*ekstasis*), astonishment (*ekplêxis*), wonder (*thaumasion*), and the moment (*kairos*)

As the modern interpretation of sublimity abundantly shows, the most consequential way of defining sublimity is by describing its *effect* on the reader/spectator, which Longinus does in iconic fashion in 1.4. Indeed, as noted in the Introduction, the modern characterizations of sublimity all hark back in some way to Longinus's description of *hypsos* as the experience of transcendence.

Of course the effect of speech on an audience has always been an integral part of rhetoric, understood as persuasive public speaking.[58] From the outset of his treatise Longinus takes care to separate *hypsos* from this Aristotelian tradition:

> Grandeur [*ta huperphua*] produces ecstasy [*ekstasis*] rather than persuasion in the hearer; and the combination of wonder [*thaumasion*] and astonishment [*ekplêxis*] always proves superior to the merely persuasive and pleasant [*tou pros charin*: "that directed towards charm/pleasure"]. This because persuasion is on the whole something we can control, whereas amazement

---

[56] Kant writes: "We express ourselves on the whole incorrectly if we call some object of nature sublime. . . . We can say no more than that the object serves for the presentation of a sublimity that can be found in the mind" (CPJ, 5:245).

[57] In his monumental *Aesthetics from Classical Greece to the Present* (76), Beardsley writes: "The lively book *On Elevation in Poetry* (*Peri Hypsous*, usually translated "On the Sublime") is another largely pedagogical work, brilliantly carried out."

[58] Aristotle's *Rhetoric* is a case in point: the second book is devoted to a systematic discussion of human emotion and is as much an anthropological investigation as a rhetorical one.

[*ekplêxis*] and wonder [*thaumasion*] exert invincible power [*dynamis*] and force and get the better of every hearer. (1.4)[59]

Although there are some parallels with other rhetorical treatises, treatises that, like *Peri hypsous*, are concerned more with the glories of written literature (criticism) than with living speech (practical oratory), this passage nevertheless indicates Longinus's singular commitment to an aesthetics of transcendence, to an experience resembling or analogous to mystical religious experience. This involves a *dual structure* of being at once *overwhelmed* ("invincible power and force" that "get the better of every hearer") and *elevated* ("ecstasy" [*ekstasis*], literally: going outside of oneself), the structure that will come to define the experience of sublimity in the modern age. The contrast with persuasive rhetoric is instructive, for persuasion can also involve the arousal of strong emotions or affects. Longinus's contrast is thus both qualitative and quantitative. Persuasion is qualitatively different from ecstasy in the sense that it involves an emotional and rational manipulation in regard to a particular end, an extrinsic purposiveness, an instrumental relation to the social world ("something we can control"). Ecstasy, on the other hand, and the concomitant affects of amazement (or astonishment) and wonder (or awe or admiration), involve only an intrinsic purposiveness; these affects/effects are for Longinus an *end in themselves*. *Hypsos* is thus a matter of the nature of the self: the raising of the self to a feeling of its own elevation, the self's vocation to outstrip itself. Thus if a passage of persuasive rhetoric can be said to exhibit *hypsos*, it does so only insofar as it *transcends* its persuasive function – as is the case with oratory that has become "literature" (in particular, the speeches of Demosthenes, for Longinus); its aesthetic appreciation presupposes a divorce from its practical context. Persuasion is also quantitatively different from ecstasy – hence Longinus's insistence on the *intensity of affect/effect* ("invincible power"). Longinus's use of the term *charis* (charm/pleasure, but also *hêdonê* in other contexts) to denote effects of lesser intensity prefigures the modern contrast between the "mere" pleasure of the beautiful and the intense feeling produced by the sublime, which borders on pain.

Although it might appear to conflict with the criterion of ecstasy, Longinus also stresses the practical aspect of his teaching, given that the treatise's putative addressee (Terentianus) would appear to be destined for

[59] As in other places in the text, Longinus here uses a synonym for *hypsos*; this one, *ta huperphua*, literally meaning "what is grown to an exceptional size" is similar to *megethos*: "the great" or "greatness." But *ta huperphua* can also mean "supernatural" or "marvelous." Boileau perhaps takes his cue from this word in his use of *le merveilleux* in the subtitle to his 1674 translation.

public life: "You have urged me to set down a few notes on sublimity [*hypsos*] for your own use. Let us then consider whether there is anything in my observations which may be thought useful to public men [*politikoi*]" (1.2). But in what sense can *hypsos* be "useful" in a public context if it is a matter of "ecstasy" rather than persuasion? Far from disparaging public rhetoric, Longinus in fact aims to reveal its nobler vocation.[60] Longinus thus distinguishes himself from other ancient writers, particularly those who associate *ekstasis* only with poetry or who see emotional transport as merely intoxicating (Plato's *Ion*). According to Longinus, *hypsos* is "useful" to the public speaker because it conduces to the development of greatness of mind in the audience. Hence Longinus's two-fold goal in his treatise: on the one hand, to raise all the verbal arts to "the condition of poetry,"[61] that is, to the noblest of the verbal arts; and, on the other, to connect them with what is noblest and highest (or most divine) in the human being. Although Longinus does make a distinction between rhetoric and poetry based on their respective effects (in chapter 15, on the imagination [*phantasia*]), this represents merely a fine differentiation within a larger project of defining a transgeneric conception of literary value.

It is no coincidence that the term that most literally expresses the idea of transcendence, *ekstasis* ("to be or stand outside oneself"), should be given a prominent role in describing the effect of *hypsos*. The term has been variously rendered: Boileau (TS, 74) divides the meaning between two French verbs, *ravir* (ravish, enrapture) and *transporter* (transport, carry away with emotion); Grube uses a paraphrase "it takes the reader out of himself";[62] Fyfe similarly has "to transport them out of themselves";[63] in Roberts one finds "transport";[64] Russell simply employs the transliterated "ecstasy."[65] *Ekstasis* has a long and rich history in Greek culture. M. A. Screech offers the following etymological sketch of the term:

> In classical Greek *ekstasis* means a displacement or a casting down of a thing from its normal place or state. From this literal meaning it took on the sense of a form of acute distraction, brought on by a strong emotion such as terror or astonishment. Under the influence of such an ecstasy a man or woman might be vouchsafed visions from God or the gods. The verb *existemi* – to

---

[60] Malcolm Heath notes that "in reality, sublimity is beyond the reach of anyone who would wish to abuse it, since achieving it requires, not merely mastery of technique, but also the ethical development of our nature. Thus Longinus's technography is fundamentally ethical" (*Ancient Philosophical Poetics*, 174).
[61] Halliwell remarks that "[Longinus] assimilates all the texts he deals with, whatever their generic or pragmatic status, to the condition of poetry" (*Between Ecstasy and Truth*, 329).
[62] Grube, *Longinus: On Great Writing*, 4.   [63] Fyfe, *On the Sublime*, 163.
[64] Roberts, *Longinus, On the Sublime*, 43.   [65] Russell, *On the Sublime*, 462.

put something out of its place – similarly acquired the meaning of "to astonish" or "to amaze."[66]

Here *ekstasis* is explicitly related to an experience of the divine as a momentary transcendence of the human condition. Indeed, the notion of sublimity as being identified with an exceptional or extraordinary state of mind – with *intensity*, as contrasted with its normal, everyday state, from which it is displaced – is a theme that runs throughout Longinus's treatise. Terror is considered to be the strongest emotion and therefore the emotion that is most associated with a displacement from the mundane condition, such as that which accompanies a divine vision.[67] Thus the idea of the "sublime" as an aestheticized terror at the limit of the sacred has its roots in the Greek terms Longinus uses to describe the experience of sublime intensity.[68] Although Longinus does at times suggest that *hypsos* puts us in touch with the gods or the divine, his vision is largely "secular" or parareligious, meaning that it expressly adopts a human – even a humanistic – perspective. However anachronistic the use of "secular" may appear in this context, this study contends that at bottom the sublime involves an essential equivocation between aesthetic-secular and mystical-religious experience, which allows it to function as a secular analog of religious transcendence.

Longinus's use of *ekstasis* – uncommon among rhetoricians of the era – has also been traced to the influence of Philo.[69] Philo's interpretation of the Old Testament, which combined elements of Jewish exegesis and Greek Stoic thought, had a significant impact on the way *ekstasis* was used in describing the mystical experiences of Jews and early Christians, experiences that were often foreign to the Old Testament passages they were meant to illuminate.[70] In his *Who Is the Heir of Divine Things?* Philo distinguishes four meanings of *ekstasis*:

> 1) a maniac fury or some similar cause which produces unreason in old age or melancholy; 2) an intense astonishment at things which are accustomed to happen suddenly and unexpectedly; 3) a quietude of thought; 4) the best kind, i.e., an inspired state of being possessed and of madness as well, which prophets make use of.[71]

---

[66] M. A. Screech, *Ecstasy and the Praise of Folly*, 48–49.
[67] Halliwell notes that there is a partial if complex antecedent for "aestheticized terror" in theories of tragic emotion: "[There] is the vocabulary of *ekstasis* ('ecstasy,' literally a state in which the mind 'stands outside' itself, a loss or forgetting of one's 'normal' self) and the closely related term *ekplêxis*, which denotes a 'stunning' impact on the mind that is compatible with various emotions, including tragic pity and fear" (*Between Ecstasy and Truth*, 332).
[68] Burke points this out in his *Enquiry* (see Chapter 6 of this study).
[69] See Francis Goyet, TS, 160.   [70] See Screech, *Ecstasy and the Praise of Folly*, 48–49.
[71] As described by Arieti and Crossett, *Longinus: On the Sublime*, 10.

Longinus's concept would appear to be a combination of (2) and (4), astonishment and possession.[72] Hence the proximity between the Greek expression *ekstasis manikê*, "possession by a god who endows his host with prophetic powers,"[73] and *mania poiêtikê*, madness brought on by poetic passion. These terms suggest a comparison with Plato's notion of *enthousiasmos* (possession by a god), which he uses in the *Ion* to describe poetry as irrational and nonhuman: "The god takes their [the poets'] intellect away from them when he uses them as servants, as he does prophets and godly diviners . . . the god himself is the one who speaks" (534d). While Longinus dismisses this idea of "divine inspiration" as the cause or source of sublimity, he nevertheless uses the term *enthousiastikon pathos* as a (secularizing) *metaphor* to describe the second source of sublimity ("inspired emotion"); and the notion of inspiration or possession is retained in his idea of an intersubjective relation between geniuses (*zêlôsis-mimêsis*).[74]

It is thus possible that Philo was responsible for the redefinition of *ekstasis* that integrated the good type of madness and rapture, thereby providing the basis for the Christian-mystical understanding of *ekstasis* as the soul's temporary possession by God.[75] Longinus uses the term *theophoreisthai*, "to be possessed by god," twice (13.2, 15.6) in a positive light. This term is apparently quite rare;[76] however, it is found in Philo – which might be taken as evidence of a connection (the noun *theophoresis* is also found in Dionysius of Halicarnassus). Given the range of connotations just described, *ekstasis* is perhaps best understood not as an emotion or an affect but as a *structure of experience*, namely transcendence, which in Longinus is given an explicitly aesthetic interpretation.

Two other terms Longinus uses to describe the effect of *hypsos* are *ekplêxis* (astonishment, amazement) and *thaumasion* (wonder, awe). These are more properly called affects and, like *ekstasis*, also possess important resonances in ancient Greek thought. They are furthermore often closely linked in usage and meaning. Perhaps most famously, the verb "to wonder" (*thaumazein*) is used by Aristotle in his *Metaphysics* to describe the starting point of philosophy: "For from wonder [*thaumazein*] men, both now and at the first, began to philosophize, having felt astonishment [*thaumazein*] at things

---

[72] See Arieti and Crossett, *Longinus: On the Sublime*, 10.
[73] Screech, *Ecstasy and the Praise of Folly*, 51.   [74] I discuss this in detail in Chapter 2.
[75] A later version of the same structure can be found in Plotinus's notion of ecstasy, which consists in an annihilation of the self and its fusion with the One. The mystic Pseudo-Dionysius attempted to accommodate both Philonic and Dionysian structures of ecstasy: the ecstatic lover lives in Christ (transcendence) just as Christ lives in him (possession). See Screech, *Ecstasy and the Praise of Folly*, 56.
[76] See Roberts, *Longinus, On the Sublime*, 200.

which were more obvious, indeed, amongst those that were doubtful"
(982b).[77] Aristotle's aphorism echoes a passage from Plato's *Theaetetus*, in
which Socrates asserts: "This is an experience which is characteristic of a
philosopher, this wondering [*thaumazein*]: this is where philosophy begins
and nowhere else" (155d). In Aristotle's *Poetics, thaumaston* is found in the
sections on epic, where it serves to justify the presence of marvelous or
fantastic elements: "In tragedy one needs to create a sense of awe [*thaumaston*], but epic has more scope for the irrational [*alogos*] (the chief cause of awe
[*thaumaston*]), because we do not actually see the agent" (1460a).[78] Aristotle
uses *ekplêxis* to characterize the *telos* of (epic) poetry: "Say a poem contains
impossibilities: this is a fault. But it is acceptable if the poetry achieves its goal
(which has been stated), that is, if it makes this or some other part of the
work more thrilling [*ekplêktikos*]" (1460b). *Ekplêxis* is also used to describe
the aesthetic effect of *anagnôrisis* (recognition): "Better is the act done in
ignorance, and followed by recognition: there is nothing repugnant here,
and the recognition is thrilling [*ekplêktikos*]" (1454a). Thus in Aristotle,
ekplêxis is an affect tied to the cardinal element of plot, an element that is
completely absent from Longinus's theory; indeed, given his singular focus
on discrete moments (*kairos*) in texts, it is excluded a priori.

Longinus's use of *ekplêxis* and *thaumasion* to describe the intensity of
aesthetic experience thus draws on a long and rich tradition of Greek
writing, even if Longinus will highlight them in ways that are novel.
These two terms often appear in tandem in Longinus's text, as mutually
reinforcing descriptions of aesthetic intensity that apply to all instances of
hypsos. The one major exception occurs in the section on imagination/
visualization (*phantasia*), where he distinguishes between the effects of
poetry and oratory: "It will not escape you that rhetorical visualization
[*phantasia*] has a different intention from that of the poets: in poetry the
aim is astonishment [*ekplêxis*], in oratory it is clarity/vividness [*enargeia*].
Both however seek emotion and excitement" (15.1).[79] It is not clear,

[77] Aristotle, *Metaphysics*, 1.2. In his *Being and Time* (161), Martin Heidegger distinguishes mere "curi-
osity" (inauthenticity) from "the contemplation that wonders at being, *thaumazein*." In his 1929
Inaugural Lecture at the University of Freiburg entitled "What Is Metaphysics?" Heidegger writes:
"Only because the nothing is manifest in the ground of Dasein can the total strangeness of beings
overwhelm us. Only when the strangeness of beings oppresses us does it arouse and evoke wonder.
Only on the ground of wonder – the revelation of the nothing – does the 'why?' loom before us"
(http://www.stephenhicks.org/wp-content/uploads/2013/03/heideggerm-what-is-metaphysics.pdf).
[78] The notion of *thaumaston* would become an important touchstone in Italian Renaissance poetics.
See Chapter 4.
[79] In later aesthetic thought, this distinction will be expressed in the idea of "confused images," that is,
images that excite by their very lack of clarity. In his *Enquiry*, Burke cites the "confused images" of
Milton's portrayal of Satan in *Paradise Lost* as being productive of the sublime (E, 62).

however, whether Longinus is drawing a merely qualitative or also a quantitative distinction with respect to the intensity of affect/effect in this instance. That is, given that "astonishment" sounds a good deal more intense than "clarity," is the effect of poetry stronger (and thus more sublime) than oratory? Later in the section, however, Longinus reveals that he is making a (quasi-Aristotelian) argument about generic propriety:

> The poetical examples, as I said, have a quality of exaggeration which belongs to fable and goes far beyond credibility. In an orator's visualizations [*phantasia*], on the other hand, it is the element of fact and truth which makes for success; when the content of the passage is poetical and fabulous and does not shrink from any impossibility, the result is shocking and outrageous abnormality. This is what happens to the shock orators [literally: tricky/clever orators] of our own day. (15.8)

That is, the kind of astonishment/amazement that is proper to poetic *phantasia*, that which, as Longinus states in this passage, is related to fantastical elements, is no more or less sublime than oratorical *phantasia*, which aims at realism and thus requires *enargeia*, vivid and clear presentation, to achieve its end. What is appropriate and sublime in one discursive genre may be inappropriate, or even "shocking," in another.[80] But what of the relation between generic propriety and sublimity? There is perhaps an irresolvable tension in Longinus between a transgeneric concept of literary value, grounded in a general description of the effect of *hypsos* in terms of astonishment (*ekplêxis*) and wonder (*thaumasion*), and the level of specificity that Longinus often brings to his generic and contextualized characterizations of *hypsos*.[81]

An important corollary of the idea of the intensity of affect is its temporal dimension. As every reader of *Peri hypsous* knows, Longinus is interested only in particular *moments* in texts, not entire works. What is less well known is the extent to which Longinus theorizes this temporal dimension. As part of his definition of sublimity at the beginning of the treatise (1.4), Longinus uses a single Greek word, *kairos*, to describe what is

---

[80] I believe that a similar logic applies to Longinus's controversial claim that grief, pity, and fear are "low emotions" unfit to produce sublimity. See my discussion in Chapter 2.

[81] Halliwell also notes the ambiguities in Longinus's discussion of *phantasia*: "Effective rhetorical *phantasia* is said not only to persuade but to 'enslave' the hearer (15.9), a formulation that seems to hark back to Chapter 1's statement that the sublime produces ecstasy rather than persuasion. Shortly afterwards, indeed, Longinus praises a passage of Hyperides which he says has gone beyond the bounds of persuasion (15.10), which makes rhetorical visualisation sound rather like poetic *phantasia* after all" (*Between Ecstasy and Truth*, 349).

rendered variously by translators as "well-timed flash" (Fyfe), "right moment" (Russell), "suddenly" (Grube), and "happily timed" (Havell):

> Experience in invention and ability to order and arrange material cannot be detected in single passages; we begin to appreciate them only when we see the whole context. Sublimity [*hypsos*], on the other hand, produced at the right moment [*kairiôs*], tears everything up like a whirlwind, and exhibits the orator's whole power [*dynamis*] at a single blow. (1.4)

The temporal immediacy of *hypsos* is contrasted with the consideration of extended passages or entire works (the subject of poetics), which are more diffuse in their effects. Thus, presumably, narrative fulfillments – reversals, recognitions, climaxes, dénouements – while they do produce moments of intensity, are, *qua narrative* (plot), formal-structural elements at bottom. One cannot therefore properly qualify an entire work as exhibiting *hypsos*.[82] The consideration of an entire work reveals craftsmanship and compositional acumen, that is, aspects of *technê* – but not sublimity. This passage also effectively separates *hypsos* from any concept of style; for a few words or even a few sentences cannot yield much reliable information concerning style.

Generally defined as the right or opportune moment, *kairos* is a fundamental notion in Greek thought, particularly in rhetoric, but also in philosophy.[83] Dionysius of Halicarnassus explains that "in every case we must, I think, seek the proper moment [*kairos*], for this is the best criterion of charm and its opposite. But about *kairos* no rhetorician or philosopher has, so far, produced a definitive treatise."[84] Longinus's use of *kairos* in the context of his theory of *hypsos* takes on a special meaning, given his focus on the idea of aesthetic intensity.[85] The metaphors Longinus employs to

---

[82] If Longinus sometimes appears to do this (as when he compares the *Iliad* to the *Odyssey*, for example), it is only because the frequency of sublime moments allows one to judge an entire work as a superior work.

[83] According to James Kinneavy, "a strong case can be made for the thesis that *kairos* is a dominating concept in sophistic, Isocratean, Platonic, Aristotelian, and in a sense even in Ciceronian rhetoric" ("*Kairos* in Classical and Modern Rhetoric," in *Rhetoric and Kairos*, 58). On the topic of *kairos*, see also Monique Trédé's monograph *Kairos: L'à-propos et l'occasion* and W. H. Race's essay, "The Word *Kairos* in Greek Drama."

[84] W. Rhys Roberts, ed. and trans., *Dionysius of Halicarnassus On Literary Composition*, 133 (translation modified, De Comp. 12, 67–68). Dionysius further notes: "The nature of the subject, indeed, is not such that it can fall under any comprehensive and systematic treatment, nor can *kairos* in general be apprehended by science, but only by personal judgment" (134). Nevertheless, Longinus will associate *kairos* with method in the following passage: "In all production Nature is the first and primary element; but all matters of degree, of the happy moment [*kairos*] in each case, and again of the safest rules of practice and use, are adequately provided and contributed by system" [*methodos*] (2.2, Fyfe's translation).

[85] The German critic Karl Heinz Bohrer has studied the relation between Longinian sublimity and modernist aesthetics in his extensive analyses of the German terms *Augenblick* (the moment) and *Plötzlichkeit* (suddenness). In his *Suddenness: On the Moment of Aesthetic Appearance* (129), Bohrer

connote the momentary shock-effect produced by *hypsos* often analogize
sublimity to events of nature, such as thunder and lightning, as we saw
above in 12.4, and in this passage: "The crash of [Demosthenes's] thunder,
the brilliance of his lightning make all other orators, of all ages, insignif-
icant" (34.4). Longinus's figurative description prefigures the *literal* association between sublimity and the prodigies of nature in chapter 35 of the
treatise as well as the appropriation of the sublime by eighteenth-century
nature aesthetics. Indeed, any metaphor of nature used to describe the
effect of sublimity is apt to be literalized; in this sense as well, the rhetoric of
sublimity is always already "beyond rhetoric."

The momentary quality of *hypsos* would appear to commit Longinus to the
view that *kairos* is nonrelational or absolute, an interpretation that the concept
of *kairos* itself, in its meaning as "timely," as a kind of fulfillment, would clearly
contradict.[86] Clearly, familiarity with the entirety of given work is essential to
the understanding of any excerpt, the sublimity of which would escape us if we
were not aware of its specific context. Longinus certainly acknowledges this, as
when he writes "but the greatness [of this passage] depends not on the mere
form of the oath, but on place, manner, occasion [*kairos*], and purpose" (16.3).
The sublimity that attaches to a particular phrase in one context does not
necessarily carry over to another. Thus the grandeur/sublimity of the "Let
there be light" quotation depends on its placement in Genesis, where it refers
to the creation of the universe by God. Given its iconic status, its appearance in
virtually any other context would devolve into parody.[87]

1.4   Creating the sublime: genius (nature) versus art (*technê*)

So far we have seen how Longinus defines *hypsos* in terms of its expression
(as exceptional *logos*) and its effect (ecstasy, transcendence). In the last part

sees Longinus's influence on modernism as mediated though Nietzsche's aesthetic thought: "The
specific elements that we found in Nietzsche's aesthetic epiphany are already contained in
Longinus's discussion of the metaphorical repertory of sublime discourse. . . . [Longinus's] metaphor
of 'lightning' and the 'all-at-once,' the momentum, that characterize the emphatic language of
Nietzsche is repeated often in Longinus." More than any other modern critic, Bohrer has recognized
the importance of Longinian sublimity for an aesthetics of temporality. See also Bohrer, "Instants of
Diminishing Representation: The Problem of Temporal Modalities."
[86] The use of *kairos* in the New Testament (roughly contemporaneous with the generally accepted
dating of *Peri hypsous*) reveals the relational aspect in a religious context. Examples from the Gospels
include Luke 1:20: "And behold, you shall be silent and unable to speak until the day when these
things take place, because you did not believe my words, which will be fulfilled in their proper time
[*kairos*]"; and John 7:6: "Then Jesus said unto them, 'My time [*kairos*] is not yet come: but your time
[*kairos*] is always ready.'"
[87] Boileau makes this precise point in his *Réflexions critiques* (X).

of the opening section, Longinus considers *hypsos* from the perspective of its production. Classical Greek thought was dominated by two divergent conceptions of poetic production: (1) as *inspiration* (*enthousiasmos*), which, as expounded in Plato's *Ion*, holds that the poet's words have a divine provenance and thus are inherently inscrutable; (2) as *craft* or *art* (*technê*), which, as exemplified in Aristotle's *Poetics*, treats poetry as an eminently skilled activity, analyzable in terms of objective and constituent features.[88] Longinus's treatise marks a significant departure from both conceptions. Whereas Aristotle subordinates the activity of the individual artist to tradition, and the Plato of the *Ion* consigns the poet's function to that of a mouthpiece of the gods, Longinus offers what will appear to many modern readers a familiar notion: that of the creative artist.[89]

Longinus uses the nouns *megalophuia* (greatness of nature) and *megalophrosynê* (nobility of mind/soul) and the adjective *megalophuês* (great-natured) to refer to the exceptional or "heroic" writer (Longinus often employs the Greek term *hêrôs*). These terms recall Aristotle's concept of *megalopsuchos*, the great-souled man, a key concept in the *Nicomachean Ethics* (1123b1–1125a29). (Longinus also uses *megalopsuchia* to mean "great-souled.") We must, however, guard against conflating the *megalo-* terms (genius/greatness) with *megethos* (grandeur); the latter is used by Longinus as the principal synonym or equivalent for *hypsos*.[90] *Megalo-* denotes a mental quality and refers *both* to the talent or ability of the writer and to his or her moral superiority (nobility of mind). Longinus defines *megalophuia* as the capacity for *hypsos*; the mere presence of sublimity thus implies some degree of greatness or genius on the part of the writer. Genius and sublimity are mutually implicit.

Longinus begins by framing the problem of artistic production around question of whether *hypos* (or literary greatness) is more a matter of nature (*physis*) or of art (*technê*):

---

[88] Aristotle does make a few scattered remarks about the poet's ability in the *Poetics* (such as "poetry is the work of a gifted person, or of a maniac" [1455a]), but this is obviously not his focus.

[89] In his *European Literature and the Latin Middle Ages* (398), Curtius observes that "the Greeks did not know the concept of the creative imagination. They had no word for it. What the poet produced was a fabrication. Aristotle praises Homer for having taught poets 'to lie properly.' For him, as we know, poetry was mimesis. . . . But is Aristotle really the last word of antique literary criticism? Fortunately we have the treatise *On the Sublime*."

[90] Grube remarks that Longinus "uses a large number of synonyms or near synonyms for *hypsos*" ("Notes on the *Peri hypsous*," 359).

The question from which I must begin is whether there is in fact an art [*technê*] of *hypsos* or emotion [*pathos*].[91] Some people think it is a complete mistake to reduce things like this to technical rules. Genius/greatness [*ta megalophuê*, "great-natured things"], the argument runs, is a natural product, and does not come by teaching. The only art [*technê*] is to be born like that. They believe moreover that natural products are very much weakened by being reduced to the bare bones of a textbook. (2.1)

As a pedagogue, this question is of the upmost importance for Longinus, but it places him before a dilemma. If, on the one hand, *hypsos* is primarily a product of *technê*, then all that is needed to attain it is the proper understanding and application of the rules. But it is clear that, for Longinus, the kind of greatness that gives an author "eternal life" (1.3) is not reducible to rules or formulas. On the other hand, if *hypsos* is solely a function of innate talent, then the addressee of *Peri hypsous* would presumably have no need for Longinus's instruction, and there would be no justification for Longinus's statement at the outset that "two things are required of any textbook: first, that it should explain what its subject is; second, and more important, that it should explain how and by what methods we can achieve it" (1.1).[92] To reconcile these two opposing ideas Longinus develops a notion of what we would now call "genius," a concept that only explicitly emerges in eighteenth-century aesthetic thought and that is inspired in large part by Longinus. (In fact, some translators of *Peri hypsous* use "genius" to convey Longinus's idea.)

The key to Longinus's concept of "genius" is his dialectical conception of the nature/art opposition: on the one hand, nature cannot be completely divorced from *methodos* (method/system); on the other, *nature itself* can be cultivated. As Longinus states at the outset, his goal is to show "we can develop our nature [*physis*] to some degree of greatness" (1.1). Longinus thus does not see natural talent and *methodos* (method/system) as antipodes (an inherent capacity versus an acquired skill), but as mutually reinforcing:

---

[91] This passage has engendered controversy among translators. The Greek manuscripts read "art of *hypsous* and *bathous*"; but "bathos," usually translated as "profundity" or "depth," has struck many as strange in this context. The term inspired Alexander Pope's satirical *Peri Bathous, Or The Art of Sinking* (1728).

[92] The importance of the formative ideal in Longinus's theory cannot be overestimated, for the Romans treated *oratory* – that is, highly formalized public speaking – as the central pillar of their educational and civic system.

(i)   Though nature is on the whole a law unto herself in matters of emotion [*pathos*] and elevation [*hypsos*], she is not a random force and does not work altogether without method [*methodos*].

(ii) [Nature] is herself in every instance a first and primary element of creation, but it is method [*methodos*] that is competent to provide quantities and appropriate occasions [*kairos*] for everything, as well as perfect correctness in training and application.

(iii) Grandeur/genius [*megalophrosynê*] is particularly dangerous when left on its own, unaccompanied by knowledge, unsteadied, unballasted, abandoned to mere impulse and ignorant temerity. It needs the curb as well as the spur. (2.2)

With respect to the first point, nature is "not a random force" and "does not work altogether without method [*methodos*]" in the sense that it *creates* the "rule" that is recognized as such only after the fact, as something analyzable insofar as it exhibits the attributes of a system or method. Longinus's rapprochement between nature and rule or method thus resonates with Kant's theory of genius as encapsulated in the dictum: "*Genius* is the inborn predisposition of the mind (*ingenium*) *through which* nature gives the rule to art" (CPJ, 5:307, original emphasis). The idea of genius as rule-giving, as opposed to rule-following, is consonant with Longinus's dialectical formulation: on the one hand, it affirms the importance of method and system (and thus the possibility of literary criticism itself); on the other, it asserts the primacy of nature and the autonomy of the genius. "But the most important point of all is that the actual fact that there are some parts of literature which are in the power of natural genius alone must be learnt from no other source than from art" (2.3, Havell's translation). *Technê* can reveal nature. Moreover, if works of genius were merely random or inscrutable, they could not function as models, and Longinus considers the emulation of great models (*zêlôsis-mimêsis*) to be essential to the achievement of *hypsos*. Kant too will stipulate that works of genius should be "exemplary," that is, "while not themselves the result of imitation, they must yet serve others in that way, that is, as a standard of judging" (CPJ, 5:308).[93]

The second point underlines the importance of *kairos*, which Longinus associates with *methodos* and *technê* as an acquired skill or technique. If, as was observed above, *kairos* is constitutive of *hypsos*, then on this basis alone *hypsos* is revealed to be dependent on the *conscious* application of *methodos*, as opposed to these technical aspects merely being deduced *a posteriori*, as the first point implies.

---

[93] See Robert Doran, "Imitation and Originality: Creative Mimesis in Longinus, Kant, and Girard."

The third point stresses the importance of pedagogy. Longinus suggests that nature (*physis*) is not a fixed "endowment," but should be thought in terms of a dynamic process of growth. In other words, *physis*, which derives from the verb *phuein*, meaning "to grow," is malleable and subject to modification by extrinsic forces. Longinus observes that even though Euripides was "not formed by nature for grandeur [*megalophrosynê*], he often forces himself to be tragic" (15.3).[94] When Longinus says that genius may be "dangerous," if not properly trained, he is most probably referring to the misuse of rhetorical gifts in the public sphere and its potentially pernicious effects. Longinus may have been influenced by the following passage in Plato's *Phaedrus*: "If you have an innate capacity for rhetoric, you will become a famous rhetorician, provided you also acquire knowledge and practice, but if you lack any of these three you will be correspondingly unfinished" (269d). Genius thus requires "education" – what the Germans call *Bildung* – in the broadest sense: moral, intellectual, cultural, practical, spiritual. As evidenced later in the treatise, where Longinus observes that nobility of mind, one of the chief sources of *hypsos*, involves a *pattern* of thinking over an extended period of time, it is clear that Longinus conceives of education largely as inculcation: the more one is exposed to greatness in the verbal arts the better one is able to achieve it; *hypsos* is a spur to *hypsos*. But the idea of discipline or self-control is also present in the stipulation that genius "needs the curb as well as the spur." In his theory of genius, Kant similarly explains that "taste . . . is the discipline (or corrective) of genius, clipping its wings and making it well behaved or polished; but at the same time it gives genius guidance as to where and far it should extend itself if it is to remain purposive" (CPJ, 5:320).

As mentioned above, Longinus on several occasions employs the Greek word *hêrôs*, "heroes" or "demigods" (Fyfe uses both translations in his edition), to refer to great writers or geniuses. Curtius observes that "ancient Greece put the poet in the category of 'godlike men,' besides heroes, kings, heralds, priests, seers. They are called godlike because they surpass human standards. They are favorites of the gods, intermediaries between them and men."[95] Tellingly, Longinus makes no qualitative distinction between poets and other verbal artists. Thus Longinus refers to Homer, Demosthenes, and Plato (a poet, an orator, and a philosopher) in the same paragraph (36.1) as "these heroes [*hêrôsi*]" and in 4.4 to Xenophon (a

---

[94] Grube translates more freely: "[Euripides] had little natural genius, yet he forced such talent as he had to rise to tragedy very often, and in all his great passages" (*On Great Writing*, 24).

[95] Curtius, *European Literature in the Latin Middle Ages*, 398.

historian) and Plato as *hêrôsi*. This use of *hêrôsi* has a two-fold significance: on the one hand, it reinforces the idea of sublimity as a transgeneric conception of literary value; on the other, it emphasizes the association between sublimity and the moral-social ideal of high-mindedness – a recurrent theme of the modern interpretation of sublimity.

1.5 True and false sublimity

Immediately following the introductory sections but prior to the formal presentation of the sources of *hypsos*, Longinus discusses the various faults to which one is susceptible in striving for sublimity, a common practice of rhetorical treatises of the era. In effect, Longinus describes a false sublime: bombast (turgidity); the overelaboration of an inferior idea (puerility); expressions unworthy of the thought (frigidity);[96] and *parenthyrsos*: excessive, artificial, or untimely (*akairos*) emotion. Beyond being a conventional gesture, Longinus's main purpose in this discussion is to show: (1) that a less cultivated reader might be deceived as to the existence of *hypsos* and that therefore an element of *critical judgment* is required to produce and even recognize true sublimity; and (2) that since all these "lapses in dignity," as Longinus calls them, stem from the same cause, "that passion for novelty of thought which is the particular craze of the present day" (5.1, Fyfe's translation) – that is, what we would call "fashion" – true *hypsos* is what *perdures*, as opposed to the ephemeral and the transitory. These two points are developed in tandem in an often-cited passage:

> When a man of sense and literary experience hears something many times over, and it fails to dispose his mind to greatness or to leave him with more to reflect upon than was contained in the mere words, but comes instead to seem valueless on repeated occasions, this is not true sublimity; it endures only for the moment of hearing. Real sublimity contains much food for reflection, is difficult or rather impossible to resist, and makes a strong and ineffaceable impression on the memory. In a word, reckon those things which please everybody all the time as genuinely and finely sublime. When people of different trainings, ways of life, tastes, ages, and manners all agree about something, the judgment and assent of so many distinct voices lends strength and irrefutability to the conviction that their admiration is rightly directed. (7.3–4)

Longinus here introduces the concept of aesthetic judgment into his theory of *hypsos*. By contending that only by *repeated readings* ("many times over") is a critical intelligence ("a man of sense and literary experience") capable of

---

[96] Demetrius's *On Style* also discusses this fault (114–127).

separating genuine sublimity from its simulacrum, Longinus seemingly implies that the singular and individual experience of ecstasy is insufficient to determine a passage's worth, thus contradicting the spirit of the opening section. Only the transcendence of time and place can reveal true *hypsos* with any certainty; for a passage one had at first judged sublime might in fact turn out to be a false sublime. In addition, a judgment of true sublimity implies *intersubjective agreement* or universality ("those things which please everybody all the time"),[97] suggesting that authentic sublimity can never reveal itself in its own time; for one will never be able to distinguish it with any certainty from "the particular craze of the present day." A text must be a wellspring of reflection for *future* generations. Longinus often emphasizes the importance of posterity in his treatise: "Sublimity is the means by which the greatest writers have given *eternal* life to their own flame" (1.3, my emphasis); what is sublime is "worthy of eternity" in 9.3; and in the last chapter he exhorts writers "to give thought to their reputation with posterity" (44.8). Surefire proof of literary value lies in the *universal* and *transhistorical* appeal of a text, in its ability to connect readers who are temporally and culturally dispersed ("people of different trainings, ways of life, tastes, ages"). It would thus appear that Longinus here uses *hypsos* to define we call the "classical": works of lasting value and pertinence.

The tension between a time-bound, individual ecstasy and the judgment of posterity (eternity) can be expressed as that between an *intrinsic* proof of sublimity, the inviolable authenticity that inheres in the *direct* encounter with greatness, and an *extrinsic* proof of sublimity, intersubjective agreement.[98] For most of his treatise, Longinus emphasizes the intrinsic,

---

[97] The Kantian flavor of this passage is unmistakable. Longinus's ideas of "judgment" and "reflection" are particularly intriguing from a modern perspective. The phrase "more to reflect upon than was contained in the mere words" seemingly suggests or anticipates Kant's concept of reflective judgment, and "inexhaustibility of reflection" will be echoed in Kant's notion of "aesthetic ideas" (CPJ, 5:314). Rodolphe Gasché, one of the few critics to notice a connection between Longinus's treatise and Kant's theory of aesthetics, observes that "Kant's definition of aesthetic ideas as representations that occasion much thought echoes Longinus's claim that true sublimity either touches the spirit of a well-read man 'with a sense of grandeur or leave[s] more food for reflection in his mind than the mere words convey'" (*The Idea of Form: Rethinking Kant's Aesthetics*, 236–237). One could also read the phrase "real sublimity contains much food for reflection" as indicating a level beyond the narrowly aesthetic: namely the inexhaustibility and richness of *meaning*. Thus *hypsos* is not merely a matter of aesthetic sensibility but also includes a specifically *hermeneutic* aspect – interpretability – although this idea is not developed by Longinus.

[98] In the chapter that closes his *Between Ecstasy and Truth*, Halliwell asks if "the moment of sublime rapture [can] somehow contain and transmit truth, and if so what kind of truth would that be?" (*Between Ecstasy and Truth*, 332). Halliwell's analysis of a sublime "moment of truth" in Longinus as a noncognitive realization of the mind's true vocation stretches the concept of truth beyond the Platonic conception, perhaps toward a protoexistentialist one (authenticity).

experiential proof of true sublimity, as encapsulated in one of his most memorable aphorisms: "It is our nature to be elevated and exalted by true sublimity [*hypsos*]. Filled with joy and pride, we come to believe we have created what we have only heard" (7.2). This line has been much cited and commented on in the critical literature (including by Dennis and Burke).[99] But it is not often remarked that this is one of the places where Longinus explicitly defines sublimity in terms of an intersubjective *structure of experience* (author-reader), as distinct from intersubjective *agreement* (reader-reader). The reader/auditor feels "as if" he or she had produced the utterance, as if the reader (for a moment at least) feels that he or she is in possession of the same kind of mental expansiveness and elevation of spirit that made the sublime utterance possible, that the reader's mind has "merged," so to speak, with that of the author, thereby affirming the idea of a *common* human capacity ("it is our nature ... ") for elevation or transcendence. Although only geniuses may in fact be capable of *producing* sublimity, all properly cultivated individuals can at least experience it, and this experience can, over time, transform the reader/hearer "to some degree" (1.1); that is, it can attune his or her mind to elevated thoughts and expression. To hear or read the words of a genius means to receive an impression of his or her *mental disposition*.[100] The text is for Longinus a template of the writer's mind, "the echo of a noble mind" (9.1). Hence the codependence of the creative and receptive poles in Longinus's theory: the high-minded disposition (nature) of the genius produces the state (ephemeral but making a deep impression) of high-mindedness in the audience (including other would-be geniuses) via its effective expression in discourse (*logos*).[101] An exclusively technical-stylistic approach to *Peri hypsous* will thus inevitably fail to grasp this essential subjective-intersubjective orientation of Longinus's theory.

The contrast between true and false sublimity is also couched in moral terms, drawing on the Platonic appearance/reality distinction: outward display – grandiloquence, rhetorical excess, flashiness – versus inner worth (nobility of mind or soul):

> In ordinary life, nothing is truly great which it is great to despise; wealth, position, reputation, absolute power – anything in short which has a lot of

---

99 Halliwell cites one of Nietzsche's notes from 1888: "The effect of works of art is the arousal of the state of mind that *creates* art" (quoted in Halliwell, *Between Ecstasy and Truth*, 340, original emphasis).
100 This idea is explored in more detail in my discussion of *zēlōsis-mimēsis* (emulation) in Chapter 2.
101 It is thus on the productive side that the idea of heroic subjectivity is defined most effectively in Longinus; in the modern, "aesthetic" interpretation of sublimity, on the other hand, the idea of heroic subjectivity is transferred to the receptive side, to the *spectator* of natural grandeur and power, paradigmatically in Kant's account. See Chapters 10 and 11.

external trappings – can never seem supremely good to the wise man because it is no small good to despise them. People who could have these advantages if they chose but disdain them out of magnanimity are admired much more than those who actually possess them. It is much the same with elevation in poetry and literature generally. We have to ask ourselves whether any particular example does not give a show of grandeur [*megethos*] which, for all its accidental trappings, will, when dissected, prove vain and hollow, the kind of thing which it does a man more honor to despise than admire. (7.1)

This parallel between "ordinary life" and literature is not a mere analogy; it is intended to demonstrate the moral-philosophical basis of *hypsos*.[102] True grandeur of spirit is corrupted by worldly concerns and the ephemeral values to which it is subjected. If *hypsos* is ultimately about high-mind-edness, for Longinus, then the false sublime is a kind of moral corruption, in the sense of *corruptio optimi pessima*. This sentiment is echoed through-out the treatise, particularly in its final chapter, where the desire for wealth and hedonistic pleasure are denounced as the cause of decadence and cultural decline, but also in chapter 13, where, though ostensibly discussing Plato's style, Longinus recalls Plato's association of truth and the good, quoting approvingly from the *Republic*:

Men without experience of wisdom and virtue but always occupied with feasting and that kind of thing naturally go downhill and wander through life on a low plane of existence. They never look upwards to the truth and never rise, they never taste certain or pure pleasure. Like cattle, they always look down, bowed earthwards and tablewards. (13.1, passage adapted from *Republic* 9:586a)

Just as the philosopher, according to Plato, seeks the truth beyond all appearances, the great writer seeks true elevation beyond mere artifice. The metaphor of height that defines *hypsos* is here aligned with Plato's concept of truth: both reveal a common *experience of elevation or transcendence*. Therefore, those who are insensitive to sublimity are in some sense base or vulgar (in a mental not a social sense).

***

In this chapter I have argued that *hypsos* is a philosophical rather than a stylistic concept. I have criticized the technical-stylistic conception of *hypsos* as myopic and misleading, as being ultimately at odds with what

---

[102] In his *On Style*, Demetrius writes: "But just as in the sphere of ethics certain bad qualities lie close to certain good ones... so too the types of style have neighboring faulty types" (114). See also Horace's *Art of Poetry*, 25–31.

makes Longinus an important figure in literary theory and aesthetics. For although Longinus no doubt saw his work as continuing the rhetorical theory of his era, he nevertheless endeavors to push rhetoric in new directions. I have thus favored an approach to *Peri hypsous* that highlights its moral-subjective orientation and sociocultural implications, thereby setting the stage for the modern interpretation of sublimity as a secular discourse of transcendence. I have also sought to show that, while Longinus's theory would appear to be based on a simple opposition between nature and art, or between nature and culture, the reality is much more complex. While Longinus certainly privileges the natural and the psychological, his developmental concept of natural endowment, which applies both to the genius and to the ordinary person, reveals the anthropological and democratic underpinnings of *hypos*.

CHAPTER 2

Longinus's five sources of sublimity

At the heart of Longinus's theory are the five sources of *hypsos*. As remarked in the previous chapter, Longinus considers the first two "natural" sources, grand conceptions (*noêseis*) and strong emotion (*enthousiastikon pathos*), to be more fundamental than the three that derive from *technê* (art/skill): figures (*schêmata*), diction (*phrasis*), and word arrangement (*synthesis*). A detailed analysis of the sources of sublimity will thus show that the technical-stylistic interpretation of *Peri hypsous* is misguided,[1] for it ignores or deemphasizes the specifically subjective and philosophical dimension of Longinus's theory. If sublimity is primarily a quality of mind – the "echo of a noble mind" (9.1) – then the techniques for its expression are only incidental to the mental state itself; that is to say, no mere technical brilliance can substitute for a lack of mental greatness or nobility of soul. This chapter therefore treats the five sources of sublimity disproportionately, with the greatest attention given to the source that Longinus himself presents most elaborately, grandeur of thought/conception (in sections 9–15).

My discussion of the first source is divided into three parts, corresponding to the three aspects of Longinus's treatment: (1) *megalophrosynê*, high-mindedness or nobility of spirit, which I consider in light of its social, moral, and universalist implications; (2) *zêlôsis-mimêsis*, the emulation of transcendental models, which I examine in terms of an agonistic relation with tradition; and (3) *phantasia*, imagination or visualization, which I see as an index of the mind's creative capacity to transcend the sensible world – the verbal-poetic analog of the idea of transcendence in

---

[1] Such as one finds in Jeffrey Walker (2000), for example: "What *Peri hypsous* is concerned with, then, is a specialized *technê* of loftiness, a version of the 'grand style' . . . [he] chiefly focuses his *technê* on the stylistic means – figures, diction, and rhythmic composition – by which such ideas are made fully lofty and (thus) utterly enthralling, while taking his illustrations mainly from poetic discourse" (*Rhetoric and Poetics in Antiquity*, 119). This interpretation of *Peri hypsous* is the basis for the so-called rhetorical sublime.

nature, as described in chapter 35 of the treatise.[2] All three aspects characterize *hypsos* as a kind of mental transcendence.

The second part of this chapter, on emotion (*pathos*), is largely reconstructive, given that the section devoted to it in Longinus's treatise appears to be lost (or perhaps existed as a separate treatise). I contend that our understanding of the nexus between sublimity and emotion in Longinus is greatly enhanced if we see it as intrinsically connected to the idea of nobility of mind (*megalophrosynê*), on the one hand, and, on the other, to the *experience* of sublimity as an intense emotional response, thus reinforcing the intersubjective meaning of *hypsos* as the contact between two minds. Finally, as befits their secondary status in Longinus's theory, the third part of this chapter briefly treats the technical sources of sublimity – figures, diction, and word arrangement – highlighting how the antagonistic or oppositional relation Longinus conceives between nature and rhetorical artifice reinforces the primacy of the natural sources in *Peri hypsous*.

2.1 The first source of sublimity: grandeur of conception (*noêsis*)

Longinus introduces his five sources thus:

> There are, one may say, five most productive sources of sublimity. (Competence in speaking is assumed as a common foundation for all five; nothing is possible without it.)

(i) The first and most important is the power [ability] to conceive great thoughts [*to peri tas noêseis adrepêbolon*]; I defined this in my work on Xenophon.

(ii) The second is strong and inspired emotion [*to sphodron kai enthousiastikon pathos*]. (These two sources are for the most part natural [*authigeneis*, literally: "self-generated"]; the remaining three involve art [*technê*].)

(iii) Certain kinds of figures [*schêmata*]. (These may be divided into figures of thought and figures of speech.)

(iv) Noble diction [*phrasis*]. This has as subdivisions choice of words and the use of metaphorical and coined words.

(v) Finally, to round off the whole list, dignified and elevated word arrangement [*synthesis*, composition]. (8.1)

In Longinus's elaboration of each of these five sources we can observe a twofold project: (1) to show how each contributes to the *production* of *hypsos*; and (2) to show how each contributes to the *effect* of *hypsos*. These

---

[2] I discuss this in Chapter 3.

two aims, the one pedagogical (creatively oriented) and the other analytical (receptively oriented), are sometimes fused together, so that one is unsure if experiencing the effect of *hypsos* is not also the surest guide to achieving it.

Longinus considers *noêseis*, grand thoughts/conceptions, to be the most important element of *hypsos*, both creatively, as the product of a mental disposition, and receptively, insofar as the author affects the reader's own capacity for *noêseis* through the experience of sublimity in the author's text. *Noêsis* comes from the noun *nous* (mind/intellect) and the verb *noein* (to think). It denotes the intellectual part of the mind (*noêtikos* means "intellectual") and survives in modern English in the adjective "noetic." Plato contrasts *noêsis* with *dianoia* (also translated as "thought"): the latter relates to scientific, mathematical, or logical knowledge, whereas the former denotes the direct apprehension of transcendent entities and is associated with wisdom.[3] It is thus important to note that Longinus conceives of "thought" in the sublime as *noêsis*, a notion that suggests transcendence and creativity (as in the English verb "to conceive"), as opposed to the more pedestrian *dianoia*, which, in rhetorical treatises such as Demetrius's *On Style*, refers to the subject matter of a discourse.

As mentioned above, Longinus divides grandeur of thought/conception into three aspects: *megalophrosynê* (nobility of mind or soul), *zêlôsis-mimêsis* (zealous imitation or emulation), and *phantasia* (imagination or visualization). In addition to these three aspects, there is also a short section on "amplification," which, given its more technical nature, would appear to be misplaced. Indeed, in his wrap-up of this section, Longinus refers only to the three previously mentioned aspects, minus amplification. It would seem, however, that Longinus considers amplification an intensifying rather than an essential factor, for he writes:

> There are innumerable varieties of amplification.... The orator should realize, however, that none of these will have its full effect without sublimity. Passages expressing pity or disparagement are no doubt an exception; but in any other instance of amplification, if you take away the sublime element, you take the soul away from the body. Without the strengthening influence of the sublimity, the effective element in the whole loses all its vigor and solidity. (11.2)[4]

---

[3] See Plato, *Republic*, Book 6 (the analogy of the divided line).

[4] Kant will make a similar argument in his theory of genius, with the concept of "spirit" (*Geist*): "One says of certain products, of which it is expected that they ought, at least in part, to reveal themselves as beautiful art, that they are without *spirit* [*Geist*], even though one finds nothing in them to criticize as far as taste is concerned" (CPJ, 5:313, original emphasis). See the first part of Chapter 3 for a more detailed discussion of this idea (mediocrity versus genius) in Longinus.

In discussing how sublimity can enhance the element of amplification, Longinus reverses his normal procedure. Since the expression of "pity or disparagement" in a passage can attain its "full effect" through amplification without thereby being sublime,[5] Longinus effectively separates the "full effect" of a passage from its sublime effect, implying that, unlike the other three aspects, amplification (the "body") is not a constitutive element of sublimity (the "soul"). In this sense, amplification is treated much like the technical sources, whose artifice is redeemed by sublimity.[6]

Noêsis is not only the most important source of *hypsos*; it also appears to be the *sine qua non* of the Longinian sublime, at least insofar as grandeur of conception is understood as high-mindedness (*megalophrosynê*), the most important of its three aspects. Longinus remarks that "sublimity often occurs apart from emotion" (8.2), thereby implying that it never occurs apart from elevated thought. The autonomy of the first source is emblematically expressed in the following passage on the "silence of Ajax": "Thus even without being spoken, a simple idea will of its own accord excite admiration by reason of the greatness of mind that it expresses; for example, the silence of Ajax in 'The Summoning of the Spirits' is grand, more sublime than any speech!" (9.2).[7] Of course, the silence of Ajax could not have been indicated without discourse; but Longinus's point is that sublimity is principally a manifestation of the mental qualities of the writer, not a property of language per se. A passage that exhibits sublimity is indicative of the mental grandeur of the individual who produced it; *hypsos* is the effective *expression* of high-mindedness (in art and in life):[8]

> The first source, natural greatness [*megalophuês*], is the most important. Even if it is a matter of endowment rather than acquisition, we must, so far as is possible, develop our minds in the direction of greatness and make them always pregnant with noble thoughts. You ask how this can be done. I wrote elsewhere something like this. "Sublimity [*hypsos*] is the echo of a noble mind [*megalophrosynê*]." . . . First then we must state where sublimity [*hypsos*] comes from: the orator must not have low or ignoble thoughts.

[5] But in all other cases, elevation of thought is required for amplification to be (fully) effective.
[6] See the last section of this chapter.
[7] This phrase bears a striking resemblance to a passage in Demetrius's *On Style* (line 253): "Brevity in fact is so useful in this style [the forceful] that a sudden lapse into silence often adds to the forcefulness, as in Demosthenes, 'I certainly could – but do not wish to say anything offensive . . .' His silence here is almost more effective than anything anyone could have said" (*Aristotle/Longinus/Demetrius*, 497).
[8] Longinus sometimes offers real-world examples, such as Alexander the Great (9.4). Although a lacuna interrupts this passage (omitting Alexander's name), Boileau completes it in his translation (TS, 84).

> Those whose thoughts and habits are small and servile all their lives cannot possibly produce anything admirable or worthy of eternity. Words [*logoi*] will be great if thoughts are weighty. (9.1–3)

This passage makes clear that *hypsos* is not simply a matter of a momentary state of mind, a mental event, but of a *pattern* of thinking; that is, one's expressive capacity is conditioned by having certain kinds of thoughts or a particular nature.[9] Rhetorical technique is thus subordinate to the thought it conveys, even if they are ultimately indissociable (that is, the former must always be adequate to the expression of the latter). By thinking great and noble thoughts over an extended period one is "impregnated" with *megalophrosynê* and, after a period of gestation, great words are "born."

Most striking in the above-quoted passage is the homology Longinus asserts between mental expansiveness and moral height in the couplets low/ignoble and small/servile. Elevated thoughts are contrasted, on the one hand, with those that are "small" (in terms of extension, magnitude, and scale), and, on the other, with those that are "ignoble" and "servile" (moral qualifications). The mental (noetic) is inextricable from the moral in Longinus's theory. A vulgar or low-minded individual is incapable of elevated thought and thus of elevated discourse (presumably, as we saw in the previous chapter, such an uncultivated individual would also have difficulty appreciating *hypsos*). One does not, however, *learn* to have elevated thoughts; it is not acquired through *methodos* (system or method); one *becomes* the sort of person to whom elevated thought and discourse come "naturally." Even if genius as such cannot be taught, mental or spiritual cultivation is nevertheless required. Longinus thus establishes a direct causal link between the particular mental/moral disposition of the genius and his or her products; the greatness of the writer's words and works is indicative of the dignity and nobility of his or her character (certainly a controversial assertion today, where it is generally held that there is no necessary correlation between a writer's moral being and the quality of his or her work – in other words, a great writer or artist can also be a miscreant).[10]

---

[9] Indeed, this brings to mind the "expressive" or "author-centered" theory of art, of which, as M. H. Abrams contends in *The Mirror and the Lamp: Romantic Theory and the Critical Tradition* (1953), Longinus can be considered the first theorist. Longinus inspires the Romantic concept of the self-expressive ego and the concomitant exaltation of the artist: "In the final analysis, therefore, the supreme quality of a work turns out to be the reflected quality of its author" (Abrams, *The Mirror and the Lamp*, 73).

[10] Philosophers, it would appear, are held to different standards, as the controversy over Heidegger's Nazism shows.

The surest way to elevate one's thinking is to expose oneself as much as possible to elevated thought – hence the abundance of examples of *hypsos* in the treatise: their value is not merely illustrative but also formative. If some writers appear more talented or gifted than others, it is because they have realized, through constant striving, their innate potential for mental elevation to a superior degree. It is for this reason that they are considered worthy of emulation; they are exemplars of human possibility.[11] Nevertheless, we must keep in mind that Longinus is addressing himself to his pupil, Terentianus, and that he had stated at the outset that his aim is to show how "we can develop our nature [*physis*] to some degree of greatness" (1.1). In effect, Longinus is proposing a democratized theory of genius: one does not have to be a true genius to claim some measure of greatness or sublimity for oneself; all should *strive* to transcend themselves in the sublime (in chapter 35, Longinus will claim that we have a natural desire for transcendence).[12]

This line of thinking suggests a sociological dimension. Is *megalophrosynê, nobility* of mind, such as Longinus defines it, indicative of a specific class ethos (namely, that of the aristocracy)? As noted in the previous chapter, D. A. Russell observes that "at no point in their history did *hypsos* and its cognates quite lose their moral and social connections." However, although Longinus sometimes uses a person with high social status as an example of high-mindedness (such as Alexander the Great, 9.4), those he calls "heroes" are the philosophers, the poets, the historians, and the orators, that is, those whose social backgrounds are merely incidental to their nobility of spirit. Thus there is no class-based hierarchy implied in Longinus's conception of *hypsos*; there is rather a hierarchy of mentalities, which may or may not correspond to particular social strata, even if one nevertheless assumes that the world in which Longinus lived associated nobility of mind with the aristocratic class (understanding "noble" as a social designator) and low or vulgar thoughts with the plebian or slave mentality (as the final section of *Peri hypsous* suggests). With respect to the modern history of the sublime, Longinus's effective separation of sublimity from social determinants in his notion of the hero-writer will have important repercussions. It prefigures the exaltation of the genius in Romanticism, and, more generally, the idea of nobility of spirit as an intrinsic mental quality announces the ideal of a meritocratic society – an aristocracy of talent.[13]

---

[11] As we will see in the next section, Longinus holds that even a great author like Plato requires a model, namely Homer, to achieve sublimity.

[12] See Chapter 3.

[13] For example, the French phrase *génie oblige*, attributed to the nineteenth-century piano virtuoso and composer Franz Liszt, echoes and effectively replaces the aristocratic *noblesse oblige*.

Longinus introduces the second aspect of grandeur of thought thus: "Plato, if we will read him with attention, illustrates yet another road to sublimity [*hypsos*] besides those we have discussed. This is the way of imitation and emulation [*mimêsis te kai zêlôsis*] of the great writers of the past" (13.2). The idea of *zêlôsis-mimêsis*, literally "zealous imitation," was a commonplace of the circle of rhetorical theorists around Caecilius of Calacte, Longinus's interlocutor. It is thought to have originated in the work of Dionysius of Halicarnassus and is sometimes termed "Dionysian imitatio."[14] In his *On Imitation*, Dionysius describes *mimêsis* as "an activity receiving an impression of a model through inspection of it"[15] and *zêlôsis* as "an activity of the soul moved toward admiration of what seems fine."[16] This notion of mimesis, the imitation of a model, represents a radical departure from Aristotle's concept of *mimêsis* as representation (although Aristotle's concept has a behavioral aspect as well, as expressed in *Poetics* 4). *Zêlôsis-mimêsis* is specifically subjective; it does not denote the imitation of particular literary forms, rhetorical devices, and so forth; it involves the mediation of another subject, an *intersubjective* relation.

The coupling of *mimêsis* with the *zêlôsis* (zeal), which some translators render with the single term "emulation," is as significant for the anthropological dimension of Longinus's theory as it is for the aesthetic.[17] George Kennedy observes that "in Hellenistic and later rhetoric, *zêlos* becomes an important aspect of literary imitation; for it refers to the zeal on the part of the writer to equal or excel the quality of great writers of the past."[18] *Zêlôsis* thus explicitly connotes an element of competition or *rivalry* that Longinus sees as crucial to achieving *hypsos* in literature and in life more generally (35.1–5). For Longinus, the example of past greatness is both a model to be admired – an exemplar – and a rival to be bested, even if the "rivalry" involves a merely imaginary relation to an ideal. It thereby subverts the notion, which will become dogma in the eighteenth and nineteenth centuries, that creative originality is inherently opposed to the idea of imitation.[19] Seeking to preserve its creative dimension, Longinus

[14] See the excellent collection *Creative Imitation and Latin Literature*, ed. David West, Tony Woodman, and Anthony John Woodman, especially D. A. Russell's chapter, "De Imitatione."
[15] According to George B. Walsh, "*mimêsis* means 'taking an impression' from something (*apotyposis*), as if the soul of the imitator were shapeless matter, upon which the model author (or his conjured image) might impose his more distinct shape" ("Sublime Method: Longinus on Language and Imitation," 266).
[16] Quoted in Kennedy, *Classical Rhetoric*, 164.
[17] Longinus also uses *zêlos* (instead of *zêlôsis*) in ch. 14 and elsewhere.
[18] Kennedy, *On Rhetoric*, 161.
[19] Indeed, the influence of one writer over another is often termed "inspiration," in modern parlance, rather than imitation, a distinction that is supposed to preserve an aspect of originality. But Longinus can be seen precisely as offering a theory of inspiration.

distinguishes *zêlôsis-mimêsis* from mere copying: "In all this process there is no plagiarism. It resembles rather the reproduction of good character in statues and works of art" (13.3–4).[20] *Zêlôsis-mimêsis* thus has strong echoes in Kant's distinction between *Nachfolge*, often translated as "emulation," and *Nachahmung* (imitation/copying) in his theory of genius.[21]

Interestingly, Longinus describes *zêlôsis-mimêsis* as a secularized version of the doctrine of divine inspiration, *enthousiasmos* (literally: "ecstasy arising from possession by a god"),[22] such as one finds in Plato's *Ion*: "These beautiful poems are not human, not even *from* human beings, but are divine and from gods ... poets are nothing but representatives of the gods, possessed by whatever possesses them" (534e, original emphasis).[23] In Longinus's *zêlôsis-mimêsis* one is possessed not by a god, but by another; "inspiration" becomes a mere metaphor:

> Many are possessed by a spirit not their own [*theophoreisthai*, "to be possessed by god"]. It is like what we are told of the Pythia at Delphi: she is in contact with the tripod near the cleft in the ground which (so they say) exhales a divine vapor, and she is thereupon made pregnant by the supernatural power and forthwith prophesies as one inspired. Similarly, the genius [*megalophuia*] of the ancients acts as a kind of oracular cavern, and effluences flow from it into the minds of their imitators [*zêlountes*]. Even those previously not much inclined to prophesy become inspired and share this enthusiasm which comes from the greatness [*megethei*] of others. (13.2)[24]

[20] As Russell notes, the text is uncertain at this juncture: "The reproduction of good character" could also be read as "the reproduction of beauty of form" (*Ancient Literary Criticism*, 476, n. 1).

[21] Kant would have been familiar with Longinus's notion of *zêlôsis-mimêsis*, if not directly, then through Edward Young's *Conjectures on Original Composition* (1759, translated into German in 1760). Young observes that: "Imitation is inferiority confessed; emulation is superiority contested, or denied; imitation is servile, emulation generous; that fetters, this fires; that may give a name; this, a name immortal" (*Edward Young's "Conjectures on original composition,"* 60; Longinus is mentioned fifteen times in the work). Making a threefold distinction between *copying, imitating,* and *following* (or emulation, *Nachfolge*), Kant endeavors to explain the influence that geniuses exercise on one another: "The product of a genius (in respect of that in it which is to be ascribed to genius, not to possible learning or schooling) is an example, not for imitation (for then that which is genius in it and constitutes the spirit of the work would be lost), but for emulation [*Nachfolge*] by another genius, who is thereby awakened to the feeling of his own originality, to exercise freedom from coercion in his art in such a way that the latter thereby itself acquires a new rule, by which talent shows itself as exemplary" (CPJ, 5:318). See Sanford Budick's *Kant and Milton* for an exhaustive discussion of Kant's concept of *Nachfolge*. See also Robert Doran, "Imitation and Originality: Creative Mimesis in Longinus, Kant, and Girard."

[22] As we saw, Longinus uses this term as an adjective to describe the second source of sublimity, *enthousiastikon pathos.*

[23] There is a vigorous debate about how to interpret Plato's *Ion*. For an overview, see Stephen Halliwell, *Between Ecstasy and Truth,* 166–179.

[24] This passage anticipates Nietzsche's notion of Dionysian inspiration (which is, of course, itself based on classical models).

As an extended metaphor or analogy, the passage suggests a structural homology. Just as the gods "inspired" the poet in the theory of *enthousiasmos*,[25] the great writer of the past "inspires" the literary aspirant. By replacing the divine with a human model, even as he emphasizes the structural continuity of transcendence in the "inspirational" and divine-like power of the genius, Longinus divinizes the human and humanizes the divine – a major theme of the treatise (in chapter 9 Longinus remarks: "Homer, or so it seems to me, has done his best to make the men of the Trojan war gods, and the gods men" [9.7]).[26] Intensifying his metaphorical operation, Longinus superimposes the image of "pregnancy," echoing the section on *megalophrosynê* ("make them pregnant with noble thoughts" [9.1]), thereby underlining the idea of development from an embryonic to a mature state, the model of which is nature itself (Longinus's metaphor recalls a passage in Plato's *Symposium*).[27]

The veneration for past models may, at first glance, appear to devalorize the creative potential of the present, subordinating it to an assumed superiority of the past. But such an understanding belies the dialectical import of *zêlôsis-mimêsis* in Longinus's creation aesthetics, which manifests at once a conservative respect for tradition, in the idea of the model, and a desire for the subversion of tradition, in the agonistic relation of rivalry – the constant threat of deviation from or challenge to prevailing cultural and aesthetic norms (which, in the modern era, often takes the form of artistic manifestos). The fact that Longinus has been interpreted both as an arch classicist (Boileau) and as a Romantic revolutionary (Harold Bloom) testifies to this dual or dialectical aspect.

This dialectic is nowhere more clearly or emblematically expressed than in Longinus's description of Plato's attempt to surpass Homer:

> Plato could not have put such a brilliant finish on his philosophical doctrines or so often risen to poetical subjects and poetical language, if he had not tried, and tried wholeheartedly, to compete for the prize against Homer, like a young aspirant challenging an admired master. To break a lance in this way may well have been a brash and contentious thing to do, but the competition

---

[25] Plato writes: "It's a divine power that moves you, as a 'Magnetic' stone moves iron rings. . .. This stone not only pulls those rings, if they're iron, it also puts power *in* the rings, so that they in turn can do just what the stone does – pull other rings – so that there's sometimes a very long chain of iron pieces and rings hanging from one another" (*Ion*, 533d–e, original emphasis).

[26] Longinus often indulges in theological language, as when he writes that "[noble emotion] inspires and possesses our words with a kind of madness and divine spirit" (8.4). And Longinus describes Demosthenes "in a sudden moment of inspiration [*empneustheis*] as if possessed by the divine" (16.2, Fyfe's translation; Havell has: "In a sudden moment of supreme exaltation he bursts out like some inspired prophet").

[27] See Elizabeth Pender, "Spiritual Pregnancy in Plato's *Symposium*."

proved anything but valueless. As Hesiod says, "this strife [*eris*] is good for men." Truly it is a noble contest [*agôn*] and prize of honor, and one well worth winning, in which to be defeated by one's elders is itself no disgrace. (13.4)[28]

Plato's critique of Homer can thus be seen as owing as much to a sense of rivalry and competition as to philosophical principles – hence the agonistic element in imitation. "To contest the prize with Homer" means not only to rival him on the level of literary expression but also to rival Homer's preeminent place in Greek culture, to be "like Homer" in stature, not in terms of any actual resemblance of their respective oeuvres (even if this spirit of competition inspired Plato to infuse his philosophical works with poetic elements).[29] In other words, Plato wishes to emulate Homer by replacing or displacing him, by becoming a touchstone for Greek culture in his stead.[30] Although it might seem paradoxical that "imitation" could lead to such patent dissimilarity, the dialectic between admiration and creative deviance is the essence of sublime *competition*. It is the very striving to surpass or transcend that is important – the formative nature of competition – rather than actual success ("to be defeated by one's elders is itself no disgrace").[31]

In short, Longinus is claiming that the spirit of competition is concomitant with the creative urge. Comparing Aeschylus and Euripides, Longinus writes: "The ambitious/competitive Euripides did not shirk even these risks" (15.5). Significantly, the notion of "competition" returns again in the important discussion of nature in chapter 35: "Nature made man ... to be both a spectator and an enthusiastic contestant in its competitions" (35.2). The metaphor or analogy of athletic games suggests more broadly that rivalry is fundamental to human nature, that the competitive striving for greatness – self-transcendence through rivalry – defines our *telos* as human beings. Aristotle writes in his *Rhetoric* that "the great-souled are emulous" (1388b); that is, having a competitive nature is part of what it means to be great-souled.

---

[28] Longinus appears to contradict himself in the last sentence, since he had earlier criticized those "who put their trust in the maxim that 'failure in a great attempt is at least a noble error'" (3.3).

[29] Malcolm Heath similarly observes: "Longinus ... holds that Plato's philosophy, as well as his style, was shaped by his emulation of Homer" (*Ancient Philosophical Poetics*, 172).

[30] Halliwell notes that "Plato perceives poetry as a potent cultural rival, an opponent in what Socrates famously calls the 'ancient quarrel' (607b)" (*The Aesthetics of Mimesis*, 56). See also Alexander Nehamas's discussion of Plato's view toward poetry in his essay "Plato and the Mass Media" (in *Virtues of Authenticity*, 279–299).

[31] One could, in this context, cite the work of Harold Bloom – the most Longinian of contemporary critics – whose notion of the "anxiety of influence" (a theory of poetic creation) takes Longinus's agonistic notion of *zêlôsis-mimêsis* as its starting point. Bloom speaks of the "creative envy" that "becomes the ecstasy, the Sublime of the sign-system of poetic language" (*"Poetry, Revisionism, Repression,"* 333).

Longinus's use of the terms *eris* (strife) and *agôn* (contest) serves to further emphasize the anthropological dimension of his theory. The quotation from Hesiod ("this strife [*eris*] is good for men") refers to the opening of *Works and Days*, which identifies two kinds of *eris*:

> So, after all, there was not one kind of Strife [*eris*] alone, but all over the earth there are two. As for the one, a man would praise her when he came to understand her; but the other is blameworthy: and they are wholly different in nature. For one fosters evil war and battle, being cruel: her no man loves; but perforce, through the will of the deathless gods, men pay harsh Strife [*eris*] her honor due. But the other is the elder daughter of dark Night, and the son of Cronos, who sits above and dwells in the ether, sets her in the roots of the earth: and she is far kinder to men. She stirs up even the shiftless to toil; for a man grows eager to work when he considers his neighbor, a rich man who hastens to plough and plant and put his house in good order; and neighbor vies with his neighbor as he hurries after wealth. This Strife [*eris*] is wholesome [or good] for men. And potter is angry with potter, and craftsman with craftsman, and beggar is jealous of beggar, and minstrel of minstrel.[32]

Eris (the origin of the modern English word *eristic*) is the goddess of strife, discord, and rivalry. Although this goddess is usually represented in a negative light, as delighting in the bloodshed of wars she has caused, Hesiod sees a good and a bad *eris*. The good *eris* is the motivational source of human achievement, a productive rivalry that incites effort toward (socially) beneficial ends. One could describe the bad and the good *eris* respectively as conflict and competition. The first engenders war and destruction, while the second fosters wealth and success. By using a single term, *eris*, for two opposing concepts, Hesiod emphasizes their structural identity. Indeed, competition always involves some level of conflict; and conflict, particularly when it escalates or intensifies, necessarily implies a kind of competition.

The Greek idea that competitiveness is a fundamental part of creativity was emphasized by Nietzsche, in an early essay aptly entitled "Homer on Competition":

> The whole of Greek antiquity thinks about grudge and envy differently from us and agrees with Hesiod, who first portrays one Eris as wicked, in fact the one who leads men into hostile struggle-to-the-death, and then praises the other Eris as good who, as jealousy, grudge and envy, goads men to action, not, however, in the action of a struggle-to-the-death but the action of *competition*. The Greek is *envious* and does not experience this

[32] Hesiod, *Works And Days*, 11–24 (my emphasis).

characteristic as a blemish, but as the effect of a *benevolent* deity: what a gulf of ethical judgment between him and us![33]

Using Hesiod's thesis as a basis for his ethico-cultural critique of modernity, Nietzsche sees the positive conception of the eristic or agonistic as indicative of the strength and superiority of ancient Greek culture, which celebrated ambition, envy, and rivalry, while we moderns weakly (and perhaps even hypocritically) consider these to be character defects: "Hellenic popular teaching commands that every talent must develop through a struggle, whereas modern educators fear nothing more than the unleashing of so-called ambition."[34] Nietzsche thus follows Longinus closely with regard to the cultural implications of the concept of creative emulation.

The third aspect of grandeur of conception, *phantasia*, translated as "imagination" or "visualization," possesses a rich history in Greek rhetoric and philosophy, though its relation to modern notions of the imagination is often difficult to discern. Indeed, what we now call "imagination" is expressed in a variety of Greek terms; and *phantasia* often means something quite different from "imagination."[35] In rhetoric, *phantasia* denotes the orator's ability to influence an audience through the conjuring of images. The listener "sees" in the mind's eye what he or she is hearing; the things described are experienced *as if* they were actually present. Longinus sees this capacity as one of the exemplary ways of attaining *hypsos*:

> Another thing which is extremely productive of grandeur, magnificence, and urgency, my young friend, is visualization [*phantasia*]. I use this word for what some people call image-production [*eidolopoiiai*]. The term *phantasia* is used generally for anything which in any way suggests a thought productive of speech; but the word has also come into fashion for the situation in which enthusiasm and emotion make the speaker *see* what he is saying and bring it *visually* before his audience. (15.1, translator's emphasis)

By making a distinction between the philosophical – and specifically Stoic – conception of *phantasia* and the rhetorical use of this notion in his own time,[36] Longinus's text testifies to a shift toward a new conception

---

[33] Friedrich Nietzsche, "Homer on Competition," 190, original emphasis.
[34] Nietzsche, *On the Genealogy of Morality*, 192.
[35] Fortunately, two important studies have greatly increased our knowledge of this term: Murray Bundy's *The Theory of the Imagination in Classical and Medieval Thought* (1927); and Gerard Watson's *Phantasia in Classical Thought* (1988). Both authors consider *phantasia* to be a precursor of the modern concept of the imagination and see Longinus's treatise as one of the principal texts in which such a connection becomes manifest.
[36] Watson remarks that "Longinus was aware of the Stoic technical definition of *logike phantasia*, as one 'in which what is presented can be conceived in speech'" (*Phantasia in Classical Thought*, 67). D. A. Russell also takes this view (*"Longinus" on the Sublime*, 120).

of the imagination. The philosophical use of the term centered on its role in cognition. Plato writes in the *Sophist*: "What we call appearing [*phantasia*] [is] the blending of perception [*aisthêsis*] and belief [*doxa*]" (264b). But Plato also speaks of *phantasia* in terms of prophetic "visions" in the *Timaeus* (72a). Aristotle, in contrast, treats *phantasia* as a faculty that mediates between *aesthêsis* (sensation) and *nôus* (intellect/thinking). However, in neither case is the imagination considered a primary mental function (as it will later be in Kant, for example).[37] The Stoic philosophers for the first time give *phantasia* a prominent place in their philosophical system. Since they see knowledge as derived from the senses, the Stoics consider *phantasia*, understood as sensible presentation, to be crucial in the production of language. Hence Longinus's reference to "a thought productive of speech."

Longinus is less interested in the epistemological implications of *phantasia* than in its significance for literary creation: namely, the autonomy of the imaginative capacity, its ability to *produce* and not merely reproduce images. For *phantasia* not only makes absent things present; it also creates things no mind has seen in actual perception. Discussing Euripides, Longinus writes: "The poet himself saw the Erinyes, and he has as good as made his audience see what he imagined" (15.2). Commenting on the passage, Gerard Watson observes that "what [Longinus] says about Euripides and the Furies is particularly interesting as a parallel to what Philostratus has to say on picturing the despair of Ajax and on *phantasia* producing *even what it had not seen*."[38] The idea of a "productive imagination" paves the way for the modern concept of the imagination and the related notions of originality, creativity, and, of course, genius.[39] Indeed, for Longinus, images of the greatest extent and power are to be found not

---

[37] Dan Flory observes that "Aristotelian epistemology thus makes imagination a necessary feature of perception, as well as cognition, but still limits imagination to the role of a secondary mental capacity" ("Stoic Psychology, Classical Rhetoric, and Theories of Imagination in Western Philosophy," 147).

[38] Watson, *Phantasia in Classical Thought*, 68, my emphasis. Halliwell, however, writes of the "exaggerated view that the concept of *phantasia* came in antiquity to challenge the predominance of *mimêsis* [that is, representation] in critical and philosophical aesthetics" (*The Aesthetics of Mimesis*, 308). Indeed, nowhere in his treatise does Longinus compare *phantasia* with representational mimesis. Nevertheless, Halliwell does concede that one finds in Longinus's text a "remarkable sensitivity that stretches the understanding of literary creativity well beyond anything found in most texts in the mimeticist tradition" (*The Aesthetics of Mimesis*, 311).

[39] Thus Kant, in his *Anthropology*, draws a distinction between the "reproductive imagination," which operates as a relation to the world, and the "productive imagination," which creates "in an original way (not imitatively)" (APP 7:246). Kant further states that the word *phantasy* must not be mixed with memory, for then "memory would be *unfaithful*" (APP 7:182, original emphasis). It is rather connected with creativity: "Fantasy, that is, the creative power of imagination" (APP 7:182).

in the external world but in the visionary capacity of the mind; *phantasia* is thus an essential part of *hypsos* precisely because it transcends sensibility.

As noted in Chapter 1, Longinus also makes an important distinction between the oratorical and poetic *use* of images: "It will not escape you that rhetorical visualization has a different intention from that of the poets: in poetry the aim is astonishment [*ekplêxis*], in oratory it is clarity [*enargeia*]. Both, however, seek emotion and excitement" (15.2). This is one of the few passages in his treatise where Longinus makes a discursive-generic distinction with regard to *hypsos*. The effectiveness of oratory (particularly juridical oratory) requires a more realistic presentation of images; its images affect by their *vividness* (*enargeia*). Poetical images, on the other hand, have more scope for the marvelous or the fantastical: "The poetical examples, as I said, have a quality of exaggeration which belongs to fable and goes far beyond credibility. In an orator's visualization [*phantasia*], on the other hand, it is an element of fact and truth which makes for success; in oratory it is always one of reality and truth" (15.8).[40] Longinus thus suggests that, since there is a type of *phantasia* appropriate to oratory and a type appropriate to poetry, to confuse them would be incongruous and unsublime.[41]

In the Latin rhetorical tradition *phantasiai* (visualizations) is translated by the term *visiones*, but the idea remains substantially the same as that expressed in Longinus. In his *Institutio Oratoria*, Quintilian (35–100 AD) makes this connection to Greek rhetoric explicit:

> There are certain experiences which the Greeks call *phantasiai*, and the Romans *visiones*, whereby things absent are presented to our imagination with such extreme vividness that they seem to be actually before our very eyes. . . . Some writers describe the possessor of this power of vivid imagination whereby things, words and actions are presented in a most realistic manner, by the Greek word *euphantasiotos* [blessed with imagination]; and it is a power which all may readily acquire if they will.[42]

Like Longinus, Quintilian appears to consider the ability to produce vivid images to be both a natural capacity ("*blessed* with imagination") and a faculty that can be developed ("a power which all may acquire"). The nexus Longinus posits between *phantasia* and emotion will have a strong

---

[40] Demetrius similarly observes: "Anything unclear and unfamiliar is unconvincing" (*On Style*, 221; *Aristotle/Longinus/Demetrius*, 479–481). Aristotle makes a similar contrast between tragedy and epic. See *Poetics*, 1460a.

[41] As mentioned in the previous chapter, there is a tension between Longinus's transgeneric concept of literary value and his genre- and context-specific analyses.

[42] Quintilian, *Institutio Oratoria*, 6.2.29 (quoted in Flory, "Stoic Psychology," 156).

influence on modern criticism, particularly on John Dennis and Giambattista Vico.[43]

2.2 The second source of sublimity: vehement/inspired emotion (*pathos*)

As noted above, Longinus considers the second source of sublimity, *to sphodron kai enthousiastikon pathos* (literally: vehement and god-possessed passion), to be virtually on a par with the other "natural" source of sublimity, grandeur of conception (*noêsis*). In fact, Longinus sometimes treats emotion as if it were sublimity itself.[44] However, unlike the other sources, which are discussed in the order they are announced, the examination of *pathos* does not occur in the expected place: after the section on grandeur of thought and before the treatment of the technical sources. It is possible that Longinus displaced it to the end of the treatise, for the last line of the extant text reads: "'Best to let things be,' and proceed to our next subject. This was emotion [*pathos*], to which I promised to devote a separate treatise. It occupies, as I said, a very important place among constituents of literature in general, and sublimity [*hypsos*] in particular ..." (44.12, the text breaks off abruptly). But this section (or treatise) has been lost, if indeed it ever existed. In any event, Longinus does offer a good number of observations, which, in the words of one critic, represent "the most extensive treatment of emotion in the verbal arts" of the period.[45]

After introducing his five sources of *hypsos*, Longinus makes a point of criticizing Caecilius for failing to discuss emotion in his *Peri hypsous*. He considers two possibilities for this oversight: either Caecilius confuses *hypsos* and *pathos* ("now if he thought that sublimity and emotion were one and the same thing and always existed and developed together, he was wrong" [8.2]); or he believed that emotion was unimportant or irrelevant to the production of *hypsos* ("on the other hand, if Caecilius thought that emotion had no contribution to make to sublimity and therefore thought it not worth mentioning, he was again completely wrong" [8.3–4]). Longinus rejects the second view out of hand. With respect to the first possibility, however, Longinus takes some care to refute it, which may indicate that such a confusion or fusion between *hypsos* and *pathos* was

---

[43] See Chapter 5.
[44] As G. M. A. Grube notes, Longinus often "speaks as if [a] particular aspect [of sublimity] were the thing itself" ("Notes on the *Peri hypsous*," 357).
[45] Whitney Shiner, *Proclaiming the Gospel: First-Century Performance of Mark*, 59.

common in his day and that a more subtle differentiation was needed –
despite the fact that, as mentioned above, Longinus himself sometimes uses
hypsos and *pathos* interchangeably.[46]

Longinus offers two arguments for why *hypsos* and *pathos* should be
considered distinct: (1) low emotions, "pity, grief, and fear," have nothing
in common with elevation and have a correspondingly low effect; (2) *hypsos*
can occur without *pathos*. Both points have proved controversial among
commentators.

In regards to the first point, it is indeed difficult to comprehend the
designation of grief, pity, and fear as "low emotions" unworthy of sublime
dignity, particularly given the association, in Aristotle's *Poetics*, of pity and
fear with the beneficial effects of tragedy. It is inconceivable that Longinus
could consider the tragic emotions to be low or vulgar; examples taken
from tragedy are considered to be among the most sublime, and he singles
out Sophocles's *Oedipus Rex* as a supremely great work.[47] Doreen Innes
holds that Longinus regards certain emotions as low because they are
intrinsically unheroic: "Heroes do not ask for pity; they do not show
grief and fear."[48] The advantage of this interpretation is that it emphasizes,
as I have tried to do, the importance of high-mindedness (*megalophrosynê*)
in Longinus's theory. However, I believe that one can make the case that,
in Longinus's view, it is not these emotions *as such* that are low or vulgar,
but rather the context in which they appear that determines their relative
"lowliness": "I should myself have no hesitation in saying that there is
nothing so productive of grandeur as noble emotion *in the right place*" (8.4,
my emphasis).[49] Clearly there are limits to what can count as "noble
emotion" (that is, some emotions are intrinsically lowly and therefore
unsuited to the production of *hypsos*), but, as Longinus's insistence on
kairos amply shows, he is quite cognizant of the idea that emotion, perhaps
more than other sources of sublimity, is highly dependent on the manner

---

[46] For example: "Thus sublimity [*hypsos*] and emotion [*pathos*] are a defense and a marvelous aid
against the suspicion which the use of figures engenders" (17.2).

[47] "Take tragedy: would you rather be Ion of Chios or Sophocles? ... No one in his senses would
reckon all Ion's works put together as the equivalent of the one play *Oedipus*" (33.5). However,
Longinus clearly regards at least some kinds of pity as "low." Halliwell observes that "the Odyssey's
scenes of 'lamentation and pity' (τὰς ὀλοφύρσεις καὶ τοὺς οἴκτους) are associated, at least
obliquely, with Homer's ebbing powers (9.12)" (*Between Ecstasy and Truth*, 353, n. 53).

[48] Doreen Innes, "Longinus, Sublimity, and the Low Emotions," 325.

[49] John Dennis appears to argue as much when he writes: "But Religion does not only heighten those
Passions which are great in themselves, as Admiration and Terror are; for Admiration raises the
Soul, and every Thing that is terrible, is certainly great to him to whom it is terrible, but it ennobles
those which are commonly base and dejected" (CW I, 230).

and circumstances of its use.[50] If, for example, pity and fear were employed for sensationalist purposes far removed from the noble designs of tragedy – Longinus denounces the "shocking and outrageous abnormality" characteristic of "shock orators" (15.8) – then these would indeed appear as low emotions.

This broadly contextualist (as opposed to strictly essentialist) view of emotion in Longinus is confirmed by the way in which Longinus treats fear/terror in other sections of his treatise, both explicitly, as specifically conducive to sublimity and, implicitly, in the sublime effects of *ekstasis* (ecstasy, transport) and *ekplêxis* (astonishment, amazement), which, as we saw in the previous chapter, are etymologically related to the idea of fear. In chapter 10 of his treatise, Longinus offers a compelling account of the relation between fear/terror and *hypsos*. Discussing a lyric by Sappho, Longinus observes: "She is cold and hot, mad and sane, frightened/terrified and near death. . . . A similar point can be made about the descriptions of storms in Homer, who always picks out the most terrifying aspects" (10.3). Comparing Homer with a passage from a poem by Aristeas of Proconnesus, Longinus writes: "The author of the *Arimaspea*, on the other hand, expects these lines to excite terror" (10.4); and "Homer, on the other hand, does not banish the cause of fear at a stroke; he gives a vivid picture of men, one might almost say, facing death many times with every wave that comes" (10.6). Terror and fear are thus clearly both the source ("the most terrifying aspects" in Homer) and part of the effect ("excite terror") of *hypsos*, in Longinus's estimation.[51] This is particularly significant for the later association, in Burke's theory, of sublimity with terror. Longinus's discussion of fear/terror in chapter 10 (not to mention the etymological connections noted above) is overlooked by many commentators, who insist that this aspect is a wholly modern invention.[52]

With regard to the idea that *hypsos* can occur without *pathos*, it is clear that Longinus requires this separation to preserve the autonomy of the first

---

[50] Discussing Longinus's ideas on metaphor and emotion, Marsh McCall observes how context is essential to Longinus's conception of *pathos*: "The author of *On the Sublime* says that a metaphor, or even a string of them, is never too strong a figure if used at times of high emotion and real sublimity, but when emotion is at a lower key it is sometimes better to soften the intensity of the metaphor" (*Ancient Rhetorical Theories of Simile and Comparison*, 54).

[51] Longinus is not alone among ancient rhetoricians is asserting a connection between powerful eloquence and fear. Discussing the "forceful style," which, as observed in Chapter 1, many have likened to the sublime, Demetrius observes: "What shocks is always forceful, since it inspires fear" (*On Style*, 283, *Aristotle/Longinus/Demetrius*, 511).

[52] Terror, as Debora Shuger notes, was also considered to be part of the grand style: "This style is striking, elaborate, obscure, and terrifying" ("The Grand Style and the *genera dicendi* in Ancient Rhetoric," 24).

source of sublimity (grandeur of conception). Examples of sublimity that are bereft of emotion include the following observation about oratorical genres: "In orators, encomia and ceremonial or exhibition pieces always involve grandeur and sublimity, though they are generally devoid of emotion" (8.2–8.3). Here a genre distinction indicates not the particular use of emotion, but whether it should be used at all.

I should emphasize that Longinus is not speaking about emotion *tout court*, but, as was stated above, *to sphodron kai enthousiastikon pathos*: vehement and inspired (god-possessed) emotion. Realizing that there is often a fine line separating strong emotion from its opposite, affectation, Longinus cautions (in the section devotion to the faults incident to sublimity) that there is a fault particular to emotional passages, what he calls *parenthyrsos* ("false enthusiasm"; Russell and Fyfe translate it as "pseudo-Bacchanalian"):

> It consists of untimely [*akairos*] or meaningless emotion where none is in place, or immoderate emotion where moderate is in place. Some people often get carried away, like drunkards, into emotions unconnected with the subject, which are simply their own pedantic invention. The audience feels nothing, so that they inevitably make an exhibition of themselves, parading their ecstasies before an audience which does not share them. (3.5)[53]

Longinus appears to be criticizing the notion of the "inspired bard." Indeed, Longinus's image of the drunkard recalls Plato's use of the same image in the *Ion* to describe the "enthusiasm" of the rhapsode.[54] But this passage also emphasizes the intersubjective dimension of *hypsos*, in the idea that the audience should "share" the emotions of the speaker, which is not unlike what Plato describes: "In the same way the Muse makes some people inspired herself, and then through those who are inspired a chain of other enthusiasts is suspended" (*Ion*, 533e). Discussing metaphor, Longinus similarly observes: "[Strong and appropriate emotions] never allow the hearer leisure to count the metaphors, because he too shares the speaker's enthusiasm" (32.4).

The antidote to excessive emotion or affectation is *spontaneity*, that is, allowing an emotion to arise organically from the context, as opposed to "putting in the emotion," so to speak, as if *pathos* were a kind of

---

[53] Longinus lists another fault, tumidity, the desire to "outdo elevation" (3.4), which he describes as "one of the hardest faults to guard against ... for often when they think themselves inspired, their supposed ecstasy is merely childish folly" (3.3). Longinus breaks off this discussion by remarking that he has reserved the topic of emotion "for another place" (3.5).

[54] "When once they launch into harmony and rhythm, they are seized with Bacchic transport, and are possessed" (*Ion*, 534a).

embellishment or tool – hence Longinus's censure in the above-cited passage of *akairos*, "untimely" emotion. As we have seen, Longinus often emphasizes the importance of *kairos* (the right moment) in emotional sublimity: "For emotion carries us away more easily when it seems to be generated by the occasion [*kairos*] rather than deliberately assumed by the speaker, and the self-directed question and its answer represent precisely this momentary quality of emotion" (18.2); "the right occasions [*kairos*] are when emotions come flooding in and bring the multiplication of metaphors with them as a necessary accompaniment" (32.1). Similarly: "The result is that he seems to be giving not a premediated speech but one forced on him by the circumstances" (22.2); and "the use of this figure is appropriate when the urgency of the moment gives the writer no chance to delay" (27.2). Sublimity thus involves *authentic* emotion through *kairos* (the nature of which we explored in Chapter 1), in contrast to the strategic or manipulative use of emotion in persuasive rhetoric.

Although Longinus sharply criticizes excessive or inappropriate emotion, he in no way wishes to dampen the emotional intensity of *hypsos*. This is emphatically demonstrated in Longinus's comparison of the *Iliad* and the *Odyssey*, one of the most sustained discussions of *pathos*. This section will become well known as one of the inspirations for Giambattista Vico's *Scienza nuova* (*New Science*), particularly Book 3: "Discovery of the True Homer." Since Vico's notion of the sublime is based on the pathetic rather than the noetic dimension of Longinus's theory, Vico is keen to highlight passages such as the following, where strong emotion becomes the key index of sublimity:

> [Homer] made the whole body of the *Iliad*, which was written at the height of his powers, dramatic and exciting, whereas most of the *Odyssey* consists of narrative [*mythos*], which is characteristic of old age. Homer in the *Odyssey* may be compared to the setting sun: the size/grandeur [*megethos*] remains without the force. He no longer sustains the tension as it was in the tale of Troy, nor that consistent level of sublimity [*hypsos*] which never admitted of falling off. The outpouring of the passions [*pathê*] crowding one another has gone; so has the versatility, the realism/actuality [*alêtheia*], the abundance of imagery taken from life. We see greatness [*megethos*] on the ebb. It is as though the Ocean were withdrawing into itself and flowing quietly in its own bed. Homer is lost in the realm of the fabulous and incredible. In saying this I have not forgotten the storms in the *Odyssey*, the story of Cyclops, and a few other episodes; I am speaking of old age – but it is the old age of a Homer. The point about all these stories is that the mythical element predominates in them over the realistic. . . . There is a second reason for discussing the *Odyssey*. I want you to understand that the decline in

emotional power in great writers and poets turns to a capacity for depicting manners [*êthos*]. The realistic description of Odysseus' household forms a kind of comedy of manners. (9.13–14)

Because of the greater violence of its emotions, the *Iliad* must have been written in Homer's prime. The *Odyssey*, on the other hand, shows a great author in decline, and therefore must have been composed in old age, when the passions are less intense. (Vico uses this contrast to speculate that the epics were by different authors writing at different formative moments in Greek history, of which they served as emblematic expressions.)[55] Longinus does not say that the *Odyssey* is entirely devoid of sublimity ("in saying this I have not forgotten about the storms in the *Odyssey*, the story of Cyclops, and a few other episodes"), simply that it has fewer sublime moments, thereby dulling the overall effect. (This is one of the few places, in fact, where Longinus implies that his analysis of *hypsos* can apply to the effect of an entire work.) Longinus employs the metaphor of the sunset – redolent of his use of light metaphors throughout to connote sublimity – to illustrate how he conceives of the decline of a great genius: "Homer in the *Odyssey* may be compared to the setting sun: the size/ grandeur [*megethos*] remains without the force." Emotion would thus appear to be a key ingredient in creating the *intensity* that sublimity requires.

This passage also unfolds a series of oppositions that relates *hypsos* to traditional literary categories. Longinus contrasts the *drama* of the *Iliad* with the *narrative* of the *Odyssey*, associating drama with "the outpouring of the passions [*pathê*] crowding one another." One presumes that by "narrative" Longinus means storytelling, the mere recounting of events as opposed to their direct presentation via dialogue or vivid description. Narration diminishes the emotional impact, insofar as it places the audience at a distance from the events. Longinus contrasts the dramatic *pathos*

---

[55] Vico writes: "Thus Homer composed the *Iliad* in his youth, that is, when Greece was young and consequently seething with sublime passions, such as pride, wrath, and lust for vengeance, passions which do not tolerate dissimulation but which love magnanimity; and hence Greece admired Achilles, the hero of violence. But he wrote the *Odyssey* in his old age, that is, when the spirits of Greece had been somewhat cooled by reflection, which is the mother of prudence, so that it admired Ulysses, the hero of wisdom" (NS, 879). Vico thus sees Longinus's comparison as a confirmation of his theory of historical cycles (*corso* and *ricorso*). The true Age of Heroes, of the sublime, is represented by the *Iliad*, whereas the *Odyssey* shows Greek culture in decline. The violent and spontaneous nature of the passions, the source of the sublimity of the "earlier" epic, cannot be the product of the same stage of mental development represented by the *Odyssey*. See Chapter 5 for a discussion of Vico.

of the *Iliad* with the everyday realism or *êthos* of the *Odyssey*.[56] *Êthos* belongs to "lower, more human, even comic genres."[57] Longinus thus prefers the vivid realism or actuality (*alêtheia* also means "truth") of the *Iliad* to the mythical or fantastical character of the *Odyssey* ("Homer is lost in the realm of the fabulous and incredible").[58] Although it would appear that literary genres or modes that deal with more mundane concerns – the pastoral, the novel, and so on – are generically less inclined, or not at all inclined, toward sublimity, how to characterize the modern development of literary representation toward the realistic *êthos* of the novel and away from the *pathos* of epic and tragedy? Erich Auerbach's conception of modern realism as the "mixture of styles," the combination of *sublimitas* and *humilitas*, of lofty pathos and everyday circumstances, offers a compelling way of understanding this historical evolution. According to Auerbach, the Gospels (written around the same time as Longinus's treatise) provide a counter-model of how sublimity and the highest passion – that of Christ on the Cross – can not only cohere with but can become entirely enmeshed with, and inextricable from, mundane reality (Jesus's humble milieu). As the fulfillment of the Christian mixture between the lofty and the lowly (in both a social and an aesthetic sense), modern realism will thus become, for Auerbach, a sublime realism, one in which *pathos* and *êthos* are seamlessly intertwined.[59]

2.3   The technical sources of sublimity

The discussion of the three technical sources takes up almost half of the extant text. Chapters 16–29 treat figures (*schêmata*); chapters 30–32 and 37–38 examine diction (*phrasis*) (chapters 33–36 contain a digression, which will be discussed in Chapter 3 of this study); and chapters 39–43 are devoted to word arrangement/composition (*synthesis*).

[56] Synthesizing Aristotle and Longinus, Thomas Gould observes: "If *pathos* and *êthos* are polar opposites among the great virtues in poetry, and *êthos* means a hero's ideal qualities, then *pathos* must mean a hero's unique qualities or his passionate responses to his unique situation. *Êthos* is the representation of serene and godlike stances and actions; *pathos* angry, turbulent, energetic actions, like those of Achilles in the *Iliad*" (*The Ancient Quarrel Between Poetry and Philosophy*, 65).
[57] D. A. Russell, *Ancient Literary Criticism*, 489, note 2.
[58] This appears to reverse what Longinus had said about the difference between poetry (whose sublimity derives more from the fantastical) and oratory (whose sublimity stems from its vivid realism). But, one could argue that the intrageneric contrast between the *Iliad* and the *Odyssey* brings out distinctions that have a different resonance on the intergeneric level.
[59] See Robert Doran, "Literary History and the Sublime in Erich Auerbach's *Mimesis*."

The section on figures is perhaps the most revealing of the three from the standpoint of Longinus's theory of *hypsos*; for, in addition to showing how figures might contribute to sublimity, Longinus also takes care to point out how figures also constitute a *danger* to sublimity. That is, Longinus often finds himself denigrating figures by *opposing* their artifice to the naturalness of thought and emotion. For example, Longinus writes: "Sublimity and emotion are a defense and a marvelous aid against the suspicion which the use of figures engenders. The artifice of the trick is lost to sight in the surrounding brilliance of beauty and grandeur, and it escapes all suspicion" (17.1). Clearly "artifice" is here given a negative connotation; the use of the word "suspicion" is most telling, as if Longinus were trying to pit a rhetoric of transcendence against a rhetoric of persuasion, the latter of which habitually employs "devices" to "trick" the audience. In other words, sublimity presupposes a nobler vocation for rhetoric, one that is endangered by the (overly) clever use of figures.

Thus even if "grandeur results from the total contribution of many elements" (40.1), including the technical elements, Longinus clearly intends to grant a *moral* privilege to nature, or at least to the *appearance* of naturalness: "For art [*technê*] is only perfect when it looks like nature and Nature only succeeds when she conceals latent art" (22.1). Kant will make a similar statement in his third *Critique*: "Nature was beautiful, if at the same time it looked like art; and art can only be called beautiful if we are aware that it is art and yet it looks to us like nature" (CPJ, 5:306).[60] For Longinus, art will only *look* like nature when it is in effect an expression *of* nature, that is, of nobility of thought and emotion.

Longinus thus conceives of the relation between the natural and the technical sources antagonistically, as in this – highly metaphorical – passage:

> As fainter lights disappear when the sunshine surrounds them, so the sophisms of rhetoric are dimmed when they are enveloped in encircling grandeur. Something like this happens in painting: when light and shadow are juxtaposed in colours on the same plane, the light seems more prominent to the eye, and both stands out and actually appears much nearer. Similarly, in literature, emotional and sublime features seem much closer to the mind's eye, both because of a certain natural kinship and because of their brilliance. Consequently, they always show up above the figures and overshadow and eclipse their artifice. (17.2)

---

[60] See Chapter 12.

Here sublimity and emotion are seen as operating *apart from* figures (or from *technê* more generally), as if the figures were a kind of nuisance or necessary evil. But perhaps Longinus means to say that a few sublime moments can *redeem* the "sophisms of rhetoric" a writer might lapse into. Longinus puts forward a similar argument in the digression on genius versus mediocrity (33–34),[61] except that here he would seem to be offering a path to redemption for the *mediocre* writer (to the extent that a nongenius can achieve a measure of *hypsos*).

At other moments, Longinus speaks of *technê* as involving "risk" and "audacity" that need to be checked by sublimity. For example: "As I keep saying, acts and emotions which approach ecstasy provide a justification for, and antidote to, any linguistic audacity" (38.5). The "linguistic audacity" thus does not contribute to sublime ecstasy (*ekstasis*); on the contrary, it is the ecstasy, the sublime effect, that "justifies" and compensates for (is the "antidote to") the (too) bold use of figures. Longinus makes a similar point when he writes: "I would add – and I said the same about figures – that strong and appropriate emotions and genuine sublimity are a specific palliative for multiplied or daring metaphors, because their nature is to sweep and drive all these other things along with the surging tide of their movement" (32.4). It is almost as if Longinus were attempting to describe an *anti*rhetorical sublime, a sublime that seeks to redeem the negative aspects of persuasive rhetoric: its sophistry, its trickery, its audacity, and above all, its artifice.

Paradoxically, the sections specifically devoted to *technê* are less dialectical than those on genius (2.1–3; 33–34), in which *technê* qua *methodos* (method/system) was conceived as essential and complementary to nature, rather than as antagonistic. It would thus appear that Longinus wanted to deepen his commitment to the moral ideal of nature in the production of sublimity by opposing it to a concept of *technê* as unnatural artifice.

***

In elucidating his five sources of *hypsos*, Longinus sets out to account for moments of transcendence in the verbal arts without devolving, on the one hand, into simple mysticism, that is, the theory of *enthousiasmos*, which, while it contains a subjective element, makes it utterly opaque, or, on the other, into genre theory (poetics) or technical (rhetorical-stylistic) analysis, which fail to capture the subjective conditions of transcendence.

---

[61] See Chapter 3.

Throughout my exploration of the sources of sublimity, I have emphasized how Longinus plays with theological metaphors to develop a protoaesthetics at the limit of religious experience. I have also stressed the reversibility of the creative (theory of genius) and receptive (affect, influence) standpoints in Longinus's theory, in order to reveal the importance of the intersubjective dimension, namely the *communicability* of *hypsos* as a mental disposition of high-mindedness.

CHAPTER 3

Longinus on sublimity in nature and culture

Commenting on Longinus's wide-ranging critical intelligence, Stephen Halliwell notes that *Peri hypsous* is "the only major document in the history of Western literary criticism and theory whose frame of reference extends all the way from sensitivity to the individual words, even individual syllables, of texts to a sense of the infinite spaces that lie (in thought) 'outside the cosmos.'"[1] In this final chapter on *Peri hypsous*, we will explore how, in two famous digressions, chapters 35 and 44, Longinus extends his theory of sublimity far beyond the purview of the verbal arts, into the realms of nature and the cultural-historical. These digressions are highly consequential for the modern interpretation of sublimity: chapter 35 is the impetus behind the association between sublimity and the aesthetics of nature, in particular the idea of infinity; while chapter 44 is the source of the cultural-critical dimension of sublimity, of the idea that a loss of sublimity of mind engenders cultural decline or decadence.

The first part of this chapter contends that Longinus's discussion of the grandeur of nature should be understood, first, as further development of his concept of sublime rivalry (*zêlôsis-mimêsis*); and second, as a crucial statement of the anthropological significance of *hypsos* – of how sublimity reveals humankind's natural vocation for transcendence, the constant striving beyond the limits of the sensible world or toward the divine. The second part of this chapter explores how Longinus's critique of cultural decline is firmly rooted in his earlier discussion of high-mindedness (*megalophrosynê*) and how this critique inscribes Longinus's theory of sublimity in a humanist tradition of civic engagement and concern for posterity.

---

[1] Stephen Halliwell, *Between Ecstasy and Truth*, 327.

3.1   The grandeur of nature

Longinus's digression on the grandeur of nature in chapter 35 forms part
of a larger argument on the nature of genius (32.8–36.4), which is itself a
digression interrupting the discussion of metaphor.[2] The impetus for the
return to the topic of genius (which had been treated at the outset of the
treatise) is an assertion by Caecilius that Longinus obviously feels has not
been adequately refuted thus far: "[Caecilius] had the audacity to declare
Lysias in all respects superior to Plato. . . . In preferring Lysias to Plato he
thinks he is preferring a faultless and pure writer to one who makes many
mistakes. But the facts are far from supporting his view" (32.8). This
section thus forms part of Longinus's larger defense of Plato against
Atticist attacks, one of the principal aims of the treatise.[3] Longinus here
turns the tables on Caecilius by arguing that flawed genius is preferable to
perfect mediocrity – an argument that can be read as a reaffirmation of
the superiority of the natural over the technical sources of sublimity.[4]
Longinus contends that the technical sources are in themselves insufficient for attaining sublimity and that even technical perfection pales in
comparison with true genius's grandeur of conception and emotional
intensity. If a genius like Plato exhibits technical deficiencies, these
should be seen as a *necessary by-product* of sublimity, for striving for
greatness inevitably involves audacity and risk: "Mediocre natures,
because they never run any risks and never aim at the heights . . . remain
to a large extent safe from error, while in great natures their very greatness
spells danger" (33.2). Longinus thereby concludes:

> Freedom from error does indeed save us from blame, but it is only greatness
> that wins admiration. Need I add that every one of those great men redeems all
> of his mistakes many times over by a single sublime stroke? Finally, if you
> picked out and put together all the mistakes in Homer, Demosthenes, Plato,
> and all the other really great men, the total would be found to be a minute
> fraction of the successes which those heroic figures have to their credit. (36.1–2)

In other words, genius can flourish despite technical shortcomings,
whereas even perfection cannot save the mediocre writer. Put another
way, mere technical proficiency, which can be taught according to a system

[2] In his translation, D. A. Russell puts the section under the subheading: "Digression: Genius versus
Mediocrity."
[3] See Chapter 1.
[4] This passage will become an important force in the eighteenth-century "beauties versus blemishes"
debate. See George Dickie, *The Century of Taste: The Philosophical Odyssey of Taste in the Eighteenth
Century*, 123–141.

(*methodos*), has little to do with genius per se, which, as we saw, is chiefly a function of *megalophrosynê* (grandeur/nobility of mind). As a consequence, literary criticism cannot content itself with merely technical observations, but must instead go to the core, so to speak; that is, it must seek to understand the true sources of greatness/sublimity, which lie in the mental disposition of the writer (the subjective conditions of transcendence).

The influential paragraph on the grandeur of nature (35.2–5) does not directly address the issue at hand; it rather intensifies the concept of genius/ greatness in a kind of extended analogy, an analogy that takes us very far afield indeed. One can in fact read this passage as an attempt to define the anthropological origins of sublimity.[5] Perhaps for the first time in any text, human *telos* is described in specifically "aesthetic" terms:

> What then was the vision which inspired those divine writers who disdained exactness of detail and aimed at the greatest prizes in literature? Above all else it was the understanding that nature made man to be no humble or lowly creature, but brought him into life and into the universe as into a great festival, to be both a spectator and an enthusiastic contestant in its competitions. She implanted in our minds from the start an irresistible desire for anything which is great and, in relation to ourselves, supernatural/divine. The universe therefore is not wide enough for the range of human speculation and intellect [*theôria*]. Our thoughts often travel beyond the boundaries of our surroundings. If anyone wants to know what we were born for, let him look round at life and contemplate the splendor, grandeur, and beauty in which it everywhere abounds. It is a natural inclination that leads us to admire not the little streams, however pellucid and however useful, but the Nile, the Danube, the Rhine, and above all the Ocean. Nor do we feel so much awe before the little flame we kindle, because it keeps its light clear and pure, as before the fires of heaven, though they are often obscured. We do not think our flame more worthy of admiration than the craters of Etna, whose eruptions bring up rocks and whole hills out of depths, and sometimes pour forth rivers of earth-born spontaneous fire. A single comment fits all these examples: the useful are readily available to man, it is the unusual that excites our wonder. (35.2–5)[6]

Although Longinus does not explicitly employ the term *hypsos* in this passage (because *hypsos*, as a live metaphor, applies only to the human

---

[5] Chapter 35 is thus somewhat analogous, in terms of the logic of the treatise, to Aristotle's discussion of the origins of mimesis and poetry in *Poetics* 4. I differ with Russell's somewhat dismissive observation that this section largely brings together philosophical commonplaces (see Russell, "Commentary," in *"Longinus": On the Sublime*, 165–166). The passage may indeed do so, but its power lies in the *way* in which it does so, namely how it contributes to Loginus's *theory* of sublimity.

[6] The contrast between the "useful" and the "aesthetic" will be echoed in many seventeenth- and eighteenth-century writers.

realm),[7] he nevertheless suggests that the possibility of sublimity in the verbal arts is grounded in our *spontaneous* attraction to natural grandeur, which is thus revelatory of an *innate* desire for transcendence: "[Nature] implanted in our minds from the start an irresistible desire for anything which is great and, in relation to ourselves, supernatural." We need only consider our attitude toward the overwhelming in nature to realize "what we were born for," that is, our ultimate purpose, our human *telos*, which is conceived as a realization of our god-like nature, a transcendence of the finite self: "Other literary qualities prove their users to be human; sublimity raises us towards the spiritual greatness of god" (36.1).[8] Here Longinus appears to refer more to humanity as a species rather than to the individual genius. In other words, as manifested in the universal appeal of the effects of awe and wonder, *all* participate in some way in this striving for greatness or sublimity. Although Longinus does not specifically use the term "infinity," he clearly suggests the idea of a limitless expansion of the mind: "Our thoughts often travel beyond the boundaries of our surroundings." Thus, despite its focus on external nature, I contend that chapter 35 should be read as a further elaboration of, or contribution to, the first source of sublimity, *grandeur* of conception (*noêsis*): "The universe therefore is not wide enough for the range of human speculation and intellect." This idea will, in effect, find its fulfillment in Kant's argument concerning our vocation for the supersensible in the Mathematically Sublime.[9]

Generally speaking, this passage describes natural grandeur in terms of magnitude. Nevertheless, one could make the case that Longinus also implies a concept of natural power, in the example of the volcano (Longinus elsewhere [1.4] employs the Greek word *dynamis* [power] to describe the effect of sublimity): "Etna, whose eruptions bring up rocks and whole hills out of depths, and sometimes pour forth rivers of earth-born spontaneous fire." No doubt Mount Etna has great extent, but Longinus specifically draws our attention to the preternatural *force* of the volcano, its capacity to rearrange the Earth's geology and to spontaneously create menacing rivers of fire. At the very least, it is certainly an example

---

[7] As was remarked in Chapter 1, this is due to the fact that, like the English term "elevation," *hypsos* functions only as a metaphor when applied to qualities of the human mind or human expression, such as language. Since Longinus is referring to natural objects, using *hypsos* (height, elevation) to designate such objects would be semantically improper, even if, in those languages that use the Latinate term, the term "sublime" can also refer to objects of nature.

[8] Malcolm Heath notes that "assimilation to the divine was identified as the goal of human life by a strong philosophical tradition" (*Ancient Philosophical Poetics*, 179). What distinguishes Longinus is the specifically aesthetic valence he gives to this idea.

[9] See Chapter 10.

that suggests power in a way that the other examples – large rivers and the ocean – do not.

One of the most interesting aspects of the passage is Longinus's emphasis on the language of competition, which recalls the discussion of *zêlôsis-mimêsis* (emulation) in 13.2–14.3. Longinus draws on the – apparently often-used[10] – metaphor of the festival competition (athletic or literary), to express the productive value of sublime rivalry (*eris, agôn*): "Nature made man to be no humble or lowly creature, but brought him into life and into the universe as into a great festival, to be both a spectator and an enthusiastic contestant in its competitions."[11] In other words, nature made humans competitive and rivalrous as a spur to self-transcendence; the experience of an overpowering wonder or awe as one is held in thrall to a natural prodigy incites us to a kind of rivalry with nature itself, as if natural grandeur challenged us to go beyond it, thus demonstrating, as in Kant's thought, the superiority of the human mind over natural determination.[12] We are elevated precisely by being over-whelmed – the dual transcendence-structure of sublimity.

The first modern writer to seize on the importance of this passage in Longinus was the British theologian and cosmogonist Thomas Burnet, in his *The Sacred Theory of the Earth* (1681/1684). There is no doubt that Burnet had read Longinus. He mentions the term "sublime" on numerous occasions, and in ways that recall Longinus. He also picks up on the Genesis reference in Longinus's treatise: "'In the beginning, God created the heavens and the earth.' A very short, but sublime sentence of few words, but which express and imply as much good sense and sound philosophy as could be contained in many volumes."[13] By far the most interesting of Burnet's aperçus on Longinus is his extended paraphrase of chapter 35, which would become the rallying cry of the natural sublime in the eighteenth century:

> The greatest objects of Nature are, methinks, the most pleasing to behold; and next to the great concave of the Heavens, and those boundless Regions where the Stars inhabit, there is nothing that I look upon with more pleasure than the wide Sea and the mountains of the Earth. There is something

---

[10] See Heath, *Ancient Philosophical Poetics*, 179, n. 55.
[11] The idea of being both "spectator" and "contestant" is consonant with Longinus's insistence on the reversibility of the creative and receptive standpoints in his theory of *hypsos*.
[12] Kant conceives of a similarly agonistic relation to nature (its "contrapurposiveness") in the sublime. See Chapters 9 and 10.
[13] Thomas Burnet, *The Sacred Theory of the Earth*, 487.

august and stately in the Air of these things, that inspires the mind with great thoughts and passions. We do naturally, upon such occasions, think of God and his greatness: and whatsoever hath but the shadow and appearance of INFINITE, as all things have that are too big for our comprehension, they fill and overbear the mind with their Excess, and cast it into a pleasing kind of stupor and admiration.[14]

Burnet connects the experience of natural grandeur with Longinus's first two sources of sublimity ("inspires the mind with great *thoughts* and *passions*"), though it is the noetic that certainly prevails in this passage. The experience of mental limits is at the same time the threshold of the divine.[15] Burnet also follows Longinus in not employing the term "sublime" to refer to nature, instead using "great."[16] While the competitive aspect that Longinus describes is not explicitly present in this passage, Burnet nevertheless intimates the idea of being challenged to strive beyond limits: "too big for our comprehension"; "overbear the mind." The negativity of the "overbearing excess" is combined with the positivity of the elevation ("pleasing kind of stupor"), and thus for the first time in modernity the dual, overwhelming-exalting structure of sublimity is understood as *complex pleasure* (pleasure mixed with pain). For by qualifying stupor and admiration as "pleasing," Burnet implies that they temper a negative emotion, such as fear. This is no doubt what inspired John Dennis's oxymoron "delightful horror."[17]

While Burnet's aim is primarily theological and specifically Christian ("God and his greatness"), he nevertheless offers an account of how "infinity" and all that is "too big for our comprehension" can be experienced aesthetically, thereby suggesting a secular access to the divine.[18] In her classic study *Mountain Gloom, Mountain Glory*, Marjorie Hope Nicolson relates that, prior to the revival of Longinus in Burnet and others, natural grandeur (especially mountains) was considered ugly and utterly irreligious. Aesthetic reflection on natural grandeur thus had the effect of

---

[14] Burnet, *The Sacred Theory of the Earth*, 158. The phrase "the terrible and the sublime are exchanged for the gentle and useful" (Burnet, *The Sacred Theory of the Earth*, 81) is also inspired by chapter 35 of Longinus's treatise.

[15] This is also the literal meaning of the term "sublime": sub-*limen*, under the threshold.

[16] At the time – that is, before Boileau's translation – the term "sublime" was not generally used to render Longinus's *hypsos* in English. John Hall's 1652 translation (the first into English) was entitled *Of the Height of Eloquence*.

[17] See Chapter 5.

[18] This idea of the "appearance of infinity" will become an important feature of Kant's account of the Mathematically Sublime. See Chapter 10.

valorizing and divinizing certain objects of nature, while secularizing a type of religious experience.[19]

Chapter 35 is one of the most iconic and consequential parts of *Peri hypsous*. It leads directly to the appropriation of the concept of sublimity by the aesthetics of nature in the late seventeenth and eighteenth centuries. In particular, Longinus's description of mental expansiveness in terms of boundlessness, as going beyond the finite universe in the encounter with natural grandeur, will become a staple of eighteenth-century aesthetics, culminating in Kant's third *Critique*. By demonstrating that grandeur of mind (*megalophrosynē*) is also, and perhaps even more primordially, manifested in the contemplation of the great and powerful in nature (as a function of our natural desire for transcendence), Longinus's treatise establishes the anthropological basis of sublimity.

3.2   Sublimity and cultural decline

In his *The History of the Decline and Fall of the Roman Empire* (1776–1789), Edward Gibbon cites Longinus as a contemporary witness to the decay of Roman culture:

> The sublime Longinus, who, in somewhat a later period and in the court of a Syrian queen preserved the spirit of ancient Athens, observes and laments this degeneracy of his contemporaries, which debased their sentiments, enervated their courage, and depressed their talents.[20]

Of course, Gibbon was referring to the third-century critic Cassius Longinus, whom he took to be the author of *Peri hypsous* (an attribution that, as mentioned above, few accept today). Nevertheless, the relevant point is that Gibbon, in a well-known and widely influential work, links the concept of sublimity to a critique of cultural decadence and decline. The inspiration for this assertion was most probably William Smith's popular 1739 translation of *Peri hypsous*, the introduction to which concludes that "genius can never exert itself or rise to sublimity, where virtue is neglected, and the morals are depraved."[21]

---

[19] In his *A Secular Age* (2007), Charles Taylor cites this passage of Burnet as an example of a shift away from how "contemporary apologetics" conceived of a "human-centered way of discovering God's presence in nature," namely as "comprehensible, orderly, and human-friendly"; instead Burnet shows how nature "discloses Him in another way" (334), namely in *overwhelming* nature.

[20] Edward Gibbon, *The Decline and Fall of the Roman Empire*, 46.

[21] William Smith, *Dionysius Longinus on the Sublime*, xxxii. Edmund Burke, an acquaintance of Gibbon, also shows signs of being influenced by Smith's Introduction in his *A Philosophical Enquiry into the Origin of Our Ideas of the Sublime and Beautiful* (1757). See Chapter 6 of this study.

As I have observed repeatedly, the moral aspect of sublimity is present throughout the treatise.[22] By exposing the specifically cultural dimension of high-mindedness (*megalophrosynê*) in chapter 44, Longinus connects the individual-moral with the social dimension of *hypsos*. More than any other part of the work, this chapter demonstrates that sublimity is not merely the private experience of an aesthete who enjoys the classics but has broad, real-world, and even political implications.

Chapter 44 fits somewhat awkwardly with the rest of the text, as if it were a kind of "appendix" (D. A. Russell's translation places it under just such a heading). Indeed, it is the only place in the treatise where Longinus refers to the historical world in which he lived, which is why it has been considered key to the dating of the treatise.[23] It also diverges formally from the rest of the treatise in that it features a "dialogue" between Longinus and a nameless "Philosopher" (who some have speculated is Philo),[24] whom Longinus quotes or paraphrases at length, before offering his own response: "I shall not hesitate to add for your instruction, my dear Terentianus, one further topic, so as to clear up a question put to me the other day by one of the philosophers" (44.1). This suggests at least three possibilities: (1) the "dialogue" represents the report of an actual conversation that took place with a philosopher; (2) Longinus is staging a fictional encounter for pedagogical purposes; (3) Longinus is showing two sides of his psyche at odds with one another.[25] What we can say with certainty is that the "dialogue" enacts a rather dramatic confrontation between two divergent understandings of the reasons for the cultural decline and loss of sublimity that Longinus sees as afflicting the Rome of his time.

The Philosopher (who appears to be quite conversant with *hypsos*) wonders why there are no "sublime or really great minds, except perhaps here and there" (44.1). The reference to "except perhaps here or there" is somewhat curious. Should Homers and Platos abound in every age? Or could the Philosopher perhaps be comparing his historical moment to a "golden age," such as fifth- and fourth-century Greece?[26] Like Longinus (as analyzed in the previous section), the Philosopher contrasts true greatness

[22] Alexander Nehamas (*Virtues of Authenticity*, 280) has written that "Plato simply does not distinguish aesthetics from ethics." The same might be said of Longinus, who takes Plato as his model in many respects.
[23] Heath disputes this assumption in his article "Longinus, *On Sublimity*."
[24] See James Arieti and John M. Crossett, *Longinus: On the Sublime*, 254–256 (Appendix C: Could Philo Have Been One of the Philosophers?).
[25] On this last possibility, see Paul Fry, *The Reach of Criticism*, 62 ff.
[26] Heath notes (referring to the Philosopher's quoted speech) that "the association of democracy, war, and eloquence is especially apposite with reference to classical Greece" ("Longinus, *On Sublimity*," 55).

of mind with mere competence: "Minds which are strikingly persuasive and practical, shrewd, versatile, and well-endowed, with the ability to write agreeably" (44.1). The Philosopher is thus not referring to a lack of intelligence or education, but to the absence of transcendent genius, as had existed in past eras. "There is a universal dearth of literature" (44.1), bemoans the Philosopher, and there can only be dearth where there has previously been abundance. However, while the present always appears lacking when compared to a great or exemplary past,[27] what Longinus is concerned specifically with here is the idea of cultural *decadence* or *decline*.

According to the Philosopher, the causes of the current predicament are social and political in nature. He therefore insists on the role of the political system in hindering or fostering the development of sublimity of mind and its literary expression. The idea that "democracy" (in this case, the Roman Republic) is the political system best suited to the cultivation of great literature was apparently a commonplace of the time:

> "Are we to believe," [the Philosopher] went on, "the common explanation that democracy nurtures greatness, and great writers flourished with democracy and died with it? Freedom, the argument goes, nourishes and encourages the thoughts of the great, as well as exciting their enthusiasm for rivalry with one another and their ambition for the prize." (44.2)

According to this view, literary greatness and democracy go hand in hand; the latter conditions the former. Thus the responsibility for the dearth of greatness lies not in the individual, but in the sociopolitical order, regarded as an antecedent cause. Democracy promotes greatness through the "freedom" (certainly a relative term from a modern perspective) it affords its citizens. The rationale for why such political or civic freedom should provide fertile conditions for sublimity is twofold. The first, and largely implied, rationale is that freedom of thought is a necessary condition of grandeur of thought, in terms of its cultivation and/or realization ("freedom ... nourishes and encourages the thoughts of the great"). If political freedom equals freedom of thought, then sublimity requires political freedom in order to flourish. The second rationale is based on the first: since, in a democracy, each is judged according to his ability rather than by birth, democratic freedom encourages ambition and rivalry, which, as we have seen, are key components in achieving sublimity. However, unlike the emulation of the illustrious figures of the past

---

[27] "'My good friend,' I replied, 'it is easy to find fault with the present situation; indeed it is a human characteristic to do so'" (44.6).

(*zêlôsis-mimêsis*), the Philosopher is here speaking about a more pedestrian form: rivalry with one's contemporaries.

The first rationale is emphasized a few lines later when the Philosopher describes the current Roman political system as "justified slavery" (44.3), that is, a form of tyranny, in which "we ... [are] swathed round from our first tender thoughts in the same habits and customs, never allowed to taste that fair and fecund spring of literature, freedom. We end up as flatterers in the grand manner" (44.3, the term "grand" [*megalo*-] marks an ironic contrast with sublimity). Political oppression restricts the mental processes to more rudimentary forms, which, having become habitual, lead to an overall mental degradation. Since one can survive in such a political environment only by flattery, that is, through constant dissimulation and dissembling, one's freedom of thought and moral compass – in other words, one's capacity for high-mindedness (*megalophrosynê*) – is correspondingly affected.

Longinus, it will be recalled, says something similar in 9.3 regarding the cultivation of nobility of mind: "Those whose thoughts and habits are small and servile all their lives cannot possibly produce anything admirable or worthy of eternity." Longinus's use of the term "servile" in this instance would seemingly support the Philosopher's contention that a slave mentality inhibits mental growth and thus sublimity. It is therefore curious that this is presented as part of an overall argument that Longinus will *reject*; just as Longinus will also seemingly reject the idea that freedom excites "rivalry" and "ambition for the prize" – exactly the kind of competitive language that Longinus indulges in elsewhere in the treatise. The Philosopher concludes that "one might describe all slavery, even the most [politically] justified, as a cage for the soul, a universal prison" (44.5, the image of a "cage for the soul" is obviously a metaphorical inversion of Longinus's idea of the unboundedness of the mind in chapter 35). Thus both the impediments and spurs to sublimity put forth by the Philosopher seemingly cohere with the thrust of the views that Longinus advanced previously in the treatise, and yet Longinus dismisses this entire line of reasoning.

Longinus begins his retort by turning "slavery" into a metaphor:

> I wonder whether what destroys great minds is not the peace of the world, but the unlimited war which lays hold on our desires, and all the passions which beset and ravage our modern life. Avarice, the insatiable disease from which we all suffer, and love of pleasure – these are our two slave-masters. (44.6)

While Longinus here appears to shift the debate about the decline of great literature from external factors to the inner moral disposition of man, or from a context-bound to an essentializing conception, his argument is actually quite subtle. For he says that avarice is a disease "from which we *all* suffer," indicating that, even if love of money and pleasure do not characterize everyone's disposition (presumably, Longinus is excluding himself, his student, and the Philosopher from this lament), all in a given society are negatively affected if such vices are pervasive. And by referring to "our modern life," Longinus draws attention to the particularity of his historical moment. He can thereby be read as saying that the general moral disposition of a society conditions the development and expression of sublimity of an individual member. Even a great mind, Longinus seems to be saying, would have difficulty rising above the general tenor of his or her age.[28] Sublime minds or minds with great potential are corrupted ("what destroys great minds") by the contagion of vices and the corresponding enervation or atrophy of the mental powers: "Avarice is a mean disease" (44.6).

As Longinus develops his critique, expressed in condemnatory and pessimistic language, it becomes clear that for him the principal vice from which all others flow is excessive wealth: "I cannot see how we can honor, or rather deify, unlimited wealth as we do without admitting into our souls the evils which attach to it" (44.7). The other vices – "greed, pride, and luxury" (44.7) as well as "insolence, lawlessness, and shamefulness" (44.7), and even "idleness" (44.11) – are a function of it. Like the Philosopher, Longinus insists on the insidious power of bad habits: "These evils then become chronic in people's lives, and, as the philosophers say, nest and breed" (44.7);[29] "the ruin of their lives is gradually consummated in a cycle of such vices" (44.8). That is to say, corruption begets corruption in a personal and cultural death spiral – the exact inversion of the virtuous cycle of good mental habits of high-mindedness that Longinus had earlier argued (9.3) was essential to the attainment of *hypsos* in the verbal arts.

As for the particular ethos or cultural morality Longinus seeks to extol in this chapter, it appears to be one that is specifically rooted in the ideal of sublimity as temporal transcendence. This is confirmed in the last part of his diatribe, which centers on the idea of the everlasting or the immortal:

> Men will no longer open their eyes or give thought to their reputation with posterity. . . . Greatness of mind [*psychika megethê*] wanes, fades, and loses its

---

[28] Heath thinks that "the determinist slant of [Longinus's] political explanation is incompatible with Longinus's conviction that we can and should try to develop our natures to achieve sublimity" ("Longinus and the Ancient Sublime," 21).

[29] Longinus appears to be quoting Plato here, as Russell suggests in a footnote: "And when everything else is gone, won't the violent crowd of desires that has nested within him inevitably shout in protest?" (*Republic* 9, 573e).

attraction when men spend their admiration on their mortal parts and neglect to develop the immortal. (44.8) ... Amid such pestilential corruption of human life, how can we expect that there should be left to us any free, uncorrupt judge of great things of permanent value? (44.9)

Notably, Longinus does not appeal to any specifically religious values as an antidote to the economic materialism of his contemporaries. There is no invocation of the gods or the divine, despite the fact that the treatise is certainly not lacking in theological language.[30] Instead, Longinus exhorts readers to rise above the mediocrity and short-sightedness of their age, recalling the definition of *hypsos* from the first chapter of the treatise: "Sublimity is ... the means by which the very greatest poets and prose writers have given *eternal* life to their own fame" (1.3, my emphasis). Writing for eternity should be the sole and unique goal for the hero-writer, who prefers posthumous glory to contemporary recognition. Writing for one's contemporaries subjects one to ephemeral values; thus the type of emulation advocated by the Philosopher (rivalry with one's contemporaries) fails to incite *sublime* competition, rivalry with those whose words have proved everlasting and universal. For the mark of a truly great or sublime text is, as Longinus earlier noted, its ability to "please all peoples at all times" (7.4).

The hero-writer is, for Longinus, the light and guide for successive generations and thus for culture itself. As an index of permanent, incorruptible value, *hypsos* is coextensive with what is meant by the concept of the "classical"; that is, a cultural touchstone, a *living presence*, such as what Hans-Georg Gadamer has observed regarding this term: "What we call 'classical' is something retrieved from the vicissitudes of changing time and changing taste ... a consequence of something enduring, of significance that cannot be lost and is independent of all circumstances of time ... a kind of timeless present that is contemporaneous with every other age."[31] While this passage would accurately describe Longinus's conception, we must nevertheless not lose sight of the dialectical dimension of *hypsos*: that classical greatness is not to be thought of in terms of never-to-be-surpassed models, a recipe for cultural fossilization, but as an impetus to greatness and sublimity – transcendence – *in the present*.

***

This chapter has explored how Longinus's intense focus on subjective factors in his theory is intimately connected to, on the one hand, the

---

[30] See 36.1.   [31] Hans-Georg Gadamer, *Truth and Method*, 256.

anthropological implications of our spontaneous attraction to natural grandeur, namely *our vocation for transcendence*, and, on the other, the sociocultural implications of a loss of sublimity, not only of literary greatness per se, but also of "greatness of mind" (*psychika megethê*) (44.8) more generally. The linkage between sublimity and cultural critique will become an important element of the modern concept of sublimity, recurring most notably in Vico,[32] Burke, and Kant. And the relation Longinus posits between natural grandeur and the transcendence of sensible limits will become the basis for the modern association of sublimity with infinity and boundlessness. Although the discussions of natural magnitude and cultural decline may appear somewhat disconnected from the rest of the treatise, I contend that these digressions should be seen not only as an integral part of the work but also as the fulfillment of the moral philosophy inherent in the critical concept of *hypsos*. As Russell observes: "[Longinus] unites his stylistic ideals under a moral ideal – the man of dignity and integrity who does his duty in human society and understands his station as a citizen of the cosmos."[33]

---

[32] Massimo Lollini observes that "the last chapter of Longinus's treatise was very important for Vico. In it, Longinus laments the dearth of great and noble writers in the first century of the imperial period. . . . This is the analytical scheme that figures in Vico's reflections on the decline of poetry in the time of the 'ragione spiegata'" (*Le muse, le maschere e il sublime: G. B. Vico e la poesia nell'età della "Ragione Spiegata,"* 192–193, my trans.).

[33] Russell, Introduction, *"Longinus" On the Sublime*, xliii.

PART II

Sublimity and modernity

To be taught to despise danger in the pursuit of honor and duty . . . these are the circumstances of men that form what I should call a natural aristocracy, without which there is no nation.

– Edmund Burke[1]

---

[1] Burke, "An Appeal From the New to the Old Whigs" (1791), 652.

CHAPTER 4

Boileau: the birth of a concept

The modern history of the sublime is generally thought to begin in 1674, with the appearance of Nicolas Boileau's translation of Longinus's *Peri hypsous* (*On the Sublime*). The sudden availability of the treatise in French, the most important vernacular language of the era, coupled with Boileau's authority as an eminent critic, played an essential role in the treatise's sudden rise to prominence after more than a century of relative obscurity.[1] However, what is not widely or sufficiently appreciated is the significance of Boileau's introductory Preface, which, even more than the translation itself, created the conditions under which the concept of the sublime could be adopted, first by the literary criticism of the time, and then by the emerging field of what is now called "aesthetics."

Indeed, Boileau occupies a singular position in the discourse of the sublime – he is at once the midwife, champion, and popularizer of this concept – and yet the exact nature of his contribution to the theory of sublimity is still a matter of great debate. This chapter thus explores the various aspects of Boileau's efforts to promote and defend the concept of sublimity. The first section studies the relation between Boileau and Longinus, arguing that the Longinian sublime was not an "invention of Boileau" (as some commentators have alleged) but the result of insightful interpretation. The second treats how the sublime is related to the concepts of *le merveilleux* and the *je ne sais quoi* in neoclassical aesthetics. The third interprets the biographical part of Boileau's Preface as a key to understanding Boileau's conception of sublimity of mind, namely through the association of sublimity with the protobourgeois ideal of the *honnête homme*. The fourth section analyzes how Boileau, by arguing that Longinus's *hypsos* is a matter of transcendence, not style, emancipates it

---

[1] Some additional editions have recently come to light. See Eva Madeleine Martin, "The 'Prehistory' of the Sublime in Early Modern France: An Interdisciplinary Perspective." A survey of pre-Boileauean references to Longinus's *On the Sublime* can be found in Emma Gilby, *Sublime Worlds: Early Modern French Literature*, 2–4.

from the rhetorical conception of the grand style, thereby establishing "the sublime" (*le sublime*) for the first time as a critical concept. The fifth examines the "quarrel" between Boileau and the ecclesiastic Pierre-Daniel Huet over the sublimity of the "Let there be light" (*fiat lux*) quotation in Longinus, showing how Boileau uses the suggestion of a Christian dimension to the sublime to posit a continuity between sacred and secular literature. The final section explores how, by applying the concept of the sublime to the "Qu'il mourût" quotation from Corneille's *Horace* – a modern tragedy that celebrates ancient heroic virtue – Boileau seeks to bridge the Quarrel of the Ancients and the Moderns.

4.1   Boileau and Longinus

No one who had read Longinus's treatise prior to Boileau's French edition had thought to suggest that its central term, *hypsos*, was an important new concept – or a "concept" at all. Starting with Francesco Robortello's *editio princeps* (1554), the treatise's sixteenth- and early seventeenth-century editors assumed that *hypsos* referred to a category of style, the sublime or high style of the classical rhetorical tradition (with its tripartite division of low, middle, and high styles). These early editions employed the adjective *sublimis*, rather than the substantive *sublimitas* in their descriptive Latin titles.[2] Although the use of the adjective *sublimis* in these early editions played a crucial role in preparing the way for the eventual adoption, in the Romance languages and in English (though not in German),[3] of the Latinate noun for the title of Longinus's treatise, it is noteworthy that these Latin titles failed to inspire the first English and Italian translators to use the word "sublime" in any form. John Hall's 1652 translation – the first in English – is entitled *Of the Height of Eloquence*, and, despite the proximity of Italian to Latin, Niccolò Pinelli's 1639 edition (published in Padua) similarly prefers *Dell'altezza del dire* (*On the Height of Speech*). Moreover, these titles use "height," not as a concept, but in order to modify "eloquence" or "speech." A title such as "On Height" (the most literal

---

[2] These editions are: F. Robortello (Basel, 1554), P. Manutius (Venice, 1555), F. Porto (Geneva, 1569), G. de Petra (Geneva, 1612), G. Langbaine (Oxford, 1636, Latin and Greek, Latin translation by de Petra). See the Bibliography to this volume for the Latin titles of these editions.

[3] The first mention of the word "sublime" in the title of an English edition occurs in 1698, in an anonymous translation entitled *An Essay upon Sublime Translated from the Greek of Dionysius Longinus Cassius the Rhetorician; Compar'd with the French of the Sieur Despreaux Boileau* (printed by Leon Litchfield at Oxford). But the term "sublime" did not immediately take hold in English critical writings.

translation of *Peri hypsous*) would no doubt have made as little sense to contemporary readers as "On the Sublime."[4]

Boileau's translation and explanatory Preface were thus largely responsible for the shift in attitude toward Longinus's treatise: prior to 1674, Longinus was considered an able rhetorician, an expounder of the grand style, whose various pronouncements could be cited without reference to any central, organizing concept;[5] after 1674, Longinus is the source of the critical concept of the sublime, a literary critic on a par with Aristotle and Horace, even a "Philosopher worthy to be put in Comparison with the Socrates's and Cato's" (WB II, 5), as Boileau describes him in his Preface.

Commentators have long debated the question of whether Boileau is, as he presents himself in the Preface, merely a faithful interpreter of Longinus, the first modern to understand the critical concept of the sublime, or whether he is an innovator himself, the true inventor of the concept of sublimity.[6] Many follow the lead of Samuel Monk, who asserts that "the Longinus who is of value for this study is really the creation of Boileau."[7] That is to say, Boileau's importance lies not in his having drawn attention to the Longinian sublime – for Longinus's treatise, in Monk's view, contains no such *concept*. Rather it lies in Boileau's *fashioning* of a concept of sublimity, which, according to Monk, Longinus was incapable of articulating himself, due to his rhetorical-technical bent. Monk is thus unwilling to accept Boileau's contention that a non- or

---

[4] Ernst Curtius remarks: "The word *hypsos* means height not sublimity. High literature, great poetry and prose – that is the subject" (*European Literature*, 398).

[5] If we take, for example, René Rapin's *Réflexions sur la Poétique d'Aristote et sur les ouvrages des Poètes anciens et modernes* (*Reflections on Aristotle's Poetics and on the Works of Ancient and Modern Poets*), published in 1674, the same year as Boileau's translation (republished in 1675 as *Les Réflexions sur la poétique de ce temps et sur les ouvrages des poètes anciens et modernes*), we find five references to Longinus's treatise, none of which invokes the term "sublime," or an equivalent, as a concept. At one point, Rapin refers to the sublime style: "Demetrius et Longin les proposent sans cesse pour modèles à ceux qui s'étudient au genre sublime" (45). Commenting on Longinus's key concept of *zêlôsis-mimêsis* (emulation), Rapin observes: "And I knew a painter, one of the most celebrated of our time, who read from Homer to elevate his mind before he set himself to work" (*Réflexions sur la poétique de ce temps*, 49, my translation). (Similarly Rapin notes: "Car la grande poésie doit estre soutenue par de grandes pensées et par de grands sentiments dont on ne peut se former d'idée que par le commerce des Anciens" [*Réflexions sur la poétique de ce temps*, 46]). One could also cite Bouhours, who writes: "Je veux qu'il imite les grands modèles de l'antiquité, pourvu qu'il tache de les surpasser en les imitant" (quoted in George Doncieux, *Le Père Bouhours*, 229).

[6] Hence the title of Cronk's chapter: "Inventing *le sublime*: Boileau's *Traité du sublime*" (chapter 4 of Cronk, *The Classical Sublime*).

[7] Monk, *The Sublime*, 28. According to Francis Goyet, the supposed novelty of Boileau's version of Longinus consisted simply in "revalorizing" concepts that are otherwise unremarkable when considered in context: "After 1674, Longinus is declared exceptional. In rediscovering Longinus, Boileau and his contemporaries literally invent the concept of the sublime, just as one 'invents' a treasure: by rummaging in the attic of rhetoric, by revalorizing what the previous era had devalorized" (TS, 8, my translation).

transrhetorical conception of sublimity can be ascribed to Longinus – hence Monk's description of *Peri hypsous* in precisely the way Boileau so pointedly disparages: "[Longinus's] treatment of the subject is primarily rhetorical; the essay is a discussion of style, and only incidentally does Longinus allow his deeper penetrations to find expression."[8] Perhaps no other statement has done more to promote the stereotype of Longinus as a purveyor of the so-called "rhetorical sublime" (that is, sublimity as reducible to verbal *technê*), a deeply ingrained misprision that the first part of this study has systematically endeavored to refute.[9] Even if Monk almost begrudgingly recognizes a "latent aesthetic aspect"[10] in Longinus's treatise, he is nevertheless blind to its specifically theoretical or conceptual import. Regardless, however, of whether one sees Boileau's reading of Longinus as creative misinterpretation (à la Monk) or as a highly insightful reading of Longinus (as I do), all agree that Boileau's advocacy was key to the emergence of the sublime as a critical concept.

It is certainly significant that Boileau published Longinus's treatise in a collection of his own texts. Boileau's title reveals the extent to which he saw *Peri hypsous* as part of his oeuvre: *Œuvres diverses du sieur D*** Avec le Traité du Sublime ou du merveilleux dans le discours. Traduit du grec de Longin* (Various Works of Monsieur D ... With the Treatise on the Sublime or the marvelous that strikes in discourse. Translated from the Greek of Longinus). With this collection – which also included the work for which Boileau is best known today, *Art poétique* (a compendium of neoclassical precepts) – Boileau binds his own critical fortunes to those of Longinus. Nicholas Cronk goes so far as to suggest that "given that nearly one fifth of the *Art poétique* is a translation of Horace, and that Longinus was far less known than Horace in the classical period, there is a sense in which contemporaries might have looked upon the *Traité du sublime* as the truly original work and seen the *Art poétique* as a mere reworking of Horace."[11] This seemingly extreme view nevertheless points to an important fact: namely the extent to which Boileau will become increasingly identified with Longinus in the eyes of his contemporaries.

The motivations behind Boileau's embrace of Longinus and the sublime have spurred much debate among contemporary scholars of neoclassicism,[12]

---

[8] Monk, *The Sublime*, 12.
[9] Théodore Litman, in his *Le sublime en France (1660–1714)*, asserts that Boileau "progressively detaches himself from the purely rhetorical method of Longinus," which "can be reduced to rules" (76, my translation).
[10] Monk, *The Sublime*, 12.   [11] Cronk, *The Classical Sublime*, 98–99.
[12] Gordon Pocock has noted "Boileau's ... standing as a representative rather than an individual" (*Boileau and the Nature of Neo-Classicism*, 1).

particularly concerning the question of whether the concept of the sublime, such as it was understood in seventeenth-century France, was incompatible with the neoclassical ideals of rules, reason, and *le bon sens* (good sense) and as such represented a subversive force. Although it might appear prima facie absurd that a first- (or third-) century treatise could threaten to destabilize a literary-critical movement whose program was based on the veneration of antiquity, we must nevertheless account for the singular effect of Longinus's treatise on French neoclassicism. In his *The Shock of the Ancient* (2011), Larry Norman insightfully describes the debate as follows:

> In recent decades, a second, less pacifying, view of the Ancient party's redeployment of Longinus has developed. Boileau's sublime is here presented as a radical rupture with the dictates of his age. It is out of joint with the time. The anachronistic quality of the sublime, though, can be viewed alternately as regressive or progressive, reactionary or revolutionary. Reactionary, when seen as a return to the aesthetic values of antiquity itself, or much more recently, to the neo-Platonism of the Renaissance and its metaphysics of poetic inspiration. Revolutionary, when seen as the first step toward the elaboration of an eighteenth-century philosophy of the sublime, from Addison to Burke and Kant. Or viewed even more progressively, as a pre-Romantic élan preparing the future rejection of poetic rules. Or even as the first seeds of twentieth-century modern and postmodern art.[13]

In other words, the putatively subversive quality of the Longinian sublime can be a function either of its seemingly archaic status (but then why would other ancient or Renaissance concepts not be seen as similarly radical?) or of its belonging to an aesthetic regime that the neoclassical critics could not possibly have grasped. Obviously, Boileau and his contemporaries could not have seen the sublime as "revolutionary" in the sense of an anticipation of Burke and Kant, though intellectual history often obscures this fact.[14] Similarly, if *Peri hypsous* is the only extant text in which the concept of the sublime is found, it is difficult to see how the sublime could represent a "return to the aesthetic values of antiquity." That is to say, since it is a purely *modern* discovery (it is not mentioned in any extant sources from the period), the treatise appears as strangely disconnected from antiquity, as if it were anachronistic in some originary sense. This is especially true given that *Peri hypsous* is not easily integrated into the traditional models of

---

[13] Larry Norman, *The Shock of the Ancient*, 198. Norman appears to be agnostic on the question of whether "Boileau's sublime" is more Boileau than Longinus.

[14] Arthur Danto has demonstrated in his notion of "narrative sentences" (as in his eponymous essay) the casual anachronism of intellectual history, as in phrases like "Petrarch opened the Renaissance," which presuppose a future perspective unavailable to the historical agent.

rhetoric or poetics (both ancient and Renaissance);[15] its concerns are more "aesthetic" (receptivity, creativity, subjectivity) than properly "rhetorical," and it does not deal with genre theory.

Nevertheless, many twentieth-century and contemporary commentators have seen the publication of Boileau's *Œuvres diverses*, pairing the "backward-looking" *Art poétique* with the "forward-looking" *Traité du sublime*, as emblematic of an epic battle between, as Théodore Litman puts it, "reason and genius, the rules and the sublime, common sense and enthusiasm, order and disorder,"[16] as if Longinus (or Boileau's Longinus) somehow represented the antithesis of traditional neoclassical values.[17] On this view, the very concept of a "neoclassical sublime" would therefore be an oxymoron, or, as Monk expresses it: "The sublime that came into existence in 1674 was the offspring of two minds so startlingly unlike as those of the Greek critic and the author of the *Art poétique*."[18] More recently (2007), Francis Goyet has contested this commonplace, arguing that the "*Traité du sublime* and the *Art poétique* share the same vision of literature in general, and of poetry in particular."[19] I am inclined to side with Goyet on this point; there is no need to posit a disjuncture between the two works – a "rupture" at the heart of neoclassicism.[20] A conservative movement by nature, neoclassicism would not have embraced *Peri hypsous* if it did not in some sense see Longinus as a kindred spirit.

4.2   Boileau and neoclassical poetics: *le sublime, le merveilleux*, and the *je ne sais quoi*

When we consider the title Boileau gives to his edition of Longinus – *Traité du Sublime, ou le Merveilleux qui frappe dans le Discours* (Treatise on the Sublime, or the Marvelous That Strikes in Discourse) – we perceive first that, as mentioned above, the main title establishes the subject of the

[15] Longinus does, however, treat the difference between oratorical and poetic *phantasia* in chapter 15 of *Peri hypsous*. See Chapter 2.

[16] Litman, *Le Sublime en France*, 70 (my translation). Against Jules Brody (in *Boileau and Longinus*), who endeavors to demonstrate the overall unity of Boileau's oeuvre, Litman argues that Boileau's thought is far from coherent.

[17] I rather agree with Jeffrey Barnouw, who seeks to show (in an article on John Dennis) "how the Longinian sublime could be integrated with 'neo-classical' conceptions from the start, and further, how deeply this classical sublime – far from being a matter of mere rhetorical or artistic-technical scope – is moral in constitution" ("The Morality of the Sublime: To John Dennis," 33).

[18] Monk, *The Sublime*, 28.

[19] Francis Goyet, "Raison et Sublime dans le premier livre de l'*Art poétique* de Boileau," 137 (my translation).

[20] The two works are often complementary; the *Art poétique* contains five mentions of "sublime."

treatise as "the sublime," that is, a critical *concept*. Second, the subtitle or alternate title (as the "ou" indicates) explicitly separates the sublime from its prior association with the grand style. For, if the sublime is a kind of "marvelous" that "strikes" in discourse, then it is something manifested *in* or *through* discourse and not an objective property *of* discourse itself. In other words, as Boileau will argue, sublimity is a matter of *transcendence*, not style. Boileau also repeats this language in his Preface to define the sublime as "something extraordinary and marvelous that strikes us in a Discourse and makes a work elevate, ravish, and transport us" (WB II, 7) (cet extraordinaire et ce merveilleux qui frappe dans le discours, et qui fait qu'un ouvrage enlève, ravit, transporte) (TS, 70). *Le merveilleux* is thus being used as a kind of equivalent or substitute for sublimity, a use that is eminently strategic.

Boileau clearly adapts his notion from the Italian *la meraviglia*, an axial notion in sixteenth- and seventeenth-century Italian poetics (a formative influence on French neoclassicism) that recalls many of the same attributes of the Longinian sublime. It was associated with the affects of wonder and awe;[21] it also had religious connotations that suggested a kind of transcendence: *le merveilleux chrétien*.[22] Françoise Graziani, one of the few scholars to have studied this relationship to Italian poetics, notes that

> the multiple meanings of the term marvelous had already been lost in the French language of the seventeenth-century, meanings that had allowed Boileau to translate the Greek *thaumaston* with a single word, as Italian was able to do.... In his preface, Boileau can still assert that what Longinus means by the sublime is nothing other than the "marvelous that strikes in discourse"; this assertion means little to today's reader, who, because of an inversion of perspective resulting from the concept's success, better understands the concept of the *sublime*. But it vividly demonstrates that the concept of the marvelous was one of the structural elements of the culture of a late seventeenth-century reader.[23]

Boileau's readers would thus have immediately understood the critical implications of his rapprochement between the sublime and marvelous, even if the contemporary reader no longer appreciates its importance.

---

[21] Eugenio Refini notes that "terms like *meraviglia, stupor* and *estasi* became the keywords of an idea of artistic and poetic creation which perfectly fits in with the Longinian notion of the sublime" ("Longinus and Poetic Imagination in Late Renaissance Literary Theory," 37).

[22] "The long tradition of *le merveilleux chrétien* had sanctioned the poetic use of angels, spirits, and devils so long as they did not violate Christian theology. Poetry, critics believed, demanded the marvelous, and Christian marvels carried the presumption of truth, as opposed to the fictive mythologies of pagan writers" (David Morris, "Gothic Sublimity," 309).

[23] Graziani, "Le miracle de l'art: Le Tasse et la poétique de la *meravigla*," 122, n. 9 (my translation).

For the Italian Renaissance critics, such as Giambattista Marino (1569–1625), *la meraviglia* defined the purpose or end of poetry: "è fine del poeta la meraviglia."[24] Prior to Marino, Francesco Patrizi (1529–1597), who discusses Longinus's *On the Sublime* extensively in his *Della poetica* (1586), entitles a section of this work: "Che il mirabile è forma e fine della poesia" (That the marvelous is the form and the end of poetry).[25] A Platonist highly critical of Aristotle's poetic theory, Patrizi bases his theory of *la meraviglia* on Longinus. However, the vast majority of his contemporaries looked to Aristotle's definition of the epic in his *Poetics* in terms of *thaumaston*, often translated as "awe." Since the Italian critics were keen on affirming the preeminence of the epic, a genre in which Italian literature particularly excelled (Dante, Ariosto, Tasso), passages such as the following in Aristotle's *Poetics* became touchstones: "In tragedy one needs to create a sense of awe [*thaumaston*], but epic has more scope for the irrational [*alogos*] (the chief cause of awe [*thaumaston*])" (1460a). Thus Aristotle, through the criterion of awe (*la meraviglia*), could be invoked to argue for the superiority of epic poetry, even if Aristotle himself saw tragedy as the higher art form.

But it was most probably Torquato Tasso's concept of *la meraviglia* that most influenced Boileau's conception. In his *Discorsi del poema eroico* (*Discourses on the Heroic Poem*, 1587, published in 1594),[26] Tasso endeavored to raise the status of the epic by reconciling the seemingly antithetical notions of *la meraviglia* and verisimilitude, both derived from Aristotle.[27] Tasso's theory also bears the traces of Longinus's influence.[28] The proximity between Longinus's *hypsos* and Tasso's theory of *la meraviglia* is thus not mere coincidence. Graziani comments suggestively that

---

[24] Quoted in Paolo Cherchi, "Marino and the *Meraviglia*," 64.

[25] Another treatise published the same year, *Discorso del furor poetico* (1587), by Lorenzo Giacomini, also bases its poetic theory on Longinus, in particular on Longinus's concept of *phantasia*. See Eugenio Refini, "Longinus and Poetic Imagination in Late Renaissance Literary Theory."

[26] "The *Discourses on the Heroic Poem*, for all of its unevenness and imperfections of their writing, have generally been held a major contribution to late Renaissance critical theory. They had an immediate and lasting influence not only in Italy but in England and France" (Irene Samuel, Introduction to Tasso, *Discourses on the Heroic Poem*, xx).

[27] "The verisimilar and the marvelous are very different in nature ... different almost to the point of being antithetical; yet both are necessary in a poem, though to join them takes the art of an excellent poet" (Tasso, *Discourses on the Heroic Poem*, 37).

[28] Tasso, whose Greek was not sophisticated, became familiar with Longinus through Robortello's brief Latin introduction to his *editio princeps* (1554), as well as through Pagano's Latin translation of 1572. Tasso also read P. Vettori's commentary on Demetrius's *De elocutione* (1562), which contains many references to Longinus. See Graziani, "Le miracle de l'art," 122, n. 9.

one can take *meraviglia* to mean aesthetic transport, surprise, the taste for novelty, or the elevation of the soul as well as the intuitive communication between the reader (through the emulation that accompanies admiration) and the enthusiasm [inspiration] of the creative act.... For Tasso, *la meraviglia* is not a simple aesthetic pleasure, but an ensemble of sentiments resulting in the reader's recognition and appropriation of the power contained in the poet's *altezza d'ingegno*.[29]

The major elements of Longinus's theory are evoked here. *Transport, surprise*, and *elevation* are all terms that Boileau uses to describe the sublime (both in his translation and in his Preface). Like the Longinian sublime, *la meraviglia* connotes an aesthetic feeling beyond mere pleasure (or charm), by which the reader is lifted to the mental and moral heights of the *altezza d'ingegno*,[30] the genius's nobility of mind (Longinus's *megalophrosynê*). Even more striking is the notion of an "intuitive communication" between the genius and the audience, the intersubjective element that, as noted previously, is essential to Longinus's theory of sublimity: through the emulation (Longinus's *zêlôsis-mimêsis*) of the genius, the reader is raised to a higher mental plane, resulting in a realization – or in the case of the talented individual, an appropriation – of the genius's creative power.[31]

Louis Marin has recently argued that "Boileau's marvelous is caught up in a major confrontation within aesthetics: on the one side mimetic representation, governed by the imitation of either nature or its ideal order (in Kant's terms, the mechanism of *reproductive* imagination); and on the opposite side, a notion of *phantasia* or image-making (Kant's *productive* imagination)."[32] However, far from using the marvelous to challenge the prevailing regime of representation, both Boileau and Rapin categorically assert – following Aristotle's idea of poetic probability and in agreement with Tasso – that the marvelous must be verisimilar. In his *Art poétique*, Boileau writes:

> Never offer the spectator anything unbelievable:
> What is true is sometimes not verisimilar.
> An absurd marvel is for me without charm:
> An incredulous mind cannot be moved.

---

[29] Graziani, "Le miracle de l'art," 130–131 (my translation).
[30] *Altezza* (height) specifically recalls Longinus's *hypsos* (literally: elevation/height).
[31] Cf. Rapin's *Réflexions sur la poétique*, 23. In his edition, Boileau translates *thaumaston* by *admiration*, which is etymologically related to *merveilleux* (*mirabile* in Latin), though "admiration" (or *admirable*, in Italian) has lost much of its connection to the marvelous for modern readers.
[32] Louis Marin, "1674: *On the Sublime, Infinity, Je ne sais quoi*." 342.

(Jamais au spectateur n'offrez rien d'incroyable:
Le vrai peut quelquefois n'être pas vraisemblable.
Une merveille absurde est pour moi sans appas:
L'esprit n'est point ému de ce qu'il ne croit pas.) (AP III, 49–50)[33]

Moreover, Marin sees *le merveilleux* as intrinsically connected to the *je ne sais quoi*, a phrase much commented on in the seventeenth century: "Boileau also introduced to France the *je ne sais quoi*, the ineffable, indescribable 'I-know-not-what' of the aesthetic sublime."[34] Marin is the principal purveyor of the view that there is a relation of identity between the *je ne sais quoi* and the sublime in French neoclassicism. However, this relationship is far more oblique than Marin imagines. For one thing, the *je ne sais quoi* has nothing whatsoever to do with elevation or grandeur of spirit, an essential element of sublimity. And, unlike the sublime, it has no necessary relation to the idea of transcendence. Popularized by the French neoclassical critic Dominique Bouhours (1628–1702) (its origin can be traced to the Spanish philosopher and writer Baltasar Gracián [1601–1658]),[35] the *je ne sais quoi* concerns primarily a social sentiment or an aesthetic judgment for which no rational grounds can be found: "Une personne plait et se fait aimer dès qu'on la voit, sans qu'on sache pourquoi on l'aime" (a person immediately pleases and inspires love, without our knowing why), explains Bouhours.[36] Thus, although Boileau does use a variant of the *je ne sais quoi* on one occasion in his translation of Longinus's treatise,[37] and although Bouhours sometimes describes it in terms that are indistinguishable from those used to describe the experience of sublimity,[38] the *je ne sais quoi* principally relates to the idea of taste (*le goût*): since no rule can

---

[33] My translation. The opposition between truth and verisimilitude refers to the Quarrel of the *Cid*, in which Corneille held that the principle of verisimilitude does not apply to his play, since it is based on historical truth.

[34] Marin, "1674," 340.

[35] See Benjamin Riado, *Le Je-ne-sais-quoi: Aux sources d'une théorie esthétique au XVII e siècle*, where he notes that the phrase itself is an effect of translation: "Le vocable 'je ne sais quoi' n'a jamais existé sous la plume de Gracián qu'en langue française, c'est donc à ses traducteurs que l'on doit l'apparition" (77).

[36] Bouhours, *Entretiens d'Ariste et d'Eugène*, 265, my translation.

[37] "Car tout ce qui est véritablement sublime, a cela de propre, quand on l'écoute, qu'il élève l'âme, et lui fait concevoir une plus haute opinion d'elle-même, la remplissant de joie et de *je ne sais quel* noble orgueil" (my emphasis, TS, 81, *On the Sublime*, 7.2).

[38] "It sometimes excites violent passions and produces very noble sentiments in the soul" (Il excite quelquefois de violentes passions dans l'âme, il y produit quelquefois de très nobles sentiments) (Bouhours, *Entretiens d'Ariste et d'Eugène*, 265, my translation).

account for the feeling of pleasure or displeasure, taste is "ineffable."[39] Hence the importance of the *je ne sais quoi* for the development of irrationalism in modern thought, as Alfred Bäumler outlined it in his classic 1923 study, *Das Irrationalitätsproblem in der Ästhetik und Logik des 18. Jahrhunderts bis zur Kritik der Urteilskraft* (*The Problem of Irrationality in Aesthetics and Logic of the Eighteenth-Century through the Critique of Judgment*).[40] Although Bäumler talks extensively about the *je ne sais quoi* in neoclassical criticism,[41] he never once mentions the sublime in the entire book; the *je ne sais quoi* (and irrationalism more generally) and the sublime are thus hardly inseparable or mutually implicit concepts, as Marin suggests.[42]

The most important intersection between the *je ne sais quoi* and the sublime lies in the fact that both imply a privileged place for *feeling* (*le sentiment*) that is at odds with the traditional reliance on poetic rules (genre criticism). Boileau writes in one of his *Réflexions* that the sublime is not "quelque chose qui se prouve et qui se démontre; mais c'est un Merveilleux qui saisit, qui frappe, et que se fait sentir" (something that can be proven or demonstrated; but a Marvellous that arrests our attention, that strikes, and is felt) (TS, 150, my translation). However, this was not perceived as a contradiction; for "taste" always corresponded to convention (tradition); judgment by feeling cohered with judgment by rule (concept). As Bäumler notes, "the all-powerful prestige of Antiquity rendered taste superfluous."[43]

---

[39] I am thus in complete agreement with Cronk's observation that, while "it is to be expected that there is a certain overlap between" the sublime and the *je ne sais quoi*, "Marin's claim that the *sublime* is in some sense a 'narrower' version of the *je ne sais quoi* is not convincing – in fact, the reverse is true. Boileau's concept of *le sublime* embraces the ineffability of Bouhours's *je ne sais quoi*, and much more besides, most notably a Platonist notion of enthusiasm" (*The Classical Sublime*, 109, original emphasis).

[40] Alfred Bäumler's study has been recently translated (1995) into French by Olivier Cossé as *Le problème de l'irrationalité dans l'esthétique et la logique du XVIIIe siècle*. There is as yet no English translation.

[41] For Bäumler, the *je ne sais quoi* is simply a prototype for the concept of taste: "Cette esthétique de la 'délicatesse' et du 'je ne sais quoi,' par opposition à la vérité et à la 'raison' précède immédiatement l'apparition du concept du goût dans la théorie esthétique" (*Le problème de l'irrationalité*, 42).

[42] In a recent book (Fr. 2011/Eng. 2013), Jacques Rancière appears to agree with the critique of Marin I pursue here: "Surely, representative logic was familiar with the *je ne sais quoi* and the touch of genius that had to be added to the most learned application of the rules of art. Partisans of the Ancients even used it as a weapon to repel the criticism of the Moderns. And this is the reason Boileau excavated the treatise *On the Sublime*, attributed to Longinus. Some of our contemporaries have sought to locate the ruin of the representative model and the watchword of modernity in sublime disproportion. But this is a misunderstanding to say the very least, for the sublime was not discovered by champions of modernity" (*Aisthesis: Scenes from the Aesthetic Regime of Art*, 10).

[43] Bäumler, *Le problème de l'irrationalité*, 43 (my translation). The ancients were not merely models because they were ancients, "but because they satisfied in the purest manner the atemporal exigencies of reason" (Bäumler, *Le problème de l'irrationalité*, 45, my translation).

The greatness of a Homer or a Virgil is *confirmed*, not asserted by a judgment of feeling. The sublime simply allows for *a new manner of describing* the aesthetic value of literary works: namely, a *positive* way of demonstrating the superiority of neoclassical taste, as opposed to the primarily negative manner of judgment based on conformity to the rules. The influence of the *je ne sais quoi* on criticism was thus short-lived. As Cronk observes, "it was clearly the *sublime* which was found to be the more comprehensive solution to the prevailing critical problems."[44]

4.3   Sublimity and the *honnête homme*

In discussing Boileau's Preface to his edition of Longinus, modern commentators tend to focus almost exclusively on the formal definition of sublimity contained in the final paragraphs, thereby treating the bulk of the Preface as superfluous, as simply a laudatory flourish intended to introduce and recommend a somewhat obscure figure to Boileau's contemporaries. However, I contend that Boileau's interest in the heroic life and character of Cassius Longinus has substantive theoretical implications, namely for the idea of sublimity of mind, and that these paragraphs should therefore be seen as an integral part of Boileau's interpretation of Longinian *hypsos*.[45]

Boileau begins his Preface by discussing the fragmentary state of *Peri hypsous*, situating it with respect to the other works of Cassius Longinus (third century AD), whom Boileau took to be the author of the treatise.[46] He declares *Peri hypsous* superior in eloquence to the critical writings of Aristotle and Hermogenes, making the memorable remark, later echoed by Alexander Pope,[47] that "in speaking of the Sublime, he is himself most sublime" (en parlant du Sublime il est lui-meme très sublime [TS, 65]). Paragraphs two to four recount the heroic episode of Cassius Longinus's execution at the hands of the Romans (Cassius Longinus was condemned for his role as an advisor to Queen Zenobia of Palmyra, who led a revolt against the Roman Empire in 273 AD).[48] The fifth paragraph draws a parallel between Cassius Longinus's real-world heroics and the state of mind implied by the concept of sublimity. In the sixth paragraph, Boileau laments that the high-minded character of

---

[44] Cronk, *The Classical Sublime*, 109, italics in the original.

[45] I agree with Marin when he notes that "interpreting the sublime *work* as inextricably fused with a sublime *life*, Boileau emphasizes the elevated and powerful status of Longinus as orator, critic, minister of state, and philosopher" ("1674," 341, original emphasis). Marin does not, however, draw out the implications of this fusion for the theory of sublimity.

[46] It was not until the nineteenth century that doubt was cast on this attribution.

[47] Pope writes that Longinus "is himself that great Sublime he draws" ("Essay on Criticism").

[48] I am counting Queen Zenobia's letter to Emperor Aurelius as a separate paragraph.

Longinus's treatise may not be appreciated by his contemporaries, accustomed as they are to the "debauchery and excesses of modern poets" (WB II, 6) (accoutumés au débauches et aux excès des poètes modernes [TS, 69]) – thus reminding us of the incipient Quarrel of the Ancients and the Moderns, and of Boileau's use of Longinus in defense of the ancients.[49] The seventh paragraph was actually the final paragraph of the first edition (1674) and is the most often cited. It distinguishes Longinian *hypsos* from the grand or sublime style, thus treating *le sublime* for the first time as a critical concept. Paragraphs eight and nine were added in 1683, in response to an attack by Pierre-Daniel Huet on the sublimity of *fiat lux* ("Let there be light," Longinus's example cited by Boileau).[50] The final paragraph, with its well-known example taken from Corneille's *Horace* (*Qu'il mourût*), was included beginning in 1701.

Several passages in the opening paragraphs indicate that Boileau understood the Longinian sublime as a state of mind or disposition. Perhaps the most suggestive is the following:

> The Man of Honour is to be seen everywhere in it, and there's something in the Sentiments which shews not only a sublime Wit [mind/spirit], but a Soul elevated very much above what is common.

> (Le caractère d'honnête homme y paraît partout; et ses sentiments ont je ne sais quoi qui marque non seulement un esprit sublime, mais une âme fort élevée au-dessous du commun). (TS, 68)

This English translation of the text, from 1711, obscures the key seventeenth-century terms *honnête homme* ("man of honor") and *je ne sais quoi* (discussed above). The advent of the moral and social ideal of the *honnête homme* is linked historically to the decline of the warrior-aristocracy after the Fronde (the failed rebellion of the French nobles in 1648–1653) and the consolidation of monarchical power under Cardinal Richelieu and Louis XIV. By suggesting that Longinus not only has a "sublime mind" (esprit sublime), that is, a mind capable of great thoughts and expression, but also a nobility of character that "elevates" him morally above ordinary men (une âme fort élevée au-dessous du commun), Boileau associates the seventeenth-century concept of the *honnête homme* with Longinus's idea of *megalophrosynê*, an idea that, as was argued in Part I, undergirds Longinus's subjective theory of literary practice.

In the context of this study, Boileau's invocation of the *honnête homme* is of signal importance. It refers to a mental/spiritual quality that transcends social

---

[49] The "Quarrel" would erupt into full view a few years later in Charles Perrault's *Parallèle des Anciens et des Modernes en ce qui regarde les Arts et la Science* (1688).

[50] I discuss this in detail below.

class, thus enabling an aesthetic appropriation of the grandeur of spirit associated with the warrior-nobility. As many warriors are transformed into courtiers by royal absolutism, their natural superiority over the rising bourgeoisie is attenuated, and in response a concept of the upstanding and cultured man emerges. The warrior is "civilized" – that is, he loses the heroic spirit derived from military glory; the bourgeois, on the other hand, is "ennobled" through aesthetic elevation.[51] Thus the "heroic ideal" is not so much "replaced" as it is reappropriated and transformed in the sublime, even as the language used to describe this idea reveals a nostalgia for the warrior-nobility.

By associating a progressive social category with sublimity, Boileau prefigures the democratizing role the sublime will play in eighteenth-century aesthetics, namely in the bourgeois appropriation of nobility/ elevation of mind. In this vein, Boileau strongly emphasizes the heroic nature of Cassius Longinus, who suffers death with Christ-like magnanimity: "This great man shew'd a wonderful Constancy at his Execution, insomuch, that at the last Moment he comforted those whom his misfortune had touch'd with Pity and Indignation" (WB II, 4) (Ce grand personnage souffrit la mort avec une constance admirable, jusqu'à consoler en mourant, ceux que son malheur touchait de pitié et d'indignation [TS, 68]). And in the next sentence (cited above) he compares Longinus with Socrates and Cato (95–46 BC), archetypal heroic figures who committed suicide rather than submit to tyrannical pressure.[52]

4.4 Sublimity beyond rhetoric: *le sublime* versus *le style sublime*

The masterstroke of Boileau's Preface is certainly its carefully drawn distinction between *le sublime* and *le style sublime*.[53] The function of this

---

[51] This social transformation can described positively or negatively, depending on the perspective adopted. In a book on *Don Quixote*, David Quint writes of "the general transformation of the European aristocracy in the early-modern period from an independent, warrior-nobility to a courter class attendant on centralizing monarchs, a phenomenon described alternately by Lawrence Stone as a 'crisis of the aristocracy,' and by Norbert Elias as a 'civilizing process'" (Quint, *Cervantes's Novel of Modern Times: A New Reading of* Don Quixote, 144). The works to which Quint refers are Lawrence Stone, *The Crisis of the Aristocracy, 1558–1641*; and Norbert Elias, *The Civilizing Process*, vol. 1: *The History of Manners*; vol. 2: *Power and Civility*.

[52] No doubt influenced by Boileau's Preface, references to Cato as an example of sublimity will become a virtual commonplace. It can be found in John Baillie's *An Essay on the Sublime* (1747), Burke's *Enquiry* (E, 45), and Kant's *Observations on the Feeling of the Beautiful and Sublime* (O, 2:224).

[53] Litman notes that "this distinction that Boileau makes between the sublime and the sublime style has been as influential as the translation of Longinus's text itself" (*Le sublime en France*, 72, my translation).

distinction is twofold: on the one hand, it liberates the sublime and Longinus's treatise from the narrow confines of rhetoric; on the other, it argues for the sublime to be considered as a *critical concept*, thereby introducing the term into modern thought. The following paragraph, which appears near the end of the original 1674 Preface, effectively inaugurates the modern history of sublimity:

> It must be observed then that by the Sublime he [Longinus] does not mean what the Orators call the Sublime Style, but something extraordinary and marvelous that strikes us in a discourse and makes it elevate, ravish and transport us. The sublime style requires always great Words, but the sublime may be found in a Thought only, or in a Figure or Turn of Expression. A thing may be in the Sublime Style and yet not be Sublime, that is, have nothing extraordinary or surprising in it. (WB II, 7)

> (Il faut donc savoir que par Sublime, Longin n'entend pas ce que les orateurs appellent le style sublime: mais cet extraordinaire et ce merveilleux qui frappe dans le discours, et qui fait qu'un ouvrage enlève, ravit, transporte. Le style sublime veut toujours de grands mots; mais le Sublime peut se trouver dans une seule pensée, dans une seule figure, dans un seul tour de paroles. Une chose peut être dans le style sublime, et n'être pourtant pas Sublime, c'est-à-dire n'avoir rien d'extraordinaire ni de surprenant.) (TS, 70)

In this brief but iconic passage, Boileau makes a number of important and consequential claims:

1. He explicitly distances Longinus from "the orators," a metonymy for rhetoric – a move prefigured, as we saw, by the long encomium to (Cassius) Longinus as a heroic figure comparable to Socrates (a philosopher) and Cato (a statesman). The so-called rhetorical sublime is therefore already beyond rhetoric from the moment of its appearance as a critical concept.[54]

2. The sublime is a kind of marvelous happening *in* language ("le merveilleux qui frappe *dans* le discours"); that is, sublimity shows itself as a force that language *conveys*, without its being a property of, or reducible to, the particular words used. Boileau thus follows

---

[54] Thus I differ with Nicholas Cronk, who writes that "to speak of severing a literary-critical term from its rhetorical origins is not meaningful in the context of French neoclassicism. It would make perhaps more sense to think of Boileau attempting to redefine a given critical term within the overall domain of rhetoric and poetics" (*The Classical Sublime*, 83). I think Cronk misses the extent to which Boileau does indeed endeavor to explicitly separate Longinus from classical rhetoric (the *genera dicendi*). Of course, one could always accuse Boileau of being self-deceived, but this would, I think, be beside the point.

Longinus's privileging of the natural – namely the noetic – over the
technical sources of sublimity (*technê*).[55]

3. As in Longinus, Boileau suggests that the surest sign of sublimity is its
    effect on the reader: the reader/listener experiences a kind of *transcen-
    dence*, which leaves no doubt as to the authenticity of the cause. The
    dual, overwhelming-exalting structure of the sublime is inscribed in
    the terms *enlève, ravit,* and *transporte,* which together are meant to
    translate Longinus's *ekstasis* (going-outside-oneself): these terms con-
    note a kind of violence to which one is subjected (*ravir* means "to
    ravish"), but also the idea of being "carried away" (*transporter*) or
    "uplifted" (as noted above, Boileau spoke earlier in the Preface of
    Longinus's *elevation* of soul: "une âme fort élevée").

4. The sublime is not to be confused with the grand or sublime style, which
    (typically) features pompous language and elaborate phrases (*grands
    mots*). The hallmark of the sublime is its *simplicity,* thereby introducing
    a contrast (not unlike that found in Longinus's treatise)[56] with the
    vanity of writers who merely seek a grand effect, but without grandeur
    (like *les précieuses*). In his *Art poétique,* Boileau remarks: "Be artfully
    simple / sublime without pride, pleasant without artifice" (Soyez simple
    avec art / Sublime sans orgueil, agréble sans fard), thereby connecting
    poetic-aesthetic and moral values in the sublime. The idea of simplicity
    is already contained in Longinus's Atticism (as discussed in Chapter 1);
    thus Boileau found in Longinus a powerful ally in the Quarrel between
    the Ancients (Attic simplicity) and the Moderns (the ornate).[57]

5. Probably the most surprising claim in this excerpt is the idea that a
    passage can be in the sublime style and yet not be sublime in the
    Longinian sense, as if the sublime style were actually *opposed* to the
    sublime proper, as if *true* sublimity is *never* found in the high style,
    since it lacks the cardinal virtue of simplicity, or that the grand style is a
    kind of false sublime.[58] Certainly Boileau's examples suggest such an
    interpretation, though Boileau still implies that the sublime could, in

---

[55] Longinus promotes naturalness over artifice: "For art [*technè*] is only perfect when it looks like
nature, and Nature only succeeds when she conceals latent art" (*Peri hypsous*, 22.1).

[56] See Chapter 2.

[57] The connection between simplicity and sublimity can also be found in Kant, who writes:
"Simplicity (artless purposiveness) is, as it were, the style of nature in the sublime" (CPJ, 5:275).

[58] In the *Art poétique,* Boileau appears to mock the sublime style:

De figures sans nombre égayez votre ouvrage;
Que tout y fasse aux yeux une riante image:
On peut être à la fois et pompeux et plaisant;
Et je hais un sublime ennuyeux et pesant. (AP III, 287–290)

principle, cohere with the sublime style ("the sublime *may* be found"). Boileau is also basing his conception of sublime simplicity on the style of the Bible, namely the *sermo humilis* (the sublime low style) of the New Testament and the sparse, paratactic style of the Book of Genesis, hence his highlighting of Longinus's citation of "Let there be light" (discussed below). Thus the historical tension (beginning with Saint Augustine) between the ancient hierarchy of styles and genres, generally accepted by neoclassicism,[59] and biblical simplicity (*sermo humilis*) plays itself out in Boileau's text. For Boileau, the sublime represents a way to legitimate in aesthetic terms the simple style of the Bible, which would otherwise be difficult to judge according to the traditional genres of antiquity.[60]

6. Last, Boileau notes that sublimity is often "found in a Thought only, or in a Figure or Turn of Expression" (dans une seule pensée, dans une seule figure, dans un seul tour de paroles). Longinus writes that "you often find sublimity [*hypsos*] in a single idea, whereas amplification always goes with quantity and a certain degree of redundancy" (12.1). Thus, beyond the ideas of simplicity and brevity of expression, Boileau here invokes a concept of aesthetic temporality: sublimity does not show itself over the course of entire works or in long passages, but is something that happens in singular *moments* (Longinus's *kairos*) in texts. This will also be borne out in Boileau's examples (*fiat lux, Qu'il mourût*). The temporal element was already effectively implied in the words "strike" (*frappe*) and "surprising" (*surprenant*), which connote instantaneousness. Boileau translates *Peri hypsous* 1.4 using similar terms to indicate intensity and suddenness: "Car il ne persuade pas proprement, mais il ravit, il transporte, et produit en nous une certaine admiration mêlée d'étonnement et de surprise" (TS, 74). *Etonnement* was closer to "stupeur" than to surprise in seventeenth-century French. That it was considered a very strong term is shown by Descartes's description of it in his *Les passions de l'âme* (1649), in which he states that *étonnement* is an "excess of admiration" (un excès d'admiration)

---

[59] Gordon Pocock notes that "*Genres* were ranked in a more-or-less agreed order of merit. At the top came the great Classical *genres* of Epic and Tragedy, though opinions might differ as to which was the more 'noble'" (*Boileau*, 4, italics in the original).

[60] As Erich Auerbach observes: "In antique theory, the sublime and elevated style was called *sermo gravis* or *sublimis*; the low style was *sermo remissus* or *humilis*; the two had to be kept strictly separated. In the world of Christianity, on the other hand, the two are merged, especially in Christ's Incarnation and Passion, which realize and combine *sublimitas* and *humilitas* in overwhelming measure" (*Mimesis*, 151).

and thus "can only be a bad thing" (qui ne peux être que mauvais).[61] This notion of temporal intensity also supports Boileau's antistylistic stance; for if the sublime can be found in a "single" word, figure, or thought, then style is largely irrelevant.

We should also note that an important but often neglected feature of neoclassical criticism is its holistic nature. Manners, attitudes, and morals were considered of a piece with the examination of poetic-discursive practices – hence Boileau's effort to draw out the sociocultural implications of the sublime, to show how this notion, as an emblem of heroic values, could be integrated into the economy of the modern self.[62] Neoclassical criticism involves nothing less than an implicit theory of the self from the perspective of its expressivity – as the ideal of the *honnête homme* amply demonstrates. Thus in the twelfth of his *Réflexions critiques* (1710–1713) Boileau offers another definition of *hypsos*, one that reprises many of the elements in the passage cited above, but with added emphasis on the idea of sublimity of mind and a more explicit description of the dual transcendence-structure of sublimity:

> The Sublime is a certain force of discourse, able to elevate and ravish the soul, which derives from the grandeur of thought and the nobility of feeling, or from the magnificence of words, or from harmonious, lively, and animated expression; that is, from one of these considered separately, or what makes the perfect Sublime, from all three taken together.

> (Le Sublime est une certaine force de discours, propre à élever et à ravir l'âme, et qui provient ou de la grandeur la pensée et de la noblesse du sentiment, ou de la magnificence des paroles, ou du tour harmonieux, vif et animé de l'expression; c'est-à-dire d'une de ces choses regardées séparément, ou ce qui fait le parfait Sublime, de ces trois choses jointes ensemble.) (TS, 155)[63]

The *elevating* (*élever*) and *overwhelming* (*ravir*) effect on the reader is a result of the transmission or communication of the writer's grandeur of soul ("la grandeur la pensée et de la noblesse du sentiment"), which constitutes the "force" or power of sublime writing.[64]

---

[61] René Descartes, *Les passions de l'âme*, 144, my translation.

[62] I do not, of course, deny Boileau's careful attention to the technics of poetry and eloquence in his conception of sublimity; but Boileau follows Longinus in considering art (*technê*) as a secondary aspect of sublimity.

[63] My translation.

[64] I think Boileau misconstrues Longinus by implying that linguistic figures can be sublime without grandeur or nobility of conception, though he does say that the "perfect sublime" is found in the synthesis between technique and nature.

4.5   The quarrel of *fiat lux*: Boileau contra Huet[65]

In the original 1674 text, Boileau offers only one example of sublimity, the famous *fiat lux* (Let there be light) passage found in Longinus's treatise. The example would become emblematic of the Boileauean-Longinian conception of sublimity,[66] not least due to the lively three-decade debate it sparked between Boileau and the ecclesiastic Pierre Daniel Huet (1630–1721) over the propriety of using a passage from the Bible to illustrate sublimity.

The passage in question is found in chapter 9 of *Peri hypsous*, where Longinus discusses the first source of sublimity, grandeur of conception (*noêsis*):

> The lawgiver of the Jews, no ordinary man – for he understood and expressed God's power in accordance with its worth – writes at the beginning of his *Laws*: "God said" – now what? – "Let there be light," and there was light; "Let there be earth," and there was earth. (9.9)

Boileau seizes on this example as the perfect illustration of his contrast between sublimity of style and the sublime proper:

> As for Example, *The Sovereign Arbiter of Nature with one Word only form'd the Light*; this is in the sublime style, and yet is far from being Sublime, because there's nothing very marvelous in it, and which might not be easily thought and expressed on that Occasion by any one; but God said, *Let there be Light, and there was Light*, is an extraordinary Turn of expression which so well denotes the Obedience of the Creature to the Orders of the Creator, that it is truly Sublime, and has something Divine in it. (WB II, 7)

> (Par exemple, *Le souverain arbitre de la nature d'une seule parole forma la lumière*. Voilà qui est dans le style sublime : cela n'est néanmoins Sublime ; parce qu'il n'y a rien là de fort merveilleux, et qu'on ne pût aisément trouver. Mais *Dieu dit : Que la lumière se fasse, et la lumière se fit.* Ce tour extraordinaire d'expression qui marque si bien l'obéissance de la créature aux ordres du créateur, est véritablement sublime, et a quelque chose de divin.) (TS, 70–1)

---

[65] I borrow this subtitle from the excellent discussion by Gilles Declercq, "Boileau-Huet: la Querelle du *Fiat lux*."

[66] "In hailing the *fiat lux* passage as the pinnacle of sublimity, eighteenth-century critics were following Boileau rather than Longinus" (David Morris, *The Religious Sublime*, 38). Hence the title of Baldine Saint Girons's *Fiat lux: Une philosophie du sublime* (1993).

As the only citation from the Bible found in Longinus's treatise, "Let there be light" is hardly representative of the texts Longinus comments on. Boileau's choice of example, the sole example of sublimity in the 1674 edition, is therefore highly strategic: (1) it perfectly embodies the ideal of simplicity of expression, in particular biblical simplicity (parataxis or the *sermo humilis*); (2) it conveys the substantive point that sublimity is analogous with, and in some circumstances identical to, religious transcendence (thus "Let there be light" is, from an aesthetic perspective, not an example of sublimity because it connotes divinity; rather it connotes divinity because it is an example of sublimity ["it has *something* Divine in it"]); (3) it credits Longinus with having posited a *continuity* between the sacred and secular literature, both on the level of literary expression and the effect on the reader; Boileau thereby divinizes literature (poetry), by associating it with the *fiat lux*, even as he secularizes Scripture, by subjecting it to literary-critical analysis. Thus, from the very moment of its inception as a critical concept, the sublime operates at the ambiguous frontier between the secular and the sacred.

This blurring of the category distinction between religion and "rhetoric" (or literary criticism) is no doubt what prompted Huet, in his *Demonstratio Evangelica* (1678), to argue that "Let there be light" cannot be considered sublime: "What Longinus quotes here [9.9] from Moses as a sublime and figured expression seems to me quite simple. It is true that Moses is speaking about a grand thing, but he expresses it in a way that is not at all grand."[67] Huet attacks the very notion of sublimity – namely, as referring to the grand style – that Boileau's use of *fiat lux* was designed to dispel! For Huet, the concept of sublimity is inextricably tied to rhetoric and is therefore an improper term for the analysis of Scripture, which is beyond all human *technê*. In effect, he criticizes Boileau for holding up the sublimity of *fiat lux* as an aesthetic as opposed to a religious ideal.

Although Huet devotes just two pages (out of a 780-page tome) to a discussion of Longinus's *fiat lux*, it was sufficient to provoke a stern riposte from Boileau, in the form of two paragraphs added to the Preface of his next edition of Longinus (1683). Without mentioning Huet by name, Boileau remarks:

> What shall we then say of one of the most learned Men of our Age, who having the advantage of the Gospel Light, did not find out the Beauty of this Passage, but has presum'd to advance in a Book he wrote in Defense of the

---

[67] Huet, *Demonstratio Evangelica*, 65–66.

Christian Religion, that Longinus was mistaken in thinking these words Sublime. (WB II, 7–8)

(Mais que dirons-nous d'un des plus savants hommes de notre siècle, qui éclairé des lumières de l'Evangile, ne s'est pas aperçu de la beauté de cet endroit, a osé, dis-je, avancer, dans un livre qu'il a fait pour démontrer la religion chrétienne, que Longin s'était trompé lorsqu'il avait cru que ces paroles étaient sublimes ?) (TS, 71)

In effect, Boileau is accusing Huet of a lack of aesthetic sensibility or at least of not recognizing that a text such as the Bible, in addition to its importance for religious devotion, also possesses an aesthetic dimension – hence Boileau's use of the term "beauty" in this passage as a metonymy for the concept of "aesthetics," which he did not possess (and of course at this time beauty and sublimity were not yet opposed concepts).

Boileau also deploys an additional argument, citing the Preface to a 1672 translation of Genesis (thus two years prior to Boileau's original edition of the *Traité du Sublime*) in which the translator comments, approvingly, on Longinus's use of *fiat lux*:

The translators of the first book of Genesis in their Preface ... have mention'd this Passage of Longinus, to show how much Christians ought to be convinc'd of a Truth so clear, that a Pagan himself could not help being sensible to its Power by the light of Reason only. (WB II, 8)

(Dans leur préface ... [les traducteurs] ont allégué le passage de Longin, pour montrer combien les chrétiens doivent être persuadés d'une vérité si claire, et qu'un païen même a sentie par les seules lumières de la raison.) (TS, 71)

Boileau was no doubt sensitive to the contention – forcefully expressed in the years leading up to his 1674 edition of Longinus – that the Christian tradition made modern Europe superior to pagan antiquity.[68] Thus here Boileau claims that the quotation from Genesis reveals Longinus to be a proto-Christian, thereby strengthening his hand in the Quarrel of the Ancients and the Moderns; for although a "pagan," Longinus was nevertheless able, through the notion of sublimity (and "reason" – thus hardly a *je ne sais quoi*), to perceive Christian truth *avant la lettre*.[69] It is as if, for

---

[68] Norman (*The Shock of the Ancient*, 67) identifies Desmarets de Saint-Sorlin as the most influential advocate of this position, which provided succor to the cause of the Moderns against the Ancients.

[69] Thus, as Dietmar Till, observes, "as a pagan author Longinus became, paradoxically, the most important authority for the sublimity of the Bible. In the 18th century numerous [Protestant] theological works cite Longinus" ("The Sublime and the Bible: Longinus, Protestant Dogmatics, and the 'Sublime Style,'" 63–4).

Boileau, the sublime were providing aesthetic support to religion (the sublimity of the Bible) – an experiential recognition of a religious truth – rather than the reverse.[70]

In the same year that the expanded version of Boileau's Preface appeared, Huet responds in a lengthy letter entitled: "Lettre de M. Huet à M. Le Duc de Montausier, Dans laquelle il examine le sentiment de Longin sur le passage de la Genèse : *Et Dieu dit : Que la lumière soit faite, et la lumière fut faite*" (1683). In this letter, which would not be published until 1706,[71] Huet lays out a systematic view of sublimity as a counterweight to Boileau's conception. He distinguishes four types: "The sublimity of terms, the sublimity of expression, the sublimity of thought, and the sublimity of things" (le sublime des termes, le sublime du tour de l'expression, le sublime des pensées et le sublime des choses).[72] The first two, as Huet explains them, correspond fairly exactly to Longinus's technical sources of sublimity (figures, diction, and word arrangement). The third, sublimity of thought, is covered by Longinus's first source of sublimity. The fourth, the sublimity of things, which, Huet claims, is not found in Longinus, is described as transcending the bounds of rhetoric:

> The sublime of things depends only on the grandeur and dignity of the subject, *without the speaker having to resort to any artifice* to make it appear as grand as it is. . . . The sublimity of things is the true sublime, the sublime of nature, the original sublime, and the others are only sublime by imitation and by art. The sublime of things has sublimity in itself; the others have it only by proxy.

> (Pour le sublime des choses, il dépend uniquement de la grandeur et de la dignité du sujet que l'on traite, *sans que celui qui parle ait besoin d'employer aucun artifice* pour le faire paraître aussi grand qu'il est. . . . Ce sublime des choses est le véritable sublime, le sublime de la nature, le sublime original, et les autres ne le sont que par imitation et par art. Le sublime des choses a la sublimité en soi-même, les autres ne l'ont que par emprunt.)[73]

In other words, the first three types involve some kind of human *technê*, unlike the sublimity of things, which is "of nature" and therefore of God. "Let there be light" would therefore be an example of the sublimity of things, since, according to Huet, "things" means subject matter, and it

---

[70] Dennis, Burke, and Kant do much the same thing.
[71] It was published by Jean Leclerc in Amsterdam.   [72] Huet, *Mémoires*, 286, my translation.
[73] Huet, *Mémoires*, 287, 288 (my translation, italics added).

is the grandeur of the subject matter itself, not the particular words used, that makes it sublime.[74] Huet's attempt to separate grandeur of "subject matter" from grandeur of thought is highly dubious in the case of *fiat lux*, and his dichotomy between nature and art (*technê*) simply reproduces the same dichotomy as found in Longinus (as we saw in Chapter 2). Huet might argue that the "subject matter" of "Let there be light" can be expressed in a number of equally effective ways (as its translation into different languages can attest), without thereby affecting the sublimity of God's creative act. Still, the subject matter or thought cannot be expressed in just *any* way. As Longinus observes, there are "expressions which are below the dignity of the subject" (43.1); that is, sublimity cannot *solely* be a function of the subject matter, and this is precisely Boileau's point – that the expression must be adequate to the idea. But Huet is unable to account for this in his system.

Since it took some time for Huet's "Letter" to surface, Boileau responds only many years later. Written in 1710, the tenth of Boileau's *Réflexions critiques* deploys a new argument against Huet:

> To properly judge the Beautiful, the Sublime, and the Marvelous in discourse, one should not simply consider what one says, but who is speaking, the manner in which something is said, and the occasion on which something is said; thus one should consider *non quid sit, sed quo loco sit* [not what, but in what situation]. Who in fact can deny that something said in one context can appear low and trite, while the same words said in another context can appear grand, noble, sublime, and more than sublime?

> (Pour bien juger du Beau, du Sublime, du Merveilleux dans le discours, il ne faut pas simplement regarder la chose qu'on dit, mais la personne qui la dit, la manière dont on la dit et l'occasion où on la dit ; enfin il faut regarder, *non quid sit, sed quo loco sit*. Qui est-ce en effet qui peut nier qu'une chose dite en un endroit paraîtra basse et petite, et que la même chose dite en un autre endroit deviendra grande, noble, sublime et plus que sublime ?) (TS, 153–4, my translation)

This emphasis on "the occasion on which something is said" (*non quid sit, sed quo loco sit*) is an effective rebuttal to Huet; for it shows that Huet's insistence on subject matter is, in fact, an insistence on context; it is a matter of the combination of the *context* or *moment* and the words

---

[74] Huet might be taking his cue from Demetrius's *On Style*, in which the author writes: "Some subjects are forceful in themselves, so that those who speak them are thought to be forceful, even if they do not speak forcefully" (240).

used that creates the sublimity of "Let there be light." Boileau's use of "occasion" (same word in French) refers to the following passage of *Peri hypsous*: "But the greatness [of this passage] depends not on the mere form of the oath, but on place, manner, occasion [*kairos*], and purpose" (16.3). In short, Boileau is using Longinus's concept of *kairos* (discussed in Chapter 1) to complete his defense of sublimity. In the second *Réflexion*, Boileau had observed: "*Out of place*, the sublime is not only not a beautiful thing, but sometimes even becomes a great puerility" (Le sublime *hors de son lieu*, non seulement n'est pas une belle chose, mais devient quelquefois une grande puérilité). Although Boileau still considers the manner of expression to be important, he now emphasizes that its effectiveness is conditioned by context, timing, and appropriateness (*kairos*). Boileau had implicitly made this very point some ten years earlier in the final revision of his Preface, with the inclusion of an example from Corneille.

4.6 Boileau and the heroic ideal: Corneille's *Qu'il mourût*

One could interpret the addition of what would be the final paragraph of the Preface in 1701 as a further development of the "Quarrel of *Fiat Lux*," despite the fact that Boileau's new example purposefully avoids the religious domain. No doubt believing that the religious aspects of the debate with Huet had obscured his main points, but also wishing to affirm ownership of a concept that, by 1701, had become inextricably linked to his name, Boileau offers his own *modern* example of sublimity, as opposed to one taken from Longinus: the phrase *Qu'il mourût* from Pierre Corneille's 1640 play *Horace*. Like *fiat lux*, this example will later become iconic in French literature and criticism, particularly in the nineteenth century.[75]

Boileau's choice of an example from a contemporary French author operates at several levels simultaneously: (1) at a time when the Quarrel between the Ancients and the Moderns is still raging, it demonstrates how the "ancient" category of the sublime might apply to a contemporary literary work, thus reconciling in some respect the ancient and the modern;[76]

[75] In *Les Misérables*, for example, Victor Hugo often pays tribute to Boileau's discussion of the sublime, as in the following passages: "Le cri: *Audace !* est un Fiat Lux" (II, 134); "De même qu'on dit de Corneille: Où a-t-il trouvé *Qu'il mourût* ?" (II, 553).
[76] But as Norman suggests, this use of sublimity may be less due to any perceived "authority" that Longinus might be said to possess as an ancient than to his "wonderful remoteness." Norman asserts

(2) as a heroic utterance, it emphasizes the association between sublimity and nobility of mind (a *topos* of the discourse of the sublime), thereby connecting Boileau's discussion of the heroic figure of Cassius Longinus to his formal definition of sublimity; (3) it emphasizes, like the *fiat lux* example, but in a clearer and more effective way, the temporal intensity of the sublime and its dependence on context (Longinus's *kairos*); (4) as the *ne plus ultra* of simplicity, it further develops Boileau's antistylistic conception of sublimity. In fact, years later, in the tenth of his *Réflexions critiques*, Boileau will use another example from Corneille, the single word "Moi" (TS, 151), from his play *Médée* (1635) – thus even "simpler" than *Qu'il mourût!*[77]

Since context is part of what is at issue, I quote the passage from the 1701 Preface in full:

> In this Tragedy, the three first Acts of which are in my Mind the Master-piece of that illustrious writer, A Woman who had been present at the Combat of the three *Horatij* with the *Curatij*, but went away from the Place too soon and had not seen the End of it, came too hastily to old *Horace* their Father, and told him two of his Sons were killed, and the third finding he was not able to make any Resistance afterwards fled, upon which this old Roman full of Love to his Country, without mourning for the Death of his two Sons who had died so gloriously, grieved only for the shameful Flight of the last, who, says he, by so base an Action had fixed an eternal Stain on the Name of Horace, and their Sister who was present, saying to him, *What would you have had him do against Three?* He replied briskly, *Die [Qu'il mourût]*. A short Answer; yet there is nobody who hears the Word *Die [Qu'il mourût]* but is sensible of the Heroic Grandeur contained in it, which Expression is the more Sublime for being so simple and natural; and because we see that the old Hero speaks from the very Bottom of his Soul: If instead of *Die [Qu'il mourût]* he had said, *Let him follow the example of his brethren,* or *Sacrifice his life to the interest and Glory of his Country,* a great deal of the Force of his Answer had been lost, for 'tis even the *Simplicity* of it that makes the *Dignity*: such things are what Longinus calls the *Sublime,* and such Things as there that he would have admired in *Corneille* had he been his Contemporary. (WB II, 9)

that the "unattractive image of the authoritarian Ancient party is little more than a polemical distortion carefully crafted by its contemporary adversaries [that is, the partisans of the Moderns]" (*The Shock of the Ancient*, 64).

[77] In *Le Rouge et le Noir* (*The Red and the Black*), Stendhal invokes Boileau (ironically) when he writes: "Eh bien! je me dirai comme Médée: *Au milieu de tant de périls, il me reste* MOI." (I shall say to myself like Medea: "Midst all these perils, I have still MYSELF.")

Obviously *Qu'il mourût* has nothing sublime about it *in itself*, that is, detached from its context – unlike *fiat lux* it has no determinate meaning – which is why Boileau describes *at length* the circumstances in the play that render such a simple phrase grand. It is *the moment* at which the phrase is uttered – including its unexpected brevity – that creates the sublime effect, more so than the phrase itself, and yet the phrase is also the perfect encapsulation of that moment (that is, it is adequate to its object). While *Qu'il mourût* is far from banal, it does not carry its context with it as a kind of appendage, as does *fiat lux*.

Perhaps most important, *Qu'il mourût* brings to the fore in exemplary manner the nexus between sublimity and heroic high-mindedness, an aspect that had been lacking from the definitional part of Boileau's Preface. Indeed, the idea of heroic *sacrifice* connects this example to the biographical section of the Preface, where, as we saw, Cassius Longinus is linked to the real-life sacrificial figures of Socrates and Cato. Boileau's citing of *Horace* brings the old-style noble heroism in line with the new social dispensation of the *honnête homme*: one submits to or sacrifices oneself for the monarchical state in the same way that a Horace sacrificed himself for Rome. Known for his depiction of heroic characters, it is no accident that, among the moderns, Corneille is seen as the author best able to embody the Longinian concept of sublimity. The Corneille example also conveys the significance of the historical shift described above, whereby the "crisis of the aristocracy" is reconciled with the "civilizing process." By implicitly connecting Corneille's heroic *Qu'il mourût* with the social ideal of the *honnête homme*, Boileau emphasizes the shift from mental elevation (nobility of mind) being conceived as pertaining exclusively to the warrior-nobility to its appropriation by the rising bourgeoisie through the aesthetics of the sublime.

***

Boileau's introduction of *le sublime* into the modern critical lexicon has necessitated a lengthy discussion, one that belies the perfunctory treatment the French critic most often receives in studies of the sublime as the exemplar of the so-called rhetorical sublime. As I have endeavored to show, Boileau is not merely the popularizer of Longinus; he also profoundly understood the moral-subjective dimension of sublimity: as the expression of heroic high-mindedness in literature (Corneille's *Qu'il mourût*) and in life (Socrates, Cato, Cassius Longinus); as the dual experience of transcendence, of "being ravished and elevated" (propre à élever et à ravir l'âme); and as an aestheticized form of religious experience (*fiat lux*).

At a time of social transition when the figure of the *honnête homme* came to fill the vacuum left by the outmoded warrior-nobility, Boileau perceived the democratizing implications of the sublime, the idea of a bourgeois appropriation of aristocratic values, a theme that will be taken up in Burke's and Kant's theories.

CHAPTER 5

Dennis: terror and religion

The English critic and writer John Dennis (1657–1734) plays a much larger role in the development of the modern theory of the sublime than is generally recognized.[1] Not only was Dennis the first critic writing in English to integrate Longinus's *Peri hypsous* and the concept of the sublime into his critical program (he was satirized as "Sir Tremendous" in a play by Alexander Pope),[2] but, as this chapter argues, he also developed to a large degree many of the elements of the so-called aesthetic sublime: the exaltation of Milton's *Paradise Lost* as an archetype of modern sublimity;[3] the concept of mixed pleasure ("delightful horror"); the emphasis on strong emotion ("Enthusiastik Passion") as the essence of sublimity; the nexus between sublimity and terror (Dennis's example of the "wrath of God" reappears in both Burke and Kant). Thus, like Boileau, Dennis is a *pivotal* figure in the theory of sublimity and as such merits careful attention, even if his criticism exerts relatively little influence today.

The first section of this chapter discusses several of Dennis's journal entries from a trip to the Alps in 1688, in which he recounts his experiences in terms that will come to define the basic lines of eighteenth-century aesthetic thought. In the second section, I explore how Dennis, seeking to demonstrate the superiority of modern Christian-influenced literature –

---

[1] Exceptions would be chapters on Dennis in Samuel Monk's classic study of the sublime and in David Morris, *The Religious Sublime*. I should also mention important articles by Jeffrey Barnouw, "The Morality of the Sublime: To John Dennis" (1983) and, more recently, Ann Delehanty, "Mapping the Aesthetic Mind: John Dennis and Nicolas Boileau" (2007). This said, Dennis remains an obscure figure in contemporary literary criticism, despite being called in 1720 "the greatest Critik of this Age" (quoted in Morris, *The Religious Sublime*, 47). According to his biographer, H. G. Paul, "in the first decade of the eighteenth century ... [Dennis] was generally recognized as England's foremost critic" (*John Dennis: His Life and Criticism*, 109).
[2] In *Three Hours after Marriage* (1717), by Alexander Pope, John Gay, and John Arbuthnot. Although Longinus had aroused some interest in late seventeenth-century England, it was Dennis who established the tradition of sublimity in English criticism.
[3] "Dennis first made Milton and Longinus the inseparable companions they became throughout the eighteenth century" (Morris, *The Religious Sublime*, 67).

paradigmatically *Paradise Lost* – over the pagan literature of the ancients, develops the religious resonances of the dual transcendence-structure of sublimity by converting Longinus's noetically oriented view of the sublime into a pathetically oriented one. For, where Dennis departs from contemporary critics is in his singular focus on *emotion*, which is not the refined feeling (*le sentiment*) that had been habitually associated in French neoclassicism with high literature, but the violent, unbridled passions encountered in moments of religious terror. The third section studies the relation between terror and the imagination in Dennis's account, highlighting the ways in which it anticipates similar discussions in Burke and Kant. In the final section, I study the important parallels between Dennis and his Italian contemporary Giambattista Vico (1668–1744), in particular how their common pathetic interpretation of the Longinian sublime led them to develop anthropogenetic theories of poetry.

5.1 "Delightful horror"

Our examination of Dennis's theory of sublimity begins with a sojourn in the Alps, more than a decade before the critical works for which Dennis would become known. In a journal entry describing his ascent, we find the first recorded formulation of complex pleasure in modern intellectual history:

> 1688 – In the very same place Nature was seen Severe and Wanton. In the mean time we walk'd upon the very brink, in a literal sense, of Destruction; one Stumble, and both Life and Carcass had been at once destroy'd. The sense of all this produc'd different motions in me, *viz.* a delightful Horror, a terrible Joy, and at the same time, I was infinitely pleas'd, I trembled. (CW I, 380)

Although this experience is not "aesthetic" in any traditional sense – it is not produced by the contemplation of natural magnitude or power but by the prospect of falling from a craggy precipice – Dennis's description would come to define an aesthetic experience of affective intensity as the conjoining of contrary feelings: delight/ horror; joy/terror; pleasure/fear (trembling). Although Dennis does not attempt to explain how this paradoxical feeling is possible, how fear or terror can result in a feeling of pleasure, the fact that Dennis is describing *actual experience* lends to his ruminations an aura of authenticity.

Another journal entry from the same year describes complex feeling in properly aesthetic terms:

[Nature] moves us less where she studies to please us more. I am delighted, 'tis true at the prospect of Hills and Valleys, of flowery Meads, and murmuring Streams, yet it is a delight that is consistent with Reason, a delight that creates or improves Meditation. But transporting Pleasures follow'd the sight of the *Alps*, and what unusual transports think you were those, that were mingled with horrors, and sometimes almost with despair? (CW I, 381)

Here Dennis appears to sketch the major division of eighteenth-century aesthetics, that between the beautiful and the sublime:[4] beautiful objects in nature merely please; they produce effects of calm "meditation";[5] the grandeur of the Alps, on the other hand, engenders a more intense, mixed feeling, "pleasures ... mingled with horrors," which will define the sublime. In the idea of "a delight that is consistent with Reason," Dennis would appear to be making a veiled reference to neoclassical aesthetics, with the implication that this thought, restrained by the Cartesian ideas of *la raison* and *le bon sens*, is therefore incapable of accounting for the kind of emotional transport provoked by the sight of the Alps.

It is significant that this division between simple and complex feeling is first articulated with respect to the experience of nature, rather than of art, even if, as we saw in Chapter 3 with Thomas Burnet's *The Sacred Theory of the Earth* (1684), a text with which Dennis would have certainly been familiar, Longinus is nevertheless the model for the introduction of the idea of transcendence into the encounter with nature.[6] Burnet had observed in a Longinus-inspired passage that "whatsoever hath but the shadow and appearance of INFINITE, as all things have that are too big for our comprehension, they fill and overbear the mind with their Excess, and cast it into a pleasing kind of stupor and admiration."[7] In the same work, Burnet also observes that "the terrible and the sublime are exchanged for the gentle and useful; the cataract is sloped away into a placid stream"[8] and calls Milton "our great, sublime, and philosophical poet."[9] Thus some of the views Dennis would later weave into a coherent literary theory were already in the air, so to

---

[4] According to Marjorie Hope Nicolson, Dennis "make[s] the first important distinction in English literary criticism between the Sublime and the Beautiful" (*The Aesthetics of the Infinite*, 279).

[5] Kant will echo this idea in his third *Critique*: "The taste for the beautiful presupposes and preserves the mind in calm contemplation" (CPJ, 5:247).

[6] See Nicolson's *The Aesthetics of the Infinite* for an exhaustive study of this transformation.

[7] Burnet, *Sacred Theory*, 158.

[8] Burnet, *Sacred Theory*, 81. Longinus had made the same distinction between the useful and the overwhelming in nature (35.2–5).

[9] Burnet, *Sacred Theory*, 488.

speak, even if the oxymoronic quality of Dennis's "delightful horror" is far more suggestive than Burnet's formulations. Clearly under the influence of Dennis, Joseph Addison will write in a travelogue covering the years 1701–1703: "At one Side of the Walks you have a near Prospect of the *Alps*, which are broken into so many Steeps and Precipices, that they fill the Mind with an agreeable kind of Horror, and form one of the most irregular mis-shapen Scenes in the World."[10] Such reflections set the stage for Addison's famous *Spectator* articles of 1711–12.

5.2 Recasting the Longinian sublime: "Religious Ideas" and "Enthusiastik Passion"

Dennis's critical reputation rests largely on his two important works of literary theory, *The Advancement and Reformation of Modern Poetry* (1701) and *The Grounds of Criticism in Poetry* (1704). The principal aim of these works is to show how modern poetry can, with the aid of Christian revelation, equal and even excel that of the ancients.[11] Like his mentor and friend John Dryden (1631–1700), Dennis saw Longinus's treatise as an ally and guide in his effort to define a new poetic orthodoxy.[12] Joseph Levine notes that "Longinus gave [Dryden] the chance to argue for all those features of a modern poem that could not find easy precedent in the examples or precepts of the ancients."[13] Indeed, one of the principal goals of Dennis's critical project is to defend and explicate the greatness of Milton's *Paradise Lost*,[14] a task that neoclassical and Aristotelian theory was incapable of fulfilling.[15] Dennis thus employs the Longinian sublime as

[10] Joseph Addison, *Remarks on Several Parts of Italy: In the Years 1701, 1702, 1703*, 261.
[11] "Some of the Moderns, who have been great Admirers of their Contemporaries, which is a modest Expression for themselves, will by no Means allow, that the Ancients have excell'd us" (CW I, 208). The Quarrel of the Ancients and the Moderns was discussed in Chapter 4.
[12] According to Dennis, "the Greatest Criticks among the ancients [are] *Aristotle, Hermogenes*, and *Longinus*" (CW I, 340, italics in the original).
[13] Joseph M. Levine, *Between the Ancients and Moderns: Baroque Culture in Restoration England*, 65. But Morris argues that "although Dryden had much admired Longinus and the sublime, Dennis was the first English critic to make sublimity the keystone of his poetics" (Morris, *The Religious Sublime*, 55).
[14] Morris asserts that Dryden's Preface to his operatic version of *Paradise Lost* (1677), "initiated the fashion of considering Longinus and Milton together" (*The Religious Sublime*, 45). Barnouw observes that "Dennis's idea of the sublime was part of a program of criticism which opened the way for full recognition of the greatness of *Paradise Lost*" ("The Morality of the Sublime: To John Dennis," 42).
[15] Gustavo Costa writes that "the best critical talent of Italy and England [sought] to assert the validity of such poets as Dante, Shakespeare, Tasso, and Milton, strikingly similar in their Longinian sublimity, but unacceptable to French classicism" ("Longinus' Treatment of the Sublime in the Age of Arcadia," 80).

a kind of wedge, allowing him to cite the authority of an ancient while simultaneously asserting the novelty of a modern.[16]

There is also a nationalistic motive in Dennis's critical project. The epic was considered the premier literary genre of the early modern era, not least because of its role in the formation of national identity.[17] H. G. Paul notes in his biography of Dennis that "in 1668 Dryden had contended for the English as opposed to the French, and for the moderns against the ancients, and had based his arguments partly on patriotic grounds."[18] As the French neoclassical writers lamented the lack of a great national epic, the English critics of the late seventeenth and eighteenth centuries looked to *Paradise Lost* as a touchstone. Dennis's criticism is thus a manifesto not only for the greatness of Milton but also for the greatness of English poetry and culture.[19]

Unlike Longinus's transgeneric conception of sublimity, which includes poetry (epic, lyric, tragedy) as well as prose genres (philosophy, history, oratory), Dennis saw great literature almost exclusively in terms of poetry. Thus there is little to distinguish Dennis's theory of sublimity from his theory of poetry, though he certainly does not consider all poetry to be sublime. What makes poetry sublime rather than mundane, according to Dennis, is the extent to which it draws on religion for inspiration. Dennis is concerned that modern poetry has become too secular and therefore lacks a moral basis. At the beginning of his *The Grounds of Criticism*, Dennis declares that he aims to "restore Poetry to all its Greatness," because "Poetry is miserably fall'n" (CW I, 328). Only by drawing upon what Dennis calls "Religious Ideas" can modern poetry hope to rival that of the ancients. Dennis thus aims "to shew the mutual Dependence that the Greater Poetry has on Religion, and Religion on the Greater Poetry" (CW I, 331). That is, not only does religion improve poetry, but the greatest poetry conduces to a religious sensibility: "The use of Religion in Poetry was absolutely necessary to raise it to the greatest exaltation, of which so Noble an Art is capable, and on the other side, that Poetry was requisite to Religion in order to its making more forcible Impressions upon the minds of men" (CW I, 325). However, instead of simply asserting the priority of sacred over secular literature – a "religious sublime," to cite David Morris's

---

[16] Dennis in fact uses the term "sublime" somewhat sparingly; this is partly due to the fact that, despite Boileau's advocacy of the word, the "sublime" had not yet become a critical concept in England.

[17] See David Quint, *Epic and Empire*.   [18] Paul, *John Dennis: His Life and Criticism*, 123.

[19] In this vein we should not forget that, as Morris notes, "the tradition of English empiricism, from Bacon (whom Dennis quotes) to Locke (whose ideas and vocabulary he adopts), powerfully affected Dennis's critical methods" (*The Religious Sublime*, 58).

formulation – Dennis argues that the greatest secular poetry is necessarily religious.[20] Just as Boileau had established a continuity between secular and sacred writing by avering that the biblical "Let there be light" and Corneille's "Qu'il mourût" were equivalent in their sublimity, Dennis uses the Longinian sublime to establish a religious vocation for secular literature, thereby blurring, but not collapsing, the distinction between the sacred and the secular. Despite the iconic status that Boileau had conferred on *fiat lux*, Dennis is much more forthright than Boileau in drawing out the consequences of the nexus between sublimity and religion. In fact, Dennis separates himself *on religious grounds* from the neoclassical critics who preached the superiority of Greek and Latin antiquity as sources and models.[21] Milton is not only the greatest English poet; because he had the benefit of Christian revelation, Milton is also "better than the best of the Ancients" (CW I, 331).[22]

Dennis constructs his theory of sublimity and poetry on the basis of two concepts, "Religious Ideas" and "Enthustiastik Passion," which correspond, respectively, to Longinus's first two sources of sublimity: grand conceptions (*noêseis*) and strong emotion (*enthoustiastikon pathos*). Since the greatest passion can only be excited by the grandest idea, and since the grandest ideas (the highest, noblest, and most expansive) are religious, then it is Religious Ideas that are chiefly responsible for poetic sublimity/greatness: "The strongest Enthustiastik Passions, that are justly and reasonably rais'd, must be raised by Religious Ideas" (CW I, 339). The sublimity of *Paradise Lost* thus lies in the power of its Religious Ideas, namely figures derived from Scripture or the Christian tradition that have a great emotional effect on the reader.

Dennis is far from an orthodox Longinian, however, expressing his frustration that: (1) the Greek critic had not stated more clearly that the greatest ideas are Religious Ideas; and (2) Longinus considered *pathos* to be less fundamental than *noêsis*. Despite these manifest differences, Dennis contends that Longinus in fact supports his position.[23] With respect to

---

[20] See Morris's chapter on Dennis in his *The Religious Sublime*.

[21] Nevertheless, as I noted in Chapter 4, some neoclassical writers, such as Desmarets de Saint-Sorlin, emphasized how Christianity made modern Europe culturally superior to pagan antiquity.

[22] But Milton is also the best of the moderns (including Shakespeare, whom Dennis also lauds): "One of the Moderns . . . who has often transcendentally soar'd above both Ancients and Moderns, and that is *Milton*" (CW I, 211).

[23] Concerning the lack of a substantial definition of sublimity in *Peri hypsous*, Dennis observes: "It seems plain to me, that [Longinus] had no clear and distinct Idea of it [sublimity]; and consequently Religion might be the thing from which 'tis chiefly to be derived, and he but obscurely knew it" (CW I, 360).

Religious Ideas, Dennis observes: "All the Examples which [Longinus] gives of Sublimity in his Chapter on the Loftiness of the Conceptions . . . are taken from the *Grecian* Religion" (CW I, 357, italics in the original). With regard to Enthustiastik Passion, specifically Longinus's claim (*On the Sublime*, 8.2) that the sublime can occur without emotion, but never without grandeur of thought, Dennis reasons:

> Now *Longinus* had a notion of Enthusiastick Passion, for he establishes it in that very Chapter for the second Source of Sublimity. Now *Longinus*, by affirming that the Sublime may be without not only that, but ordinary Passion, says a thing that is not only contrary to the true nature of it, but contradictory to himself. For he tells us at the beginning of the Treatise, that the Sublime does not so properly persuade us, as it ravishes and transports us, and produces in us a certain Admiration, mingled with Astonishment and with Surprize, which is quite another thing than the barely pleasing, or the barely persuading; that it gives a noble Vigor to a Discourse, an invisible Force, commits a pleasing Rape upon the very Soul of the Reader. . . . Now I leave the Reader to judge, whether *Longinus* has not been saying here all along that Sublimity is never without Passion. (CW I, 359)

To reach his conclusion that Longinus in fact considers emotion to be the *sine qua non* of the sublime, Dennis must rearrange the general scheme of Longinus's theory. "Enthustiastik Passion" migrates from being a source of sublimity to being the effect of which "Religious Ideas" are the source or cause: "These are the Effects that *Longinus* tells us, the Sublime produces in the Minds of Men . . . so that take the Cause and Effects together, and you have the Sublime" (CW I, 223, original emphasis). Although the implied symmetry might seem to belie the priority Dennis grants to emotion, it is clear that the noetic is subservient to the pathetic in Dennis's account. The above-quoted passage also demonstrates Dennis's understanding of the dual transcendence-structure of sublimity: as overwhelming force and as emotionally uplifting or ennobling. The last sentence is in fact a literal translation of Boileau's rendition of *On the Sublime*, 1.4.[24] Dennis intensifies Boileau's version by highlighting the terms "ravish" (from the French "ravir" – to overwhelm by force) and "transport" (from the French "transporter" – to elevate or move emotionally) and by adding the interpretative oxymoron "pleasing Rape" (akin to "delightful horror") to connote

[24] "Car il ne persuade pas proprement, mais il ravit, il transporte, et produit en nous une certaine admiration mêlée d'étonnement et de surprise" (TS, 74). D. A. Russell's English translation of Longinus's original reads: "Grandeur [*ta huperphua*] produces ecstasy [*ekstasis*] rather than persuasion in the hearer; and the combination of wonder [*thaumasion*] and astonishment [*ekplêxis*] always proves superior to the merely persuasive and pleasant" (1.4).

complex pleasure. Following Boileau's use of "surprize" (*surprise*) in tandem with "astonishment" (*étonnement*) to translate Longinus's *ekplêxis*, Dennis emphasizes the momentary sense of shock or suddenness that accompanies terror, which he makes explicit in the following passage: "Fear then, or Terror, is a Disturbance of the Mind proceeding from an Apprehension of an approaching Evil, threatening Destruction or very great trouble to us or ours. And when the Disturbance comes suddenly with surprise, let us call it Terror; when gradually, Fear" (CW I, 356). Thus, according to Dennis, the concept of aestheticized terror is not new, but was already present or implied in rhetorical and literary-critical descriptions of the sublime effect.

Although Dennis, like Burke after him, tends to emphasize the over-whelming force of the sublime over its uplifting effects, he nevertheless sees the ennobling or moral effect of sublimity as fundamental to his effort to reform poetry: "Poetry is the noblest of all Arts, and by consequence the most instructive and most beneficial to mankind" (CW I, 334). Combining his understanding of Longinus's concept of nobility of mind (*megalophrosynê*) with Horace's dictum "to instruct and to please," Dennis defines poetry as "that Art, by which a Poet excites passion ... in order to satisfy or improve, to delight and reform the Mind, and so make Mankind happier and better" (CW I, 336). Dennis qualifies satisfy/delight as a "subordinate" and improvement/reform as a "final" end: "Poetry attains its final end, which is reforming the minds of men, by exciting of Passion" (CW I, 337). Emotional excitation is thus not an end in itself, but leads directly to a spiritual "reformation."[25] The repeated references to "men" and "mankind" in these passages suggest a more general cultural reformation – and thus a cultural critique – rather than one that merely concerns the individual.[26]

Dennis can also be said to make an anthropological point, in his claim that Religion "reformed" men by means of passion before the advent of philosophical reflection:[27]

> For whereas Philosophy pretends to correct human Passions by human Reason, that is, things that are strong and ungovernable, by something that is feeble and weak; Poetry by the force of the Passion, instructs and informs the Reason: which is the Design of the true Religion. (CW I, 337)

[25] "The very Violence of the Passions contributes to our Reformation" (CW I, 337).
[26] Dennis may in fact be obliquely referring to the Protestant Reformation in England.
[27] See the last section of this chapter for a discussion of the anthropogenetic dimension of Dennis's theory.

Passion thus represents a *superior* means of moral improvement, "because it moves more powerfully" than reason; and reason cannot be expected to control something stronger than itself: "God himself, who made the soul, and best understands its nature, converts it by its Passions" (CW I, 337) – hence the poetic (aesthetic) nature of religious texts. In other words, the sublime allows Dennis to establish the greatness of religious texts – *qua texts* – from an aesthetic (secular or parareligious) standpoint, that of literary criticism itself. Unlike Pierre Daniel Huet, who criticized the use of a poetic or rhetorical concept of sublimity to understand Scripture, Dennis sees the sublime as revealing a common purpose between secular and sacred writing: the elevation of the mind and the ennoblement of the soul, via an overpowering emotional effect (the dual structure of sublimity). Morris observes that Dennis's irrationalism is not tantamount to religious mysticism:

> [Dennis] sought literary explanations for the superiority of the Bible. The sublime provided a particularly fortunate discovery for this purpose. Its emphasis on transport and passion accounts for aspects of great poetry which cannot be wholly judged by reason. At the same time it permits a nonmystical and nonmechanical appreciation of exalted poetry.[28]

Great secular poetry could thus, through the sublime, have a similarly transformative effect to Scripture – which is no doubt how Dennis understood passages in Longinus such as "sublimity raises us towards the spiritual greatness of god" (36.1).

Finally, Dennis's Longinian-inspired emphasis on emotion as the chief criterion of poetic value leads him to posit a notion of artistic originality that will soon be echoed in the myriad theories of genius propagated in the eighteenth century:[29] "Milton was the first, who in the space of almost 4000 Years, resolved, for his Country's Honour and his own, to present the World with an Original Poem; that is to say, a Poem that should have his own Thoughts, his own Images, and his own Spirit." If Milton had imitated the ancients or followed the rules, observes Dennis, he would have been a "Copyiest instead of an Original." However, Milton does not so much break the rules as he is "above them all." *Paradise Lost* is therefore "the most lofty, but the most irregular Poem, that has been produc'd by the

---

[28] Morris, *The Religious Sublime*, 63.

[29] Morris speaks of a "projected essay on poetic genius" (*The Religious Sublime*, 50), which was never realized. Paul writes that "Dennis went beyond the common thought of his time by insisting in some of his writings that poetry should be considered and studied as the product of a creative mind" (*John Dennis: His Life and Criticism*, 131). This clearly reveals the impact of Longinus's thought on genius, as expounded in Part I of this study.

Mind of Man" (CW I, 333).[30] How a notion of "irregularity" could become a positive term of aesthetics indicates the extent of the break with neoclassical criticism – and the singular influence of the Longinian sublime.

5.3   Terror and the imagination

According to Dennis, the hierarchy of literary genres is determined by the intensity of emotional effect they engender. The higher genres – epic, tragedy, greater lyric – excite "great Passion," while the lower genres – comedy, satire, the lesser ode, the elegy, the pastoral – excite at correspondingly lower emotional key (CW I, 338). However, even the higher genres cannot sustain their sublimity at every moment but often contain mundane passages. Dividing passion into two types, the "Vulgar" and the "Enthusiastik," Dennis separates the everyday from the exceptional or extraordinary emotions, those "that belong not to common life" (CW I, 338). Unlike the "vulgar" emotions, the higher passions are not universal: "The Enthusiastik [passions] are more subtle, and thousands have no feeling or notions of them" (CW I, 339). Feeling these passions requires "Greatness of Soul and Capacity" (that is, Longinus's *megalophrosynê*): "The greater the Soul is, and the larger its Capacity, the more it will be moved by religious Ideas" (CW I, 340). This idea that we must be prepared by culture for the sublime was noted by Longinus (7.3) and will be echoed by Kant in his third *Critique*.[31]

Dennis lists six types of Enthustiastik Passion: Admiration, Terror, Horror, Joy, Sadness, Desire. The strongest of these, and thus the most apt for achieving the end of poetry, is *terror*. Since Dennis had argued that Longinus's first source of sublimity, grandeur of thought, is coextensive with Religious Ideas, it is easy for him to assert a nexus between terror, religion, and grand conceptions: "All the Examples that Longinus brings of the loftiness of thought, consist of terrible Ideas," and "everything that is terrible in Religion, is the most terrible thing in the World," such as the "Vengeance of an angry God" (CW I, 361).[32]

---

[30] Milton himself had referred to Longinus in his *Of Education* (1644): "A gracefull and ornate Rhetorick, taught out of the rule of Plato, Aristotle, Phalereus, Cicero, Hermogenes, Longinus. To which Poetry would be made subsequent, or indeed rather precedent, as being less suttle and fine, but more simple, sensuous, and passionate" (quoted in James Egan, "Rhetoric and Poetic in Milton's Polemics of 1659–60," 97–98). Milton's reference to "passion" is especially noteworthy in the context of this chapter.

[31] See Chapter 12.

[32] This idea would make a great impression on Burke, who augments the second edition of his *Enquiry* with a section on "Power," in which he discusses the relation between fear and religion (and

With regard to the problem of how we can experience terror as pleasurable – that is, as *aestheticized* terror rather than as simply painful, a question that will haunt Burke's and Kant's accounts – Dennis takes his lead from this well-known passage from Lucretius's *De rerum natura:*

> It is sweet, when the winds disturb the waters on the vast deep,
> To behold from the land the great distress of another;
> Not because it is a joyous pleasure that any one should be made to suffer,
> But because it is agreeable to see what from what evils thou thyself art free.
> (2.14)[33]

Thus Dennis comments:

> As Terror is perhaps the violentest of all the passions, it consequently makes an Impression which we cannot resist, and which is hardly to be defaced: and no passion is attended with greater Joy than Enthustiastik Terror, which proceeds from our reflecting that we are out of danger at the very time that we see it before us. (CW I, 361)

Dennis's acceptance of the idea that "reflecting" on one's safety is what allows one to experience joy seemingly contradicts his devaluation of reason in favor of passion. Nevertheless, unlike Burke, who needed to define aesthetic terror in ways that would distinguish it from real, non-aesthetic terror, Dennis is speaking here only about poetic representation; there is no question of "real" terror.[34] Thus Dennis only needs to distinguish the grandeur or sublimity of a poetic evocation from the ordinary discussion of the same object:

> So Thunder mention'd in common conversation, gives an idea of a black Cloud, and a great Noise, which makes no great impression on us. But the Idea of it occurring in Meditation, sets before us the most forcible, most resistless, and consequently the most dreadful Phaenomenon in Nature: So that this Idea must move a great deal of Terror in us, and 'tis this sort of Terror that I call Enthusiasm. And 'tis this sort of Terror, or Admiration, or Horror, and so all of the rest, which express'd in Poetry make that Spirit, that Passion and the Fire, which so wonderfully please. (CW I, 339)

Dennis is most probably adapting this argument from Boileau, who, in his debate with Huet (discussed in Chapter 4), contrasts a mundane description

---

authority in general). Burke's discussion moved Kant to devote several paragraphs to this idea in his third *Critique*. See Chapter 11.
[33] Translated by Watson (London, 1851). This passage became a standard reference for many eighteenth-century theorists, including Dubos, Burke (E, 44), Kant (APP, 7:238), and Schiller.
[34] See my discussions of "virtual terror" in Chapters 6 and 11.

with a sublime one, noting that simplicity is a necessary but not a sufficient condition of sublimity.[35]

Invoking the notion of *phantasia* as developed in the rhetorical tradition, particularly by Longinus, where it denotes the use of vivid imagery,[36] Dennis explains how the presentation of "Religious Ideas," that is, supernatural beings and events, could provoke terror, even if such things are obviously beyond experience and are thus not an evil that could threaten us. Starting from the premise that "the nearer the Evil is, the greater still is the terror," Dennis describes how "the Imagination being fill'd with that Agitation, sets the very things before our Eyes; and consequently, makes us have the same Passions that we should have from the Things themselves" (CW I, 218).[37] The image must not be static but in "violent Action or Motion," so as not to allow the mind "leisure to reflect upon the Deceit" (CW I, 362). Dennis is thus committed to the view that the imaginative force of the poet can create images that appear to be real and affect us *as if* they were real: for this "sudden agitation surprises the soul and gives it less time to reflect; and at the same time causes the Impressions that the Objects make to be so deep, and their Traces to be so profound, that makes them in a manner as if they were really before us" (CW I, 362–363). In describing the power of the imagination, Dennis goes much further than Longinus in specifying the nature and type of ideas that are proper to sublimity, and by correlating particular elements with specific emotions, Dennis opens the way for sublimity to be understood objectively in terms of certain kinds of objects.[38]

Although Dennis sometimes comes close to outlining an aesthetics of religion, his abiding concern is to defend poetry from religious attacks. Dennis thus takes pains to explain how sublime terror is not merely subjugating but also leads to an elevation and "ennoblement" of the soul:

> But Religion does not only heighten those Passions which are great in themselves, as Admiration and Terror are; for Admiration raises the Soul, and every Thing that is terrible, is certainly great to him to whom it is terrible, but it ennobles those which are commonly base and dejected. (CW I, 230)

With regard to the idea that religion transforms passions that are "commonly base and dejected," Dennis is almost certainly referring to Longinus's

---

[35] See Boileau, *Réflexion* X (TS, 154).   [36] See Chapter 2.

[37] Jean Dubos will develop this idea a few years later in his *Réflexions critiques sur la poésie et la peinture* (1719), a work that will strongly influence Burke's *Enquiry*.

[38] As Mats Malm notes: "The primary effect of *Peri hupsous* was to connect the sublime to a certain set of motifs and scenes, often strongly passionate (a terrifying storm, a battle of gods, or even the torments of love), but this effect was itself dependent upon the promotion of the rhetorical figure *phantasia*." Thus, over the course of the eighteenth century, "the sublime became even more loosely connected to language and text" (Malm, "On the Technique of the Sublime," 8).

controversial statement that the sublime does not involve "low emotions" such as "pity, grief, and fear" [8.3].[39] For Dennis, religion necessarily transforms such emotions, by connecting them with the highest values. Dennis thus approvingly paraphrases Longinus's observation in 7.2 that sublimity "exalts the Soul, and makes it conceive a greater Idea of itself, filling it with Joy, and with a certain noble pride, as if itself had produc'd what it barely reads" (CW I, 360). Grandeur of mind is achieved most effectively by terror, for terror forces us to consider the greatness and power of the cause (archetypally the divine), thereby expanding our mind accordingly. The dual experience of sublime terror allows us to sense *our own power* – an idea that will be exploited to great effect by Burke and Kant.[40]

5.4   Sublime anthropogenesis in Dennis and Vico

Dennis's effort to account for genius of a great pagan author such as Homer, who, unlike Milton, did not have the benefit of Christianity, required that he link his theory of poetry to a more general theory of man, lest he be forced to aver either that there was no poetic genius before Christianity (an absurdity) or that pre-Christian poetic genius was nevertheless divinely inspired (blasphemy). Dennis's theory of poetry and sublimity thus necessitated the development of an anthropological perspective. Morris observes that "looking to man himself for the source of poetry, Dennis concluded that history and human nature both prove that poetry originates in strong passion."[41] Although Morris's recognition of a secular-anthropological perspective in Dennis is somewhat at odds with his thesis about the "religious sublime," I believe that Morris is correct in suggesting a fusion of the aesthetic and the anthropological levels in Dennis's thought. Dennis's efforts to connect his idea of strong emotion to the primitive (prerational) mindset reveal a fundamental, anthropogenetic dimension to his poetic theory.

Although the thesis of the primitive origins of poetry is typically attributed to the Italian philosopher and rhetorician Giambattista Vico, Jeffrey Barnouw notes that "[Dennis] anticipates Vico in his sense of the primitive mentality of early men, the all-encompassing character of their religion, which ensured the coherence and stability of their culture and polity."[42] Like Dennis, Vico in his *Scienza nuova* (1725/1744) finds his inspiration in

---

[39] See my discussion in Chapter 2.
[40] Interestingly, Burke's only reference to Longinus in the 1757 version of the *Enquiry* is a gloss on the same passage in Longinus (7.2). See Chapters 6 and 11.
[41] Morris, *The Religious Sublime*, 49, original emphasis.
[42] Barnouw, "The Morality of the Sublime: To John Dennis," 37.

the pathetic aspect of Longinus's theory of sublimity.[43] Indeed, what Morris says of Dennis can also be said of Vico: "For Longinus, the interaction of passion and imagination *contributed* to the sublime; for Dennis, it *created* the sublime."[44] For Vico, too, sees the conjunction of emotion and imagination as the essence of sublimity: "[Homer] is celestially sublime in his poetic sentences, which must be expressions of true passions [*passione*] or in virtue of a burning imagination [*fantasie*] must make themselves truly felt by us ... Reflections on the passions themselves are the work of false and frigid poets" (NS, 825). Vico also speaks of Homeric "sentences filled with sublime passions [*passioni sublimi*]" (NS, 895).[45]

Basing their respective theories on the idea that poetry is the natural language of the passions, both Dennis and Vico view an investigation into the origins of poetry as essential to the understanding of human development. Both associate sublimity with primitive poetry, which they see as expressing an immediate relation between feeling (sensibility) and religion. Vico thus observes that the "poetry [of the first men] was at first divine, because ... they imagined [*immaginavano*] the causes of the things they felt and wondered [*sentivano ed ammiravano*] at to be gods" (NS, 325). The following passage from Dennis bears a striking resemblance to Vico's theory:

> Poetry is the natural Language of Religion ... Religion at first produc'd it, as a Cause produces its Effect. In the first Ages of writing among the *Grecians*, there was nothing writ but Verse, because they wrote of nothing but Religion, which was necessary for the cementing of the Societies which in those times were but just united; and Nature had taught them, that Poetry was the only Language in which they could worthily treat of the most important Parts of Religion. (CW I, 364, italics in the original)

Like Vico, Dennis thinks that prose and logical thinking characterize a later stage in the development of civilization: "As soon as Religion was sufficiently imprinted in the Minds of Men, and they had leisure to treat of human things in their Writings, they invented prose" (CW I, 364). In a

---

[43] Vico's contribution to the theory of sublimity is rarely acknowledged. Notable exceptions are Baldine Saint Girons's *Le sublime de l'antiquité à nos jours* (2005), which devotes a chapter to the Neapolitan philosopher, and Massimo Lollini's monograph *Le muse, le maschere e il sublime: G. B. Vico e la poesia nell'età della "Ragione Spiegata"* (1994).

[44] Morris, *The Religious Sublime*, 66, original emphasis.

[45] David L. Marshall notes that "the word that more often than any other qualifies the true nature of poetic form in the *Scienza nuova* is *sublime*" (*Vico and the Transformation of Rhetoric*, 106). Indeed, this term is not merely evaluative in Vico but also signifies a combination of creative ingenuity, emotional power, and heroic élan.

proto-Nietzschean observation, Dennis holds that the advent of philosophy with Socrates destroyed religious belief and with it great poetry:

> Thus upon the Establishment of Moral Philosophy, the Credit of the
> Oracles was diminish'd considerably, and Apparitions, Visions, etc. were
> condemn'd and exploded, and with them down went the greater Poetry; for
> you will find upon Inquiry, that there was no Poet among the *Grecians*, who
> was born after the Death of *Socrates*, who writ with a great Spirit. (CW I,
> 241, italics in the original)

Similarly, according to Vico, the most consequential transformation in
human cultural evolution occurs between what he calls the Age of Heroes
(epic poetry) and the Age of Men (philosophy), when the sublimity of
mind engendered by imagination (*fantasia*) is destroyed by the development of "reflection" (*riflessione*), the rational capacity: the imagination
atrophies, and poetry loses its capacity to signify the transcendent. Only
Christianity can rescue poetry from its absorption into what Vico called the
"barbarism of reflection" (NS, 1106).[46]

There is thus a great deal that unites the thought of Dennis and Vico
with respect to the sublime. Vico too emphasizes terror as the most
productive emotion: "The frightfulness of the Homeric battles and deaths
gives to the *Iliad* all its marvelousness" (NS, 827). And just as the Christian
epic *Paradise Lost* is the archetypal sublime poem for Dennis, the pagan
epic *Iliad* plays the same role for Vico; it best exemplifies the primacy of
"passion" that characterizes the Age of Heroes. The fact that Vico focuses
on an ancient exemplar, while Dennis chooses a modern archetype, marks
the difference between the pessimism of the former and the optimism of
the latter with respect to modernity. Nevertheless, Vico can be said to
evince a more hopeful view of how the primitive Age of Heroes can
connect with the modern age (Age of Men) through the sublime. In an
address (in Latin) to the Royal Academy of Naples in 1732 entitled, *De
mente heroica* (*On the Heroic Mind*), Vico proclaims:

> "Hero" is defined by philosophers as one who ever seeks the sublime [*Heros
> enim philosophis definitur qui sublimia appetit*]. Sublimity is, according to
> these same philosophers, the following, of the utmost greatness and worth
> [*Sublimia autem iisdem ipsis sunt haec optima maxima*]: first, above nature,
> God Himself; next within nature, this whole frame of marvels spread out
> before us, in which nothing exceeds man in greatness and nothing is of more

---

[46] That is, a barbarism that symmetrically resembles the earlier period dominated by the "barbarism of
sense," in its potential violence and savagery.

worth than man's well-being, to which single goal each and every hero presses on, in singleness of heart.[47]

By "heroic mind" (Longinus's *megalophrosynê*) Vico means the celebration of a will-to-transcendence: the natural desire to achieve greatness as a consequence of striving toward the divine. But the occasion of this speech – an address to university students – also emphasizes the formative and egalitarian dimension of sublimity, thereby linking a concept of transcendence to the establishment and preservation of civil society. Whereas sublimity in the Age of Heroes is expressed in the poetic mindset that gave rise to the Homeric epics, sublimity of mind – heroism of thought – in the modern world represents a (democratic) reappropriation of imaginative self-creation.[48]

***

Although Dennis's literary criticism may no longer speak to a modern audience, Dennis's place in the development of the theory of sublimity, as this chapter has argued, can hardly be underestimated. Boileau transformed the sublime into a critical concept, thereby extricating it from its rhetorical meaning as a kind of style. Dennis goes one step further: by emphasizing the pathetic interpretation of sublimity – sublimity as terror – thereby endowing sublimity with a quality that makes it *incompatible* with beauty and reason, Dennis extricates sublimity from neoclassicism, thus preparing the way for the aesthetic opposition between the sublime and the beautiful that will be fundamental to Burke's and Kant's accounts.

A major aim of this chapter has been a reexamination of Dennis's rapprochement between religion and poetry in the sublime, in particular with regard to Morris's claim that "John Dennis provided England … with a thorough and articulate theory of the religious sublime," a claim that can be misleading.[49] For Dennis does not aim to describe the sublimity of religion, nor does he suggest that reading *Paradise Lost* or another great

---

[47] Vico, "On the Heroic Mind," 230. The idea that the "marvels" of nature occasion the feeling of man's greatness, his mental and moral superiority over nature, is at the heart of Kant's Mathematically and Dynamically Sublime.

[48] Donald Verene compares the concept of heroism articulated in *De mente heroica* with that of the Age of Heroes thus: "The two major moments of dissolution in the *New Science* involve heroism. The first moment is the dissolution of the *universale fantastico* that structures the first two ages and its replacement by the *generi intelligibili* of the third age. The second moment is the struggle by recollective *fantasia* to produce the *New Science* in the memory-deficient world of the third age. This struggle is not the true heroism of combined thinking and acting of the second age, but the heroism of thought that Vico speaks of in *De mente heroica*" (*Vico's Science of the Imagination*, 116).

[49] Morris, *The Religious Sublime*, 47. Nevertheless, Morris's book remains one of the best scholarly treatments of the sublime.

Christian-inspired – but nonscriptural – poem is tantamount to devotional practice, religious conversion, or the direct apprehension of the divine. Rather than offering a religious version of sublimity, Dennis highlights the *structural analogy* between aesthetic transcendence and religious experience. Hence Dennis's version of the dual structure of sublimity: the paradoxical conjoining of overwhelming (sacred) terror with the elevation and "reformation" of the soul (aesthetic high-mindedness).

As I emphasize throughout this study, the theme of religion is always in some sense an inextricable part of the modern discourse of sublimity, from the *fiat lux* in Boileau to the idea of God's sublimity in Burke's *Enquiry* and Kant's third *Critique*. Dennis simply makes this relation more explicit and in the process allows us to understand, however contrary to his stated intentions, how the sublime represents a counterweight to religion, precisely by furnishing its aesthetic equivalent.

CHAPTER 6

Burke: sublime individualism

Edmund Burke's *A Philosophical Enquiry into the Origin of Our Ideas of the Sublime and the Beautiful* (1757/1759) is not only one of the major theories of the sublime; it is one of the foundational texts of modern aesthetics.[1] The first treatise to systematically compare the sublime and the beautiful, it serves as a bridge between the empiricism of early eighteenth-century British criticism (Addison, Shaftsbury, Hutcheson) and the development of philosophical aesthetics in Germany in the latter half of the eighteenth century (Mendelssohn, Lessing, Kant). Although the treatise is perhaps best known for its promotion of an aesthetics of terror – indeed, it is one of the mainsprings of the gothic novel and the horror genre[2] – this reputation tends to obscure Burke's multifaceted treatment of sublimity, namely his integration of theories of man and society with reflections on art and nature.

This chapter thus endeavors to explore the wider contexts and implications of Burke's *Enquiry*, specifically how Burke, by integrating empiricist with literary-critical methods of analysis, seductively recalibrates the sublime for modernity. The first section argues that the narrowness of the term "aesthetic" – a concept that was not available to Burke – can lead to

---

[1] Commentators such as Tom Furniss (1993) and Philip Shaw (2005) have attempted to link Burke's notion of sublimity (developed in the 1750s) to his late work *Reflections on the Revolution in France* (1790). Paddy Bullard has recently (2011) questioned this tendency: "Why do modern readers continue to search for connections between the *Philosophical Enquiry* and the larger body of his writings?" (*Edmund Burke and the Art of Rhetoric*, 79).

[2] Samuel Monk observes that "it was Burke who converted the early taste for terror into an aesthetic system and who passed it on with great emphasis to the last decades of the century, during which it was used and enjoyed in literature, painting, and the appreciation of natural scenery" (*The Sublime*, 87). And David Morris, in his essay "Gothic Sublimity," notes that Burke's "illustrations of the sublime have provided something like a readers' guide to the Gothic novel: vast cataracts, raging storms, lofty towers, dark nights, ghosts and goblins, serpents, madmen; mountains, precipices, dazzling light; low, tremulous, intermittent sounds, such as moans, sighs, or whispers; immense, gloomy buildings; tyranny, incarceration, torture" (300–301). Morris also points out that "the Gothic novel pursues a version of the sublime utterly without transcendence" (306) – which makes the Gothic sublime distinct from the theory of sublimity examined herein.

fundamental misunderstandings of Burke's project and that Longinus's treatise and rhetorical theory more generally play a greater role in Burke's conception of sublimity than is typically granted. The second section, on Burke's empirical methodology, aims to dispel the common assumption that the pleasure in the sublime results from the "removal" of pain. I contend that, according to Burke's own articulation, the sublime involves an irreducible *virtuality* that is somewhat at odds with Burke's presentation of elementary sensation. The third section explores Burke's opposition between the passion of self-perseveration (based on fear) and the social passions, an opposition that does not neatly map onto the distinction between the sublime and the beautiful, as Burke initially implies; for the sublime also involves the social passions, namely sympathy and ambition, the former emphasizing the social bond (empathy for the other's pain) and the latter the individualistic impulse (the agonistic quality of sublimity we observed in Longinus). The fourth section delves more deeply into Burke's association between bourgeois individualism and the sublime. Following the lead of Tom Furniss and Emma Clery, I argue that Burke treats aesthetic concepts as proxies for sociopolitical categories and that the feeling of exaltation provoked by sublime terror represents a bourgeois appropriation of the aristocratic-heroic ethos.[3] Finally, the fifth section closely examines Burke's subsection devoted to "Power," which was added to the second edition of the *Enquiry*, showing how it reveals a continuity between a religious and an aesthetic understanding of transcendence in Burke's thought.

6.1 The question of "aesthetics" and the legacy of Longinus

Burke's treatise is widely – and to some degree rightly – credited with transforming the sublime from a term primarily associated with the verbal arts into a general aesthetic category. However, this basic view masks a more complex reality.[4] For even if, methodologically speaking, Burke's approach was directly inspired by John Locke's empiricist philosophy and the critical writings of Addison, Shaftesbury, Baillie, and Hutcheson, the *Enquiry* is in fact steeped in literary theory, art criticism, and rhetoric, drawing in particular on Longinus's *On the Sublime*, Aristotle's *Poetics* and

---

[3] See Chapter 4 for a discussion of this idea in the context of neoclassicism.

[4] As noted in the Introduction to this volume, eighteenth-century criticism did not consider nature and art to be two radically separate realms requiring distinct modes of address.

Rhetoric, Jean-Baptiste Dubos's *Réflexions critiques sur la poésie et sur la peinture* (*Critical Reflections on Poetry and Painting*, 1719),[5] as well as on John Dennis's critical works, discussed in the previous chapter.[6]

The eclectic character of Burke's *Enquiry* reflects the fact that the "field" of "aesthetics" was in the process of forming at this time and had not yet acquired the more exclusive meaning we associate with it today. Although the word "aesthetics" had been coined in Germany in the early eighteenth-century (by Baumgarten), the term would not, in fact, come into general usage in the English-speaking world until 1830, after Kant's third *Critique* had been assimilated into Anglophone critical discourse.[7] Thus what does it mean for the *Enquiry* to be considered one of the founding texts of a "discipline" or area of inquiry that Burke could not have conceived as such? Although it is undeniable, from the perspective of intellectual history, that Burke played a singular role in the development of aesthetic thought, the anachronistic application of the term "aesthetics" to the program outlined by the *Enquiry* has often led to an unfortunate narrowing of focus that obscures the richness of Burke's conception of sublimity (and of beauty as well, for that matter).[8]

The protoaesthetic concept of "taste" had become an important topic in England during the decade preceding the publication of the *Enquiry*.[9] However, we must remember that the "Introduction on Taste" only appears in the second (1759)[10] edition of the *Enquiry*.[11] What interests Burke in the body of the *Enquiry* is not aesthetic judgment per se, but the relation between sensible *qualities* (aesthetic properties) and their

---

[5] This work was translated into English in 1748 by Thomas Nugent.
[6] Recent exceptions to the prevailing "aesthetic" or antirhetorical view of Burke include Paddy Bullard, *Edmund Burke and the Art of Rhetoric* (2011), and Cressida Ryan, "Burke's Classical Heritage: Playing Games with Longinus" (2012). Suzanne Guerlac observes in her 1990 book, *The Impersonal Sublime*, that "there are also significant echoes of Longinus in the *Enquiry*" (7).
[7] In his *A History of Modern Aesthetics*, vol. 1, Paul Guyer notes that "the history of what we now call aesthetics as a specialty within academic philosophy began in Britain with the *Treatise Concerning Beauty, Order, Harmony, Design* by Francis Hutchson" (98), published in 1725.
[8] See Andrew Ashfield's and Peter de Bolla's excellent Introduction to their *The Sublime: A Reader in British Eighteenth-Century Aesthetic Theory*, in which they note that, unfortunately, "pre-Kantian texts are read through the lens of the third critique, thereby dissolving the differences between the English and German traditions" (2).
[9] A critic commented in 1747 that "of all our Words lately, none has been more in Vogue, nor so long held in Esteem, as that of TASTE" (Quoted in E, xxiii).
[10] The second edition contains numerous additions and emendations, many of which are quite substantial.
[11] The "Introduction" was most probably motivated by the publication of David Hume's "Of the Standard of Taste" in 1757. It does not, however, substantially add to the eighteenth-century debate on taste, but rather, as James Boulton remarks, "reiterate[s] the commonplaces of his time" (E, xxxvi).

psychological and physiological *effects* (affects and emotions).[12] As Burke writes:

> When we go but one step beyond the immediately sensible qualities of things, we go out of our depth.... So that when I speak of cause, and efficient cause, I only mean, certain affections of the mind, that cause certain changes in the body; or certain powers and properties in bodies, that work a change in the mind. (E, 128)

Burke's critical approach can thus be called "sensationalist."[13] However, while this passage certainly describes a purely empirical approach, Burke's actual critical practice in the *Enquiry* is in fact quite protean, which explains its wide and diverse appeal.

Although the vast majority of commentators see Burke's theory of sublimity as his most important contribution to aesthetics, Rodolphe Gasché has contended in a recent essay (2012) that "beauty is perhaps the intrinsically more important and stimulating part of Burke's aesthetics."[14] Ultimately, however, since the two categories are deeply intertwined and are often defined in terms of one another in Burke's treatise, it makes little sense to speak of either in isolation. Indeed, what is important is the *oppositional relation* Burke conceives between beauty and sublimity,[15] as contrasted with neoclassical aesthetics, where sublimity is considered a superlative of beauty (or where, as previously noted, the term "beauty" functions a kind of metonymy for what we would call "aesthetics").

As argued in the first part of this study, the Longinian legacy traverses the boundary between the "rhetorical sublime" and the "aesthetic sublime." Thus Joseph Addison, one of the first English critics to draw out the implications of chapter 35 of Longinus's treatise,[16] speaks in his 1712 *Spectator* articles of a tripartite division of objects, the "great," the "beautiful," and the "uncommon," a division that is clearly based on the following passage of Longinus: "If anyone wants to know what we were born for, let him look round at life and contemplate the splendor, *grandeur* [*megalos*] and *beauty* in which everywhere it abounds.... [I]t is the *unusual* that excites our wonder" (35.4–5, my emphasis). Like Longinus, Addison does

---

[12] Monk comments that Burke "removes the perception of the beautiful and the sublime from the realm of judgment, where the French neo-classicists had sought it, as well as from the realm of sentiment, where some of his immediate predecessors had found it" (*The Sublime*, 98).

[13] Bullard dubs it "hedonistic empiricism" (*Edmund Burke and the Art of Rhetoric*, 80).

[14] Rodolphe Gasché, "... And the Beautiful? Revisiting Edmund Burke's 'Double Aesthetics,'" 26.

[15] "The ideas of the sublime and the beautiful stand on foundations so different, that it is hard, I had almost said impossible, to think of reconciling them in the same subject" (E, 113).

[16] Following the lead of Thomas Burnet's *The Sacred Theory of the Earth*. See Chapter 3.

not employ the term "sublime" to refer to nature, preferring instead the category of "the great." Only after the words "great" or "grand" have been established in the critical literature as quasi-technical terms by Addison and others does the word "sublime" come to supplant them in descriptions of transcendence in nature. This shift can be perceived in the first sentence of Part II of the *Enquiry*: "The passion caused by the great and the sublime in *nature*, when those causes operate most powerfully, is Astonishment" (E, 57, original emphasis). It is as if Burke feels that he has to use the term "great" to signal a continuity with Addison (and to some extent with Longinus, who often uses the terms "sublimity" and "grandeur" inter-changeably); but in having "the sublime" refer to nature Burke also enlarges the meaning of the term. This usage had been prepared by John Baillie's posthumously published *An Essay on the Sublime* (1747): "We have first inquired what disposition of mind was created by grand objects, the sublime of nature."[17] But whereas Baillie holds that "the vastness of the object constitutes the sublime,"[18] Burke maintains that "whatever therefore is terrible, with regard to sight, is sublime too, whether this cause of terror be endued with greatness of dimension or not" (E, 57). Magnitude is subordinate to power, since it is the latter that produces the strongest affective response. Burke's *Enquiry* thus effectively completes the linguistic evolution of the "sublime": from a term used almost exclusively in the analysis of literary texts to one that refers paradigmatically to natural objects in terms of both magnitude and power.

One of the principal continuities between Longinus and Burke lies in their respective attitudes toward the effect of sublimity on the reader/spectator. According to Burke, "astonishment... is the effect of the sub-lime in the highest degree; the inferior effects are admiration, reverence, and respect" (E 57). In other words, the sublime is what affects us most *intensely* ("the highest degree"). "Astonishment" translates the Greek *ekplêxis*, which, as we saw, is one of the main terms Longinus uses to describe the experience of sublimity, along with *thaumasion* (wonder/awe/admiration) and *ekstasis* (ecstasy/transport). Only the idea of "respect" is lacking from Longinus's account.[19] Burke's point is that, since fear/terror is

---

[17] John Baillie, *An Essay on the Sublime* (http://www.earthworks.org/sublime/Baillie/index.html, accessed October 11, 2014).

[18] Baillie, *An Essay on the Sublime* (http://www.earthworks.org/sublime/Baillie/index.html, accessed October 11, 2014).

[19] Although Burke sees "respect" as the weakest of the affects and thus as the least sublime, it will play a crucial role in Kant's second and third *Critiques*, where it serves to underscore the link between sublimity and Kant's moral theory. See Chapter 8 of this study.

the strongest passion one can feel, affects that denote experiences of the highest intensity invariably include an element of fear:

> Indeed terror is in all cases whatsoever, either more openly or latently, the ruling principle of the sublime. Several languages bear a strong testimony to the affinity of these ideas. They frequently use the same word to signify indifferently the modes of astonishment or admiration and those of terror. Θάμβος is in Greek either fear or wonder; δεινός is terrible or respectable; αἰδέο to reverence or to fear. *Vereor* in Latin is what αἰδέο is in Greek. The Romans used the verb *stupeo*, a term which strongly marks the state of an astonished mind, to express the effect either of simple fear, or of astonishment; the word *attonitus* (thunderstruck) is equally expressive of the alliance of these ideas; and do not the French *étonnement*, and the English astonishment and amazement, point out as clearly the kindred emotions which attend fear and wonder? They who have a more general knowledge of languages, could produce, I make no doubt, many other and equally striking examples. (E, 58)

The Greek Θάμβος (*thambos*), a term Burke finds in a passage from Homer's *Iliad*, which he uses as an example,[20] is semantically (through not etymologically) related to Longinus's description of the effect of sublimity in terms of *ekplêxis* and *thaumasion*, while the Latin *stupeo* (astonishment, amazement, wonder) is often used to translate Longinus's *ekstasis* (as we saw, Burnet speaks of "a pleasing kind of stupor" in his *The Sacred Theory of the Earth*).[21] Moreover, the linguistic ambivalence – the coupling of positive and negative feelings of wonder/fear and astonishment/terror that Burke sees *thambos* and its Latin and French translations as embodying – implies a notion of *complex pleasure*, the hallmark of the "aesthetic" approach to sublimity. One can thus conclude that, by positing an implicit notion of terror in ideas of astonishment, amazement, awe, and so on, Burke (who is to a large extent following Dennis on this point) thereby underlines a *continuity* rather than a break with the Longinian conception of the sublime.

6.2 Burke's empiricism: pleasure, pain, and delight

We begin our analysis of the *Enquiry* where the *Enquiry* itself begins: with an examination of the idea of complex pleasure. This idea is the crux of Burke's theory of sublimity and to a large extent conditions Kant's transcendental reinterpretation of Burke's account. We thus treat it in detail.

---

[20] See my discussion of this passage below.
[21] We noted in Chapter 1 that *ekstasis* is also associated with terror and fear.

Inspired by John Locke's *An Essay Concerning Human Understanding* (1690), Burke seeks to ground his reflections on beauty and sublimity in an empirical-psychological account of pleasure and pain. Locke had observed that:

> By the terms "pleasure" and "pain" I signify whatever delights or displeases us, whether it arises from the thoughts of our minds or anything operating on our bodies. For whether we call it "satisfaction," "delight," "pleasure," "happiness," etc., on the one side; or "uneasiness," "trouble," "pain," "torment," "anguish," "misery," etc., on the other; they are merely different degrees of the same thing, and belong to the ideas of pleasure and pain, delight or uneasiness, these being the names I shall most commonly use for those two sorts of ideas.[22]

In other words, all affects and emotions, all states of mind, insofar as they are perceived as positive or negative, can be reduced to the elemental forms of pleasure or pain. Moreover, these are, Locke argues, mutually exclusive: what is painful is not pleasurable and vice versa. Burke, on the other hand, will contend that it is possible to have a *mixed* feeling that is irreducible to one or the other pole. Burke begins his analysis by criticizing Locke's view that pleasure and pain are simply the negation of the other: pain does not "arise necessarily from the removal of some pleasure," and pleasure is not rooted in "the ceasing or diminution of some pain." He argues instead that they arise out of a state of "indifference," which is our default state of mind (Burke is clearly following Dubos's aesthetics in this respect), and thus have a "positive nature" (E, 32). Burke then qualifies the feeling resulting from the cessation of pain as "relative pleasure," for which he reserves the technical term "delight": "Whenever I have occasion to speak of this species of relative pleasure, I call it *Delight*" (E, 36, original emphasis).

The reference to "this species" is notable, for Burke allows for several forms of relative pleasure, a point that is often overlooked. In Section V of the first part, Burke states that "the cessation of pleasure affects the mind in three ways," namely indifference, disappointment, and grief (E, 37), the last two of which Burke considers to be *mixed* feelings. Although the cessation of pleasure produces a different species of relative pleasure than the cessation of pain, pleasure nevertheless predominates in both forms ("in grief, the pleasure is still uppermost" [E, 37]). Thus, to sum up, there are according to Burke three elemental states – pleasure, pain, and indifference – and two basic types of mixed states: the cessation of pain,

---

[22] Locke, *An Essay Concerning Human Understanding*, II, vii, ii.

which has one form (delight); and the cessation of pleasure, of which there are two forms (disappointment and grief).

The aim of Burke's critique of Locke is clear: to legitimate a concept of complex pleasure. However, the type of complex pleasure that truly interests Burke in this discussion is that which results from the *cessation of pain*, namely "delight," a term that will, a few sections later, be associated with the sublime. In effect, Burke is articulating the empirical-philosophical underpinnings of what John Dennis had dubbed "delightful horror."[23] The problem for Burke, as it will be for Kant, is how to define a properly *aesthetic* notion of fear or terror, that is, one that does not involve the *actual* or *direct* apprehension of danger, pain, or fear. The problem is compounded in Burke's case, since his initial definition of complex pleasure refers to *actual* pain and danger, whereas his later definition of complex pleasure expressly excludes it. The disparity between the two ways of defining "delight" threatens Burke's account in ways that are often unperceived by commentators.

Burke's first discussion of mixed pleasure is found in Part I, Section 3, where he endeavors to elucidate the "difference between the *removal* of pain and positive pleasure" (E, 33, my emphasis), as the title of the section reads. Burke uses the example of the narrow escape from danger:

> Let us recollect in what state we have found our minds upon escaping some imminent danger, or on being released from the severity of some cruel pain. We have on such occasions found ... the temper of our minds in a tenor very remote from that which attends the presence of positive pleasure; we have found them in a state of much sobriety, impressed with a sense of awe, in a sort of tranquility shadowed with horror. (E, 31)

Burke aims to establish the fact that in circumstances when pain or a threat is *removed* we feel a pleasure that cannot in any way be considered a positive pleasure; it is rather a pleasure that retains something of the effect of the pain experienced, thereby rendering the feeling more intense than simple pleasure (since pain is always more intense than pleasure).[24] As Burke concludes several pages later: "When we recover our health, when we escape an imminent danger, is it not with joy that we are affected?" (E, 38). Although there is nothing necessarily or particularly aesthetic about this example, Burke's language is strongly suggestive of the sublime

[23] Burke in fact repeats Dennis's exact phrase: "Infinity has a tendency to fill the mind with that sort of delightful horror, which is the most genuine effect, and truest test of the sublime" (E, 73).

[24] "The torments which we may be made to suffer, are much greater in their effect on the body and mind, than any pleasures which the most learned voluptuary could suggest" (E, 39).

(a term he will only start using a few sections later): "awe" translates Longinus's *thaumasion*; and "tranquility shadowed with horror" is obviously redolent of Dennis's "delightful horror." (In fact, later in the text Burke will *define* delight as "a sort of delightful horror, a sort of tranquility tinged with terror" [E 134].) The use of such language has led some – including Kant – to erroneously interpret the experience of the escape from danger as emblematic of Burke's aesthetics of sublimity.[25] However, when one examines Burke's statements in later sections about the mixed pleasure of the sublime, it is not certain that he and Kant really disagree on the point that properly aesthetic feeling should not involve any actual fear or pain; for Burke stipulates that "when danger or pain press too nearly, they are incapable of giving any delight, and are simply terrible" (E, 36).

Burke's use, in this section, of a passage from a literary text, Homer's *Iliad*,[26] demonstrates his reliance on high-cultural examples to further develop his "empirical" argument. But instead of stripping the text of its literarity (as a strictly empirical or philosophical approach might dictate), he instead exploits its richness, as in the following passage, which almost surreptitiously introduces the question of spectatorship into the equation: "As when a wretch, who conscious of his crime, / Pursued for murder from his native clime, / Just gains the frontier, breathless, pale, amaz'd; / All gaze, all wonder [*thambos*]" (E, 34).[27] While Burke is clearly interested in the affects of amazement and wonder – affects traditionally associated with sublimity since Longinus – his main reason for citing the passage is to distinguish the vantage point of the participant ("breathless, pale, amaz'd") from that of the spectator ("all wonder"): "This striking appearance of the man whom Homer supposes to have just escaped an imminent danger, the sort of mixt passion of terror and surprise, with which he affects the spectators, paints very strongly the manner in which we find ourselves affected upon occasions any way similar" (E 35). Leaving aside the question of "similarity" (of how familiar the average person would be with such a seemingly extreme situation), it would appear that Burke is here effecting a shift in perspective from direct participatory experience to spectatorial observation – a shift that would ensure the kind of distance and modification of feeling that the sublime, as an aesthetic concept, requires. The idea

[25] Kant writes in his third *Critique* of a "joyfulness on the account of liberation from a danger" (CPJ, 5:261). See Chapter 11.
[26] This departs significantly from Longinus's practice of using excerpts to illustrate the sublimity of Homer's poetry.
[27] *Iliad*, XXIV, 480–482.

of spectatorship will also become important in Burke's evocation of "sympathy," as we will see below.

Overall, Burke's commentary on Homer remains ambiguous; for he also describes the narrow escape from danger in a way that can apply to both participant and spectator: "For when we have suffered from any violent emotion, the mind naturally continues in something like the same condition, after the cause which first produced it has ceased to operate. The tossing of the sea remains after the storm" (E, 36). Burke's discussion recalls a similar observation in Aristotle's *Rhetoric*: "And *peripiteias* and narrow escapes from dangers [are pleasurable]; for all of these cause admiration [*thaumaston*, awe, wonder]" (1371b). George Kennedy, the translator, comments that in this passage "Aristotle seems to be thinking of both persons directly involved and of spectators."[28] Thus Burke could be seen as simply reproducing the same ambiguity found in Aristotle's *Rhetoric*. Although Burke will later stipulate that *actual* "suffering" from a "violent emotion" cannot give rise to the sublime, here Burke focuses only on the bare idea of mixed pleasure: the removal of pain produces an emotional aftereffect, the residue of an overexcited state, which, relieved of the external cause that prompted it, lingers on as a somewhat pleasurable sensation. Even if we assume that Burke first argues at the general empirical level (the investigation into pleasure and pain) before making the transition to the aesthetic level (how pleasure and pain specifically relate to the categories of the beautiful and the sublime), Burke seemingly puts himself in a box by *defining* "delight" – the term he later uses to characterize the feeling of sublimity – thus: "I make use of the word Delight to express the sensation which accompanies the *removal* of pain or danger" (E, 36, my emphasis). The operative word here, "removal," only makes sense when speaking of some actual pain or threat; indeed, Burke drops this language when he switches to a discussion of "delight" in the context of the sublime.

As Burke turns to his theory of sublimity and beauty, in Sections VI and VII of Part I, he makes no effort to explain the apparent shift from the empirical-physiological investigation of pleasure and pain to the analysis of aesthetic concepts. Burke simply begins to speak about the "ideas" of pain or pleasure and ceases to refer to the "removal" of danger (the last reference to "removal" in the *Enquiry* is in Section V of Part I). Section VI begins: "Most of the *ideas* which are capable of making a powerful impression whether simply of Pain or Pleasure, or of the modification of those" (E, 38,

---

[28] Aristotle, *On Rhetoric*, 96, n. 212.

my emphasis). One thus assumes that Burke is distinguishing the mere *idea* of pain from *actual* pain. Section VII, entitled "Of the Sublime" (the first mention of the sublime in the book), introduces the topic thus: "Whatever is fitted in any sort to excite the *ideas* of pain, and danger, that is to say, whatever is in any sort terrible, or is conversant about terrible objects, or operates in a way *analogous* to terror, is a source of the sublime" (E 39, my emphasis). As the word "analogous" suggests, Burke here establishes a break with his earlier analysis of actual terror, effectively creating a separation between real and virtual experience.

Burke's text is highly ambiguous on the relation between the empirical analysis of elementary sensation (Sections II–V of Part I) and the elucidation of the beautiful and the sublime in the rest of the *Enquiry*, which explains why commentators most often conflate the two characterizations of delight.[29] Gasché writes (in 2012), for example: "The feeling of the sublime thus presupposes the *removal* of the direct threat to self-preservation and the fear of death that accompanies it. . . . The feeling that makes up the sublime depends on the *removal* or cessation of another feeling."[30] As we saw, the "removal of pain" is the way Burke defines delight *initially*, but it is not the way he describes delight as it pertains to the sublime. In other words, according to the logic of Burke's presentation, all delight is not necessarily sublime, even if all sublimity necessarily involves a feeling of delight. In place of the "removal of pain," Burke substitutes a concept of aesthetic distance – the *idealization* of pain and danger.[31]

However, if delight, as it relates to the sublime, involves only the mere *idea* of pain in a condition of safety, then how is it supposed to affect us in the manner previously described? Burke writes:

> The passions which belong to self-preservation, turn on pain and danger; they are simply painful when their causes immediately affect us; they are delightful when we have an *idea* of pain and danger, without being *actually* in such circumstances; this delight I have not called pleasure because it turns

[29] Thomas Weiskel observes: "We may infer that the 'imminent danger' to which we are exposed and from which we are then released in the sublime moment is an unconscious fantasy of parricide" (*The Romantic Sublime*, 92). W. J. T. Mitchell remarks: "But this severe, indirect pleasure is exactly the sort of sensation Burke analyzes as 'delight,' the feeling that accompanies the removal of pain or its contemplation from a safe distance, and which serves as the key term in explaining how pain can become the sources of aesthetic pleasure in the sublime" (*Iconology*, 127).

[30] Gasché, ". . . And the Beautiful," 27 (my emphasis).

[31] The concept of "aesthetic distance" was coined by Edward Bullough in a 1912 article entitled "'Psychical Distance' as a Factor in Art and as an Aesthetic Principle." In a chapter on Burke in his *Critical Aesthetics and Postmodernism*, Paul Crowther notes that "distance momentarily invests the object with the character of representation rather than that of real physical existence" (123).

on pain, and because it is different enough from any *idea* of positive
pleasure. Whatever excites this delight, I call *sublime*. (E, 51, emphasis
mine except "sublime")

According to the use of the term "actually," Burke here posits a clean
dichotomy between actuality and nonactuality, or virtuality, in the experience of sublimity, a dichotomy that was completely missing from the earlier
discussion, when it was a matter of the "removal" of (actual) pain. This
passage therefore directly contradicts the example of the escape from danger
("without actually being in such circumstances"), which now appears to have
been merely heuristic rather than exemplary or illustrative. The safety condition, ensured by the mere *idea* of pain or danger, effectively replaces the
condition of the removal of pain/danger in the earlier analysis.

Paul Guyer, in his recent *A History of Modern Aesthetics* (2014), has
proposed to think this real/virtual dichotomy according to a distinction
between emotions "at play" as opposed to "at work":

> In the tradition of Dubos, Burke holds that what we directly enjoy in the
> experience of the sublime is the arousal of powerful emotions which, because
> of the remoteness of real or fictional distance, fall short of being actually
> painful. In the experience of the sublime we enjoy real emotions, but in
> conditions in which they ... can be said to be at play rather than at work.[32]

However, in what sense are emotions "real" if they are "at play"? Burke in
fact *criticizes* Dubos for not recognizing that we also take pleasure in *real* and
not only represented suffering or horror, as Dubos imagines, because reality
is more powerful than the representation.[33] Dubos had stipulated that "the
impression of the imitation differs from that of the object imitated only in its
being of an inferior force."[34] Thus, the question remains: how can emotions
"at play" (or "virtual terror" in my nomenclature) create the *intensity* of
response associated with the sublime? Aristotle observes in his *Rhetoric*: "Let
fear [*phobos*] be [defined as] a sort of pain or agitation derived from the
imagination [*phantasia*] of a future destructive or painful evil ... if they do
not appear far off but near, so that they are about to happen; for what is far
off is not feared" (1382a). But it is only with respect to *actual* pain/danger that
one can speak of a proper distance, of being too close or too far ("when
danger or pain press too nearly" [E, 36]; "when their causes immediately
affect us").[35] *Virtual* pain/fear, on the other hand, is *absolutely* removed from

---

[32] Paul Guyer, *A History of Modern Aesthetics*, vol. 1, 152.   [33] I discuss this in more detail below.
[34] Dubos, *Critical Reflections*, 23.
[35] F. R. Ankersmit, however, in his book *Sublime Historical Experience* (334–340), makes an interesting
argument about how trauma and the sublime might be seen as having an analogous structure.

any real threat (as in artistic representation or in the spectator position more generally). The bare assertion of a safety or distance condition does not thereby solve the problem of how one can experience fear without being actually afraid (the same problem Kant will encounter in his Dynamically Sublime); it merely displaces it from the empirical to the properly aesthetic realm.[36]

6.3   Burke's aesthetic anthropology of the sublime: sympathy, mimesis, and ambition

The point of the discussion of relative pleasure was to define the concept of the intensity or strength of effect/affect. In Section VI (of Part I), this idea of intensity is used to ground a more general philosophical-anthropological outlook on man and society:

> Most of the ideas which are capable of making a powerful impression on the mind, whether simply of Pain or Pleasure, or of the modifications of those, may be reduced very nearly to these two heads, *self-preservation* and *society;* to the ends of one or the other of which all our passions are calculated to answer. The passions which concern self-preservation, turn mostly on *pain* or *danger*. The ideas of *pain, sickness,* and *death,* fill the mind with strong emotions of horror; but *life* and *health,* though they put us in a capacity of being affected with pleasure, they make no such impression by the simple enjoyment. The passions therefore which are conversant about the preservation of the individual, turn chiefly on *pain* and *danger,* and they are the most powerful of all the passions. (E, 38, original emphasis)

---

[36] I am not the only one to point out the problematic nature of Burke's "virtual aesthetics" (though to my knowledge no one else has used the term "virtual" in this context). Frances Ferguson speaks of Burke's "inability or refusal to make a thorough-going distinction between objects and mental objects" or to "differentiate the response to objects to one's own representations of them" (*Solitude and the Sublime,* 2). Philip Shaw notes that "whilst at no point does Burke concede the radical possibility that sublimity is an effect of language, his argument seems constantly on the verge of declaring this possibility" (*The Sublime,* 49). Ankersmit argues that since the sublime "provokes a movement of derealization by which reality is robbed of its threatening potentialities ... Burke's description of the sublime is less the pleasant thrill that is often associated with it than a preemptive strike against the terrible" (*Sublime Historical Experience,* 336). Tom Furniss even raises the possibility of self-deception: "If the sublime is therefore a deception which the self passes upon itself, an auto-affective ruse powerful enough to suspend disbelief, we might ask why Burke, like many theorists of the eighteenth century, was so committed to it" (*Edmund Burke's Aesthetic Ideology,* 30). I have thus introduced the notion of "virtuality" in an attempt to bring some consistency to Burke's account of aestheticized terror. This is why, in my discussion of Kant's Dynamically Sublime, the most Burkean part of his theory, I will also have recourse to the concept of the virtual. See Chapter 11 of this study.

By placing the emphasis on the *strength* of the individual in contradistinction to the social, Burke lays the groundwork for a heroic subjectivity
associated with the sublime. Burke's argument can be summarized as
follows: if the strongest passion a human being can feel is fear in the face
of death (namely terror), then the instinct for self-preservation is the source
of the most intense experiences a human being can have; therefore, the
effects of the social passions, of those not principally concerned with self-
preservation, are comparatively weaker.[37] At first glance, the concepts of
self-preservation and society appear to correspond to the sublime and the
beautiful respectively. However, Burke's subsequent analysis of sublimity
in specific social passions undermines the basic individual-versus-society
dichotomy. In Section VIII, Burke divides the social passions into two
groups: the "society of the sexes" and "general society." Burke defines the
former in terms of "love" and associates it with beauty. Although love
produces "violent effects" and is often a "mixed passion," it does not
approach self-preservation as the source of the strongest emotion one
can feel (E, 40). Beauty engages other-directed feelings; sublimity is
individualistic. It is striking, from a modern perspective, that beauty
should be described as a "social quality" (E, 42); but we must keep in
mind that Burke is writing in, and in some measure against,[38] the tradition
of British moral philosophy, in particular that of Shaftesbury and his
concept of "moral beauty,"[39] and of Francis Hutcheson and his notion of
"moral sense."

It is only with regard to "general society," which is divided into the
aspects of sympathy, imitation, and ambition, that Burke will outline
certain implications for the concept of sublimity. "Sympathy" was already
a major topic during the time Burke was writing, from the art criticism of
Marivaux and Dubos to the moral philosophies of Hume, Rousseau, and
Adam Smith.[40] "Imitation" is essentially Aristotle's concept of mimesis,[41]
and it includes both the behavioral as well as the representational meanings
of the term. "Ambition" is seen by Burke as a natural corrective to

---

[37] "The passions therefore which are conversant about the preservation of the individual, turn chiefly
   on *pain* and *danger*, and they are the most powerful of all the passions" (E 38, original emphasis).
[38] See Bullard's *Edmund Burke and the Art of Rhetoric*, especially the chapter entitled "The Epicurean
   Aesthetics of the *Philosophical Enquiry*."
[39] Shaftesbury defines moral beauty as "beauty of the sentiments, the grace of actions, the turn of
   characters, and the proportions of a human mind" (*Sensus Communis* IV, ii).
[40] See David Marshall, *The Surprising Effects of Sympathy: Marivaux, Rousseau, Diderot, and Mary
   Shelley.*
[41] "Aristotle has spoken so much and so solidly upon the force of imitation in his poetics, that it makes
   any further discourse upon this subject the less necessary" (E, 49).

behavioral imitation, insofar as it introduces a concept of rivalry (inspired by Longinus's agonistic conception of sublimity). I explore the significance of each aspect in turn for Burke's theory of sublimity.

By "sympathy" Burke does not mean compassion, but something rather more akin to the modern notion of "empathy," that is, putting oneself in the place of another:

> It is by [sympathy] that we enter into the concerns of others; that we are moved as they are moved, and are never suffered to be indifferent spectators of almost anything which men can do or suffer. For sympathy must be considered as a sort of substitution, by which we are put into the place of another man, and affected in many respects as he is affected; so that this passion may either partake of the nature of those which regard self-preservation, and turning upon pain may be a source of the sublime; or it may turn upon ideas of pleasure. (E, 44)[42]

Sympathy thus defines a spectatorial attitude, a dialectic of proximity and distance. The spectator experiences joy and suffering by proxy, as it were, so that one is affected emotionally without one's person actually being implicated. In other words, sympathy entails a kind of *virtual* experience and thus fulfills Burke's condition that sublimity involve only the *ideas* of pain or fear, not their actuality. However, there is nothing specifically aesthetic about this description of sympathy. Indeed, it would appear to be indistinguishable from a properly moral sentiment, for Burke adds:

> As our Creator has designed we should be united by the bond of sympathy, he has strengthened that bond by a proportionable delight; and there most where our sympathy is most wanted, in the distresses of others. If this passion was simply painful, we would shun with the greatest care all persons and places that could excite such a passion; as some who are so far gone in indolence as not to endure any strong impression actually do. (E, 46)

The invocation of "strength" and the contrast with "indolence" connotes a heroic subjectivity that is at one with the moral meaning of sublimity. Burke thus displaces the British moral sense tradition, based on taste and beauty, with an ethics of sublime sympathy.

---

[42] Adam Smith's description of sympathy in his *Theory of Moral Sentiments* (1759), published just two years after the first edition of the *Enquiry*, owes much to Burke's account: "By the imagination we place ourselves in his situation, we conceive ourselves enduring all the same torments, we enter as it were into his body, and become in the some measure the same person with him, and thence form some idea of his sensations, and even feel something which, though weaker in degree, is not altogether unlike them.... For as to be in pain or distress of any kind excites... some degree of the same emotion, in proportion to the vivacity or dullness of the conception" (9).

In the sentences that follow, Burke shifts his focus from the question of morality to that of representation, in particular the often-debated problem of how the suffering of others can be rendered pleasurable though mimesis – an idea that goes back to Aristotle's *Poetics* 4 ("we enjoy contemplating the most precise images [*eikônes*] of things whose actual sight is painful to us, such as the forms of the vilest animals and corpses" [1448b]), which Burke paraphrases as follows: "It is a common observation, that objects which in the reality would shock, are in tragical, and such like representations, the source of a very high species of pleasure" (E, 44). In contrast to Aristotle's cognitive approach to artistic representation, Burke rejects any explanation involving reason or reflection,[43] observing (like Dennis) that "the influence of reason in producing our passions is nothing near so extensive as it is commonly believed" (E, 45).[44] Instead, Burke sees sympathy as providing the explanation for how "poetry, painting, and other affecting arts, transfuse their passions from one breast to another, and are often capable of grafting a delight on wretchedness, misery, and death itself" (E, 44). The use of "delight" signals the complex pleasure of the sublime, which will now be considered from the perspective of sympathy (thus implying that it is not necessarily related to the instinct for self-preservation).

While much is made of Burke's debt to English thought, his anthropology of the passions and theory of representation is inspired in large measure by Jean-Baptist Dubos's seminal *Réflexions critiques sur la poésie et sur la peinture* (*Critical Reflections on Poetry and Painting*, 1719).[45] With regard to the idea of imitation-qua-representation in particular, Burke reveals important continuities with Dubos's aesthetic theory, which is based on the following principle: "The more our compassion would have been raised by such actions as are described by poetry and painting, had we really beheld them; the more in proportion the imitations attempted by those arts are capable of affecting us."[46] Although he will draw very different conclusions, Burke concurs with Dubos that (1) what affects us most strongly in reality also affects us most strongly in representation; (2) artistic imitation serves to weaken the effect of what it represents; and (3) the pleasure taken

---

[43] Burke alludes to Lucretius's *De rerum natura* (2.1–4, quoted in the previous chapter) when he speaks of "the contemplation of our own freedom from the evils which we see represented" (E, 44).

[44] For Aristotle, mimesis involves a cognitive process of recognition, a perception of likeness or correspondence, such as discerning that a portrait is that of a particular person.

[45] James Boulton does an excellent job of tracing this influence in the Introduction to his edition of Burke's *Enquiry*. More recently (2014), Guyer has argued for the importance of Dubos in eighteenth-century thought. See Guyer, *A History of Modern Aesthetics*, vol. I, 78–93.

[46] Dubos, *Critical Reflections*, 2.

in artworks that evoke suffering is due principally to the effect of (sublime) sympathy rather than to imitation.

With respect to the first point, Burke endeavors to separate the effects of mimetic form from mimetic content:

> When the object represented in poetry or painting is such, as we would have no desire of seeing it in the reality; then I may be sure that its power in poetry or painting is owing to the power of imitation, and to no cause operating in the thing itself. So it is with most of the pieces which the painters call still life. In these a cottage, a dunghill, the meanest and most ordinary utensils of the kitchen, are capable of giving us pleasure. But when the object of the painting or poem is such as we would run to see if real, let it affect us with what odd sort of sense it will, we may rely upon it, that the power of the poem or picture is more owing to the nature of the thing itself than to the mere effect of imitation, or to a consideration of the skill of the imitator however excellent. (E, 49)

Burke here makes the opposite case to Aristotle's *Poetics* 4, arguing that the transformative effect of mimesis is apparent only with respect to mundane objects (objects we find uninteresting in reality), rather than those that affect us powerfully (such as Aristotle's examples of corpses and wild animals). Burke thus opposes the "power of imitation," attributable to the *form*, to the "power of the artwork," which resides in the *content*, insofar as it is an index of a possible reality. According to Burke's schema, then, the sublimity of an artwork cannot be a function of the representation itself (qua artistic form or *technê*), but only of the subject represented (Burke's position would seem to recall Huet's idea of the "sublimity of things," in his debate with Boileau).[47]

Like Dubos, Burke appears to value mimetic art mainly for its ability to approximate reality. The ideal of mimetic art should be to remove, to the extent possible, the distance between the representation and the reality of which it presents itself as an image: "The nearer [tragedy] approaches the reality, and the further it removes all idea of fiction, the more perfect its power" (E, 47). This "power" would thus not be attributable to the artwork itself (an untenable position in today's critical thought, with its wide appreciation of the role of form in the effect of an artwork).

Burke evinces a much more extreme position than Dubos concerning our enjoyment of the real – and not merely represented – suffering of others: "But be its power of what kind it will, it [mimetic art] never

[47] See Chapter 4.

approaches what it represents" (E, 47). Thus Burke asks what would happen if, on the same day "the most sublime and affecting tragedy" was to be performed by the best theater company, it was announced that an execution of a famous criminal was about to take place in the adjoining square: "In a moment the emptiness of the theater would demonstrate the comparative weakness of the imitative arts, and proclaim the triumph of real sympathy" (E, 47).[48] Reality is preferred over art because its effects are comparably stronger (although these are still "indirect," via the distancing operation of sympathy). Burke thus rejects the commonplace of "pain in the reality, pleasure in the representation," a position attributed to Aristotle's *Poetics* 4, as well as the idea that the weakening effect of mimetic representation is a sufficient explanation for the pleasure taken in the suffering of others. Not content to observe, like Dubos, that real suffering would simply be more distracting or fascinating than represented suffering, Burke asserts: "I am convinced that we have a degree of delight, and no small one, in the real misfortunes and pains of others" (E, 45).[49] By using the term "delight" Burke is invoking the sublime (as indicated in Section XVIII, "The Recapitulation," quoted above [E, 51]); but here it is not a matter of sublimity of nature or art, but of a real *human event*, thereby introducing a third category of sublime object.

Burke's answer to the question of how a negative reality can generate a positive affect is thus not tied to the question of representation at all, as he appeared to assert at the beginning of Section XIII; for the structure of sympathy is identical, whether we are speaking of real or represented suffering. By "real" Burke means both historically real and actual perceptual reality: "Whether the misfortune is before our eyes, or whether they are turned back to it in history, it always touches with delight."[50] This delight in others' misfortune is sublime: "[It] is not an unmixed delight, but blended with no small uneasiness" (E, 46). In short, Burke uses the concept of sympathy to demonstrate how real pain and suffering can produce

---

[48] In the *Anthropology*, Kant repeats Burke's pronouncement after citing Lucretius (*De rerum natura* 2:1–4): "This is why people run with great desire, as to a theater play, to watch a criminal being taken to the gallows and executed" (APP, 7:238).

[49] But this does not thereby imply that we are thereby amoral or vicious: "We delight in seeing things, which so far from doing, our heartiest wishes would be to see redressed. This noble capital, the pride of England and of Europe, I believe no man is so strangely wicked as to desire to see destroyed by a conflagration or an earthquake, though he should be removed himself to the greatest distance from the danger. But suppose such a fatal accident to have happened, what numbers from all parts would crowd to behold the ruins, and amongst them many who would have been content never to have seen London in its glory!" (E, 47–8).

[50] "Such a catastrophe touches us in history as much as the destruction of Troy does in fable" (E, 45).

relative pleasure – a backdoor way of justifying the privileging of reality over representation as the more powerful and authentic source of sublimity. The distancing structure of sympathy also coheres with the earlier stipulation that in the sublime it is the mere "idea" rather than the thing itself that affects us.

While Burke's discussions of "imitation" in the sections on sympathy treat it solely in terms of representation, the section entitled "Imitation" (Section XVI) introduces the behavioral dimension. Paraphrasing Aristotle, Burke notes that "it is by imitation far more than by precept that we learn everything; and what we learn thus we acquire not only more effectually, but more pleasantly" (E, 49).[51] It is the behavioral meaning of imitation that informs the following section on "Ambition," which begins thus:

> Although imitation is one of the great instruments used by providence in bringing our nature towards its perfection, yet if men gave themselves up to imitation entirely, and each followed the other, and so on in an eternal circle, it is easy to see that there never could be any improvement amongst them. . . . To prevent this, God has planted in man a sense of ambition, and a satisfaction arising from the contemplation of his excelling his fellows in something deemed valuable amongst them. It is this passion that drives men to all the ways we see in use of signalizing themselves, and that tends to make whatever excites in a man the idea of this distinction so very pleasant. (E, 50)

The concept of "ambition" Burke articulates here is perhaps better described as "rivalry," particularly since it is induced by imitative behavior;[52] it is what prods the individual to seek greatness. As will become clear in the next section (below), Burke's uniformly positive view of "ambition" announces a heroic individualism and celebration of bourgeois mercantilism.[53]

Burke's anthropology is thus diametrically opposed to that of Jean-Jacques Rousseau, articulated just two years earlier in the *Discours sur l'origine et les fondements de l'inégalité parmi les hommes* (*Discourse on the Origin and Basis of Inequality among Men*, 1755), with its denunciation of "amour-propre" and the "civilization" it engenders: self-comparison with others, rivalry, hatred, and the struggle for power. Instead, Burke sees

---

[51] Cf. Aristotle, *Poetics* 4 (1448b): "For it is an instinct of human beings, from childhood, to engage in mimesis (indeed this distinguishes them from all other animals: man is the most mimetic of all, and it is through mimesis that he develops his earliest understanding); and equally natural that everyone enjoys mimetic objects."

[52] As in René Girard's notion of "mimetic rivalry." See Girard's, *Deceit, Desire, and the Novel: Self and Other in Literary Structure* and *Mimesis and Theory: Essays on Literature and Criticism, 1953–2005*.

[53] This probably also explains the choice of the word "ambition" rather than "rivalry": ambition is both a more positive term and one that is more conventionally linked to bourgeois-mercantile values.

ambition as linked to the positive feeling of sublimity as a (natural) desire
for self-transcendence – thereby connecting Burke's conception to the
agonistic aspect of the Longinian sublime (discussed in Chapters 2 and 3).
In the following passage at the end of the section on Ambition, the only
mention of Longinus in the 1757 text, Burke observes:

> Now whatever either on good or upon bad grounds tends to raise a man in
> his own opinion, produces a sort of swelling and triumph that is extremely
> grateful to the human mind; and this swelling is never more perceived, nor
> operates with more force, than when without danger we are conversant with
> terrible objects, the mind always claiming to itself some part of the dignity
> and importance of the things which it contemplates. Hence proceeds what
> Longinus has observed of that glorying and sense of inward greatness, that
> always fills the reader of such passages in poets and orators as are sublime; it
> is what every man must have felt in himself upon such occasions. (E, 46–7)

Burke here alludes to a well-known phrase from Longinus's treatise: "It is
our nature to be elevated and exalted by true sublimity. Filled with joy and
pride, we come to believe that we have created what we have only heard"
(7.2). The self-exaltation in the encounter with terrible nature is thus
presented as analogous, if not homologous, with the experience of sublimity in discourse. In Longinian fashion, Burke aligns terror with the
dignity and grandeur of the self, that is to say, the "swelling" is not mere
egotism but involves an ennoblement of the soul. The words "triumph,"
"glorying," "inward greatness" emphatically connect heroic values to the
sublimity of bourgeois ambition (upward mobility). One is *elevated* by
terror; that is, sublimity allows us to *appropriate* the strength and power of
that which inspires our fear. We are simultaneously overwhelmed and
exalted, dominated and elevated, by the contemplation of "terrible
objects" – the dual transcendence-structure of sublimity. In the next
section I examine how Burke articulates the socioeconomic implications
of this aesthetic experience of transcendence.

6.4   Burke's sociopolitics of sublimity: the bourgeois hero

According to his biographer, Isaac Kramnick, Burke offers "nothing less than a
pivotal insight into the great turning point in our history – the transformation
from the aristocratic to the bourgeois world."[54] And yet, continues Kramnick,
"at the center of Burke's life and thought is an unresolved ambivalence
between his identification with what might be called an aristocratic personality

---

[54] Kramnick, *The Rage of Edmund Burke*, xii.

on the one hand, and the bourgeois personality on the other."⁵⁵ This ambivalence is effectively figured in Burke's concept of sublimity, the modern interpretation of which, as I argue throughout this study, is associated with a bourgeois appropriation of aristocratic values (grandeur/nobility of mind, heroic subjectivity).

Emma Clery notes that this aspect had been highlighted in William Smith's popular edition of the treatise, which Burke most surely read:

> The relation of the sublime to the civic humanist critique of luxury could be traced back to Longinus's founding text. In the final section of *On the Sublime* the author attributes the "Corruption of Genius" in the present age to peace, avarice and voluptuousness: "Love of Money is the disease which renders us most abject, and love of pleasure is that which renders us most corrupt." William Smith's 1739 translation employs the standard vocabulary of condemnation: when the "corruption" spreads, "the faculties of the Soul . . . grow stupid" and men cease to "cultivate Virtue;" "Life in general . . . is thrown away in Indolence and Sloth [and] deadly Lethargy." This process, once properly underway, is unstoppable, the loss of sublime genius is irredeemable, and examples of the sublime can be admired only retrospectively: this is the message Smith understood in the preface to his edition. . . . It was this conviction that led critics to regard the literature of the sublime or of elevation as the trace of all that had been lost, as a result of the refinements of modernity.⁵⁶

This notion of sublimity-as-nostalgia will become acute later in the eighteenth century (in Kant's lament concerning the "spirit of commerce" in his third *Critique*) and will intensify in the nineteenth century. But already in Burke we find the idea (anticipated by Dennis's call for a "reformation," as we saw in the previous chapter) that the sublime can be used to critique the present state of society, thus adapting Longinus's analysis of cultural decline to a modern context.

Throughout his treatise Burke systematically opposes figures of inertia – rest, relaxation, inactivity, languor, indifference – to those of action: vigor, force, and in particular, *labor*, a term that conjures the idea of economic individualism. The aristocracy is coded as degenerate for its lack of energy and work ethic: "Who is a stranger to that manner of expression so common in all times and in all countries, of being softened, relaxed, enervated, dissolved, melted away by pleasure" (E, 147–8). Thus:

> Melancholy, dejection, despair, and often self-murder, is a consequence of the gloomy view we take of things in this relaxed state of body. The best

⁵⁵ Kramnick, *The Rage of Edmund Burke*, 10.
⁵⁶ Clery, "The Pleasure of Terror: Paradox in Edmund Burke's Theory of the Sublime," 173.

remedy for all these evils is exercise or *labour*; and labour is a surmounting of
difficulties, an exertion of the contracting power of the muscles; and as such
resembles pain. (E, 133, original emphasis)

The bourgeois is elevated by having his principal activity of labor associated
with a feeling of transcendence of pain through effort and ambition.[57]
Labor is connected to sublimity via the idea of difficulty: "Another source
of greatness is *Difficulty*. When any work seems to have required immense
force or labour to effect it, the idea is grand."[58] According to Clery, "more
important than references to labour, is the claim that Burke sees labour as
an act of mastery, an overcoming of difficulty that gives rise to a heroic
sense of self. The taste for the sublime would, in this sense, offer a moral
foundation for economic individualism."[59] Indeed, Burke's cultural critique is informed by a moral contrast based on the (Protestant) ethos of
hard work.[60]

In his *Edmund Burke's Aesthetic Ideology*, Tom Furniss traces a similar
perspective to that of Clery, but with important differences:

> The theoretical assumptions which shape Burke's aesthetics emerge out of a
> larger debate about the social and political consequences of the commercial
> revolution in the first half of the eighteenth century. [Reading Burke in such
> a context] allows me to claim that Burke's rigorous distinction between the
> sublime and the beautiful in terms of absolute differences between labour
> and repose, masculine and feminine, virtue and luxury, ambition and
> imitation, is driven by the need to refute traditionalist attacks on the
> "corruptions" of middle class commerce. In effect, Burke seeks to create
> an image of the upwardly mobile man of ability (the "self-made man") as an
> heroic and virtuous laborer whose sublime aspirations are quite different
> from the beautiful but debilitating luxury of the aristocracy (and of women).
> Burke can therefore be said to work out a "revolutionary" aesthetic designed
> to establish the authenticity and authority of the middle-class ethos.[61]

Put another way, Burke treats aesthetic concepts as proxies for sociopolitical categories, surreptitiously claiming for the bourgeoisie the (heroic)
values previously associated with the nobility.[62] But this appropriation is

---

[57] In the *Anthropology*, Kant echoes Burke's contentions: "Pain is the incentive [*eigennützig*] of
activity" (APP, 7:231); "as an incentive to activity, nature has put pain in the human being that he
cannot escape from" (APP, 7:235).
[58] Like Longinus, Burke here uses "greatness" and "grand" as synonyms of sublimity.
[59] Clery, "The Pleasure of Terror," 175.
[60] Burke was born in Ireland to a Protestant father and a Catholic mother.
[61] Furniss, *Edmund Burke's Aesthetic Ideology*, 2.
[62] We saw a hint of this already in Boileau's invocation of the sublimity of mind of the *honnête homme*,
the protobourgeois man of honor and refinement. See Chapter 4.

also transformation, namely from actuality to virtuality: the ancestors of the (now degenerate) aristocracy, the heroic warrior class, metamorphose into competitive merchants and shopkeepers; war is replaced by economic strife, real violence by imaginary terror. Burke's linkage of sublimity to "self-preservation" in a situation of safety is thus the paradoxical logic of a virtual heroism.

Clery and Furniss differ, however, on the question of Burke's specific attitude toward economic individualism. Whereas Furniss sees Burke as "driven by the need to refute traditionalist attacks on the 'corruptions' of middle class commerce," and interprets Burke's theory of sublimity as "a contribution to the hegemonic struggle of the rising middle class in the first half of the eighteenth century,"[63] Clery contends that Burke's interest in sublimity also reflects an antibourgeois attitude, namely in his awareness of the dangers of mercantilism: "The sublime operates in opposition to pleasure, as an antidote for the corrupting effects of a commercial society."[64] Clery thus argues that Burke's theory of sublimity is indicative of a certain skepticism toward economic individualism, rather than simply a celebration or defense of it. On this view, Burke should be seen as projecting heroic values on a middle class that lacks it, rather than as defending the ethos of economic individualism per se (as Furniss holds). As Clery writes:

> In a primitive warrior society, private interest was always subordinated to public ends, encouraging a spirit of liberty. But in a modern commercial society, the thoughts of the majority are never lifted beyond their daily round of business and pleasure, and they become slaves to necessity and vice.[65]

Burke would therefore be aware of a radical disjuncture between the bourgeois-mercantile mentality (orientated toward profit and gain) and the warrior state of mind (the overcoming of fear in the face of death): the values engendered by a commercial society precipitate the loss of civic responsibility and solidarity previously supported by the military spirit. Kant will, in fact, make a similar argument in his third *Critique*, asserting

---

[63] Furniss, *Edmund Burke's Aesthetic Ideology*, 1.   [64] Clery, "The Pleasure of Terror," 180.

[65] Clery, "The Pleasure of Terror," 178. Clery also adduces a historical rationale for Burke's socio-political understanding of the sublime, noting that in the 1750s there was widespread anxiety with respect to the strength of Britain's military forces and the willingness of its citizens to face foreign threats (highlanders from the north and Jacobites from France). The Militia Act was passed in 1757, the same year as Burke's *Enquiry*. Seen from this perspective, Burke's warnings against the dangers of lethargy and overindulgence in luxury are not simply a critique of an outmoded aristocracy but also a warning to a complacent bourgeoisie.

that the "spirit of mere commerce . . . debases the mentality of a populace" (CPJ, 5:263).[66] Thus both Burke and Kant evince, through the aesthetics of sublimity, a certain skepticism toward the viability of translating the heroic disposition into a bourgeois context.

The divergence between Furniss and Clery can perhaps be attributed to what Kramnick calls Burke's "unresolved ambivalence" toward the aristocratic and bourgeois personalities. This tension is, however, emblematic of a more general modern ambivalence toward the decline of the aristocracy and the rise of the bourgeoisie, which, in a post–French Revolutionary context, will resolve itself into a patently antibourgeois stance, such as one finds in French novelists of the nineteenth century (Stendhal, Balzac, Flaubert), where in the form of nostalgia sublimity reveals itself as an implicit critique of the vanity, egotism, and ennui of contemporary society.[67]

6.5   Terror, power, and religion

Outside the "Introduction on Taste," by far the most lengthy and important and addition to the 1759 version of the *Enquiry* is the section entitled "Power" (Part II, Section V), a section that greatly influenced Kant's discussion of the Dynamically Sublime (the sublimity of nature considered as a power). It is the only section that discusses religion in any sustained manner, a subject Burke was reluctant to address in the first edition: "I purposely avoided when I first considered this subject, to introduce the idea of a great and tremendous being [God], as an example in an argument so light as this; though it frequently occurred to me, not as an objection to, but as a strong confirmation of my notions in this matter" (E, 67).[68] But one can also offer a more immediate explanation for why Burke neglected this topic: given that he saw the sublime as a way of "aestheticizing" (secularizing) the concept of transcendence, he needed to avoid an overtly theological perspective, such as Dennis had pursued, even if Dennis's references to "Religious Ideas" and the "Vengeance of an angry God" were all treated in the context of nonscriptural poetic expression, thus through human artifice. It is much more difficult to maintain a

---

[66] See my discussion in Chapter 11.
[67] See my forthcoming book (in progress): *Revolutionary Aesthetics: The Sublime in Nineteenth-Century France.*
[68] Indeed, Paddy Bullard, in a recent article (2012), goes so far as to suggest that "the power that interests Burke is ultimately a divine power. It is manifested in the natural magnificence of the created world, in the direct revelation of Bible and church, and in the providential disposition of the human body toward religious awe and astonishment" ("Burke's Aesthetic Psychology," 60).

secular-empirical perspective when speaking about sublimity in natural objects, given the idea of nature as made by God and thus in some sense a manifestation or reflection of the divine.

Burke has no difficulty discussing Satan, for example, in the first edition, since this theological figure is mediated by Milton's poetry: "We do not any where meet a more sublime description than this justly celebrated one of Milton, wherein he gives the portrait of Satan with a dignity so suitable to the subject" (E, 62).[69] Burke's analysis of the passage does not concern the figure of Satan itself, but the manner of its representation:

> Here is a very noble picture; and in what does this poetical picture consist? in images of a tower, an archangel, the sun rising through mists, or in an eclipse, the ruin of monarchs, and the revolutions of kingdoms. The mind is hurried out of itself, by a crowd of great and confused images; which affect because they are crowded and confused. (E, 62)

Although in this passage Burke would appear to contradict his devalorization of form in his discussion of mimesis (analyzed above), Burke is speaking precisely about how poetry can affect us in ways *other than* by mimesis (particularly given its cognitive interpretation in Aristotle). By asserting that sublime poetry affects by the *obscurity* of the images it conjures ("there are reasons in nature why the obscure idea, when properly conveyed, should be more affecting than the clear" [E, 61]; "images raised by poetry are always of this obscure kind" [E, 62]), Burke offers a competing view to Dubos's claim that poetry and painting affect us through their *clarity* (hence the affective superiority of painting in Dubos's schema).[70] For Burke, it is the *confusion* of images – which is more easily attained in poetry than painting – that produces the effect of sublimity. Thus poetic representation does not achieve sublimity through mimesis, but through an *intrinsic affective power*, which Burke elucidates in Part 5 of his *Enquiry*, where he observes that "as to words; they seem to me to affect us in a

---

[69] "He above the rest
   In shape and gesture proudly eminent
   Stood like a Towr; his form had yet not lost
   All her Original brightness, nor appear'd
   Less then Arch Angel ruind, and th' excess
   Of Glory obscur'd: As when the Sun new ris'n
   Looks through the Horizontal misty Air
   Shorn of his Beams, or from behind the Moon
   In dim Eclips disastrous twilight sheds
   On half the Nations, and with fear of change
   Perplexes Monarchs."   (*Paradise Lost*, I, 589–99)

[70] "A clear idea is therefore another name for a little idea" (E, 63).

manner very different from that in which we are affected by natural objects, or by painting or architecture" (E, 161).[71]

With respect to the experience of nature, Burke ultimately finds that religion can indeed be invoked in regards to the experience of sublimity in nature, that a balance or fusion is possible between a Christian attitude and a secular-scientific, aesthetic-empirical perspective. Reacting to a critic, who observed regarding the first edition of Burke's *Enquiry* that "it is certain, we can have the most sublime ideas of the Deity, without imagining him a God of terror,"[72] Burke, in the 1759 edition, endeavors to show how the notion of the sublimity of God can be integrated into his notion of sublimity-as-terror, without falling into an anti-Christian stance. It is not surprising that Burke chooses to respond at length, since, in effect, his critic is attempting to discredit Burke's entire theory by suggesting that if God can be seen as arousing the feeling of sublimity without this feeling thereby being connected to terror, then terror is not the sine qua non of the sublime. I thus quote Burke's response *in extenso*:

> I say then, that whilst we consider the Godhead merely as he is an object of the understanding, which forms a complex idea of power, wisdom, justice, goodness, all stretched to a degree far exceeding the bounds of our comprehension, whilst we consider the divinity in this refined and abstracted light, the imagination and passions are little or nothing affected. But because we are bound, by the condition of our nature, to ascend to these pure and intellectual ideas, through the medium of sensible images, and to judge of these divine qualities by their evident acts and exertions, it becomes extremely hard to disentangle our idea of the cause from the effect by which we are led to know it. Thus, when we contemplate the Deity, his attributes and their operation, coming united on the mind, form a sort of sensible image, and as such are capable of affecting the imagination. Now, though in a just idea of the Deity, perhaps none of his attributes are predominant, yet, to our imagination, his power is by far the most striking. Some reflection, some comparing, is necessary to satisfy us of his wisdom, his justice, and his goodness. To be struck with his power, it is only necessary that we should open our eyes. But whilst we contemplate so vast an object, under the arm, as it were, of almighty power, and invested upon every side with omnipresence, we shrink into the minuteness of our own nature, and are, in a

---

[71] Guyer notes that "Burke's position that the aim of art is emotional arousal, not cognition, and that this can be achieved directly through the associations of images or words rather than indirectly through accurate representation or description, would be of immense influence on the practice of art – one might take this to be the underlying premise of Romanticism in poetry and elsewhere – even if it did not have the same impact on aesthetic theory" (*A Modern History of Aesthetics*, vol. 1, 157). On the word/ image question, see Paul Duro's 2013 essay "Observations on the Burkean Sublime."

[72] *Monthly Review*, XVI, 475 n., quoted in E, 67, n. 17.

manner, annihilated before him. And though a consideration of his other attributes may relieve, in some measure, our apprehensions; yet no conviction of the justice with which it is exercised, nor the mercy with which it is tempered, can wholly remove the terror that naturally arises from a force which nothing can withstand. If we rejoice, we rejoice with trembling; and even whilst we are receiving benefits, we cannot but shudder at a power which can confer benefits of such mighty importance. (E, 68)[73]

Burke endeavors to argue that the *aesthetic* idea of God's power (as a "sort of sensible image") and the terror it thereby raises is both more *immediate* (because "some reflection, some comparing, is necessary to satisfy us of his wisdom, his justice, and his goodness") and *inextricable* (for nothing "can wholly remove the terror") than the positive or beneficial attributes of the Deity. Responding to his critic, Burke is forced to emphasize the overwhelming-dominating aspect of the dual transcendence-structure of sublimity ("annihilated before him," "a force which nothing can withstand") and correspondingly deemphasize the elevating-exalting aspect (even if it is nonetheless implied in the phrase "rejoice with trembling").[74] But Burke also draws a distinction (as does Kant, in his analysis of the Dynamically Sublime) between archaic religion and Christianity with regard to terror: "True religion has, and must have, [a] large mixture of salutary fear … false religions have generally nothing else but fear to support them. Before the Christian religion had, as it were, humanized the idea of the Divinity, and brought it somewhat nearer to us, there was very little said of the love of God" (E, 70). Primitive religion is based on simple terror and awe, and thus on simple pain, which, according to Burke's empirical psychology, cannot conduce to sublimity. With the advent of Christianity a concept of sublime terror – that is, *mixed* terror – emerges: the Christian is both "god fearing" (overwhelmed) and *elevated* by the contemplation of a benevolent Deity. Burke is content to conclude that it would be "endless to enumerate all the passages, both in the sacred and profane writers, which establish the general sentiment of mankind, concerning the inseparable union of a sacred and reverential awe, with our ideas of the divinity" (E, 69). In the union of "sacred and profane writers,"

---

[73] This passage was also no doubt inspired by a similar discussion in Baillie's *An Essay on the Sublime*: "And we cannot conceive a deity armed with thunder without being struck with a sublime terror; but if we regard him as the infinite source of happiness, the benign dispenser of benefits, it is not then the dreadful, but the joyous sublime we feel" (http://www.earthworks.org/sublime/Baillie/index.html, accessed October 11, 2014).

[74] Thus one could ask, with Weiskel, to what extent does the "novelty of Burke's theory lie in its determined exclusiveness," that is, its endeavor "to reduce the occasions of the sublime to the motive of terror" (*The Romantic Sublime*, 87).

Burke ultimately continues Dennis's drive to consider the sublimity of "Religious Ideas" as structuring our experience more generally, and not merely in a properly religious context.

Indeed, the analogy between religion and politics with regard to "reverential awe" was too tempting for Burke the political theorist to resist:

> The power which arises from institution in kings and commanders, has the same connection with terror. Sovereigns are frequently addressed with the title of dread majesty. And it may be observed, that young persons, little acquainted with the world, and who have not been used to approach men in power, are commonly struck with an awe which takes away the free use of their faculties. (E, 67)

Simple terror or awe in the face of political authority suggests the attitude associated with the monarchical system of government, particularly one organized according to the idea of the "absolute" nature of royal power, in which reverence for the king is equivalent to reverence for God. The doctrine of "divine-right of kingship" was in fact developed just prior to the time when the sublime emerges as a critical concept. Of course, like the sublime, the idea of "divine right" is in fact a *secularizing* concept, for it effectively replaces papal and clerical power with the idea of national-political sovereignty.[75]

Finally, according to the distinction Burke makes between true and false religion, he might be taken as implying that, following the lead of an enlightened religion such as Christianity, a modern (democratic) political system would be based on the mixed terror of sublimity: that is, not on a terror that is merely subjugating ("awe which takes away the *free* use of their faculties"), but on the combination of reverential awe and a sense of elevation (the dual transcendence-structure of sublimity).

* * *

In this chapter I have explored the multifaceted nature of Burke's theory of sublimity, with a view toward enlarging our perspective on the *Enquiry* and placing it within a historical continuum. I have emphasized how Burke's theory draws on the literary and art criticism of Dennis and Dubos, two figures who are often neglected in the effort to situate Burke's approach

---

[75] This confluence of politics and religion that Burke observes in the notion of the sublime has had a lasting influence, as indicated by the following dictionary entry for "awe," found in Merriam-Webster: "An emotion variously combining dread, veneration, and wonder that is inspired by authority or by the sacred or sublime" (http://www.merriam-webster.com/dictionary/awe, accessed August 8, 2013).

within the British empiricist tradition of Locke, Addison, Shaftsbury, and Hutcheson. In this manner, I have thus sought to expose a fundamental tension in Burke's thought: that between its "scientific" attitude – its empirical and sensationalist bent – and its literary-theoretical and cultural-critical pretensions. Hence the difficulty in squaring the empirical presentation of complex pleasure (as the "removal" of actual pain) with the properly aesthetic definition of complex pleasure in sublimity ("ideas" of pain, the virtual); or in fusing a physiological analysis privileging labor over languor with a sociopolitical account of the bourgeois-individualist appropriation of the aristocratic mindset in the sublime; or in assimilating an anthropological view of religion to a Christian-centric interpretation based on sublime authority. Nevertheless, it is by means of this tension between the scientific and the cultural that Burke's *Enquiry* defines a secular concept of transcendence based on sublime terror.

PART III

The sublimity of the mind: Kant

We express ourselves on the whole incorrectly if we call some object of nature sublime. . . . We can say no more than that the object serves for the presentation of a sublimity that can be found in the mind.[1]

– Immanuel Kant

[1] Kant, CPJ, 5:245.

CHAPTER 7

The Kantian sublime in 1764: Observations on the Feeling of the Beautiful and the Sublime

While Kant's conception of sublimity is often reduced to the few sections devoted to it in his 1790 opus *Critique of the Power of Judgment*, Kant's thinking on this topic is actually quite varied and spans virtually his entire career: from his early essay *Bemerkungen zu den Beobachtungen über das Gefühl des Schönen und Erhabenen* (*Observations on the Feeling of the Beautiful and Sublime*, 1764) to his moral theory as expressed in the *Kritik der praktischen Vernunft* (*Critique of Practical Reason*, 1788), which often employs the language of sublimity, and, in between, his *Anthropologie in pragmatischer Hinsicht* (*Anthropology from a Pragmatic Point of View*, 1798/1800), which represents more than two decades of lectures on topics relating to taste, the imagination, and the emotions.[1] Given Kant's lifelong engagement with matters aesthetic in a career characterized by intellectual shifts – conventionally divided into pre-Critical, Critical, and post-Critical phases – it is impossible to offer a comprehensive account of Kant's theory of the sublime based solely on an analysis of the third *Critique*. Part III will thus consider a wide swath of Kant's writings to better perceive the fundamental and enduring influence of the sublime on the Kantian corpus as well as to better situate Kant's conception with respect to his predecessors and successors.

We begin with a consideration of Kant's *Observations on the Feeling of the Beautiful and Sublime.* Although some scholars dismiss this relatively early work (Kant was forty) as a slight effort that merely expresses "the prejudices of an era,"[2] the *Observations* nevertheless offers fascinating

---

[1] Kant's *Anthropology* presents the contents of his lecture courses from 1772 to 1796, and, with the exception of the third *Critique*, is Kant's most elaborate presentation of his ideas relating to aesthetics, broadly conceived. Although the book can be profitably used to elucidate Kant's other more organically conceived works, it is not a mere assemblage of assorted reflections but develops its own perspective, namely the relentless pursuit of the question "What is man?" – a question Kant did not think was truly answerable.

[2] Manfred Kuehn, *Kant: A Biography*, 142.

insights into Kant's early interest in aesthetics, art, and sublimity,[3] and many of its formulations take on a new meaning when considered in light of Kant's mature thought.[4] This chapter thus dissents in part from Paul Guyer's assessment that "the interest of this work thus lies not in what it reveals of Kant's eventual aesthetic theory, which is very little, but in what it displays of his emerging moral theory, which is significant."[5] As I will endeavor to show, important continuities with Kant's later aesthetic theory do in fact emerge from the text when one considers, for example, the section of the third *Critique* on mental states or the lectures on anthropology.[6]

The first section of this chapter aims to show that the fusion of the moral and the aesthetic in the *Observations* represents a blend of British and French influences, but also an effort to grapple with the epistemology inherited from Kant's German predecessors. The second section explores how the *Observations* anticipates key tenets of Kant's theory of sublimity in the third *Critique*: specifically, the cardinal idea of mixed pleasure and the distinction between the Mathematically and the Dynamically Sublime. The third section studies how Kant's treatment of sublimity in literary texts highlights the idea of aesthetic high-mindedness (nobility of mind), thus connecting Kant's *Observations* with both Longinus's treatise and Kant's mature aesthetic theory (in particular, the Dynamically Sublime). Throughout this chapter, I insist on Kant's fusion of moral and aesthetic transcendence in the sublime as possessing a special meaning vis-à-vis his concept of human dignity.

7.1   The origins of the *Observations*

One must be prudent when approaching the topic of aesthetics in Kant, particularly in the early Kant, since, as we noted in the Introduction, the

---

[3] Indeed, this elegantly written book, considered by some to be "an early masterpiece of modern German style" (Susan Shell, "Kant as Propagator: Reflections on *Observations on the Feeling of the Beautiful and Sublime*," 465), belies Kant's reputation as an awkward and abstruse writer. The *Observations* was one of Kant's most popular publications during his lifetime, going through some seven editions.

[4] Henry Allison asserts that "this work [the *Observations*] is not an aberration, since a continuous concern with questions of taste or matters aesthetic can be traced through the surviving transcripts of his lectures, particularly the recently published lectures on anthropology, as well as the associated *Reflexionen*. And throughout these discussions Kant, like many of his contemporaries, emphasized the social nature of taste, its inherent claim to universality" (*Kant's Theory of Taste*, 2).

[5] Paul Guyer, Translator's Introduction, *Anthropology, History, and Education*, 19. However, Melissa Merritt remarks that "some commentators have tended to exaggerate the extent to which Kant draws a connection between the sublime and morality in the precritical *Observations*" ("The Moral Source of the Kantian Sublime," 49 n.). I think, however, that it would be difficult to argue that the sublime is divorced from morality in this work.

[6] See in particular Chapter 12.

concept is often used anachronistically.[7] Indeed, in pre-Kantian German thought the term "aesthetics" denoted the science of "sensibility" more generally, that is, without necessarily referring to the appreciation of nature or art, and as such was not separable from questions of cognition or morality. Alexander Baumgarten, who, as earlier noted, coined the term "aesthetics" (*ästhetisch* in German), laid the groundwork for aesthetic reflection within philosophy in his Latin treatises *Metaphysica* (1739) and *Aesthetica* (1750). According to Lewis White Beck's seminal *Early German Philosophy*, Baumgarten is the first thinker "to handle the subject matter of art with the apparatus of an established system that professed to have a place for everything, and to reason syllogistically with the recalcitrant matter of art without distorting it beyond recognition."[8] Along with his student, Georg Friedrich Meier,[9] Baumgarten advocated a cognitive approach to aesthetic feeling, a systematic "science of taste" that also served as a kind of philosophy of art (specifically of poetry).

Despite the importance of the Baumgartean model for the early development of German aesthetic thought – Kant regularly taught Baumgartean in his classes – it was quickly superseded in the mid eighteenth century by foreign imports. The growing German interest in the topics of taste, genius, beauty, sublimity, and fine art was largely stimulated by British and, to some extent, French sources, with their emphasis on empirical psychology and sensationalism.[10] Critical works by Shaftesbury, Francis Hutcheson, and Henry Home, Lord Kames were translated into German in the 1760s and were widely read. Although Burke's *A Philosophical Enquiry into the Origin of Our Ideas of the Sublime and Beautiful* (1757) was not available in German until Christian Garve's translation of 1773, Moses Mendelssohn's 1758 review of the work and his extensive discussion of it in his *Über die Mischung der Schönheiten* (*On the Mixture of Beauties*, 1758)[11] and his *Über das Erhabene und Naive in den*

---

[7] Kuehn observes that "aesthetics [in eighteenth-century Germany] was still not a very well-defined discipline, and it was a different enterprise from what we understand it to be today" (*Kant*, 345).

[8] Lewis White Beck, *Early German Philosophy: Kant and His Predecessors*, 284.

[9] Meier's *Betrachtungen über den ersten Grundsatz aller schönen Künste und Wissenschaften* (1757) mentions Longinus as well as Boileau and Dominique Bouhours.

[10] The works of the French school include Jean-Baptiste Dubos's *Réflexions critiques sur la poésie et sur la peinture* (1719), which we discussed in Chapter 6, and Charles Batteux's 1746 monograph *Les beaux arts réduits à un même principe* (*The Fine Arts Reduced to a Single Principle*), which is often credited with the coining of the term "fine art."

[11] Mendelssohn had been introduced to Burke's treatise by Lessing, just months after its initial publication. See Herman Parret's historical reconstruction in his article "From the *Enquiry* (1757) to the Fourth *Kritisches Wäldchen* (1769): Burke and Herder on the Division of the Senses."

schönen Wissenschaften (*On the Sublime and the Naïve in the Fine Sciences*, 1758)[12] acquainted his contemporaries with the basic tenets of Burke's aesthetic thought.[13] Mendelssohn's ability to translate the ideas of Burke and other English and French thinkers into a German philosophical idiom had a great impact on Kant, who could not read English.

Interestingly, Mendelssohn's *On the Sublime and the Naïve in the Fine Sciences* is concerned more with Longinus's theory than with Burke's – thus we should not discount Longinus's influence on Kant. Longinus's treatise was available in a Greek/German edition as early as 1737 (when Kant was thirteen years old), with a second edition in 1742.[14] Beck notes that "[Mendelssohn] had in fact formulated his theory of the sublime before he had read Burke."[15] Thus, the Longinian influence was primary. Nevertheless, Mendelssohn draws particular attention to Burke's articulation of "mixed sentiments": "When I wrote the 'Letters on Sentiments' I had, to be sure, a flimsy concept of the nature of mixed sentiments. But I only saw a flickering of the astonishing and myriad effects of them until I had the opportunity to read the splendid English work on the sublime and the beautiful for the *Library of Fine Sciences*."[16] Despite his enthusiasm, Mendelssohn complains that Burke was insufficiently schooled in German philosophy to successfully undertake his enterprise: "Whenever it comes down to explaining these observations on the basis of the nature of the soul, [Burke's] shortcomings become apparent. One sees that he was unacquainted with the psychology developed by German philosophers."[17]

The first fruit of this partly first-hand (through translations) and partly second-hand (through Mendelssohn) encounter with British aesthetic thought in Kant's published oeuvre was the *Observations on the Feeling of the Beautiful and Sublime*. To the modern reader of Kant, particularly to

[12] Originally published anonymously. An English translation of this essay can be found in Moses Mendelssohn, *Philosophical Writings*.
[13] It should be noted that these publications appeared before Burke's second edition in 1759, that is, before the crucial section on "Power" and the "Introduction on Taste" were added.
[14] Karl Heinrich Heinecken, *Dionysius Longin vom Erhabenen: Griechisch und Teutsch; Nebst dessen Leben, einer Nachricht von seinen Schriften und einer Untersuchung, was Longin durch das Erhabene verstehte* (Dresden, 1737/1742). Mendelssohn suggests that *Peri hypsous* was widely read in Germany at the time, noting that "[Longinus's] essays are in everybody's hands" (*Philosophical Writings*, 217). It is unclear why Mendelssohn refers to "essays" in the plural, since none of (Cassius) Longinus's (other) works are extant, unless he is thinking of the fragment *On the Chief End*, found in Porphyry's *Life of Plotinus*.
[15] Beck, *Early German Philosophy*, 326.
[16] Moses Mendelssohn, "Rhapsody or Additions to the Letters on Sentiments," in Mendelssohn, *Philosophical Writings*, 146.
[17] Mendelssohn, *Philosophical Writings*, 146.

one coming from the perspective of the third *Critique*, the treatment of the beautiful and the sublime as moral sentiments in the *Observations* appears strangely un-Kantian. Even among Kant scholars, there are conflicting views on how to situate the 1764 work. Some see the British influence (Shaftesbury, Hutcheson, Hume) as paramount.[18] Beck, on the other hand, emphasizes Kant's fusion of the moral and the aesthetic as a remnant of Christian Wolff's "one-faculty theory" of the mind (will and feeling as two aspects of a single faculty of representation),[19] an epistemology that would be fully overcome only with the advent of the Critical Philosophy.[20] Thus in the First Introduction (10: 206) to the third *Critique*, Kant will observe (without acknowledging his own prior complicity with such a view): "To be sure, philosophers who otherwise deserve nothing but praise for the thoroughness of their way of thinking have sought to explain this distinction [between the three faculties of cognition, of the feeling of pleasure and displeasure, and of desire] as merely illusory and to reduce all faculties to the mere faculty of cognition."[21] Kant's project in this late work will be precisely to separate the aesthetic from the cognitive and the ethical.[22]

We should also note the influence of Rousseau's *Emile, ou De l'éducation*, published in 1762, just two years prior to the *Observations*. Although Rousseau's profound impact on Kant's moral theory would become public only two decades later, we have direct evidence, in some fragments associated with the composition of the *Observations*, of Kant's

[18] "This brief and stylistically elegant work stems from a period in which Kant still thought, in agreement with the British moral sense tradition, that morality was based on feeling, and in which he, like many of his contemporaries, insisted on an intimate linkage between moral feeling and the aesthetic feelings of the sublime and the beautiful" (Allison, *Kant's Theory of Taste*, 1). P. A. Schillpp, on the other hand, contends (in his 1938 monograph *Kant's Pre-Critical Ethics*) that "nowhere in all these references to the 'moral feeling' or 'feeling for morality' ... does there seem to be any reason for assuming that Kant meant by the term a definitely independent 'sense' or separate 'instinct' such as the British moralists had in mind" (quoted in Paul Crowther, *The Kantian Sublime: From Morality to Art*, 12–13).
[19] Kant called Christian Wolff "the greatest of all dogmatic philosophers," in the Preface to the revised version of his first *Critique*. Beck remarks that "[Wolff] was the first philosopher to give the Germans a complete system of philosophy in their own language" (*Early German Philosophy*, 274).
[20] "Even when aesthetic experience was differentiated from the cognitive, however, its connection with the volitional remained relatively undisturbed. Thus the break with [Wolff's one-faculty theory] was not complete.... Art disciplines feeling, but, because of the relation between feeling and will, art falls under moral judgment (Beck, *Early German Philosophy*, 288).
[21] Beck writes that "the emancipation from [Wolff's one-faculty theory] required also the work of Mendelssohn and Johan Heinrich Tetens before it was finally accomplished by Kant" (*Early German Philosophy*, 288).
[22] See Chapter 9.

enthusiastic reaction to the French thinker,[23] in particular concerning Rousseau's vision of humanity: "There was a time when I believed that [learning and knowledge] constituted the honor of humanity, and I despised the people, who know nothing. Rousseau corrected me in this. This blinding prejudice disappeared. I learned to honor man."[24] The *Observations* documents this newfound respect for human dignity, and it is the category of sublimity that Kant sees as most clearly and effectively expressing man's moral and spiritual grandeur. For underlying the *Observations*, as one critic notes, is the notion that "man's dignity is the ground of the judgment that man himself is sublime."[25] This idea of the sublimity of the self – the sublimity of the mind – will prove to be crucial for Kant's *Critique of Practical Reason*, as well as for the Analytic of the Sublime in the *Critique of the Power of Judgment*.

7.2   Kant's *Observations* and Burke's *Enquiry*

Kant's *Observations* is divided into four sections: (1) "On the Distinct Objects of the Feeling for the Sublime and the Beautiful"; (2) "On the Qualities of the Sublime and the Beautiful in Human Beings in General"; (3) "On the Difference between the Sublime and the Beautiful in the Contrast between the Two Sexes"; and (4) "On National Characters insofar as They Rest upon the Different Feeling of the Sublime and the Beautiful." Only the first two sections are of interest for this study.[26]

Despite the obvious similarity in titles, there is some controversy regarding the extent to which Kant's *Observations on the Feeling of the Beautiful and the Sublime* is directly influenced by Burke's *A Philosophical Enquiry into the Origin of Our Ideas of the Sublime and Beautiful*, or whether Kant and Burke had simply drawn on common sources.[27] However, it is unlikely that Kant, known chiefly at the time for his writings on scientific subjects,

---

[23] Kant was so taken with the work that he famously missed one of his walks devouring it.
[24] Quoted in Beck, *Early German Philosophy*, 489. Beck notes that the quotation comes from "the collection of unnumbered fragments concerning the *Observations on the Feeling of the Beautiful and the Sublime*" (*Early German Philosophy*, 489).
[25] Jonathan Goldthwait, Introduction to *Observations on the Feeling of the Beautiful and the Sublime*, 25.
[26] The last two sections contain many repugnant remarks about race, gender, and national character.
[27] Paul Crowther argues that "the piecemeal affinities between Kant's and Burke's texts are probably due to common source material" (*The Kantian Sublime*, 12). On the other hand, John Boulton, in the Introduction to his edition of Burke's *Enquiry*, writes that "certain isolated observations and phrases point unmistakably to Burke's influence" (E, cxxvi).

would have composed a book comparing the beautiful and the sublime (for which no model existed in German), without Burke's example. The use of the term "observation" in Kant's title indicates that this will not be a properly philosophical or scientific "inquiry," as with Burke. Kant remarks that he approaches the topic "more with the eye of an observer than of the philosopher" (O, 2:207).[28] And whereas Burke treats our "ideas" of the sublime and the beautiful, Kant's title highlights the term "feeling" (*Gefühl*).[29] As the first line of the *Observations* reads: "The different sentiments of gratification or vexation rest not so much on the constitution of the external things that arouse them as on the feeling, intrinsic to every person, of being touched by them with pleasure or displeasure" (O, 2:207). Here Kant anticipates somewhat his subjectivist theory of aesthetics, separating the judgment of objective qualities (that is, by concepts) from judgment by an immediate feeling. In practice, however, Kant does not follow this intuition, since he proceeds by correlating subjective effects with specific objective features such as magnitude, simplicity, and so on.

Unlike Kant's later writings, the beautiful and the sublime are not truly opposed in the *Observations*; they are merely differentiated.[30] That is, Kant can conceive of combinations of beauty and sublimity, whereas in the third *Critique* they are, for the most part, mutually exclusive judgments. (I say "for the most part" since the idea of sublimity in fine art – sublimity-within-beauty – will be an important exception.)[31] Kant emphasizes at the outset that the beautiful and the sublime are both examples of "finer feeling" (O, 2:208), a distinction that in the third *Critique* will be thought according to the difference between the merely agreeable and the properly aesthetic judgments of the beautiful and the sublime.[32] Such "finer" sentiments require cultivation: "Of whichever sort these finer feelings that we have thus far treated might be, whether sublime or

---

[28] It may also be a reference to Rousseau's *Emile*, which "famously announces itself to be a mere collection of 'disordered' and 'almost incoherent' 'observations'" (Susan Shell, "Kant as Propagator," 456).

[29] "Kant uses the term 'feeling' to pick out particular instances of pleasure and displeasure; he subsequently – and much more frequently – uses it to denote the subjective disposition which enables us to find things pleasurable or displeasurable" (Crowther, *The Kantian Sublime*, 9).

[30] Susan Shell comments that in the *Observations* "beauty and sublimity thus represent two interrelated principles of life, one pointing toward a kind, natural harmony, the other toward spiritual uplift" ("Kant as Propagator," 457).

[31] See Chapter 12.

[32] From the third *Critique*: "The agreeable, the beautiful, and the good therefore designate three different relations of representations to the feeling of pleasure and displeasure. . . . Agreeableness is also valid for nonrational animals; beauty is valid only for human beings" (CPJ, 5:209–10).

beautiful, they have in common the fate of always seeming perverse and absurd in the judgment of those who have no feeling attuned to them" (O, 2:224).[33] This anticipates Kant's insistence, in the third *Critique* (§29), that the feeling of the sublime in particular requires a high degree of culture.[34]

Kant initially distinguishes the beautiful from the sublime as follows:

> The sight of a mountain whose snow-covered peaks arise above the clouds, the description of a raging storm, or the depiction of the kingdom of hell by *Milton*, arouses satisfaction, but with dread [or horror, *Grausen*]; by contrast, the prospect of meadows strewn with flowers, of valleys with winding brooks, covered with grazing herds, the description of Elysium, or *Homer's* description of the girdle of Venus also occasion an agreeable sentiment, but one that is joyful and smiling. For the former to make its impression on us in its proper strength, we must have a *feeling* of the *sublime*, and in order to properly enjoy the later we must have a *feeling* for the *beautiful*. (O, 2:208, original emphasis)

Kant makes several key points in this passage, of which we find echoes in his mature theory of sublimity. Like Burke, he stipulates that the sublime is a complex feeling (conjoining "enjoyment" with "dread," that is, pleasure mixed with pain), as opposed to the simple feeling of the beautiful ("joyful" and "smiling").[35] Milton is assigned a privileged place as an exemplar of the sublime, suggesting that Kant, like Dennis and Burke before him, sees *Paradise Lost* as the archetypal sublime poem.[36] One can also perceive in the juxtaposition of a tall mountain (a magnitude) and a "raging storm" (a power) the outlines of a distinction that will play a major role in the third *Critique*, that between the Mathematically and the Dynamically Sublime. In fact, some paragraphs later, Kant will explicitly anticipate his treatment of the Mathematically Sublime by observing that "the mathematical representation of the immeasurable magnitude of the universe, metaphysical considerations of eternity, of providence, of the immortality of our soul contain a certain sublimity and dignity" (O, 2:215). Where the third

[33] Burke asserts in the "Introduction on Taste" appended to the second edition (1759) of the *Enquiry* that the "vulgar" (those oriented toward sense pleasure or ego satisfaction) are insensitive to the "delicate and refined play of the imagination" (E, 23).
[34] See Chapter 12.
[35] Kant also notes that "the sublime *touches*, the beautiful *charms*" (O, 2:209, original emphasis), a comparison he will repeat almost verbatim in the third *Critique* (5:245).
[36] *Paradise Lost* was first translated into German in 1732 by Johann Jacob Bodmer. Sanford Budick observes that "in the *Observations* Kant's Miltonic references are of an uncommon order both of specificity and of generalizing power" (*Kant and Milton*, 28). See also Annemarie Lina Voss, "John Milton's *Paradise Lost* in Germany: Reception and German-language criticism" (Ph.D. thesis, Ball State University, 1991).

Critique will diverge is with regard to the Burkean parallelism between sublimity in nature and in literature that Kant here affirms: "The *sight* of a mountain" and the "*depiction* of the kingdom of hell by Milton" are equally sublime.[37] Kant also uses Milton to make a point about the intensity of the sublime: "The sentiments of the sublime stretch the powers of the soul more forcefully and therefore tire more quickly. One will read a pastoral longer at one sitting than Milton's *Paradise Lost*" (O, 2:212, note b).

Kant distinguishes three types of sublimity: (1) the terrifying (mixed with dread, melancholy, or loneliness); (2) the noble (quiet admiration); and (3) the magnificent (mixed with beauty). "The feeling of [the sublime] is sometimes accompanied with some dread or even melancholy, in some cases merely with quite admiration, and in yet others with a beauty spread over a sublime prospect" (O, 2:209). Only the "terrifying sublime" appears to correspond to Burke's theory, and then only loosely, since Kant does not refer to the idea of self-preservation. Kant also says that "the sublime must always be large," thereby designating magnitude as the sine qua non of sublimity, and, in a nod to neoclassical aesthetics, notes that the "sublime must be simple" (O, 2:210). Offering examples of the three types of sublimity, Kant observes, first, that a great height and a great depth are both sublime; the former induces feelings of nobility and admiration, while the latter, terror and shuddering (O, 2:210);[38] second, the Egyptian Pyramids are noble; and third, St. Peter's Basilica in Rome is magnificent; its grandeur is mixed with beauty. Kant, who never ventured beyond Germany, bases many of his observations on literary reports, in this case D. Friedrich Hasselquist's *Reise nach Palästina in den Jahren 1749–1752* (*Journey to Palestine in the Years 1749–1752*), published in 1762. Both the Pyramids and St. Peter's will be reprised as examples in the third *Critique* (but Kant's analysis in this work will be based on a more recent travelogue).[39] Kant also makes some finer distinctions within the "terrifying sublime": "The quality of the *terrifying sublime*, if it becomes entirely unnatural, is *adventurous*. Unnatural things, in so far as the sublime is thereby intended, even if little or none of it is actually found, are *grotesqueries*" (O, 2:213–14). Later, Kant says that Homer and Milton exemplify the

---

[37] Although Kant's third *Critique* will allow for a notion of the sublime in literature or art, it will be conditioned by the idea of formal beauty. See Chapter 12. See also APP, 7:243, for a similar statement.

[38] Presumably a great depth produces terror because of the idea that one might fall into an abyss. This obliquely recalls John Dennis's sojourn in the Alps, where he remarked upon the "pleasant horror" that attends the experience of being on a mountain precipice. See Chapter 5.

[39] CPJ, 5:252. See my discussion in Chapter 10.

adventurous sublime, while Ovid's *Metamorphoses* are examples of grotesqueries (O, 2:215). Indeed, one of the most interesting aspects of the
Observations is its abundant remarks on specific literary texts and genres,
which will be echoed in the section on the "aesthetically sublime" – the
sublimity of mental states – in the third *Critique*.[40]

7.3 Sublimity, morality, and literary representation

Unlike Longinus, Boileau, or Burke, Kant does not analyze literary expression per se, but rather speaks more generally about themes and images that
characterize particular genres or are exemplified in individual works. Thus
Kant describes tragedy as sublime and comedy as beautiful. In tragedy, one
finds "magnanimous sacrifice for the well-being of another, bold resolve in
the face of danger, and proven fidelity" (O, 2:212). In other words, tragedy
is sublime because it involves the representation of noble or high-minded
sentiments. Tragedy also affects us through sympathy: "The misfortune of
others stirs sympathetic sentiments in the bosom of the onlooker and
allows his magnanimous heart to beat for the need of others. He is gently
moved and feels the dignity of his own nature" (O, 2:212). Despite this
passage, which is reminiscent of Burke,[41] Kant does not consider sympathy
to be a sublime or a genuinely moral sentiment; it is rather a weaker feeling
associated with the beautiful: "A certain tenderheartedness that is easily led
into a warm feeling of sympathy is beautiful and lovable, for it indicates a
kindly participation in the fate of other people, to which principles of
virtue likewise lead. But this kindly passion is nevertheless weak and blind"
(O, 2:215).[42] Sympathy offers a weak basis on which to ground morality,
because it cannot decide between competing ethical demands. Only the
"strict duty of justice" (O, 2:216) – the idea of "duty" anticipates Kant's
mature moral theory – can properly orient our moral compass.

In a passage that parallels a similar discussion in the third *Critique*, Kant
uses literary examples to separate moral content from aesthetic effect:

> Even the vices and moral failings often carry with them some of the traits of
> the sublime or the beautiful, at least as they appear to our sensory feeling,
> without having been examined by reason. The wrath of someone fearsome is
> sublime, like the wrath of Achilles in the *Iliad*. In general, the hero of
> *Homer* is *terrifyingly sublime*; that of *Virgil*, by contrast, *noble*. Open

---

[40] See Chapter 12.   [41] See E, 46 and my discussion in Chapter 6.
[42] This coheres with the views on sympathy expressed in Kant's later writings, including in the second
and third *Critiques*.

brazen revenge for a great offense has something grand in it, and however
impermissible it might be, yet in the telling it nevertheless touches us with
dread and satisfaction. (O, 2:212)

Here Kant appears to distinguish to some extent the aesthetic from
the moral: one can be aesthetically uplifted by the representation of
something that is nevertheless worthy of condemnation according to our
moral judgment. It is the association with heroic grandeur (a "great
offense") that makes such representations sublime; hence the choice of
examples from the genre of the epic, with its larger-than-life scale.[43]
But Kant also makes similar observations regarding nobility of mind in
the novel (which will be echoed in the third *Critique*): "A person of calm
and self-interested industry does not have, so to speak, the organs to be
sensitive to the noble feature in a poem or in heroic virtue; he would
rather read a Robinson than a Grandison, and holds Cato to be an
obstinate fool" (O, 2:224). Kant's citation of the heroic figure of Cato
connects his account to those of Boileau and Burke.[44]

What is perhaps most striking in the *Observations* is Kant's systematic
association between sublimity and morality, which anticipates his later
thought. For example: "Subduing one's passions by principles is sublime";
"among moral qualities, true virtue alone is sublime" (O, 2:215); "truthful-
ness is sublime. . . . He [the melancholic] has a lofty feeling for the dignity
of human nature. He esteems himself and holds a human being to be a
creature who deserves respect" (O, 2:221). The notion of "respect" will
become a key term in Kant's moral philosophy; it is also the feeling that
Kant associates with sublimity in the third *Critique*. As mentioned above,
the idea that the sublime is associated with the "dignity of human nature"
is at the center of both Kant's early aesthetic theory as well as his emerging
moral thought.

Beauty, on the other hand, is considered a weak moral sentiment that
barely deserves the name. The moral distinction between beauty and
sublimity is well illustrated in the following passage:

Hence I can call them *adoptive virtues*, but that which rest on principles,
genuine virtue. The former are beautiful and charming, the latter alone is
sublime and worthy of honor. One calls a mind in which the former

---

[43] Kant thus seemingly rejects the understanding of mimesis that prompted Plato (in the *Republic*) to
declare such representations dangerous, since they might be taken for models of behavior.

[44] Burke writes: "Scipio and Cato are both virtuous characters; but we are more deeply affected by the
violent death of the one, and the ruin of the great cause he adhered to, than with the deserved
triumphs and uninterrupted prosperity of the other" (E, 45–6). And Boileau calls Longinus a
"philosopher worthy to be put in Comparison with the Socrates's and Cato's" (WB II, 5).

sentiments rule a *good heart* and the people of that sort *good-hearted*; but one rightly ascribes a *noble heart* to one who is virtuous from principles, calling him alone a *righteous* person. (O, 2:217–18, original emphasis)

The proximity between sublimity and a strong concept of morality largely coheres with Kant's later moral theory, and it would appear to explain in part Kant's recourse to the language of sublimity in the *Critique of Practical Reason*. In addition, the idea of nobility or the heroic, associated here with genuine virtue (virtue from principles), is used throughout the *Observations* to express the cast of mind designated by sublimity (even if "the noble" is also considered by Kant to be a type of sublimity). Thus, in terms of the states of mind or "temperaments" that Kant analyzes, he opposes the "sanguine," which he associates with the beautiful, to the "melancholic," which he associates with sublimity. The "melancholic" exhibits heroic qualities: "He defies danger and has contempt for death" (O, 2:222) and is "noble and generous" (O, 2:221).

***

Although the *Observations* is a work that is perhaps more of historical interest, it is not of mere historical interest. For a careful reading reveals myriad continuities with and amplifications of Kant's mature thought, namely: (1) the moral distinction between beauty and sublimity, which anticipates many passages in the second *Critique*; (2) the importance of Milton's *Paradise Lost* as an index of the poetic sublime, which is carried over in passages in the *Anthropology* and the third *Critique*; (3) Kant's strong association of the sublime with the heroic or noble cast of mind, which finds its fulfillment in the Dynamically Sublime; and 4) an aesthetically inflected concept of human dignity, which will become foundational for both Kant's moral and aesthetic philosophy.

CHAPTER 8

The sublime in Kant's Critique of Practical Reason

The advent of what is called Kant's Critical Philosophy, in his massive *Critique of Pure Reason* (1781/1787), is certainly one of the most crucial turning points in Western thought. By "critique" Kant means the self-examination of reason, considered in terms of its limits, powers, and legitimate domains of application. Given the systematic character of Kant's Critical Philosophy, it is difficult, if not impossible, to comprehend one part, such as the theory of sublimity, in isolation. Hence, we must have a general sense of the principal goals, assumptions, and terminology of the Critical Philosophy to understand how the sublime fits within it.

Kant saw his first *Critique* as a "Copernican Revolution" in that it endeavored to reconcile the claims of the two major strands of modern philosophy: rationalism (Descartes, Leibniz, Spinoza), which taught that knowledge is derived from reason alone and is thus independent of sense experience (for example, proofs of God's existence); and empiricism (Berkeley, Locke, Hume), which held that knowledge is derived from the senses, and is therefore relative and contingent. Kant's defense of "synthetic a priori knowledge" was designed to integrate these seemingly irreconcilable positions: on the one hand, he argued, against the rationalists, that genuine knowledge (cognition) is limited to what is derivable from experience, and, on the other, against the empiricists, that knowledge derived from experience is both necessary and universal, given that the a priori "conditions of possibility" of such knowledge are rationally demonstrable. According to Kant, then, one can have no *knowledge* of supersensible (noumenal) entities or ideas (God, freedom, immortality), though we can still *think* them in logically suitable ways (as obeying the law of noncontradiction, for example).

Kant's account of cognition as transcendentally structured was a breakthrough insofar as it staked out a middle path between the skepticism of the empiricists and the dogmatism of the rationalists. However, in asserting that the world corresponded to our cognitive apparatus (the idealist view), rather than the other way around (the realist view), Kant introduced the controversial idea of the "thing-in-itself" (*Ding an sich*): the idea that we can know things only as they appear to us in the sensible manifold, not how they are "in themselves" (that is, independent from their appearance). Later philosophers found this disjuncture between phenomenal appearances and an unknowable – yet thinkable – noumenal reality to be the most challenging and questionable aspect of Kant's philosophy, and the debate around it continues to this day.[1]

While there are a few sparing uses of the adjective "sublime" (*erhaben*) in the first *Critique*,[2] the sublime really only enters the Critical Philosophy with the *Critique of Practical Reason* (*Kritik der Praktischen Vernunft*, 1788), which, since it was published just two years before the third *Critique*, shows greater affinities with the latter work than does the 1785 *Groundwork of the Metaphysics of Morals* (*Grundlegung zur Metaphysik der Sitten*). The overlap in vocabulary – and even in conception – between the second and third *Critiques* suggests that Kant was most probably thinking about the third *Critique* as he was writing the second.

This chapter argues, first, that the sublime plays both a supportive and substantive role in Kant's moral theory, rather than a merely ornamental or incidental one; second, that this role is defined in terms of a transcendence-structure (overwhelming-elevating, inferiority-superiority) that is common to both morality and sublimity; and third, that the moral examples Kant adduces to illustrate his theory are best thought of as mixed aesthetic/moral judgments of sublimity – similar to the "aesthetically sublime" of the third *Critique* – as opposed to the category of the "moral sublime" as put forward, divergently, by Robert Clewis and Melissa Merritt.

8.1   The role of the sublime in the second *Critique*

One of the recurring questions in Kant's Critical Philosophy is that of how human freedom relates to the causal realm of nature, given that these two realms (the intelligible and the sensible) are separate and distinct in Kant's thought.[3] In the (second) introduction to the third *Critique*, Kant observes that "there is an incalculable gulf fixed between the domain of the concept of nature, as the sensible, and the domain of the concept of the super-sensible, so that from the former to the latter (thus by means of the

---

[1] See, for example, Ralf Meerbote's 1972 essay, "The Unknowability of Things in Themselves."
[2] A word search reveals ten uses of "erhaben" and none of "das Erhabene" in the German original of the *Critique of Pure Reason*.
[3] Like most of his contemporaries, Kant subscribed to a mechanist or determinist view of nature.

theoretical use of reason) no transition is possible" (CPJ, 5:175–6). This is, in fact, one of the motivating factors behind the composition of the *Critique of the Power of Judgment*: the desire to bridge the "gulf" between nature and freedom. In the *Critique of Pure Reason*, Kant had addressed the problem through the idea of "spontaneity." In the words of Terry Pinkard, we "*spontaneously* (that is, not as a causal effect of anything else) bring certain features of our conscious experience *to* experience rather than deriving them *from* experience."[4] But this concept of freedom was limited in that it was described only *negatively* in this work. While revising his first *Critique*, Kant seeks to forge a more positive account of freedom and the noumenal by focusing on the moral or practical realm, first in the *Groundwork* and then in the *Critique of Practical Reason*. As Kant observes in the latter work:

> For, the moral law proves its reality, so as even to satisfy the *Critique* of speculative reason, by adding a positive dimension to a causality thought only negatively, the possibility of which was incomprehensible to specula-tive reason, which was nevertheless forced to assume it; it adds, namely, the concept of a reason determining the will immediately (by the condition of a universal lawful form of its maxims), and thus is able for the first time to give objective though only practical reality to reason, which always became extravagant when it wanted to proceed speculatively with its ideas, and changes its *transcendent* use into an *immanent* use (in which reason is by means of ideas itself an efficient cause in the field of experience). (CPaR, 5:48, original emphasis)

Kant distinguishes between the theoretical or speculative use of reason and its practical or moral use, with regard to freedom, by comparing the negative sense of the former, as something that had to be "assumed," to the positive sense of the later, as "the concept of a reason determining the will immediately." In other words, a moral consciousness (practical reason) can experience its freedom *directly* or *immanently*;[5] its existence is objective and not merely presupposed, as in theoretical reason, which cannot estab-lish the objective reality of its ideas (the rationalist error alluded to above).

This idea of an "experience of freedom" will play a fundamental role in Kant's theory of sublimity in the third *Critique*,[6] where the supersensible

---

[4] Terry Pinkard, *German Philosophy*, 27, original emphasis.
[5] "In this way it can be understood why in the entire faculty of reason *only the practical* can provide us with the means for going beyond the sensible world and provide cognitions of a supersensible order and connection, which, however, just because of this, can be extended only so far as is directly necessary for pure practical purposes" (CPaR, 5:106, original emphasis).
[6] Hence the title of Paul Guyer's *Kant and the Experience of Freedom*.

also receives a positive description. But even in the second *Critique*, the sublime (*das Erhabene*) is invoked, quasi-systematically, as a way to describe the practical freedom of the moral law (which Kant terms "a law of causality through freedom" [CPaR, 5:47]), in such phrases as: "The purity and sublimity of the moral law" (CPaR, 5:71); "the sublimity of our own supersensible existence" (CPaR, 5:88); "it is something very sublime in human nature to be determined to actions directly by a pure rational law" (CPaR, 5:117). These uses of *das Erhabene* are striking and appear to suggest a role for the concept of sublimity in Kant's mature ethical thought.[7]

In his *The Kantian Sublime: From Morality to Art*, a landmark work that is among the first (and still the most detailed) to explore the relation of the sublime to Kant's ethical thought, Paul Crowther endeavors to understand why Kant, in the second *Critique*, seeks to "reserve the term sublime exclusively for the moral domain" and "why Kant should imagine that moral consciousness is so *uniquely* worthy of the term 'sublime.'"[8] Crowther concludes that Kant's use of the sublime is intended to demonstrate or convey the *superiority* of practical over theoretical rationality.[9] On this reading, the use of the term "sublime" in the second *Critique* would be primarily understood in an adjectival sense as a kind of superlative or term of emphasis – an amplification of the idea of superiority – with no conceptual meaning or specific domain of application, that is, as a term that does not substantively contribute to Kant's moral theory.

We must thus consider the following interpretative possibilities: (1) the use of some form of the term *das Erhabene* (sublimity/elevation) is merely rhetorical, that is, a stylistic embellishment intended to more eloquently describe Kant's moral vision; (2) the use of the term represents a (perhaps unwitting) aesthetic influence over Kant's moral theory; (3) Kant develops a concept of moral elevation – moral sublimity – that is distinct both from its aesthetic counterpart in the third *Critique* and also from the fusion of moral and aesthetic sentiments that characterized the *Observations*. While these are not mutually exclusive possibilities (that is, there may be some purely stylistic or rhetorical uses, while other uses are more substantive; or some of these options may be combined), the question of the sublime in

---

[7] One of the earliest discussions is M. C. Nahm's 1957 article: "'Sublimity' and the 'Moral Law' in Kant's Philosophy."
[8] Crowther, *The Kantian Sublime*, 26, 27, original emphasis.
[9] "Morality with its cosmological presuppositions gives us a fuller dimension of completeness to our view of self and world which theoretical reason strives toward but cannot itself demonstrate" (Crowther, *The Kantian Sublime*, 36).

Kant's moral philosophy is not a simple one, particularly given the inclination to view this notion through the lens of the third *Critique*.

8.2   Respect and the moral law: the structural analogy between sublimity and morality

According to Lewis White Beck, "the sublimity of the moral law is more than a metaphor for Kant"; for "not only does [Kant] use the language of the aesthetics of the sublime in describing the moral law, but he gives an analogous interpretation of the origins of the feelings of sublimity and respect."[10] I aim to show that this "analogy" is the key to understanding Kant's use of sublimity in the *Critique of Practical Reason*.

Indeed, it is no coincidence that the section of the second *Critique* where the language of sublimity figures most prominently is also the section that is devoted to an analysis of *respect (Achtung)*, a term that will be used to describe the feeling of sublimity in the third *Critique*. This section, "On the Incentives of Pure Practical Reason," deals with the motivational disposition associated with the moral law – the categorical imperative that each should act in such a way that his or her actions can be universalized without contradiction.[11] The question Kant seeks to address is the following: if, as he asserts, "what is essential to any moral worth of actions is *that the moral law determine the will immediately*" (CPaR, 5:71, original emphasis), how does this in fact happen? In other words, how can the will be in fact determined by an abstract idea? Although rarely commented on by scholars, the role of the sublime in addressing this question is important not only for the second *Critique*, but also for the nexus between morality and aesthetics that carries over into the third *Critique*.

To understand this role, we must first analyze what Kant means by "moral worth" and by the "immediate" determination of the will. If one performs an action that is simply *in accordance with* the moral law, that is, by means of a feeling (an incentive) that does not stem from the law itself, then one's action contains mere *legality* (mere conformity to the law) but not *morality*, strictly speaking.[12] Only an action done *for the sake of the law*

---

[10]   Lewis White Beck, *A Commentary on Kant's* Critique of Practical Reason, 220. However, Beck does not go into detail on this point.

[11]   The centrality of the moral law in the second *Critique* should not, however, lead us to reductive conclusions about Kant as a stern and rigid formalist. Allen Wood, for example, speaks of "the exaggerated emphasis usually placed on the Formula of Universal Law in expounding Kant's approach to moral reasoning" (*Kant's Ethical Thought*, 5).

[12]   Guyer stresses that this is not about holding human beings to an impossibly lofty standard: "We can earn esteem for the purity of our motivation, but no demerit, let alone punishment, merely for the

possesses "moral worth"; for only in such a case is an action a manifestation of freedom as a rationally (as opposed to a sensibly) determined act. Therefore, only the moral law itself can be an incentive to morality. This brings us to the problem inherent to the concept of moral autonomy: how we can have an *interest* in following the moral law that is not dependent on something outside it, such as is found in the realm of the senses, in which case morality would be a form of *heteronomy* rather than *autonomy*?[13] Compounding the problem, Kant holds that the question of *how* the moral law can be an incentive to moral action – that is, how it can be the "determining ground of the will" (CPaR, 5:72) – is inscrutable, as inscrutable as the question of how the freedom of the will itself is possible (for it would require knowledge of the noumenal, which for Kant is impossible). Thus, Kant asserts: "What we shall have to show a priori is ... not the ground from which the moral law in itself supplies an incentive but rather what it effects (or, to put it better must effect) in the mind insofar as it is an incentive" (CPaR, 5:72). That is to say, the fact that the moral law is an incentive must be presupposed; the very concept of the moral law requires it. What is left to discover, then, given that the moral law *is* an incentive, is what "effect" this incentive has on the mind, or what effect this incentive "must" have in order for the moral law to have a causal effect in the phenomenal realm: in other words, what *feeling* can the noumenal-practical produce?[14]

Kant observes that the incentive of the moral law appears initially as a *negative* feeling, insofar as it suppresses all (sensible) inclinations and impulses that disagree with it. These must disagree with it a priori, since "there is no *antecedent* feeling in the subject that would be attuned to morality" (CPaR, 5:75, original emphasis); that is, since it is based on reason, morality must be "free from any sensible condition" (CPaR, 5:75). From the perspective of the moral law, then, sensibility is an antagonist; it is inimical to rational freedom. As creaturely beings, we are necessarily subject to the inclinations of sense; thus the moral law's stern command is experienced as a restraint and hence as painful.[15] Drawing on the Rousseauean contrast between two forms of self-love, *amour de soi*

---

typical impurity of our motivation; we earn demerit only for evil deeds, not impure motives" (*Kant*, 248).
[13] See Kant's *Groundwork of the Metaphysics of Morals* (G, 4:433).
[14] As Stephen Darwall puts it: "The manifestation of moral action in the phenomenal realm must have a cause in the agent's psychology, which Kant supposes must be a feeling" ("Kant on Respect," 184).
[15] However, the injunction against inclinations is not identical to the suppression of *desire*, for we should desire the good, even if our inclinations, conditioned by sense, lead us astray. Wood notes that for Kant "all action ... requires both feeling and desire"; an action is moral if it is based on

(self-preservation) and *amour-propre* (egotism), Kant describes rational self-restraint in terms of an opposition between *Eigenliebe*, love for oneself or self-esteem ("*benevolence* toward oneself"), and *Eigendünkel*, self-conceit ("*satisfaction with oneself*") (CPaR, 5:73, original emphasis).[16] *Eigendünkel* is akin to the notion of "pride," which, according to Christian doctrine, is the greatest of all sins (as in Dante's *Inferno* from the *Divine Comedy*). Kant's concept of self-conceit is a bit broader, insofar as it connotes the general tendency to raise one's personal propensities above the moral law ("if self-love makes itself law-giving" [CPaR, 5:74]),[17] but it also includes an element of social evil.

To the extent that both forms of self-love are based on inclination, they are somewhat less strictly oppositional in Kant than in Rousseau. With respect to *Eigenliebe*, love for oneself (the "good" type of self-love, according to Rousseau, *amour de soi*), pure practical reason only "infringes upon" or "restricts" it, in order to direct it to be in conformity with the moral law, in which case it becomes "rational self-love" (CPaR, 5:73). In regards to self-conceit (vanity, egotism, pride), on the other hand, no rapprochement is possible; the moral law simply "strikes down" or "humiliates" it. Only the latter gives rise to the moral feeling of *respect (Achtung)*, which is "the sole and also the undoubted moral incentive" (CPaR, 5:78). Allen Wood notes that "respect is basic to Kantian ethics because it is the feeling that corresponds to rational self-restraint."[18] In other words, we would have no psychological incentive to restrain our inclinations in response to the moral law save for the respect for this law itself. The mere redirection of love for oneself or self-esteem does not conduce to a truly moral attitude, since it does not require self-restraint but only an "infringement" on its impulses, which are not in radical conflict with the moral law.

Qua incentive, however, respect must, in addition to the pain of self-restraint, also possess a *positive* aspect:

> Since this law [the moral law] is still something in itself positive – namely, the form of an intellectual causality, that is, of freedom – it is at the same

---

"rational (not empirical) feelings and desires." Thus: "Moral action, which always sets ends, always involves a rational desire for them" (*Kantian Ethics*, 36).

[16] Frederick Neuhouser (in *Rousseau's Theodicy of Self-Love: Evil, Rationality, and the Drive for Recognition*, 61) notes that Kant's "appropriation" of the doctrine of amour-propre for his moral philosophy has a "narrower" purpose than in Rousseau.

[17] Darwall writes that Kant's self-conceit is "the radical idea that something has objective normative significance *because it is what one wills subjectively* – that one has a unique authority or standing to create reasons for acting independently of and unconstrained by the moral law" ("Kant on Respect," 185, original emphasis). See also Stephen Darwall, "Two Kinds of Respect."

[18] Wood, *Kant's Ethical Thought*, 46.

time an object of *respect* inasmuch as, in opposition to its subjective antagonist, namely the inclinations in us, it *weakens* self-conceit; and inasmuch as it
even *strikes down* self-conceit, that is, humiliates it, it is an object of the
greatest *respect* and so too the ground of a positive feeling that is not of
empirical origin and is cognized a priori. (CPaR, 5:73, original emphasis)

The supremacy – or absoluteness – of the moral law vanquishes the
pseudo-supremacy of self-love (which, *qua* pseudo-supremacy, is self-
conceit),[19] thereby awakening respect for this law. But only when the
moral law completely destroys or humiliates our self-conceit is it the
object of the "greatest respect," in other words, the sublime (hence everyday morality would not necessarily be experienced as sublime).[20]
Paradoxically, then, the manifestation of the moral law as affective incentive is *dependent* on self-conceit. This is because morality implies a loss of
(childlike) innocence, the inevitable development of self-conceit. As Wood
remarks: "The *innocent* will *can* respect nothing, because it lacks the self-
reflection presupposed both by self-esteem and self-conceit. It *does not need*
to respect anything because its inclinations, which are in a natural (if
fragile) harmony with the good, do not yet need to be checked by reason."[21]
We are all susceptible to self-conceit as the very condition of being rational,
and, by the same token, we are all in principle capable of *transcending* this
condition.

The image of "striking down" in this passage resonates with Burke's
evocation of the sublimity of God's almightiness: "We shrink into the
minuteness of our own nature, and are in a manner *annihilated before
him*" (E, 68, my emphasis). In fact, using the language of sublimity, Kant
directly suggests an analogy between the moral law and the divine when
he observes that "one can in turn never get enough of contemplating
the majesty of this law, and the soul believes itself *elevated* in proportion
as it sees the holy elevated above itself and its frail nature" (CPaR, 5:77,
my emphasis). The experience of the moral law is therefore none other
than the dual transcendence-structure of sublimity: it simultaneously
humiliates (dominates by force) and elevates (exalts toward high-
mindedness). As a kind of "holiness," the moral law is a quasi-religious

---

[19] "This propensity to make oneself as having subjective determining grounds of choice into the
objective determining ground of the will in general can be called *self-love*; and if self-love makes itself
lawgiving and the unconditional practical principle, it can be called *self-conceit*" (CPaR, 5:74,
original emphasis).

[20] In a personal email, Crowther argued the following: "The fact is that respect, as Kant presents it, can
be grumbly and low key. . . . Everyday morality doesn't always transport us to the sublime. You don't
have to bring the sublime into it" (September 26, 2014).

[21] Wood, *Kant's Ethical Thought*, 47, original emphasis.

substitute for God, thus drawing on and emphasizing the quasi-religious nature of the sublime.

Respect also connotes the dual transcendence-structure of sublimity insofar as it is a *mixed feeling*:

> As *submission* to a law, that is, as a command . . . it therefore contains in it no pleasure but instead, so far, displeasure in the action. On the other hand, however, since this constraint is exercised only by the lawgiving of his *own* reason, it contains something *elevating*, and the subjective effect on feeling, inasmuch as pure practical reason is the sole cause of it, can thus be called *self-approbation*. (CPaR, 5:80–1, original emphasis)[22]

Thus respect combines the pain in the destruction or weakening of self-conceit (that is, self-restraint) with the positive feeling in the majesty of the moral law itself and its implicit comparison with the lowliness of our sensible nature: "Hence the moral law unavoidably humiliates every human being when he compares it with the sensible propensity of his nature" (CPaR, 5:74).[23] The dual humiliation-elevation structure is a function of the dual nature of Kant's conception of the human being: "Humiliation on the sensible side – is an elevation of the moral – that is, practical – esteem for the law on the intellectual side" (CPaR, 5:79). Humiliation "is" elevation – the paradoxical experience of sublimity. Commenting on the above-quoted passage (CPaR, 5:73), Wood highlights the role of sublimity: "[Respect] does this [strikes down self-conceit] only through the awe and wonderment we feel at the dignity of our sublime vocation as rational beings which we must strive to live up to."[24] Although I read the passage slightly differently (that respect is the *result of* the destruction of our self-conceit, not its cause, which is the moral law itself),[25] the important point is that "awe and wonderment" – classic expressions of the effect of sublimity since Longinus – are transformed

---

[22] The words Kant highlights are quite revealing about his conscious use of sublimity/elevation in his moral theory. The verb "to elevate" (*erheben*) comes from the same root as the adjective "sublime" (*erhaben*).

[23] In the *Groundwork*, Kant speaks explicitly of *pleasure* as it relates to the moral law: "It is admittedly required that his reason have the capacity to *induce a feeling of pleasure* or of delight in the fulfillment of duty, and thus there is required a causality of reason to determine sensibility in conformity with its principles" (G, 4:460, original emphasis).

[24] Wood, *Kant's Ethical Thought*, 47. Crowther comments similarly: "On these terms, then, respect not only provides an incentive which assists the moral law's capacity to determine the will, but also enables it to amplify into metaphysical awareness of our ultimate vocation – to be free rational legislators in a supersensible order of existence" (Crowther, "Authentic Moral Commitment: Kant's Phenomenology of Respect," manuscript version).

[25] "This feeling [respect] (under the name of moral feeling) is therefore produced solely by reason [practical reason]" (CPaR, 5:76).

by Kant into a moral sentiment via the mixed feeling of respect. Kant expresses this idea more poetically in a famous passage at the end of the second *Critique*, where the structural analogy between sublimity in nature and the sublimity of the moral law becomes most explicit: "Two things fill the mind with ever new and increasing admiration and reverence [*Ehrfurcht*] the more often and more steadily one reflects on them: *the starry heavens above me and the moral law within me*" (CPaR, 5:161, original emphasis). Beck comments that "what the starry heavens awake in us only indirectly is produced directly by the contemplation of the moral law, sublime in itself, and of the moral agent who embodies the law; the humility thus induced in man is itself sublime."[26] The sublimity of morality in Kant, here evoked cosmically, can thus be said to recall the *sermo humilis*, the humble sublimity – the sublime morality – of the Gospels.[27]

Kant is certainly not unaware that his use of the sublime to articulate his moral theory might engender misunderstandings relating to the aesthetic connotations of the term, connotations he himself had explored in the *Observations*. In a passage from the same section of the second *Critique*, Kant seeks to preempt inappropriate associations:

> *Respect* is always directed to persons, never to things. The latter can awaken in us *inclination* and even *love* if they are animals (e.g., horses, dogs, and so forth), or also *fear*, like the sea, a volcano, a beast of prey, but never *respect*. Something that comes nearer to this feeling is *admiration*, and this as an affect, amazement, can be directed to things also, for example, lofty mountains, the magnitude, number and distance of the heavenly bodies, the strength and swiftness of many animals, and so forth. But none of this is respect. (CPaR, 5:76, original emphasis)

Kant's main point in this passage is that respect *can never be directed to things*, that it is a feeling that can apply *only* to human beings – which would appear to put him at odds with the use of respect to describe the effect of sublimity in the third *Critique*. But there is no actual inconsistency on this score, since, as Kant will insist in the later work, the feeling of the sublime is not actually directed toward things in the world, but rather toward our own mental disposition or vocation. In addition, although it would appear that Kant is here opposing aesthetic to ethical feeling, rather than underlining their continuity or proximity as he does in the third *Critique*, the invocation of the specifically aesthetic meaning of the sublime

---

[26] Beck, *A Commentary on Kant's* Critique of Practical Reason, 282.
[27] See Erich Auerbach's analysis of the *sermo humilis* in his *Literary Language and Its Public in Late Latin Antiquity and in the Middle Ages*.

in this context ("lofty mountains" and "heavenly bodies" are conventional figures of sublimity) is nevertheless significant. For Kant is implicitly suggesting a certain parallel between the aesthetic experience of the sublime in nature and the moral attitude – which is precisely why he takes care to distinguish them. This passage is actually a gloss on the following remark in Burke's *Enquiry*: "Astonishment is the effect of the sublime in the highest degree; its inferior effects are admiration, reverence, and respect" (E, 53). In describing a moral sentiment that is analogous to the aesthetic feeling of the sublime, Kant simply reverses Burke's hierarchy: what is least in terms of aesthetic intensity, according to Burke, becomes greatest in terms of ethical feeling, according in Kant. The poles are reversed but the structure of sublime transcendence (humiliation-elevation) remains the same.

One thus sees why Kant will so naturally connect respect to the feeling of the sublime in his third *Critique*: the sublime, more effectively than the beautiful, is opposed to the interest of sensibility and thus to self-conceit. For particularly in the Dynamically Sublime, the subject is elevated above all attachment to material life, that is, above self-love as the instinct for self-preservation; it makes us "regard those things about which we are concerned (goods, health, and life) as trivial" (CPJ, 5:362). Hence Kant's remark, in the third *Critique*, that "the feeling of the sublime in nature is *respect* for our own vocation," namely our vocation for the supersensible: "The superiority of the rational vocation of our cognitive faculty over the greatest faculty of sensibility" (CPJ, 5:257). And in the third *Critique* Kant also notes that "the satisfaction of the sublime does not so much contain positive pleasure as it does admiration or respect" (CPJ, 5:245). The mixed feeling of respect associated with the effect of the moral law in the second *Critique* thus *reappears* as the mixed feeling associated with the effect of the sublime in the third *Critique*, the difference being that, in the case of its aesthetic manifestation, it *does not determine the will*. In the case of the Dynamically Sublime, respect is simply the feeling that the will *could* be so determined.[28]

8.3   Sublime morality or moral sublimity?

As was noted at the beginning of this chapter, it is one thing to say that the concept of sublimity *illuminates* important aspects of Kant's moral theory, namely the feeling of respect and the dual structure of humiliation-exaltation (moral transcendence), but it is quite another to suggest that

---

[28]   I discuss this in detail in Chapter 11.

the sublime actually helps *define* Kant's moral theory, without interrogating how a putatively aesthetic concept can play such a role. In an effort to clear up some of the ambiguities of Kant's presentation, two commentators, Robert Clewis and Melissa Merritt, have recently invoked the category of the "moral sublime," a category found nowhere in Kant.

Clewis, in his 2009 book *The Kantian Sublime and the Revelation of Freedom*, contends that

> by "moral sublime," I refer to the effect on consciousness when the moral law, or some representation or embodiment thereof, is observed or perceived aesthetically rather than from a practical perspective. That is, an experience of the sublime is one of the moral sublime if and only if something moral, such as an idea, object, mental state, act, event, or person, elicits the sublime in an aesthetic judge who observes, imagines, hears, or somehow reflects on that object.[29]

Prima facie, Clewis appears to want to replace Kant's category of the "aesthetically sublime" (the sublimity of mental states described in the General Remark to §29 in the third *Critique*, and especially CPJ, 5:271) with that of the "moral sublime," but upon further examination his aims appear to be broader.[30] In any case, it is not clear how the "moral sublime" could function as a category in Kant's oeuvre in the way that Clewis understands it, for it seemingly implies either (1) that the sublime in the second *Critique* has only an aesthetic and not a practical significance ("perceived aesthetically rather than from a practical perspective"), which, as we have seen, is definitely not the case; or (2) that the moral law, when considered from a purely practical perspective, is not sublime, and yet Clewis notes that "Kant's description of the sublimity of 'the moral law within me' is surely based on an experience of the moral sublime."[31] But the idea of the "sublimity of the moral law" in this passage does not mean an aesthetic (or observer) apprehension of the moral law, as Clewis imagines, but a practical one. As Kant remarks, "this is how the genuine moral incentive of *pure practical reason* is constituted; it is nothing other than the pure moral law itself insofar as its lets us discover the *sublimity of our own supersensible existence*" (CPaR, 5:88, my emphasis). Thus it is unclear to me what Clewis is attempting to argue here.[32]

---

[29] Clewis, *The Kantian Sublime*, 84.   [30] See Chapter 12.   [31] Clewis, *The Kantian Sublime*, 85.

[32] The explanation for the confusion may lie in the fact that, as Clewis notes in his Introduction: "I do not attempt to fill in what happened in Kant's development between the middle of the 1760s and the writings of the 1790s. This task would require me to go beyond my knowledge of Kant as well as necessitate more pages than can be contained in this book" (*The Kantian Sublime*, 2). But if this is

In her reading of Kant (2012), Merritt distinguishes the category of the "moral sublime" from the "natural sublime" (that is, Mathematical and Dynamical sublimity). Unlike Clewis, her "moral sublime" seems to exclude rather than include what goes under the heading of the "aesthetically sublime," the sublimity of mental states (she calls enthusiasm, a Kantian term that Clewis privileges, a "fraudulent mode of the sublime").[33] The main problem with her account, in my view, is that it attempts to resolve Kantian ambiguities in ways that clearly go against the Kantian text. For example, she writes that "the natural sublime is enjoyed through admiration, whereas the moral sublime is enjoyed through respect,"[34] thus transforming the second *Critique* distinction between morality and aesthetics (CPaR, 5:76, discussed above) into a general claim that can also be applied to the third *Critique*. But this is incorrect; for in the third *Critique* Kant writes that "admiration *or* respect" (CPJ, 5:245, my emphasis) describes the experience of the sublime in nature. Thus, while I agree with her assertion that "our capacity to appreciate the sublime in nature is grounded in the development of sound moral disposition,"[35] I think that, given the manifest differences between the second and third *Critiques* on these questions, totalizing the Kantian sublime according to various "modes" that span the entire Kantian corpus (such as "moral sublime" and "natural sublime")[36] creates more problems than it solves.

As both Clewis and Merritt contend, though in ways I find problematic, there are many overlaps in conception between the second and third *Critiques*, particularly in regard to "aesthetically sublime" (the General Remark to §29 in the latter work), which is one of the few places in which Kant directly addresses the issue of how aesthetics relates to morality:

> From this it follows that the intellectual, intrinsically purposive (moral) good, judged aesthetically, must not be represented so much as beautiful but rather as sublime, so that it arouses more the feeling of respect (which scorns charm) than of love and intimate affection, since human nature does not agree with that good of its own accord, but only through the dominion that reason exercises over sensibility. (CPJ, 5:271)

---

the case, then it is imprudent to apply the category of the "moral sublime" to pronouncements of the second *Critique*, written in the 1780s.
[33] Merritt, "The Moral Source of the Kantian Sublime," 47 (figure 3.1).
[34] Merritt, "The Moral Source of the Kantian Sublime," 48.
[35] Merritt, "The Moral Source of the Kantian Sublime," 49. Kant makes this point in §29 of the third *Critique*. See Chapter 12.
[36] See Merritt's Figure 3.1, "The Moral Source of the Kantian Sublime," 47.

According to Kant, the mental state of the morally good should, when judged aesthetically – that is, from an observer, not an agent perspective – be *represented* as sublime, so that the observer feels a respect for the example of rational self-legislation, which is akin to the (direct) effect of rational self-legislation itself. This would also appear to point the way to a conception of sublimity in literature and art to the extent that they can offer such images (and narrative would be more apt for this task).[37]

The opposition between sublimity/respect and beauty/love in the above passage from the third *Critique* has parallels in the second: "It is very beautiful to do good to human beings from love for them and from sympathetic benevolence ... but this is not the genuine moral maxim of our conduct, the maxim befitting our position among rational beings as *human beings*" (CPaR, 5:82, original emphasis). This recalls a similar passage from the *Observations*: "A certain tenderheartedness that is easily led into a warm feeling of sympathy is beautiful and lovable, for it indicates a kindly participation in the fate of other people, to which principles of virtue likewise lead. But this kindly passion is nevertheless weak and blind" (2:215). In both instances Kant describes sympathy as a "beautiful" sentiment, as contrasted with true moral virtue – implicitly the sublime. The second *Critique* thus continues Kant's aesthetico-philosophical critique of sympathy on a transcendental level: moral action should be motivated by the majesty and sublimity of the moral law alone, which includes an element of negativity associated with respect for the moral law, not by any sympathetic attunement to individuals (as in Hume's and Adam Smith's theories of moral sentiments).

Kant contrasts sympathy or love with the concept of *duty*, a key term in the second *Critique*, which he explicitly associates with sublimity: "*Duty!* Sublime and mighty name that embraces nothing charming or insinuating but requires submission" (CPaR, 5:86, original emphasis). Here again, the charm or pleasantness of the beautiful is contrasted with the strength of character that sublime duty requires, namely the ability to elevate oneself above or struggle (heroically) against one's inclinations by submitting (willfully) to a self-given law. Duty is simply another name for actions performed for the sake of the moral law alone: actions done *from duty* have true moral worth, whereas those done merely *in conformity with* duty are simply lawful and cannot therefore be qualified as moral per se.

---

[37] I thus disagree with Crowther who observes: "Kant's attitude to the sublime in his Critical ethics is one that serves to locate it wholly beyond the artistic and aesthetic sphere" (*The Kantian Sublime*, 36). As I assert below, I believe that many of Kant's examples in the second *Critique* presuppose a mixed moral-aesthetic judgment.

Invoking a parallel between Kant's aesthetic and moral theories, Paul Guyer notes that the ability of the sublime to override personal interests – *moral* disinterestedness (that is, imperviousness to sensibility) – makes it much more consequential for morality than the *aesthetic* disinterestedness of the beautiful:

> The disinterestedness of our response to the sublime seems more like a form of moral disinterestedness in which private interests are overridden by some higher interest than like the purely aesthetic disinterestedness of the beautiful, in which personal interests are supposed to be simply disengaged without being overridden by any other interest, higher or not.[38]

It is notable that Guyer contrasts the moral disinterestedness of the sublime with the "*purely aesthetic* disinterestedness of the beautiful," as if the sublime were in some fundamental sense a mixed moral-aesthetic feeling (Guyer does not develop this thought). In addition, although Guyer is discussing the third *Critique* in this instance, the continuity he suggests between Kant's moral philosophy and the third *Critique* demonstrates how the sublime can also contribute to Kant's moral theory (and not only the reverse): the "higher interest" (the pervasive height metaphor of the sublime) is, in the second *Critique*, the moral law itself, while in the third *Critique* it is our supersensible vocation. In both cases, the sublime connotes our ability to transcend sensibility, which points at once to the sublimity of morality and to the moral implications of sublimity.

Nevertheless, it is important to note that not all acts called sublime are necessarily moral:

> By exhortations to actions as noble, sublime, and magnanimous, minds are attuned to nothing but moral enthusiasm and exaggerated self-conceit; by such exhortations they are led into the delusion that it is not duty – that is, respect for the moral law . . . which constitutes the determining ground of their actions . . . but it is as if those actions are expected from them, not from duty but as bare merit. (CPaR, 5:84–5)

Kant attacks the idea of *moral enthusiasm* in this passage, which he sees a certain use of the term "sublime" as potentially supporting. Kant defines moral enthusiasm as "an overstepping of the bounds [undertaken on principles] that practical reason sets to humanity" (CPaR, 5:85). Knowing that the idea of enthusiasm has traditionally been associated with sublimity, particularly in the early eighteenth-century British writers he read extensively, Kant endeavors to disassociate the two concepts, so as

---

[38] Guyer, *Kant and the Experience of Freedom*, 223.

to purify, as it were, the concept of the sublime for his moral theory. Kant is thus keen on highlighting the ambiguity of enthusiasm. On the one hand, it tends toward fanaticism, which is anathema to his rational moral theory; on the other, toward the heroic: "The [moral] enthusiasm of [the Stoics] was more heroic while that of the [novelists and sentimental educators] is of a more insipid and languishing character" (CPaR, 5:86). Thus, while Kant will in the General Remark (in the third *Critique*) call enthusiasm "aesthetically sublime," it is clear, from the perspective of the *Critique of Practical Reason*, that it is not morally sublime and that the idea of "moral enthusiasm" is an oxymoron in Kant.[39]

If sublimity is understood in terms of enthusiasm, as a passion that overrides reason, then it is not an appropriate mode of representation for moral actions. On the other hand: "Actions of others that are done with great sacrifice and for the sake of duty alone may indeed be praised by calling them *noble* and *sublime* deeds, but only insofar as there are traces suggesting that they were done wholly from respect for duty and not from ebullitions of feeling" (CPaR, 5:85, original emphasis). Kant here essentially redefines the category of the heroic in moral terms. The truly heroic act, one that deserves to be called sublime, is not one done according to a passionate disposition or because of exaggerated self-love, but in response to a rational command. The hero is one who manifests supreme moral strength, particularly in a situation of *moral adversity*, when the conflict between sensibility and the moral law is the most acute and requires the greatest effort (as in, for example, risking or sacrificing one's life for a moral principle).[40] This passage also anticipates the virtual heroism of the Dynamically Sublime, the ability to aesthetically transcend the sensible attachment to life.[41]

Although in the second *Critique* Kant might appear to throw together, rather nonchalantly, sublimity and morality, Kant is not insensitive, as we saw with the notion of respect, to the threat posed by such a confusion, as when he writes: "The determination of the will directly by reason alone is the ground of the feeling of pleasure, and this remains a pure practical, not aesthetic, determination of the faculty of desire" (CPaR, 5:116). Even if Kant is here using the term "aesthetic" in a pre–third *Critique* manner, it

[39] At least until *The Conflict of the Faculties* (1798) (contained in Kant, *Religion and Rational Theology*). See Chapter 12.

[40] That is to say, it is not the nature of the act itself that determines its sublimity, but the nature of its motivation; thus an identical act of self-sacrifice can be a product of moral enthusiasm or duty, but only the latter is truly moral and morally sublime.

[41] See Chapter 11 of this study.

nonetheless reveals the importance of the "purity" of moral consciousness for Kant (a pendant to the "purity" of aesthetic judgment in the third *Critique*). The pleasure or self-regard taken in the performance of a moral action cannot be seen as a moral incentive, since this would precisely contradict Kant's idea of a moral act as one done for the sake of the moral law alone: "Now, consciousness of a determination of the faculty of desire is always the ground of a satisfaction in the action produced by it; but this *pleasure*, this satisfaction with oneself, is not the determining ground of the action" (CPaR, 5:116, my emphasis). Kant uses the term "subreption" – a term that will figure in the discussion of sublimity in the third *Critique* – to describe the illusion of mistaking the feeling of satisfaction in an action done for the sake of the moral law for the satisfaction in the determination of the will that gave rise to the action.[42]

*** *** ***

If the central question of Kant's moral philosophy is that of how we can rise above sensible determination (that is, achieve autonomy), the sublime, precisely as the transcendence of sensibility, has both a moral and an aesthetic significance. This chapter has therefore argued that the role of the sublime in the *Critique of Practical Reason* is structural, that Kant uses the dual (humiliating-elevating) structure of sublimity as a *secular concept of transcendence* to help define his moral theory. The great unsettled question in this examination is whether, or to what extent, the effect of an *example* of moral sublimity is aesthetic or moral, for Kant is indeed equivocal on this point. I have therefore suggested that if a moral example can elevate us both morally and aesthetically, it can then be said to be a mixed aesthetic/moral judgment of sublimity, rather than an example of the "moral sublime," a highly problematic category that is not found in Kant. I shall return to this issue in Chapter 12, in my discussion of affects and mental states.

---

[42] "There is always present here the ground of an error of subreption (*vitium subreptionis*) and, as it were, an optical illusion in the self-consciousness of what one *does* as distinguished from what one *feels* – an illusion that even the most practiced cannot altogether avoid" (CPaR, 5:116, original emphasis). Notably, Kant qualifies this "illusion" as sublime: "It is something very sublime in human nature to be determined to actions directly by a pure rational law, and even the illusion that takes the subjective side of this intellectual determinability of the will as something aesthetic and the effect of a special sensible feeling (for an intellectual feeling would be a contradiction) is sublime" (CPaR, 5:117).

CHAPTER 9

The sublime in Kant's Critique of the Power of Judgment

The theory of the sublime reaches its apotheosis in Kant's *Kritik der Urteilskraft* (*Critique of the Power of Judgment*, 1790). By attaching an "Analytic of the Sublime" to his Critical Philosophy, Kant indicated that this notion was integral to an understanding of the foundations of human thought, action, and feeling, thereby solidifying its status as a key concept in both aesthetics and modern intellectual history. Due to the complexity and importance of Kant's theory of sublimity in the third *Critique*, I have spread my examination over four chapters: Chapter 9 deals with how the sublime fits within the new theoretical armature established by the *Critique of the Power of Judgment* – namely reflective judgment and the purposiveness of nature – as well as with the contrast between judgments of beauty and sublimity; Chapters 10 and 11 explore the relation of the sublime to the experience of nature in Kant's account, the Mathematically and the Dynamically Sublime; and Chapter 12 studies the importance of culture in Kant's theory of sublimity, including Kant's contention that we must be prepared by culture for the sublime, the neglected concept of the "aesthetically sublime," and Kant's treatment of sublimity in art.

In this chapter, divided into two sections, I begin by offering a general examination of Kant's theory of aesthetic judgment – necessary if we are to understand Kant's specific account of sublimity – and then proceed to address several points of controversy regarding Kant's systematic confrontation between the beautiful and the sublime: form versus formlessness, simple versus complex pleasure, and objective versus subjective grounding. I argue first that, despite appearances, the sublime is not the *symmetrical* opposite of the beautiful, and second, against the idea advocated by some commentators that the sublime should be seen as a "mere appendix" to the critique of taste (the beautiful); instead, I see the sublime as not only an integral part of the Analytic of Aesthetic Judgment (Division I) but in some ways as even *more* consequential for Kant's overall aims in the Critical

Philosophy than the beautiful,[1] in particular because of the importance of the transcendence-structure of the sublime for Kant's conceptions of morality, religion, and culture – connections that will be fleshed out in the following chapters.

9.1   Reflective judgment and the purposiveness of nature

We have seen that, prior to the writing of the third *Critique*, Kant considered the project of a critique of taste a strictly empirical endeavor, a task for psychological or anthropological investigation rather than a properly philosophical (that is, transcendental) one. Despite his high regard for Alexander Baumgarten's philosophy (he often taught Baumgarten's *Metaphysica* in his classes), Kant could not vouchsafe the idea of an aesthetic judgment expressible in terms of a priori principles. Thus in 1781, in his *Critique of Pure Reason*, Kant asserts in an often-cited footnote:

> The Germans are the only ones who now employ the word *aesthetic[s]* to designate what others call the critique of taste. They are doing so on the basis of a false hope conceived by that superb analyst Baumgarten. He hoped to bring our critical judging of the beautiful under rational principles, and to raise the rules for such judging to the level of a lawful science. Yet that endeavor is futile. For, as far as their principal sources are concerned, those supposed rules or criteria are merely empirical. Hence they can never serve as determinate a priori laws to which our judgment of taste must conform. It is, rather, our judgment of taste which constitutes the proper test for the correctness of those rules or criteria. Because of this it is advisable to follow either of two alternatives. One of these is to stop using this new name *aesthetic[s]* in this sense of critique of taste, and to reserve the name *aesthetic[s]* for the doctrine of sensibility that is true science. (In doing so we would also come closer to the language of the ancients and its meaning. Among the ancients the division of cognition into *aisthêtá kai noêtá* [sensed or thought] was quite famous.) The other alternative would be for the new *aesthetic[s]* to share the name with speculative philosophy. We would then take the name partly in its transcendental meaning, and partly in the psychological meaning. (CPuR, A 21, note)

---

[1] This does not mean, for example, that Kant's section on beauty as a "symbol of morality" is not important. It is simply that, seen in conjunction with the previous chapter on the second *Critique*, the third *Critique* can be read as proposing a more proximate or intimate relation between morality and sublimity than between morality and beauty. Thus Henry Allison observes that "according to the terms of Kant's own analysis, the sublime stands in an even more intimate relation to morality than does the beautiful," even if Allison ultimately sees Kant as "deeply ambivalent" toward the sublime, hence its seemingly "parergonal" status in the third *Critique* (*Kant's Theory of Taste*, 303).

Kant endeavors in this passage to separate two meanings of the term "aesthetic(s)": (1) as *elementary sensation* (*Empfindung*), the matter of empirical intuition (sound, color, and so on); and (2) as *feeling* (*Gefühl*), namely pleasure and displeasure, the basis for a critique of taste. Thus in the *Critique of Pure Reason*, Kant employs the term "transcendental aesthetic" in the first sense: this work treats the conditions of sensible knowledge and is a pendant to "transcendental logic," which establishes the conditions and limits of logical knowledge.[2] Kant's *Observations*, like Burke's *Enquiry* before it, represents an empirical investigation of aesthetics considered as feeling.

Just seven years after having dismissed the possibility of "bring[ing] our critical judging of the beautiful under rational principles," Kant had changed his mind, coming around to a more Baumgartian view concerning the possibility of a critique of taste within philosophy. The reason for this shift lay in Kant's discovery of the a priori principle of the "purposiveness" (*Zweckmäßigkeit*) of nature, through which he was able to raise the concept of taste to the level of a transcendental inquiry. The principle of the *purposiveness of nature*, the idea that nature shows itself as particularly suitable for our judging faculty – that is, as manifesting a kind of "design" that appears intentional vis-à-vis our judging faculty, even if it cannot be considered intentional in any empirical sense – allowed Kant to connect aesthetic feeling to an a priori concept. With this principle in mind, Kant set out to write a *Foundation of the Critique of Taste*, as an early version of the *Critique of the Power of Judgment* was called. This initial project was expanded to include teleological judgment, or "objective purposiveness," a pendant to the "subjective purposiveness" – purposiveness without a purpose – of aesthetic judgment. The principle of purposiveness allowed Kant to conceive of a new kind of judgment, which he termed *reflective judgment*, judgments of singularity, as distinguished from *determinant judgment*, judgments by concepts, the type described in the *Critique of Pure Reason*.

Most important, from the perspective of Kant's Critical Philosophy, the a priori principle of the purposiveness of nature, in both its aesthetic and teleological modes,

---

[2] Lewis White Beck notes that "from the beginning, there was an ambiguity in the notion of feeling – it covered both sensation (*Empfindung*) and feeling proper (*Gefühl*). This ambiguity continued throughout the history of Wolffian aesthetics and appeared again in the two quite distinctly different meanings Kant attached to the word *Aesthetik* – the analysis of sensible cognition (intuition) and the analysis of taste" (*Early German Philosophy: Kant and His Predecessors*, 288).

provide[s] the mediating concept between the concepts of nature and the concept of freedom, which makes possible the transition from the purely theoretical to the purely practical, from the lawfulness in accordance with the former to the final end in accordance with the latter. (CPJ, 5:196)

By connecting the supersensible (the intellectual realm of freedom) to the sensible (empirical laws discovered and expressed by pure reason) in terms of the purposiveness of nature, a judgment of *reflection*, whether aesthetic or teleological, allows us to impute a design to nature (though this assertion is in no way theoretically demonstrable), thereby forging a link between self-determining human thought and conduct (freedom) and the mechanistically causal realm of nature.[3] The idea that nature is meant for us, either for our pleasure (the beautiful) or as a spur to rational transcendence (the sublime), or for our scientific need to perceive organization and systematize (or totalize) objects of inquiry, introduces a unity between feeling, cognition, and morality, or, in the words of Lewis White Beck, shows "how the realm of ends can coexist with the realm of nature."[4] Thus despite the fact that Kant's third *Critique* stresses the independence of aesthetic judgment, it would indeed be a gross misunderstanding to see the aesthetic in Kant as somehow walled off from the ethical or even the cognitive. As recent Kant scholarship has emphasized, the sublime in particular reveals a close and unique connection between aesthetics and moral consciousness in Kant's thought.[5]

The third *Critique* represents Kant's first real rethinking of the concept of judgment since the *Critique of Pure Reason*, where it was defined as "the faculty of subsuming under rules; that is, of distinguishing whether something does or does not stand under a given rule (*casus datae legis*)" (CPuR, A 132/B 171). Since there are no rules for judgment itself (thereby avoiding the infinite regress of rules for the application of rules, and so on), Kant

---

[3] In the second *Critique* Kant notes that the concept of freedom is the "*keystone* of the whole structure of a system of pure reason, even of speculative reason" (CPaR, 5:3, original emphasis).

[4] Beck, *Early German Philosophy*, 497. Beck thought that "this task was brilliantly executed in its second part, the Critique of Teleological Judgment," but that "the connection of [the third Critique's] first part, the 'Critique of Analytic Judgment,' to this final goal is exceedingly tenuous. . . . 'The Critique of Aesthetic Judgment' does complete, in an aesthetic sense, so to speak, the critical philosophy even if it does not do so in the logically systematic way Kant pretended" (*Early German Philosophy*, 497). The recent interest in the sublime is, I think, at least partly attributable to the desire to address this problem. For at least as far as morality is concerned, the sublime is obviously far more consequential than teleological judgment.

[5] Allison goes so far as to remark that the sublime is "crucial for Kant's understanding of morality, reflecting what I term the 'Stoic side' of his moral theory" (*Kant's Theory of Taste*, 9). Rodolphe Gasché, however, argues that the sublime "is equally about cognition in a very broad and elementary sense, and not primarily about morality, as so many commentators are inclined to believe" (*The Idea of Form*, 124).

stipulates that judgment is simply a "peculiar talent which can be practiced only, and cannot be taught" (CPuR, A 133/B 172). The idea that judgment transcends the rule (though not lawfulness itself) will be quite consequential for the conception of reflective judgment in the third *Critique*. In the later work, Kant defines judgment as the "faculty for thinking of the particular as contained under the universal" (CPJ, 5:179), thus eliminating the condition of "subsumption" from the general definition of judgment and allowing for a bifurcated conception: "If the universal (the rule, the principle, the law) is given, then the power of judgment, which subsumes the particular under the universal . . . is *determining*. If, however, only the particular is given, for which the universal is to be found, then the power of judgment is merely *reflecting*" (CPJ, 5:179). A reflecting or reflective judgment of taste is therefore a judgment of *singularity*: it judges *this* rose (a particular) as opposed to *a* rose (a universal). In other words, it is the judgment of an *event*: it happens only once, and, unlike empirical or scientific concepts, it is not applicable to other cases. Just because I find a particular rose beautiful, it does not then follow that all roses are beautiful – and the same holds for the sublime, which is also a judgment of reflection (though not a judgment of taste). Reflective judgment, then, does not proceed mechanically, according to a universal, a concept, but rather "technically" or "artistically," that is, with a measure of *freedom*, from the particular to indeterminate concepts (or the possibility of conceptualization). The very indeterminacy of a judgment of reflection is what preserves its singularly and its freedom.

Although reflective judgment is judgment in the absence of determinate laws or rules, it is not thereby chaotic or anarchic. Alluding to Kant's reference to a "free lawfulness" (CPJ, 5:240) or "lawfulness without law" (CPJ, 5:241), Paul Guyer describes it as "produced by the free rather than rule-governed conformity of the imagination to the law of a 'higher' cognitive faculty."[6] Henry Allison, on the other hand, perhaps thinking more of CPJ, 5:287,[7] characterizes reflective judgment as a kind of ordered limitlessness: "exhibit[ing] a pattern or order (form), which suggests an indeterminate number of possible schematizations (or conceptualizations), none of which is fully adequate, thereby occasioning further reflection or engagement with the object."[8] On this view, aesthetic reflection connotes

---

[6] Paul Guyer, *Kant and the Experience of Freedom*, 206.

[7] "Since the freedom of the imagination consists precisely in the fact that it schematizes without a concept, the judgment of taste must rest on a mere sensation of the reciprocally animating imagination in its *freedom* and the understanding in its *lawfulness*" (CPJ, 5:287, original emphasis).

[8] Allison, *Kant's Theory of Taste*, 51.

the idea of a *striving for but never arriving at a determinant concept.* In any case, it is important to note that reflective judgment *involves concepts* even if it is not a judgment *by concepts.* Aesthetic judgment might therefore be characterized as *paracognitive.* Hence Kant's idea of a "technique of nature" (*Technik der Natur*): "We shall in the future also use the expression 'technique' where objects of nature are sometimes merely *judged as if* their possibility were grounded in art, in which case the judgments are neither theoretical nor practical" (FI, 20:200–1, original emphasis). Nature is regarded *as if* it were art or technique, that is, *as if,* like a work of art, it had been specially designed for our judging faculty, without there being any objective or theoretical claim made concerning nature itself. Reflective judgment, then, functions much like a regulative or "as if" judgment, thereby recalling the account of "empty propositions" (those with no objective validity but must merely be assumed) in the first *Critique* (in the Appendix to the Transcendental Dialectic).[9]

That nature rather than fine art should be the principal or at least the most immediate focus of Kant's aesthetics is a crucial point in Kant's critical system, for only nature provides examples of "pure" aesthetic judgments, in Kant's estimation,[10] that is, those bereft of the human intentionality that characterizes works of art and that constrains judgments of taste by introducing a concept of a purpose. The seeming marginalization of art in Kant's aesthetic theory has been the source of much disagreement – and consternation – among Kant scholars and commentators on the sublime.[11]

The concept of reflective judgment helps explain how we can aesthetically judge without such a judgment having to depend on particular attributes of objects that are expressible in terms of determinate rules, such as the objectivist idea of beauty as inhering in certain qualities such

[9] The Appendix is called: "Of the Regulative Employment of the Ideas of Pure Reason." For the relation between regulative and reflective judgment, see Beatrice Longuenesse, *Kant and the Capacity to Judge*, 163–6 and Allison's discussion of Longuenesse in *Kant and the Claims of Taste*, 16–20.

[10] However, this idea is somewhat compromised by the chart Kant places at the end of the Introduction, which connects, in a fourfold: feeling of pleasure/displeasure, power of judgment, purposiveness, and art.

[11] Gasché sums up the view of many when he writes that "Kant's aesthetics is unquestionably an aesthetics of nature" (Gasché, *The Idea of Form*, 1). Fiona Hughes, however, finds it "arguable that Kant is mistaken in the exclusion of artworks and [in assuming] that [art] is unnecessary for his wider account" (*Kant's Critique of Aesthetic Judgment*, 87). Guyer, on the other hand, contends that "it would be a mistake to think that such judgments [of nature] should be the norm for all aesthetic judgments; rather Kant begins with them because they are the *simplest* cases of aesthetic judgment" (*Kant*, 312, original emphasis). However, Guyer's view seemingly neglects the problem of the "purity" (CPJ, 5:252–3) of aesthetic judgments, on which Kant bases much of his argument. See Chapter 12.

as proportionality and symmetry (the neoclassicist "rules of art" would also fall under this rubric).[12] For, to apply a concept of beauty to an object (which either corresponds to it or not) is to confuse a universal judgment of cognition with a singular judgment of beauty or sublimity, which is based on *immediate* feelings of pleasure and displeasure. However, unlike what Kant calls the "agreeable," "that which pleases the senses in sensation" (CPJ, 5:205), which is combined with an *interest* in the object (that is, a desire for it), the pleasure in the judgment of the beautiful comes not from sensation, but from the harmony of the imagination and the understanding in the *disinterested* contemplation of the object. It is thus an "intellectual" as opposed to a strictly sensorial pleasure (since the pleasure comes from the act of judging-reflecting itself). In the judgment of the sublime, on the other hand, which also involves an act of reflection, the faculties of the imagination and the understanding are in *disharmony*; the sublime pleases *against the interest* of the senses and therefore involves an element of displeasure. The beautiful and the sublime thus represent two ways of rising above mere sensibility and empirical interest – namely disinterestedness and contra-interestedness – two ways of achieving subjective autonomy in the aesthetic.

I have yet to discuss what is perhaps the most controversial claim of Kant's aesthetic theory: the seemingly contradictory idea that an aesthetic judgment can at once be entirely subjective and singular (that is, be based on a feeling of pleasure or displeasure without the mediation of a concept) and yet also *claim* universal (or objective) validity or assent – what Kant calls the "*universal validity* of a *singular* judgment" (CPJ, 5:281, original emphasis). On one level, Kant appeals to common language usage, pointing out that in the simple judgment "this rose is beautiful," it is implied both that "I find this rose beautiful" and that "the beauty of this rose should be recognized by everyone" (but not "roses are beautiful," which would not be a singular judgment of feeling). Without a shared sense of beauty, our aesthetic judgment would be private and as such noncommunicable. Without singularity, there would be no actual *experience* of beauty (or sublimity). Thus with reflective judgment, judgment by *indeterminate* concepts, Kant can have it both ways, as it were: a judgment grounded on feeling that, by being reflective, is nevertheless related to concepts (principally to an indeterminate concept of purposiveness – purposiveness without purpose) and

---

[12] Thus Kant does not have to change his mind regarding the impossibility of judging by rules or determinate concepts, a view he had held since before the writing of the first *Critique*. As mentioned above, Kant had for a long time thought that aesthetic judgments were merely empirical, not transcendental.

can thereby claim universal validity on a transcendental basis.[13] In discovering an a priori principle of taste, Kant is therefore able to ground the idea of intersubjective agreement, what Kant calls "*sensus communis*" (common sense/common sensibility), or universal "communicability,"[14] with regard to aesthetic judgment, judgment by feeling.[15]

In the judgment of the beautiful, the feeling of pleasure or satisfaction in purposive form (ideally of nature) is a result of the *harmony* produced between the faculties of the imagination (the faculty of presentation) and the understanding (the faculty "for the cognition of the general of rules" [FI, 20:201]). Since a judgment of beauty proceeds from the particular to the universal, the pleasure occurs when the imagination's grasping of (purposive) form engages the faculty of understanding in an act of reflection (rather than subsumption), meaning that it involves indeterminate as opposed to determinate concepts. A judgment of sublimity, on the other hand, involves not the purposiveness of nature, but the *purposive use* of a representation of nature for our highest faculty, namely reason,[16] both pure and practical (that is, the Mathematically and Dynamically Sublime, respectively). Although not a judgment of taste, due to its mixture of pleasure and emotional agitation, a judgment of sublimity is nevertheless aesthetic: it involves reflection and subjective purposiveness without a concept (purposiveness without purpose).

9.2 The sublime versus the beautiful: form (*Form*), feeling (*Gefühl*), and purposiveness (*Zweckmäßigkeit*)

The Analytic of the Sublime occupies a relatively small part of the third *Critique*. Although it is not much shorter, in terms of the number of pages devoted to it, than the Analytic of the Beautiful, its seven dense sections (§23–§29) appear to many commentators to fit awkwardly within the

---

[13] However, the idea that certain aesthetic judgments, namely the sublime, require prior cultivation does introduce a sociocultural element into the equation. See Chapter 12 of this study.

[14] Samuel Weber has recently emphasized that it is indeed a state of mind that is communicated: "No knowledge, however, is actually communicated in the aesthetic judgment of beauty or the sublime: rather, a certain state of mind (*Gemütszustand*) that is felt to be indissolubly linked to a singular representation is experienced as being potentially communicable, which is to say, capable of being communicated universally" (*Benjamin's –abilities*, 13). I discuss *Gemütszustand* in Chapter 10.

[15] Kant specifically stipulates that this "common sense" is not to be confused with common understanding (CPJ, 5:238). Though today we say "everyone has his or her own taste" (that is, taste is a strictly individual affair, a relative judgment), eighteenth-century thinkers generally believed in the uniformity of aesthetic judgments, in their shared, intersubjective nature.

[16] "The faculty of the *determination* of the particular through the general (for the derivation of principles)" (FI, 20:201, original emphasis).

general framework of Kant's exposition. The comparatively more elaborate and systematic presentation of the beautiful has prompted critics to
view the Analytic of the Sublime as a kind of afterthought or supplement
that does not add much of substance to the basic arguments of Kant's
aesthetic theory – despite the fact that, as has been amply demonstrated
in the previous two chapters, the sublime had been an integral part of
Kant's thinking prior to the writing of the third *Critique*. Kant himself
has lent support to such a view by famously calling the sublime "a mere
appendix to the aesthetic judging of the purposiveness of nature" (CPJ,
5:246), a remark used by many to justify their neglect of the sublime
in favor of the beautiful.[17] However, as I shall argue later in this chapter,
this statement, when considered in context, does not actually support the
treatment of the sublime as marginal or of secondary importance in
Kant's account.

Kant introduces his discussion of the sublime in §23 with a brief, point-
by-point comparison between the sublime and the beautiful.[18] First the
similarities. Both are singular judgments (*this* raging storm, *this* rose),
and both claim universal or intersubjective validity. Insofar as both are
judgments of reflection, they do not involve subsumption under concepts,
but are "nevertheless still related to concepts, although it is indeterminate
which" (CPJ, 5:244). Both the beautiful and the sublime are judgments
based on *feeling* (of pleasure and displeasure/pleasure, respectively); and
they ultimately "please for themselves" (CPJ, 5:244); that is, they exhibit
purposiveness for the judging faculty alone (subjective purposiveness,
reflective aesthetic judgment), rather than for some extrinsic end (objective
purposiveness, reflective teleological judgment). In §24 Kant notes that the
four modalities that organized his presentation of the beautiful – quantity
(universally valid), quality (disinterested), relation (subjectively purposive), modality (necessary) – also apply to the sublime, albeit with certain
caveats,[19] with the difference that the sublime requires the division into the
Mathematical and the Dynamical.

The principal differences between the two judgments relate to form,
feeling, and purposiveness. The beautiful involves the purposiveness of

[17] One commentator who resists this characterization is Hughes. See her *Kant's Critique of Aesthetic Judgment*, 78.
[18] Kant entitles §23 "Transition from the faculty for judging the beautiful to that for judging the sublime."
[19] Sublimity is less universal in fact than the beautiful (see Chapter 12); sublimity involves a contra-purposiveness that goes *against* the interest of sense (see this chapter); sublimity involves the purposive *use* of a contrapurposive representation of nature (see this chapter); the necessity of judgments of sublimity is linked to morality (see Chapter 12).

form for subjective judging, "which consists in limitation" (CPJ, 5:244).[20] By contrast, the judgment of the sublime "is to be found in a formless object insofar as *limitlessness* is represented in it, or at least at its instance, and yet it is also thought as a totality" (CPJ, 5:244). Three interrelated conditions are thus enumerated: formlessness, limitlessness, and the idea of totality; the first depends on the second, and the second on the third. In the encounter with an object of great magnitude it is pure reason's demand for totality of presentation that occasions the perception and feeling of limitlessness: that is, the imagination "presents" such an object by its very failure to present it. The "formlessness" of the object is simply a function of the absence of limits it displays (in other words, the magnitudinous object need not be intrinsically formless). Reason can be said to "cause" the formlessness to appear by introducing limitlessness into the representation through its demand of totality of presentation. The sublime, then, does not involve mere formlessness but *boundless* formlessness, that formlessness that is associated with excessive magnitude. In sum, the overwhelmingly large object exhibits limitless formlessness by being referred to a rule of reason (the demand of totality), which, as in the beautiful, does not in any way determine the object (cognition): "The beautiful seems to be taken as the presentation of an indeterminate concept of the understanding, but the sublime as that of a similar concept of reason" (CPJ, 5:244).

Although in this section (§23) Kant purports to address the sublime in general, his discussion corresponds for the most part to what he calls the Mathematically Sublime, the judgment of the aesthetic estimation of magnitudes. The focus on boundlessness and formlessness (in particular, the reference to the rational idea of "totality") appears to leave out the Dynamically Sublime, the aesthetic judgment of nature as a power; for it is not immediately clear how – or even if – natural power specifically involves these two conditions (moreover, the Dynamically Sublime derives from the rational demand for "autonomy," as opposed to totality). Adding to the confusion, Kant later stipulates (perhaps as a nod to the Dynamically Sublime) that the object involved in a judgment of sublimity "can be formless" (CPJ, 5:249). Formlessness thus does not seem to be a necessary

---

[20] For a recent discussion of the notion of "form" in Kant's aesthetics, see Gasché, *The Idea of Form: Rethinking Kant's Aesthetics*: "As Kant elaborates it throughout the Third Critique, form is not an objective attribute of certain things. It is not a construct of lines that objectively draws the contours of a thing, or the delineation (*Zeichnung*) that interlaces its characteristics into the definite shape of a figure. Form names a subjective condition concerning the representability of certain things, that is, their fitness for being judged" (179).

condition for judgments of sublimity in general. However, the form/
formless dichotomy does offer Kant a clearer and cleaner contrast with
the beautiful, and it also supports Kant's general claim that the sublime is
not a judgment that applies to objects but rather to the mind.

As mentioned above, Kant is not speaking of mere formlessness, but of
boundless formlessness. Mere formlessness (that which is not associated with
the demand of totality) is simply *ugly*; it produces only displeasure.[21] The
sublime, however, involves a special kind of encounter with ugliness (and a
special kind of dissatisfaction), which, though *contrapurposive* for our
faculty of presentation, for the accord between the imagination and the
understanding (the beautiful), is nevertheless purposive for the mind as a
whole: "That which . . . excites in us the feeling of the sublime, may to be
sure appear in its form to be contrapurposive for our power of judgment,
unsuitable for our faculty of presentation, and as it were doing violence to
our imagination, but is nevertheless judged all the more sublime for that"
(CPJ, 5:245). The formal contrapurposiveness of the sublime is precisely
purposive for our rational faculty and, given the preeminence of reason in
Kant's concept of the human being, is therefore purposive for the "whole
vocation of the mind" (CPJ, 5:259), a stipulation that includes our moral
being (practical rationality). This yields the doubly paradoxical concept of
purposive contrapurposiveness (without a purpose), which contrasts with the
simple purposiveness of the beautiful: "For just as imagination and *understanding* produce subjective purposiveness of the powers of the mind in the
judging of the beautiful through their unison, so do imagination and *reason*
produce subjective purposiveness through their conflict" (CPJ, 5:258,
original emphasis). This unequal conflict – in which the higher faculty,
reason, makes its superiority felt over the lower, the imagination – allows us
to experience sublimity as a transcendence of, or freedom from, sensible
constraint (or interest) in a more direct and dramatic way than in the
beautiful (which involves a nonhierarchal, and thus harmonious, relation
between the imagination and the understanding). This *agonistic* element
of the Kantian sublime, which is constitutive of Kant's conception of
aesthetic transcendence – expressed in terms of the dual structure of the
overwhelming of our imaginative capacity and the *elevation* by our rational
capacity – is not often noted by commentators, and we will have occasion
to further explore it in the following two chapters.[22]

---

[21] Gasché notes that "the boundless formlessness of the sublime is not the symmetrical opposite
of beautiful form; the opposite of beauty is instead mere formlessness, mere absence of form . . . .
A formless thing is found ugly" (*The Idea of Form*, 123).

[22] It also connects Kant theory to that of Longinus. See Chapters 2 and 3.

As will be recalled, Kant, as early as the *Observations*, had accepted the idea, articulated by Burke and Moses Mendelssohn, that the sublime involved complex pleasure. In the third *Critique*, the dual transcendence-structure of sublimity is thus defined by a correspondingly dual affective structure: a *pain* produced by the overbearing grandeur (Mathematically Sublime) or dominating force (Dynamically Sublime) of nature, and a *pleasure* taken in the self-exaltation that accompanies the realization of reason's supersensible vocation. The question of how the combination of pleasure and pain is experienced – that is, the question of the phenomenology of the feeling of the sublime – is ambiguous in Kant's theory. Kant offers at least three different accounts of the interaction of pleasure and displeasure: as simultaneous, as alternating, and as successive (displeasure followed by pleasure).[23] Kant also describes the pleasure taken in the sublime as "indirect" and even "negative" (CPJ, 5:245). What is particularly intriguing about Kant's embrace of the conventional idea (since Burke) of complex pleasure in the sublime is its more or less explicit association with his moral philosophy, in the description of the feeling of sublimity in terms of "admiration or respect," feelings that presuppose a measure of negativity, in Kant's view. As we saw in the previous chapter, "respect" is one of the key concepts of Kant's *Critique of Practical Reason*. The use of this term thus establishes a ground of analogy (or qualified identity) between the experience of sublimity and moral feeling that Kant will exploit, particularly in the Dynamically Sublime.

The feeling of the sublime is also distinguished from that of the beautiful by being an "emotion" (*Rührung*, "to be stirred"), although the relation between *Rührung* and "admiration or respect" is not quite clear, even if all are instances of "negative pleasure." In the *Anthropology*, Kant writes that "the sublime, therefore, is not an object of taste, but a feeling of emotion [*das Gefühl der Rührung*]" (APP, 7:243). In the third *Critique, Rührung* is described as "not play [as in the beautiful] but something serious in the activity of the imagination" (CPJ, 5:245), which means that "the mind is

---

[23] With regard to simultaneity: "The feeling of the sublime is thus a feeling of displeasure from the inadequacy of the imagination ... by means of reason, and a pleasure that is thereby aroused *at the same time*" (CPJ, 5:257, my emphasis). With regard to alternation: "This movement (especially in its inception) may be compared to a vibration, i.e., to a *rapidly alternating* repulsion from and attraction to one and the same object" (CPJ, 5:258, my emphasis). In §23, Kant's description implies a unidirectional succession, from pain to pleasure: "A momentary inhibition of the vital powers and the immediately following and all the more powerful outpouring of them" (CPJ, 5:245). As Guyer notes, there is also the question as to whether complex pleasure involves separate feelings combined in one experience or one feeling that is irreducibly complex (*Kant and the Experience of Freedom*, 211).

not merely attracted by the object," as in the beautiful, "but is also reciprocally *repelled* by it" (CPJ, 5:245, my emphasis). Thus: "The mind feels itself *moved* [*bewegt*] in the representation of the sublime in nature, while in the aesthetic judgment on the beautiful in nature it is in *calm* contemplation" (CPJ, 5:258, original emphasis), a standard contrast in the literature (as we saw, this contrast was articulated for the first time by Dennis).[24] It should be noted that the English phrase "to be moved" is also a possible translation of *Rührung* (even though the German term used in the above-quoted passage is *bewegt*).[25] The idea of emotional agitation, however, seems more particularly suited to the Dynamically Sublime, the "seriousness" of which derives from seeing nature as threatening to one's well-being. It is thus not clear how a great magnitude can produce *Rührung* in the same way (or to the same extent) as a great and threatening power.

We now come to the most controversial element in the comparison between the beautiful and the sublime: the radical discontinuity between the sublime and the beautiful in regards to the ontological implications (or grounding) of each judgment:

> From this one immediately sees that we express ourselves on the whole incorrectly if we call some object of nature sublime, although we can quite correctly call very many of them beautiful; for how can we designate with an expression of approval that which is apprehended in itself as contrapurposive? We can say no more than the object serves for the presentation of a sublimity that can be found in the mind. (CPJ, 5:245)

Sublimity, then, is *of the mind*; it is a mental elevation resulting from a *transcendence* of sensibility: "The mind is incited to abandon sensibility and to occupy itself with ideas that contain a higher purposiveness" (CPJ, 5:246). A common feature of Continental and Anglo-Analytic interpretations of Kant's theory is the lack of emphasis on (or indifference to) the idea of "sublimity of mind," which I see as central both to an understanding of Kant's theory and to how it fits within the broader history of the sublime.[26] The antisubjectivism of recent Continental thinkers predisposes them to dismiss the idea that the sublime demonstrates, in the words

---

[24] See Chapter 5.

[25] This aligns the Kantian conception of sublimity with the Latin rhetorical tradition of *movere*. See Chapter 1 and Francis Goyet's *Le sublime du "lieu commun": L'invention rhétorique dans l'Antiquité et à la Renaissance.*

[26] This is not to say that these thinkers are not aware of what Kant is attempting to do. For example, Jacques Derrida writes: "All we can say is that the natural object in question can be proper, apt (*tauglich*) for the 'presentation of a sublimity.' Of a sublimity which, for its part, can be encountered as such only in the mind and on the side of the subject" (*The Truth in Painting*, 131).

of John Zammito, "a connection between aesthetic experience and the ultimate nature of the self."[27] On the Anglo-Analytic side, the resistance is often expressed as a logical conundrum. Guyer, for example, finds it "peculiar" that Kant "differentiates the judgments on the beautiful and the sublime by holding that some particular object can always be treated as both cause and grammatical subject of the former, but as cause and not grammatical subject of the latter."[28] Mary McCloskey similarly contends "we can just as well say that the 'sublime' objects are apt for outraging the imagination and thus for calling up the ideas of Reason, as we can say that beautiful objects are apt for setting the imagination and the understanding into free play."[29]

As I observed in the first chapter with regard to the translation of the Greek term *hypsos*, the German term for sublimity, *das Erhabene*, is misleading linguistically when rendered with the Latinate "sublime." *Das Erhabene*, which is actually a much closer approximation of Longinus's *hypsos*, would be more faithfully translated by "elevation." Indeed, the verbal form, *erheben*, is generally translated with a form of "to elevate" in modern English editions of Kant's works. Like *hypsos, das Erhabene*, as a *metaphor*, is not generally applied to objects, but rather to the mind or to human expression (language, art) as a term of praise ("lofty words," "elevated sentiments," and so on). Its literal use (that is, for objects) often involves rather banal observations, such as "elevated platform," and the like. It is thus not surprising that Kant finds improper or even unseemly the idea of using *das Erhabene* to refer to objects, even if Burke had used the English word "sublime" in just such a manner:

---

[27] John Zammito, *The Genesis of Kant's* Critique of Judgment, 278. This is an idea that, as I seek to show, reveals a continuity with Longinus's theory of sublimity, with his aesthetic conception of "nobility of mind" (*megalophrosynê*) and of human *telos*.

[28] Guyer, *Kant and the Experience of Freedom*, 218. But Guyer, seemingly reluctantly, comes to accept the idea that "the physical properties play a causal role in this reflection, but it is our own moral character which is ultimately the object of our pleasure. To this extent Kant is justified in denying that the property of sublimity can be properly attributed to the external objects which may stimulate our reflection" (*Kant and the Experience of Freedom*, 221).

[29] Mary McCloskey, *Kant's Aesthetic*, 98. The only justification for this differing treatment in McCloskey's mind would be a distinction between an "internal" relation of pleasure to its object in the beautiful and an "external" relation in the case of sublimity. McCloskey says that though "suggestions to this effect are thrown out by Kant," they come to naught, as Kant did not formulate "clearly" enough the "notion of the object of pleasure" (*Kant's Aesthetic*, 98). However, Kant, in the First Introduction to the third *Critique*, makes just such an intrinsic–extrinsic distinction with regard to the kinds of purposiveness that relate to the beautiful and the sublime respectively. I discuss this below.

> It is also evident from this that true sublimity [*Erhabene*] must be sought
> only in the mind of the one who judges, not in the object of nature, the
> judging of which occasions this disposition in it. And who would want to
> call sublime [*Erhabene*] shapeless mountain passes towering above one
> another in wild disorder, with their pyramids of ice, or the dark and raging
> sea, etc.? (CPJ, 5:256)

In other words: why would one use a *term of praise* for such ugly and
terrible things?[30] In Kant's understanding, *das Erhabene* connotes a mental
disposition that possesses no intrinsic relation with an object that merely
"occasions" it. If one were to substitute the word "elevation" for "sublimity" and "elevated" for "sublime" in the passage just cited, Kant's
meaning would become immediately clear; for we have indeed become
habituated to using the term "sublime" for the things Kant describes,
whereas the word "elevated," as in "the elevated ocean," for example,
would obviously be linguistically improper (though an "elevated description of the ocean" would be perfectly acceptable).[31]

In addition to the linguistic argument (largely implicit), there is also the
substantive point that in a judgment of sublimity the object is in fact
judged as *ugly*, as contrapurposive; hence there is no sense in which the
object itself could be considered sublime. On this view, then, there are two
kinds of objects: beautiful and ugly, purposive and contrapurposive. Ugly
objects divide into the simply contrapurposive and the purposively contrapurposive: that is, those that are simply ugly and those that, by virtue of
their specific contrapurposiveness (boundless limitlessness or threatening
power), are suitable to a "purposive use" for our rational supersensible
vocation (a judgment of sublimity).

The question of the ontological grounding of judgments of sublimity
thus turns on the relation between "purposiveness" and "purposive use,"
which is laid out in detail in section 12 of the First Introduction: "One can
divide all purposiveness, whether it is subjective or objective, into *internal*
and *relative* purposiveness, the first of which is grounded in the representation of the object in itself, the second merely in the contingent *use* of it"
(FI, 20:249, original emphasis). Kant elaborates:

---

[30] In §29, Kant speaks about the sublime in terms of "a judgment about this *excellence* of the objects of
nature" (CPJ, 5:264, my emphasis).

[31] In discussing the semantics of *das Erhabene*, Gasché writes: "I should point out here that *Erhabenheit*
(sublimity) suggests *Gehobenheit* (elevation, elatedness). The latter, significantly, cannot be predicated of objects of nature but refers to the position of the human being as a social and moral being,
as well as to the position of the mind" (*The Idea of Form*, 143).

The form of an object can, *first*, already be perceived as purposive for the reflecting power of judgment by itself, i.e., in the mere intuition without any concept, and then the subjective purposiveness is attributed to the thing and to nature itself; *second*, the object may, in perception, have nothing at all purposive for reflection in the determination of its form in itself, although its representation, when applied to a purposiveness lying in the subject *a priori*, for the arousal of its feeling (that, say, of the supersensible determination of the powers of the mind of the subject), can ground an aesthetic judgment, which is related to a principle *a priori* (although to be sure only a subjective one), not, as in the first case, in accordance with a *purposiveness of nature* in regard to the subject, but only in regard to a possible purposive *use* of certain sensible intuitions in accordance with their form by means of the merely reflecting power of judgment. Thus if the first judgment attributes *beauty* to the objects of nature, but the second attributes to it *sublimity* ... then no special technique of nature is to be presupposed for the latter, because it is merely a matter of a contingent use of the representation, not for the sake of the cognition of the object, but rather with a view to another feeling, namely that of the inner purposiveness in the disposition of the powers of the mind. (FI, 20:249–50, original emphasis)

Ultimately, then, the sublime reveals the *mind's own purposiveness*, namely its supersensible vocation (transcendence), which involves nature as a means to an end (hence its "relative" status). The question is: can the sublime still be integral to the theory of reflective judgment, and thus to Kant's aesthetic theory more generally, if it involves only relative purposiveness rather than intrinsic purposiveness (the purposiveness of natural form)? Given Kant's analysis above, I believe that we can answer in the affirmative. Indeed, at the end of this passage Kant observes that "the judgment on the sublime in nature is not to be excluded from the division of the aesthetic of the reflecting power of judgment, because it also expresses a subjective purposiveness which is not based on a concept of the object" (FI, 20:250).[32] Although the stipulation that the sublime is "not to be excluded" from the Critique of the Aesthetic Power of Judgment hardly sounds like an enthusiastic endorsement of its importance, Kant is merely anticipating the objection that results from his non-symmetrical treatment of the sublime and the beautiful with regard to their grounding and a priori basis. It is quite clear from Kant's statement that the sublime in fact *completes* the concept of reflective judgment in regards to the aesthetic. Kant shows how aesthetic reflection can refer both to indeterminate ideas

---

[32] Nevertheless, Allison argues that "such a 'higher purposiveness' clearly stands apart from the theory of reflective judgment and the purposiveness of nature that serves as its 'category'" (*Kant's Theory of Taste*, 311).

of reason (the sublime) and to indeterminate concepts of the understanding (the beautiful). It should be noted that the term "reflective judgment" is completely absent from the Analytic of the Beautiful, whereas this fundamental concept is discussed on several occasions in the sections on the sublime, as if the sublime were somehow more apt for its elucidation.

Regarding the commonsense perception that the feeling of sublimity is directed to nature rather than to ourselves, Kant appeals to the idea of "subreption" (a term he uses only once in the body of the third *Critique*)[33] to account for how the feeling that accompanies our rational transcendence of sensibility is transferred to the object that occasions it:[34]

> Thus the feeling of the sublime in nature is respect for our own vocation, which we show to an object in nature through a certain subreption (substitution of a respect for the object instead of for the idea of humanity in our subject), which as it were makes intuitable the superiority of the rational vocation of our cognitive faculty over the greatest faculty of sensibility. (CPJ, 5:257)

Thus when we say that an object is beautiful we are saying that the object *qua* form is purposive for our mental faculties, whereas when we judge an object sublime we are really judging the sublimity or elevation of our own minds as prompted by an object, rather than the object itself. "Subreption," then, describes the tendency of the judgment of sublimity to confuse a subjective determination with an objective one. The concept of subreption also allows Kant to reaffirm, as noted in the previous chapter, that the feeling of "*respect* is always directed to persons, never to things" (CPaR, 5:76, original emphasis). That is, the feeling of respect in the sublime is not directed to the magnitudinous or powerful object, but rather to the "idea of humanity within ourselves as subjects" (CPJ, 5:257).

We are now in a position to interpret Kant's comment that the Analytic of the Sublime is a "mere appendix" to the Analytic of the Beautiful. Let us consider the entire passage in view of our analysis:

> From this we see that the concept of the sublime in nature is far from being as important and rich in consequences as that of its beauty, and that in

[33] Another mention occurs in the First Introduction, but only as a parenthetical remark in Latin: *vitium subreptionis*. Werner Pluhar notes that the Latin *subreptionis* appears in Kant's *Inaugural Dissertation* of 1770, where Kant writes: "We may call a fallacy of subreption (by analogy with the accepted meaning) the intellect's trick of slipping in a concept of sense as if it were the concept of an intellectual characteristic" (quoted in Kant, *The Critique of Judgment*, trans. Pluhar, 114, note).
[34] Zammito goes so far as to claim that "Kant's whole theory of the sublime revolved around 'subreption' – viewing an object of nature as though it were the ground of a feeling which in fact had its source in the self" (*The Genesis of Kant's* Critique of Judgment, 280).

general it indicates nothing purposive itself, but only in the possible *use* of its intuitions to make palpable in ourselves a purposiveness that is entirely independent of nature. For the beautiful in nature we must seek a ground outside ourselves, but for the sublime merely one in ourselves and in the way of thinking that introduces sublimity into the representation of the former – a very necessary introductory remark, which entirely separates the ideas of the sublime from that of the purposiveness of *nature*, and makes of the theory of the sublime a mere appendix to the aesthetic judging of the purposiveness of nature, since by this means no particular form is represented in the latter, but only a purposive use that the imagination makes of its representation is developed. (CPJ, 5:246, original emphasis)

Kant underlines the word "nature" because he does not want to divorce the sublime from the more general concept of subjective purposiveness. The sublime is an "appendix" only in terms of its relation to the *formal purposiveness of nature*, the a priori basis for the Analytic of the Beautiful. Thus it is not the affective difference between the sublime and the beautiful (the incongruity between the "liking" of the latter and the complex feeling of the former)[35] that leads Kant to designate the sublime as an "appendix." It is the fundamental *asymmetry* – which inhibits any strictly oppositional relation – between judgments of beauty (grounded in nature, in the object) and judgments of sublimity (grounded in the mind, in its more direct and higher purposiveness). In the *Anthropology*, Kant states that "the *sublime* is the counterweight but not the opposite of the beautiful" (APP 7:243).[36] To the extent, however, that the judgment of the sublime involves the "purposive use" of representations of nature to reveal the mind's supersensible vocation, nature is still nominally "purposive" (though it does not exhibit formal purposiveness), as Kant will make clear when he states that natural grandeur and power allow us to measure ourselves against nature, thereby producing a feeling of superiority and/or independence vis-à-vis nature. As Jacques Derrida puts it, "the mind . . . contents itself with *using* nature to give us a feeling of a finality [*finalité*, purposiveness] independent of nature."[37] In other words, the idea of nature as *hospitable* (purposive)

---

[35] Allison adopts Pluhar's translation of *Wohlgefallen* as "liking," but Guyer and Matthews prefer "satisfaction" in their translation.

[36] In a similar vein, Derrida notes that "one can hardly speak of an *opposition* between the beautiful and the sublime. An opposition could only arise between two determinate objects, having their contours, their edges, their finitude. But if the difference between the beautiful and the sublime does not amount to an opposition, it is precisely because the presence of a limit is what gives form to the beautiful" (*The Truth in Painting*, 127, original emphasis). And in his essay "Economimesis" (21), Derrida similarly asserts: "The sublime is not the absolute other of the beautiful."

[37] Derrida, *The Truth in Painting*, 132.

is as important for Kant as the idea of nature as *inhospitable* (contra-purposive – as, for example, in the connection between the Dynamically Sublime and Kant's idea of "moral worth," morality in a situation of adversity, which I discuss in Chapter 11). Both the beautiful and the sublime involve seeing nature as ultimately promoting human well-being and freedom. In the sublime we seek to *transcend* nature, within and without, whereas in the beautiful we merely appreciate its seeming benevolence.[38] This feeling of transcendence Kant terms *Geistesgefühl*, spiritual feeling, "the capacity for representing a sublimity in objects" (FI, 20:250), in contrast to *Lebensgefühl*, feeling of life, associated with the beautiful.[39]

***

The main contention of this chapter is that the Analytic of the Sublime is not, as some might have it, an afterthought,[40] a "mere appendix" *in regards to the general project* of Critique of the Aesthetic Power of Judgment, that is, with respect to the development of the cardinal ideas of reflective judgment and subjective purposiveness. If Kant's analytical framework obliges him to "compare" the sublime and the beautiful, even if the latter applies to objects whereas the former refers only to the judging subject, it is because (1) both manifest a (merely) subjective purposiveness – a purposiveness without purpose – that characterizes aesthetic judgment in general and distinguishes it from teleological judgment; and (2) both are conducive to morality and thus to the bridging of the divide between nature and freedom. As the following two chapters will argue, sublimity, due to its more profound subjective implications – namely due to its more effective and pronounced mental elevation above sensible determination – is more consequential for the practical and cognitive aims of Kant's Critical Philosophy than is the beautiful, thus belying the traditional privilege granted to the beautiful in Analytic Philosophy and the resistance to the idea of sublimity of mind in Continental Philosophy.

---

[38] Guyer remarks that "both aesthetic and teleological experience give us crucial encouragement in our fundamental task of literally transforming the *natural world* into a *moral world*" (*Kant*, 308, original emphasis).

[39] In a personal email, Allen Wood characterized the difference as follows: "The feeling of life is natural and harmonious, whereas the feeling of spirit exhibits the conflict, ambiguity, dissatisfaction, and also elevation, that are part of the human condition, the privilege and also the curse of being rational" (May 4, 2012). See John Zammito's chapter "Aesthetics as the Key to Anthropology: *Lebensgefühl* and *Geistesgefühl*" (Zammito, *The Genesis of Kant's* Critique of Judgment, 292–305).

[40] Allison, for example, writes that "Kant only included a discussion of the sublime at the last minute, and even then tended to downplay its significance" (*Kant's Theory of Taste*, 307).

Judging nature as a magnitude: the Mathematically Sublime

With the division between the Mathematically Sublime (§25-§26) and the Dynamically Sublime (§28),[1] Kant endeavors to appropriate two distinct but interrelated strains of eighteenth-century aesthetic thought: the one relating to ideas of grandeur (magnitude) and the other to power (terror). As noted in the previous chapter, Kant's ability to accommodate the sublime within the Critical Philosophy stems from the two transcendental ideas he sees as underlying this division: the Mathematically Sublime relates to theoretical reason's demand for *totality*; the Dynamically Sublime to practical reason's demand for *autonomy*. Two types of transcendence are thus defined: in the first instance, the freedom of theoretical reason from the constraints of sensible intuition (the finitude of the imagination); in the second, the freedom of practical reason from the dictates of sensible inclination (attachment to life, instinct of self-preservation). Both forms of sublimity recall and reaffirm the main thrust of Kant's moral philosophy: the idea that man can transcend the limitations placed on him by his sensuous nature and natural causality, thereby realizing the essential freedom on which rational moral consciousness is grounded. Since the experience of sublimity puts us *directly* in touch with the supersensible realm of freedom, I contend that its "higher purposiveness" is more meaningful for morality than the beautiful, whose relation to morality is indirect or symbolic (as described in §59 of the third *Critique* entitled "On beauty as a symbol of morality").

The first section of this chapter explores Kant's distinction between the absolutely and the simply great, showing how this contrast helps him to define a quasi-theological concept of transcendence as a relation to infinity. The second section examines Kant's description of the mental disposition (*Geistesstimmung*) occasioned by the paradoxical experience of a finite

---

[1] Although §27 and §29 are placed under the rubric of the Mathematically Sublime (A.) and the Dynamically Sublime (B.) respectively, these in fact involve the sublime in general.

presentation of infinity, insisting on the centrality of the idea of "sublimity of mind" for Kant's account. The third section analyzes the shift in perspective in §26, in which sublime transcendence is considered from the vantage point of the imagination, in terms of a "maximum." The fourth section studies how Kant seeks to further define the concept of contrapurposiveness in nature through his treatment of the "impure" judgments of the monstrous and the colossal. Throughout this chapter, I contend that Kant's account of the feeling of mental *superiority* engendered by the *agonistic* struggle with the contrapurposiveness of natural grandeur suggests the outlines of a heroic subjectivity, which will then be more emphatically elaborated in the Dynamically Sublime.

10.1   The absolutely and the simply great

Although section §25 is entitled "Nominal Definition of the Sublime," it appears to apply only to the Mathematically Sublime. This serves to reinforce the impression, alluded to in the previous chapter, that Kant considers the Mathematically Sublime to be more exemplary of the sublime in general or at least as more primary than the Dynamically Sublime (hence the privilege granted to it by some commentators).

Kant begins §25 by asserting that "we call *sublime* that which is *absolutely great* [*schlechthin groß*]," which amounts to a positive description of what, in the earlier comparison between the sublime and the beautiful, had been characterized negatively as an intuition exhibiting limitlessness or *infinity* (a trope of sublimity for over a century).[2] Kant then proceeds by making a basic distinction between two types of natural magnitude, the "absolutely" and the "simply" great: "Simply to say that something is great is also something entirely different from saying that it is absolutely great (*absolute, non comparative magnum*)" (CPJ, 5:248). This distinction is crucial to Kant's account, since only that which, as Kant says, "*is great beyond all comparison*" (CPJ, 5:248, original emphasis) conduces to sublimity. Nevertheless, under the concept of the "simply great" (*schlechtweg groß*) Kant distinguishes a whole class of objects that, to the extent they occasion a mental expansion and thereby induce feelings of awe or astonishment,

[2] Starting with Thomas Burnet's *The Sacred Theory of the Earth* (1684). In fact, Kant will use "the absolutely great" and "infinity" interchangeably to describe an overwhelming magnitude. As far as I am aware, Kant is the only theorist of the sublime to use the terminology of the "absolute" to describe natural grandeur, a word which, like "the infinite," is often used as another name for God. However, the connection between God and natural sublimity will be addressed only in the section on the Dynamically Sublime and in the discussion of "enthusiasm" in the General Remark following §29.

are akin to sublimity.[3] In making this contrast, Kant clearly designs to separate an authentic experience of transcendence (one proximate to religious experience) from experiences that resemble it only superficially.

As part of his preliminary exposition, Kant also draws a distinction between magnitude and greatness, noting that they are "quite different concepts" (CPJ, 5:248) and that the distinction is analogous (according to the use of the term "likewise")[4] to the relation between simple greatness (a comparative judgment) and absolute greatness (a noncomparative judgment). That is, one can judge something to be a magnitude (merely to have size) without necessarily comparing it to something else: "That something is a magnitude can be cognized from the thing itself" insofar as it is a "unity" of heterogeneous elements (CPJ, 5:248). This judgment of a magnitude as a unity, though noncomparative (like the absolutely great), is nevertheless not absolute, which would require the reflective judgment associated with sublimity. The simple assessment of size instead involves *determinant* judgment ("cognized") and is therefore not an aesthetic judgment.

The judgment of comparative magnitudes, on the other hand, given that it is "grounded in a subjective purposiveness of the representation in relation to the power of judgment" (CPJ, 5:248), does involve reflective judgment. Presumably this subjective purposiveness is due to the nature of comparison itself, which entails the judging of one thing in terms of another, rather than in terms of a (determinant) concept. By this logic, then, *any* comparative judgment of magnitude – "great or small or medium-sized" – qualifies ipso facto as an *aesthetic* judgment, since "it does not bring with it any principle of cognition at all" (CPJ, 5:248). In other words, comparison is a form of reflection and can therefore claim universal agreement: "Even though the standard for comparison is merely subjective, the judgment nonetheless lays claim to universal assent; the judgments 'The man is beautiful' and 'He is great' do not restrict themselves merely to the judging subject, but, like theoretical judgments, demand everyone's assent" (CPJ, 5:248). The judgment of the simply great thereby makes the same normative claims as the beautiful and the sublime.

Although judgments such as "this mountain is great" do not prima facie appear to be comparative judgments, they nonetheless *imply* comparative

---

[3] Henry Allison, for example, calls the simply great "a kind of proto- or quasi-sublime" (*Kant's Theory of Taste*, 312).

[4] "To be great and to be a magnitude are quite different concepts (*magnitudo* and *quantitas*). Likewise, to simply say something is great. . . ." (CPJ, 5:248).

judgments of objects "of the same kind." Thus a judgment of the greatness of a mountain, however indeterminate, makes sense only by comparison with other mountains, the greatness of a river by comparison other rivers, and so on (that is, a mountain may be great among mountains but small when compared with the ocean or the cosmos): "In a judgment by which something is described simply as great it is not merely said that the object has magnitude, but rather that it is attributed to it in a superior extent than to many others of the same kind" (CPJ, 5:249). It should be noted that such judgments of comparative magnitudes are neither beautiful nor sublime, though one type, the simply great, is sublime-like. Kant offers no aesthetic classifications for these (since he would have to invent them), and it is also not clear what specific kind of pleasure would be involved in such judgments, apart from the simply great, where the pleasure is due to "the enlargement of the imagination itself" (CPJ, 5:249).[5] These judgments of comparative magnitude would appear to be marginal to our aesthetic experience; that is, we tend not to think of them as aesthetic per se, though they do involve reflective judgment without the concept of an end; they are also distinct from the mathematically determining judgment (numerical measurement), although Kant will have more to say about this last point in §25 (discussed below).

Despite a very terse and somewhat convoluted presentation, Kant's broader aim is clear: to set the stage for explaining how a judgment of the absolutely great can be both noncognitive and noncomparative, given Kant's assertion that the question "how great?" – presumably the starting point for any aesthetic estimation of magnitudes – is necessarily a comparative judgment. This leads Kant to claim, rather paradoxically, that the judgment of the absolutely great involves either a *failure of comparison* or an *absolute comparison*, which, though they appear to be diametrically opposed, actually amount to the same thing. For Kant holds that the absolutely great can be expressed *either* as "*that which is great beyond all comparison*" or as that "*in comparison with which everything else is small*" (CPJ, 5:250, original emphasis). In other words, the concept of comparison is the necessary basis of its own transcendence. Kant skirts this seeming contradiction by appealing to the concept of the supersensible as that which is absolute and thus ipso facto beyond any meaningful comparison with objects of sense. The absolutely great can therefore be judged only by its own standard, which is necessarily a "nonsensible standard" (CPJ,

[5] Paul Crowther remarks that "Kant . . . offers no criterion for distinguishing the merely overwhelming from the sublime" (*The Kantian Aesthetic: From Knowledge to the Avant-Garde*, 179).

5:261). In other words, it is one that must come from reason itself (as the faculty of the supersensible); for there is no sensible or natural standard by which the seeming absoluteness of an overwhelmingly great object might be judged: "We do not allow a suitable standard for it to be sought outside of it, but merely within it. It is a magnitude that is equal only to itself. That the sublime is therefore not to be sought in the things of nature but only in our ideas follows from this" (CPJ, 5:250). Thus the judgment of the Mathematically Sublime cannot apply to objects in the world: there are no objects of perception that are empirically immeasurable (except perhaps the universe itself, which is not perceivable as such), even if they can be formless (an aesthetic not an empirical qualification).

Despite his appeal to the absolute, Kant, as we have seen, does not wish to abandon the concept of comparison. This goes as well for Kant's idea that, in the aesthetic judgment of sublimity, the mind is in effect *measuring itself against* (that is, comparing itself to) nature. The following summary of the Mathematically Sublime (which actually comes from the section on the Dynamically Sublime) illustrates Kant's point that, unlike the logical-cognitive judgment of magnitude as a unity, and unlike an aesthetic judgment of comparative magnitudes, the judgment of the absolutely great involves a feeling of *superiority*, thus turning the tables, as it were, on nature:

> We found our own limitation in the immeasurability of nature and the insufficiency of our capacity to adopt a standard proportionate to the aesthetic estimation of the magnitude of its domain, but nevertheless at the same time found in our own faculty of reason another, nonsensible standard, which has that very infinity under itself as a unit against which everything in nature is small, and thus found *in our own mind a superiority over nature itself* even in its immeasurability. (CPJ, 5:261, my emphasis)

This is a good description of how Kant conceives of the dual transcendence-structure of sublimity. At first, the immeasurability – our inability to (aesthetically) grasp a large object phenomenally in nature – humiliates us, but this humiliation gives way to the realization of our *superiority* to nature in our supersensible capacity to grasp the same object noumenally. The judgment of the absolutely great throws us out of nature, as it were, and into the realm of ideas; consequentially everything is seen as small or *inferior* to the infinity of the mind (limitlessness of conception, in Longinus's sense).[6] Our supersensible capacity is aroused in our ability to think this absoluteness on the basis of a failure of a presentation of sense, so

---

[6] See my discussion of *On the Sublime*, 35.2 in Chapter 3.

that a *very large object* in nature appears to be *absolutely large* to our aesthetic judgment, by virtue of our inability to estimate the magnitude. The ungraspably large occasions a *failure of comparison*: we attempt to compare it to others of its class, to find a sensible standard, but discover that it has no class, not even that of immeasurability. Immeasurable objects cannot be compared, even among themselves (that is, as one being more immeasurable than the others).[7] This would seem to imply that there are no degrees of sublimity in Kant's account – that sublimity is absolute, as is the mental dignity and grandeur it engenders.[8]

Jacques Derrida describes this Kantian absolute as a "superelevation" of the mind: "*Erhaben*, the sublime, is not only high, elevated, nor even very elevated. Very high, absolutely high, higher than any comparable height, more than comparative, a size not measurable in height, the sublime is *superelevation* beyond itself."[9] Derrida's string of superlatives effectively conveys Kant's equivocation between absolute comparison and being beyond comparison. But they also capture the quasi-religious character of absolute elevation: in the Hebrew Bible, for example, 'Ēl 'Elyōn is another name for God and is usually rendered in English as "God Most High."[10] The concept of absolute elevation – superelevation – thus suggests a mixture of the theological and the rational: the sublime retains the same structure as properly religious experience insofar both are a matter of the absolute. As in Longinus, we are elevated to a God-like height ("sublimity raises us towards the spiritual greatness of god" (*On the Sublime*, 36.1); Kant's *das Erhabene* similarly expresses a secular form of religious transcendence.

In the idea of "superiority over nature," what one could call Kant's *heroic* vision of the human being as self-transcending and self-exalting comes to the fore. The experience of sublimity demonstrates that human greatness is superior to natural greatness – that human greatness alone is absolute. In our struggle with nature in its inhospitable aspects (in this case its immeasurability), which exposes the limits of our sensible nature (our inability to provide a sensible standard for certain magnitudes), the mind's encounter with the seemingly absolute greatness of nature becomes an image of its

---

[7] This goes as well for the judgment of historical catastrophes that involve immeasurable horror, paradigmatically the Holocaust. One can conceptually compare two genocides on the basis of the number of victims killed, injured, etc.; but for a judgment by feeling, an aesthetic judgment, no comparison is possible beyond a certain level. On this idea of a historical sublime, see Jean-François Lyotard, *Le différend*.

[8] On the other hand, it would appear that there could be degrees of the quasi-sublime of the simply great, corresponding to the degree of the mental expansion.

[9] Jacques Derrida, *The Truth in Painting*, 122–123.   [10] See Genesis 14.18–19.

own absolute grandeur. The attempt to grasp the immeasurable in nature can thus be seen as a kind of *challenge* or *duel*, in which the seemingly inferior party discovers itself to be superior – hence the paradox of being exalted *by* being overwhelmed. In the *Anthropology* Kant similarly notes that "the *sublime* is awe-inspiring *greatness* (*magnitudo reverenda*) in extent or degree which invites approach (in order to measure our powers against it)" (APP 7:243, original emphasis). In this idea of "measuring" or testing oneself against the grandeur of nature, Kant recognizes the fundamentally agonistic aspect of the sublime that we also observed in Longinus,[11] even if the "competition" is ultimately with oneself. It follows, then, that those whose rational-moral nature is not sufficiently cultivated or developed are incapable of such an experience of the absolutely great; they would not feel any mental elevation, only humiliation and pain (Kant will address this question of mental cultivation directly in §29).[12]

10.2 The appearance of infinity

By associating sublimity with magnitude, Kant appears to have slipped into the bad habit he repeatedly derides: that of using the term "sublime" to designate a quality of objects. However, an object we *judge* to be absolutely great is not *itself* or *in fact* absolutely great, since absoluteness, infinity, limitlessness, and so on are not phenomenally apparent. Even if there is of necessity an objective reality "behind" a singular judgment of sublimity (that of a very great object whose immeasurability makes it appear too big for our comprehension), this judgment is not therefore grounded in the object. The experience of the absolute is a product of aesthetic *judgment*, insofar as it appeals to reason, to our supersensible capacity.

An obvious objection to this premise is that the sublime might appear to be "a mere fiction or 'phantom of the brain.'"[13] Put another way: how can infinity appear? Burke had addressed this question in his *Enquiry*:

> But the eye not being able to perceive the bounds of many things, they *seem to be* infinite, and they produce the same effects *as if* they were really so. We are deceived in the like manner, if the parts of some large object are so continued

---

[11] See Longinus, *On the Sublime*, 35.2, and my discussion of it in Chapter 3.
[12] In §29 Kant also addresses the problem of squaring the necessity of judgments of sublimity (their claim to universality) with their realization (in fact). See Chapter 12.
[13] Allison, *Kant's Theory of Taste*, 314.

to any indefinite number, that the imagination meets no check which may hinder its extending them at pleasure. (E, 67, my emphasis)

Unlike Burke, Kant cannot speak of "deception," for this would involve a determinant judgment (a judgment of truth or validity). But Kant does agree with Burke that an object's boundlessness prompts the mind to present it "as if" it were infinite.[14] Kant writes that "nature is thus sublime in those of its appearances the intuition of which brings with them the *idea* of its infinity" (CPJ, 5:255, emphasis added). In other words, it is the human mind that introduces such ideas into its perception of nature.[15]

While it might seem from the foregoing that the difference between the simply and the absolutely great is that the former is phenomenal while the latter is noumenal, this would be too reductive. For the absolutely great, insofar as it has an objective correlate that occasions its judgment, is at once phenomenal *and* noumenal,[16] and therein lies another paradox of the sublime: the idea of a finite presentation of infinity (a finite object of sense that occasions an experience of subjective infinity):

> Thus nothing that can be an object of the senses is, considered on this footing, to be called sublime. But just because there is in our imagination a striving to advance to the infinite, while in our reason there lies a claim to absolute totality, as to a real idea, the very inadequacy of our faculty for estimating the magnitude of the things of the sensible world awakens a feeling of a supersensible faculty in us; and the use that the power of judgment naturally makes in behalf of the latter (feeling), though not an object of the senses, is absolutely great.... Hence it is the disposition of the mind [*Geistesstimmung*] resulting from a certain representation occupying the reflective judgment, but not the object, which is to be called sublime.... *That is sublime which even to be able to think of demonstrates a faculty of the mind that surpasses every measure of the senses.* (CPJ, 5:250, original emphasis)

---

[14] Allison makes an almost identical observation to Burke's, in his commentary on Kant: "Such objects present themselves *as if* they were absolutely great.... Thus, even though nothing in nature is really infinite, Kant is suggesting that certain of its appearances have an effect on the mind comparable to one that (*per impossible*) something actually infinite would have" (*Kant's Theory of Taste*, 323). Kant's regulative idea of the "as if" is shown here to be fundamental to the Mathematically Sublime, accounting for contradictory idea of the "appearance of infinity." I noted the proximity between regulative ideas and reflective judgment in Chapter 9.

[15] As Derrida puts it, "unlike that of the beautiful, the principle of the sublime must therefore be sought in ourselves who *project* (*hineinbringen*) the sublime into nature" (*The Truth in Painting*, 132, original emphasis).

[16] On the other hand, Crowther writes: "I have argued that the idea of infinity need not be brought into the experience of the mathematical sublime. However, whilst it need not be brought in of necessity, it can, nevertheless, play a significant *contingent* role.... Infinity may, in other words, *sometimes* play an important role in enhancing rational thought's felt transcendence of the limits of sensibility, even if this role is not logically presupposed" (*The Kantian Aesthetic*, 189).

Simply put, the experience of sublimity demonstrates, makes palpable, in the futile striving of the imagination to infinity, the mind's supersensible capacity. The failure of a presentation of sense – the "violence" (CPJ, 5:245) done to the imagination – allows us to become aware, in this very failure, of reason's demand for "absolute totality," a demand that is both necessary and impossible: necessary, because of the very nature of reason; impossible, because the demand is made of a faculty, the imagination, that cannot, by its very nature, fulfill it. The judgment of absolute greatness, of the sublime, is simply the chasm between reason's impossible demand and the inadequacy of the sensible presentation (the imagination) that occasions it. One could perhaps ask whether it is reason's demand for totality that "causes" the immeasurability or the immeasurability that "prompts" reason's demand for totality. But they really amount to the same thing seen from two different perspectives, those of reason and the imagination. In fact, §26 (which I discuss forthwith) will redescribe the Mathematically Sublime from the perspective of the imagination and the concept of the "maximum."

The passage cited above offers the clearest articulation of the idea of the "sublimity of the mind," the elevated mental disposition or state of mind, *Gemütsstimmung* or *Geistesstimmung*,[17] which, in my view, is the essence of Kant's theory of sublimity. The idea of a "faculty of the mind that surpasses every measure of the senses" echoes Longinus's statement that "the universe [*kosmos*] therefore is not enough for the range of human speculation and intellect [*theôria*]. Our thoughts often travel beyond the boundaries of our surroundings" (35.3). Indeed, the presence of this noumenal-phenomenal dynamic in Longinus puts him closer to Kant than perhaps any other theorist of the sublime. It was this reflection of Longinus that led Thomas Burnet (much admired by Newton) to make this proto-Kantian observation in 1684: "Whatsoever hath but the shadow and appearance of INFINITE, as all things have that are too big for our comprehension, they fill and overbear the mind with their Excess."[18] That Burnet's theological approach to geology and Kant's aesthetic approach to natural teleology

---

[17] "Die Stimmung des Gemüts zum Gefühl des Erhabenen erfordert eine Empfänglichkeit desselben für Ideen" (The disposition of the mind to the feeling of the sublime requires its receptivity to ideas [CPJ, 5: 265]). In addition to *Gemütsstimmung*, *Geistesstimmung* is used, as we saw above, at CPJ, 5:250. Very similar to these two terms is *Gemütszustand*, often translated as "state of mind," which Kant uses to designate a separate form of sublimity he calls the "aesthetically sublime" (as in CPJ, 5:272, which I discuss at length in Chapter 12). Kant also notes the proximity of moral consciousness to the sublime mental disposition: "In fact, a feeling for the sublime in nature cannot even be conceived without connecting it to a disposition of the mind [*Stimmung des Gemüts*] that is similar to the moral disposition" (CPJ, 5:268). See Chapter 12.
[18] Burnet, *The Sacred Theory of the Earth*, 110.

employ nearly identical terms points again to the mediating role of the sublime as a secular analogue of religious transcendence. In both Longinus and Kant, our response to natural grandeur as demonstrated by the feeling of the sublime reveals our *telos* as beings who strive – and *struggle* – to transcend the limits of nature.[19]

10.3   Presenting the maximum

The ostensible purpose of §26, "On the estimation of the magnitude of the things of nature that is requisite for the idea of the sublime," is to contrast the mathematical (logical) with the aesthetic estimation of magnitude, in regards to the concept of the maximum (*Größtes*), and furthermore to provide an account of how the aesthetic estimation of a maximum involves certain "actions" of the mind, namely apprehension and comprehension. As suggested above, this section amounts to a *redescription* of the Mathematically Sublime from the perspective of the imagination (the presentation of its maximum), as contrasted with that of reason (the absolutely great and the demand for totality). This shift in perspective allows Kant to better address the question of why there should be a limit in aesthetic estimation.

Mathematical estimation is purely conceptual ("logical estimation . . . by means of numerical concepts") and thus has no maximum: "The power of numbers goes on to infinity" (CPJ, 5:251). This type of estimation is also clearly a matter of determinant judgment (though Kant does not say so explicitly, perhaps because he thought it too obvious) and is therefore distinct from what Kant calls the Mathematically Sublime.[20] Nevertheless, Kant holds that "in the end all estimation of the magnitude of objects of nature is aesthetic (i.e., subjectively and not objectively determined)" (CPJ, 5:251), which is why it is appropriate to discuss it in this section. Mathematical estimation of objects is ultimately aesthetic because measurements presuppose "a primary or basic fundamental measure" (5:251), which can only be aesthetically given; otherwise, measurements would be completely abstract and divorced from reality. For example, the

---

[19]   Richard Rorty expresses this idea eloquently in an interview: "Kant took off from the idea that the sublime can awaken a consciousness of the ideal of reason and that, in this way, it actualizes uniqueness – and demonstrates the greatness of man before nature" (*Take Care of Freedom and Truth Will Take Care of Itself*, ed. Eduardo Mendicta, 74).

[20]   Thus, in effect, the Mathematically Sublime does not involve mathematical estimation! Kant can also be seen as clarifying what he wrote in the *Observations* on the subject of "mathematical representation": "The mathematical representation of the immeasurable magnitude of the universe . . . contain[s] a certain sublimity and dignity" (O, 2:215).

measurement 100 meters is meaningless unless one has an aesthetic and not a purely logical-mathematical sense of how long a meter is.[21] However, merely because mathematical estimation is "in the end" aesthetically based does not thereby make it an aesthetic judgment. It is still a determinant judgment insofar as it is a judgment according to a quantitative measure (numerical concepts), though, as we will see below, Kant appears to make an exception if the "aesthetic basic measure" is "vividly preserved in the imagination."

Unlike mathematical estimation, aesthetic estimation, which Kant calls measurement "by the eye" (CPJ, 5:251), is indeterminate and thus involves reflective judgment. It is also inherently *limited* by the imaginative capacity to present objects in intuition and thus reaches "a greatest [*Größtes*] ... beyond which no greater is subjectively (for the judging subject) possible" (CPJ, 5:251). As the aesthetic estimation of magnitude attains its maximum, a *feeling of transcendence* is thereby generated:

> I say that if it is judged as an absolute measure, beyond which no greater is subjectively (for the judging subject) possible, it brings with it the idea of the sublime, and *produces that emotion* which no mathematical estimation of magnitudes by means of numbers can produce (except insofar as that aesthetic basic measure is vividly preserved in the imagination), since the latter always presents only relative magnitude through comparison with others of the same species, but the former *presents magnitude absolutely*, so far as the mind can grasp it in one intuition. (CPJ, 5:251, my emphasis)

This passage may appear somewhat confusing, given what Kant had said in the previous section (§25). First, the contrast between the "relative magnitude" of estimation by means of numbers and the absolute presentation is really a moot point; for, as Kant has already stated, mathematical estimation involves determinant judgment and thus cannot give rise to the sublime (or to any aesthetic judgment, for that matter), except, as he notes parenthetically, to the extent that the "aesthetic basic" unit of measurement comes to the fore and activates the imagination rather than the understanding. Second, Kant is using the term "absolute" in a different sense than in the idea of the "absolutely great" (adverb modifying an adjective). Here it refers not to a judgment of magnitude as such, but to the manner of presenting a magnitude (adverb modifying a verb), namely as a maximum or greatest (*Größtes*) in "one intuition," which is contrasted

---

[21] And defining a meter mathematically, for example, as "the distance traveled by light in a vacuum in 1/299,792,458 of a second," or in terms of feet, simply refers to another abstraction, which, in turn, must be grounded in an aesthetic apprehension.

with the relative magnitude of numerical estimation (for example, a seven-foot-tall man is a tall man, whereas a seven-foot-tall hill is a small hill). Only aesthetic estimation presents magnitude absolutely, qua maximum, thereby producing the "emotion" or feeling associated with the sublime.[22]

Implicitly, Kant is using mathematical estimation to compare the non-aesthetic limitlessness or infinity of numerical concepts with the earlier discussion of aesthetic limitlessness or infinity of the absolutely great – a fairly straightforward contrast. More problematic, however, is the relation between the infinity of the absolutely great and the idea of a *maximum* presented absolutely. For in moving from one to the other, we encounter the following conundrum: how can the feeling of the sublime relate *both* to infinity and to the idea of the maximum that seemingly excludes it? Should one "absolute" not cancel out the other? To be consistent, Kant must hold that the grasping of the maximum in one intuition will occasion the sublime only if the magnitude *cannot be grasped* in one intuition, that is, only if it goes *beyond the maximum*.[23]

To resolve this paradox, Kant distinguishes between "two actions" of the faculty of the imagination: apprehension (*Auffassung*) and comprehension (*Zusammenfassung*).[24] Kant had defined these notions in the First Introduction to the third *Critique* (FI, 20:220–21), but §26 recalibrates them for the type of reflective judgment associated with sublimity, that is, with the presentation of a maximum. Like numerical estimation, apprehension has no maximum; it merely adds intuitions together and thus can in principle "go on to infinity" (CPJ, 5: 252). It is what one does when, confronted with a large vista, one scans up and down or from side to side, attempting to see all that one can see, without thereby attempting to bring the contents of the view together in a single intuition. Continued apprehension starts to be a zero sum game, however, since it "loses on one side as much as it gains on the other" [CPJ, 5:252], as earlier apprehensions fade and others are added. Comprehension, on the other hand, strives to hold the apprehended intuitions together in a totality, thereby reaching its maximum in the case of a very large magnitude. However, Kant does not specify under what conditions comprehension must, as it were, rein

---

[22] Lyotard remarks that there are two absolutes: "L'absolument tout quand elle [la pensée] conçoit, l'absolument mesuré quand elle présente" (*Leçons sur l'Analytique du Sublime*, 154). But these are not equal, as Lyotard asserts; the absolute of reason must take precedence.

[23] But this also means that, even in the judgment of the simply great, magnitude is presented absolutely (all at once), not comparatively.

[24] Lyotard bases his interpretation of this passage on a textual discrepancy. Kant had apparently originally written the word "composition" (*Zusammensetzung*), but this was corrected to read "comprehension" by Erdmann. See *Leçons sur l'analytique du sublime*, 131.

in apprehension. Otherwise any unobstructed vista, no matter how mundane, would be an occasion for sublimity.[25]

As an example of how apprehension and comprehension interact in the aesthetic estimation of magnitude, Kant offers two iconic examples, the Pyramids of Egypt and St. Peter's Basilica in Rome, both of which, as we saw, Kant had used in his 1764 *Observations*. Kant's use of these examples has caused a great deal of controversy and confusion in the literature. First, they are both manmade structures rather than natural objects, which conflicts with Kant's stipulation that the sublime should ideally involve "raw nature" [CPJ, 5:253].[26] (And the fact that these artificial objects are the only examples of the Mathematically Sublime that Kant addresses in any detail is even more curious.) Second, it is not certain that both are examples of sublimity, as many commentators assume. In fact, they appear to exemplify judgments of magnitude that are qualitatively different.

In his use of the Pyramids, Kant relies on the account by the orientalist Nicholas Savary in his *Letters on Egypt* (*Lettres sur l'Egypte où l'on offre le parallèle des mœurs anciennes et modernes et de ses habitants*, 1786).[27] Kant was intrigued by the following observation of Savary's: "Having arrived at the foot of the pyramid, we circled it, contemplating it with a sort of terror. When considered up close, it seems to be made of blocks of rock, but from a hundred feet, the magnitude of the stones is lost in the immensity of the structure, and they seem very small."[28] Ironically, Savary's account more directly suggests the Burkean idea of sublime terror (and might have even been influenced by Burke's theory). But Kant ignores this aspect and instead uses the example to illustrate the interaction between apprehension and comprehension:

> In order to get the full emotional effect of the magnitude of the pyramids one must come neither too close nor be too far away. For in the latter case, the parts that are apprehended (the stones piled on top of one another) are represented only obscurely, and their representation has no effect on the aesthetic judgment of the subject. In the former case, however, the eye requires some time to complete its apprehension from the base level to the apex, but during this time the former always partly fades before the

---

[25] Kant addresses this issue somewhat with the example of the Pyramids, but this concerns only the relative view of a particular object, rather than some general principle of viewing. It does not seem possible that the distinction Kant applied to the beautiful – "beautiful objects are to be distinguished from beautiful views of objects" (CPJ, 5:243) – could be applicable to the sublime.

[26] However, Kant is not against the idea of sublimity in art, as I discuss in the Chapter 12.

[27] The account of the Pyramids in the *Observations* is based on a 1762 travelogue by Swedish naturalist D. Fredrik Hasselquist, *Reise nach Palästina in den Jaren 1749–1752*.

[28] Quoted by the editor (Paul Guyer) in Kant, *Critique of the Power of Judgment*, 374.

imagination has taken in the latter, and the comprehension is never complete. (CPJ, 5:252)

Most commentators interpret this example as an illustration of the sublime, even though it does not correspond to Kant's definition. For viewing the Pyramids in the manner Kant describes involves not a failure of the imagination but a *juste-milieu* in which comprehension achieves a kind of equilibrium with apprehension. Thus the reference to "full emotional effect" appears somewhat contradictory, since, as Paul Crowther observes, the best way of achieving such an effect would be precisely to stand too close to it.[29]

On the other hand, Derrida comments that "the right place, the ideal *topos* for the experience of the sublime, for the inadequation of presentation to the unpresentable, will be a median place, an average place of the body which would provide an aesthetic maximum without losing itself in the mathematical infinite."[30] However, merely *reaching* an "aesthetic maximum," as Derrida asserts, is not the sublime, according to Kant. Only going *beyond the maximum*, beyond the limit, gives rise to the feeling of sublime transcendence.[31] Derrida continues:

> So one has to find a middle place, a correct distance for uniting the maximum of comprehension to the maximum of apprehension, to take sight of the maximum of what one cannot take and to imagine the maximum of what one cannot see. And when the imagination attains its maximum and experiences the feeling of its impotence, its inadequacy to present the idea of the whole, it falls back, it sinks, it founders into itself (*in sich selbst zurück sinkt*).[32]

Derrida appears to (con)fuse the example of the Pyramids (the "median place") with that of St. Peter's (the imagination sinking back into itself), which Kant describes thus:

> The very same thing can also suffice to explain the bewilderment or sort of embarrassment that is said to seize the spectator on first entering St. Peter's in Rome. For here there is a feeling of the inadequacy of his imagination for presenting the ideas of a whole, in which the imagination reaches its

---

[29] Crowther argues that "what Kant is actually doing is disproving Savary's claim that to experience the 'full emotional effect' of the Pyramids we must see them from neither too far away nor too near. Kant shows, rather, that if we view them from close proximity our capacity is soon overwhelmed. It is *this* which leads us to the full emotional effect" (*The Kantian Sublime: From Morality to Art*, 103).

[30] Derrida, *The Truth in Painting*, 141.

[31] But elsewhere Derrida does mention this aspect: "But the sublime, if there is any sublime, exists only by overspilling: it exceeds cise and good measure" (*The Truth in Painting*, 122).

[32] Derrida, *The Truth in Painting*, 142.

maximum and, *in the effort to extend it*, sinks back into itself [*in sich selbst zurück sinkt*], but is thereby transported into emotionally moving satisfaction. (CPJ, 5:252, my emphasis)

Only in this example does the inadequacy of the imagination to comprehend the whole that apprehension strives in a progressive way to encompass becomes manifest. There is no equilibrium, but instead a *failure* of comprehension to extend itself beyond its capacity to present the whole in a single intuition.[33] This pain of inadequation is not due to the *reaching of the maximum* (as in the Pyramids example), but rather to the *extending of the maximum* ("and, in the effort to extend it" – Derrida leaves this out), which is then converted into an "emotionally moving satisfaction" in the exhaustion of the comprehending faculty – a failure and a success, a humiliation and an exaltation. The mental expansion is sublime precisely because it involves a *transcendence* of limits, which, as I stated above, is here examined from the perspective of the imagination rather than that of reason.

Henry Allison reads the Pyramids example, convincingly in my view, as an instance of the "simply great."[34] The expansion of the imagination in the median view ("full comprehension") of the Pyramids is pleasing, generating the emotional effect Kant speaks about, but it does not occasion the complex feeling of pain mixed with pleasure that is the hallmark of the sublime and that is exemplified by St. Peter's. One finds a similar distinction in Moses Mendelssohn's 1758 essay on the sublime (which Allison does not mention), with which Kant was no doubt familiar:

> If the full dimensions of the object cannot be taken in by the senses all at once, then it ceases to be sensuously beautiful and becomes gigantic in extension. The sentiment that is then aroused is, to be sure, of a mixed nature. For well-educated minds, those used to order and symmetry, there is something repugnant about this, since the senses ultimately can perceive the boundaries, but cannot comprehend them and combine them into one idea without considerable difficulty. If the boundaries of this extension are deferred further and further, then they ultimately disappear from the senses, and, as a result, something sensuously immense emerges.[35]

---

[33] Thus Derrida appears to take the two examples as saying essentially the same thing, merging the idea of "correct distance" in viewing the Pyramids with the feeling of imaginative inadequacy one encounters in St. Peter's.
[34] "An aesthetic experience of the pyramids as simply great in Kant's sense would arguably require perceiving them at a distance that allows for full comprehension as well as distinct apprehension" (Allison, *Kant's Theory of Taste*, 318).
[35] Moses Mendelssohn, *Philosophical Writings*, 192–193.

At least three aspects of Kant's theory of sublimity are prefigured in this passage from Mendelssohn: (1) the distinction between the "gigantic" and the "immense," which is redolent of Kant's contrast between the simply and the absolutely great; (2) the proximity between sublimity and the ugly ("repugnant"), which we analyzed in the previous chapter; and (3) the use of "comprehension" to denote a totality that is exceeded ("cannot comprehend them and combine them into one idea").

One of the most neglected aspects of Kant's discussion of apprehension and comprehension is the temporal dimension, which Kant briefly analyzes in the following section (§27):

> By contrast, the comprehension of multiplicity in the unity not of thought but of intuition, hence the comprehension in one moment of that which is successively apprehended, is a regression, which in turn cancels the time-condition in the progression of the imagination and makes *simultaneity* intuitable. It is thus (since temporal succession is a condition of inner sense and of an intuition) a subjective movement of the imagination, by which it does violence to inner sense, which must be all the more marked the greater the quantum is which the imagination comprehends in one intuition. Thus the effort to take up in a single intuition a measure for magnitudes, which requires an appreciable time for its apprehension, is a kind of apprehension which, subjectively considered, is contrapurposive, but which objectively, for the estimation of magnitude, is necessary, hence purposive; in this way, however, the very same violence that is inflicted on the subject by the imagination is judged as purposive *for the whole vocation* of the mind. (CPJ, 5:258–9, original emphasis)

Kant seeks to resolve the seeming paradox of "comprehension in one moment of that which is successively apprehended," thereby superimposing a temporal concept of comprehension onto a spatial one. As a single intuition, comprehension happens in a single *moment*, whereas the apprehension on which it is based is necessarily extended in time. (This is not an issue for mathematical-logical estimation, with its infinite unfolding.) The effort to force successive apprehensions into a single, comprehensive intuition through a "regression" does "violence" to the "inner sense,"[36] which is characterized by temporal succession. The larger the magnitude, the more violence is done. In the case of the sublime, the magnitude is "absolute," that is, the comprehension has reached its maximum, hitting a stopping point that, like a broken (vinyl) record, it strives *ad infinitum* to go beyond. Thus, the sublime can be said to cancel out or absorb *infinite*

---

[36] "Outer sense is where the human body is affected by physical things; inner sense, where it is affected by the mind" (APP, 7:153). This "violence" recalls CPJ, 5:245.

time. This violence done to the imagination, which reaches an extreme form in the sublime (though it is always to some degree present even in the normal comprehension of magnitudes, as successive apprehensions are brought together), is especially contrapurposive for the imagination; but it is also for this very reason purposive: the violation of the time-condition of inner sense (the successive apprehensions) presupposes the rational requirement of comprehension *in a single instant.* By making succession appear as simultaneity, the sublime transcends time itself, again demonstrating the noumenal superiority of reason. The temporal condensation of the sublime is in effect a byproduct of reason's demand for the "totality for all given magnitudes, even for those that can never be entirely apprehended although they are (in the sensible representation) judged as entirely given, hence comprehension in *one* intuition" (CPJ, 5:254, original emphasis). In other words, the rational idea and requirement of totality reveals itself to be a *temporal idea and requirement* in addition to being a spatial one.

These considerations on the temporal dimension of sublimity allow us to read the Pyramids example in a new light. Kant says that if one is standing too close, it takes "some *time* to complete [the eye's] apprehension" (my emphasis), and, since earlier apprehensions fade as others are added, the "comprehension is never complete." No sense of the whole is given in such an operation; thus there is no experience of the absolutely great *in the flow of time.* Time is stopped, as it were, in the excessive expansion of the imagination, in its effort to comprehend a supremely great magnitude. The feeling of sublimity is thus constituted by an aesthetic temporality, that of a *moment of transcendence* (which, as we saw in Longinus, was conceived according to the concept of *kairos*).[37]

10.4   The monstrous and the colossal

As many commentators have noted, the fact that Kant chooses artificial as opposed to natural examples to illustrate the operations of apprehension and comprehension is highly curious. Although this is not the moment to discuss the question of artificial sublimity in Kant's thought,[38] one can say that, at the very least, the examples of the Pyramids and St. Peter's establish the possibility of sublimity in architecture, the type of artefact that most closely recreates the three-dimensionality and scale of natural magnitude.[39]

---

[37] See Chapter 1.   [38] See Chapter 12.

[39] These two examples are also noteworthy for having a specifically religious meaning. It is almost as if Kant were suggesting that the intermixture of the human and the divine in art is a mark of sublimity.

As if to avoid leaving the impression that his manmade examples should be taken as exemplary of his theory of the Mathematical Sublime, Kant shifts gears, emphasizing that only "raw" nature offers an experience of the sublime in the purest or strongest sense (a point that Kant had also made with regard to beauty ["free beauty," §16]):

> If an aesthetic judgment is to be *pure (not mixed up with anything teleological)* ... then the sublime must not be shown in products of art (e.g., buildings, columns, etc.), where a human end determines the form as well as the magnitude, nor in natural things *whose concept already brings with it a determinate end* ... but rather in raw nature [*an der rohen Natur*]. (CPJ, 5:252–3, original emphasis)

By detracting from its appropriateness for aesthetic reflective judgment (judgment without determinant concepts and without regard to an end), an object with a determinate end – which, as products of human intentionality, all works of art are – would inhibit the supersensible use of the object for the judgment of the sublime.[40]

However, as Kant also mentions, just because an object is an object of nature does not thereby make a judgment pure, since there are "natural things whose concept already brings with it a determinate end" (as in Kant's idea of "adherent beauty"),[41] even if these are examples of "raw" nature. Hence the concepts of the "monstrous" (*ungeheuer*) and the "colossal" (*kolossalisch*): what is judged monstrous or colossal are objects of great magnitude that are fused with a concept of their end, as if their magnitude violated (the monstrous) or almost violated (the colossal) the objective purposiveness of the object. In the *Anthropology*, Kant states that "the monstrous is greatness that is contrapurposive (*magnitudo monstrosa*). Writers, therefore, who wanted to extol the vast extent of the Russian empire have missed badly in calling it monstrous; for herein lies a reproach, as if it were too great for a single ruler" (APP, 7:243). In other words, not all contrapurposive representations of magnitudinous nature are sublime. There is purposive contrapurposiveness (the sublime), and there are varying degrees of contrapurposive contrapurposiveness, such as the monstrous and the colossal. Presumably, however, the monstrous and the colossal, like

---

[40] "A pure judgment on the sublime, however, must have no end of the object as its determining ground if it is to be aesthetic and not mixed up with any judgment of the understanding or of reason" (CPJ, 5:253). Despite this statement, Guyer argues that because Kant stipulates in §29 that the sublime requires culture Kant is actually "ambivalent" on the question of the purity of judgments of sublimity; thus "we should not take the experience of the sublime as a model for pure aesthetic experience" (*Values of Beauty*, 161). See my discussion of §29 in Chapter 12.

[41] Kant gives the example of the horse (see §16).

the simply great, could give rise to affects akin to those found in the experience of the sublime (awe, astonishment, etc.); that is, they are not entirely contrapurposive, and the colossal would appear to be less contrapurposive than the monstrous.[42] But Kant's real reason for bringing up these judgments is to make it clear that the magnitudinous nature that gives rise to the feeling of sublime transcendence, no matter how ugly or contrapurposive its oversized greatness appears, should not thereby be judged as "monstrous": "For in this sort of representation [of magnitude] nature contains nothing that would be monstrous (or magnificent or terrible); the magnitude that is apprehended may grow as large as it wants as long as it can be comprehended in one whole by the imagination" (CPJ, 5:253). That is, there may be a thin line that separates the monstrous from the sublime, but it is nonetheless absolute.

***

To sum up, the Mathematically Sublime involves two movements: (1) an *overwhelming* of our imaginative capacity, an extreme expansion of the mind, an expansion beyond limits, *beyond the maximum*; (2) an *elevation* of the self in the resulting feeling of limitlessness and freedom from sensible constraint, which is seen by the mind as an index of its supersensible vocation, its vocation for *transcendence*. The purposive contrapurposiveness of the sublime thus implies an agonistic relation to nature, a *struggle* wherein our rational self is pitted against and ultimately prevails over a seemingly indomitable foe. While this emergence of a heroic self will become more explicit in the Dynamically Sublime, we can already perceive the outlines of such a conception in the Mathematically Sublime.

---

[42] Although it is not clear if the overall effect would necessarily be pleasurable; perhaps these would give rise to a mixed pain rather than a mixed pleasure.

CHAPTER II

Judging nature as a power: the Dynamically Sublime

Commentators have often wondered why Kant thought it necessary to divide the Analytic of the Sublime into two aspects, particularly since much of Kant's general presentation of the sublime, including its contrast with the beautiful, appears to be predicated on the judgment of magnitudinous nature. There are perhaps several reasons for the addition of a section on the judgment of nature as a power: (1) it permits Kant to engage more directly with Burke's *Enquiry*, in particular with Burke's contention that sublimity is reducible to power and the terror it produces; (2) given the association, since John Dennis, of sublime terror with the idea of the wrath of God, the Dynamically Sublime allows Kant to redefine his rational approach to religion in aesthetic terms; (3) it develops the idea of aesthetic high-mindedness in the direction of the heroic, thereby forging a more direct link to Kant's moral theory. In sum, the Dynamically Sublime presents a wider and more varied set of perspectives than does the Mathematically Sublime, including a more proximate relation to culture,[1] a relation I explore in greater detail in the following chapter.

The first section of this chapter examines Kant's rewriting of Burke's theory of sublime terror, arguing that, like Burke, Kant must resort to a concept of virtuality – an added level of reflection that was not required in the Mathematically Sublime – to describe the paradoxical experience of fear-within-safety. The second section seeks to further redefine the Dynamically Sublime in terms of a "virtual heroism," as expressed in Kant's value-laden language. I also argue in this section that the Dynamically Sublime reveals certain parallels with Kant's notion of "moral worth," thus solidifying my case that sublimity is more consequential for the architectonic of the Critical Philosophy than is the beautiful. The third section treats Kant's discussion of war, arguing that Kant's putatively aesthetic preference for the figure of the warrior amounts to a

---

[1] See in particular CPJ, 5:265.

moral critique of contemporary bourgeois culture and its "spirit of mere commerce" (CPJ, 5:263). The final section studies how Kant uses the Dynamically Sublime to distinguish an enlightened-rational from a primitive-fanatical attitude toward God, in an effort to reconcile the secularizing forces of the Enlightenment with Christian experience.

11.1   *Macht* versus *Kraft*: toward an aesthetics of resistance

Kant begins his discussion of the Dynamically Sublime (§28) in a Burkean manner,[2] stating in the second paragraph that "if nature is to be judged by us dynamically as sublime, it must be represented as arousing fear" (CPJ, 5:260). In developing his concept of aestheticized fear (first emblematized, as earlier noted, in John Dennis's formula "delightful horror"), Kant must address many of the same conceptual issues that plagued Burke's account, prime among them: (1) if we are afraid of powerful nature, then the fear is simply painful and hence unaesthetic; and (2) if we are not actually afraid, then the effect of natural power is too weak to produce the intensity of effect/affect associated with sublimity. More simply put, how can we not be "actually" afraid without simply being unafraid? I contend that, if it is to fulfill these paradoxical requirements, the experience of the Dynamically Sublime must include an element of virtuality.

Kant begins the section on the Dynamically Sublime by defining "power" (*Macht*) as "a capacity that is superior to great obstacles" (CPJ, 5:260).[3] With this phrase, Kant suggests the classic definition of the hero as one who possesses a surpassing moral/physical strength, thereby establishing a heroic tone for the section. Kant further elaborates that power "is called *dominion* [*Gewalt*] if it is also superior to the resistance of something that itself possesses power" (CPJ, 5:260), thereby underlining the aspect of authority in the term *Macht*, that is, power in the sense of having power over something or someone – power as domination. Taken in the abstract, this rather general formulation could apply to nature itself (the animal kingdom), to human affairs (politics), to the relation between nature and humanity (natural disasters), or even to intrahuman relations (a combination of physical and nonphysical dominance, as in slavery, for

---

[2] Burke writes: "I know of nothing sublime which is not some modification of power" (E, 64). Burke's name is mentioned twice in the third *Critique*: in the First Introduction (FI, 20:238) and at the end of §29 (CPJ, 5:277).

[3] German has two words that can be translated as "power" in English: *Macht*, meaning power in the sense of authority or force that acts on an agent; *Kraft*, meaning power in the sense of a capacity to do something, as in the title of the third *Critique*: *Kritik der Urteilskraft*.

example).[4] Although Kant is of course only interested here in the relation between humanity and inanimate nature, the presence of these other possibilities indicates the suggestiveness of Kant's language in this section. A notable example is Theodor Adorno's comment that "by situating the sublime in overpowering grandeur and setting up the antithesis of power and powerlessness, Kant directly affirmed his unquestioning complicity with domination."[5] However, as I shall show over the course of this chapter, Kant endeavors to affirm precisely the opposite.[6]

Joining the two definitions of "power" (*Macht*) and "dominion" (*Gewalt*), Kant offers a preliminary characterization of the aesthetic encounter with natural power: "Nature considered in aesthetic judgment as a power that has no dominion over us is *dynamically sublime*" (CPJ, 5:260). This statement is somewhat misleading, however, insofar as it fails to capture, or rather elides, the paradoxical idea of a power that threatens us because it is superior to us, *and yet, despite this fact*, has no dominion over us. As Kant expresses it in the next paragraph:

> If nature is to be judged by us dynamically as sublime, it must be repre-
> sented as arousing fear (although, conversely, not every object that arouses
> fear is found sublime in our aesthetic judgment). For in aesthetic judging
> (without a concept) the superiority over obstacles can only be judged in
> accordance with the magnitude of the resistance. However, that which we
> strive to resist is an evil, and, if we find our capacity to be no match for it, an
> object of fear. Thus, for the aesthetic power of judgment nature can count
> as a power, thus as dynamically sublime, only insofar as it is considered an
> object of fear. (CPJ, 5:260)

According to this formulation, then, it would appear that nature *both has and does not have dominion over us*: we fear nature only to the extent that we find that we are "no match for it," and yet we resist it all the same. Thus if the power of nature must be perceived as *threatening* ("an object of fear") to produce a feeling of aesthetic elevation, the elevation itself derives from the *resistance* to the all-powerfulness of nature, that is, a *resistance to that which cannot be resisted*, a resistance to a superior power that, despite its superior power, has no dominion over us. In this manner we are, paradoxically, exalted by a power that overwhelms us – the dual transcendence-structure of sublimity. As Kant's later analysis will show, the solution to this paradox

---

[4] Or nonviolent protests: peaceful protesters resisting morally what they cannot resist physically.
[5] Theodor Adorno, *Aesthetic Theory*, 199.
[6] Indeed, Adorno hastens to add: "Even Kant was by no means unaware that the sublime is not quantitative grandeur as such: With profound justification he defined the concept of the sublime by the resistance of spirit to the overwhelming" (*Aesthetic Theory*, 199).

of the Dynamically Sublime involves reinterpreting it in light of the bifurcation between the physical/sensuous and moral/spiritual aspects of our being (the pendant to the bifurcation between the failure of the imagination and the transcendence of reason as the faculty of the super-sensible in the Mathematically Sublime). At this point, however, Kant's idea that the Dynamically Sublime involves encountering an "evil" – that is, an existential threat that could easily destroy us – lines up with Burke's emphasis on the instinct of self-preservation.

After asserting that natural power has dominion over us to the extent it provokes fear, but does not have dominion over us because of our capacity to resist, Kant delves into the problem of aestheticized fear, that is, the problem of how we can "consider an object as *fearful* without being afraid *of* it" (CPJ, 5:260, original emphasis). This question is intrinsically related to the problem of complex pleasure (pleasure mixed with pain), though it logically precedes it: for if one is simply or actually fearful then there can be no (aesthetic) pleasure, complex or otherwise. According to Kant, there is no contradiction if "we judge [a natural power] in such a way that we merely *think* of the case in which we might wish to resist it and think that in that case all resistance would be completely futile" (CPJ, 5:260, original emphasis). The focus on the "thinking of a case" here reveals an extra or second-order level of reflection that was not required in the Mathematically Sublime. This would appear to mean that an aesthetic encounter with powerful nature involves thinking a nonactual scenario, that is, a *virtual* scenario or "case" in which we would actually feel threatened.

To explain how the mere thought of fear is supposed to operate aesthetically, Kant offers the example of the God-fearing man: "The virtuous man fears God without really being afraid of him.... But since he does not think of such a case [of having to fear God] as impossible in itself, he recognizes God as fearful" (CPJ, 5:260). If we can think of situations in which an object could destroy us, then we can be affected by such an object, with a strength proportional to the magnitude of the power, more so than by those for which we cannot conceive of any such real possibility. Thus when I see God as fearful, I am implicitly thinking the case (seeing it as thinkable) in which I would feel actual fear, though I am not actually afraid; that is, I do not see this case as probable or likely and hence have nothing to actually be *worried about*. However, the mere "recognition" of God as fearful is not tantamount to *actually* thinking of Him as fearful; to not think of something as "impossible in itself" is a far cry from actively entertaining a possibility.

In addition to being somewhat murky on the question of what constitutes the "thinking of a case," Kant's example is not very pertinent for
aesthetic judgment; for it does not involve any identifiably aesthetic situation, such as a sensible presentation of God's power, a question that Kant
will discuss later in §28. Paul Crowther, however, seemingly takes this
example as paradigmatic for the operation of Dynamical Sublimity. After
summarizing the example of the God-fearing individual, Crowther
observes that "the might of nature is aesthetically disclosed in two ways –
through actual or through imagined fear."[7] This statement raises two
problems. First, as Crowther correctly notes, Kant states that a person in
actual fear cannot judge the sublime. Thus why would Crowther hold that
the feeling of actual fear is consistent with an *aesthetic* judgment of natural
power? Second, Crowther's idea of "imagined fear" does not truly square
with what Kant is trying to express in the Dynamically Sublime (though it
does perhaps more narrowly apply to the example of the God-fearing
man), since it makes no distinction between being in the actual *presence*
of powerful nature and mere mental conjuring. Moreover, "imagined fear"
sounds too much like "imaginary fear," which could hardly affect us in the
powerful way that the sublime requires (although it does recall Burke's
injunction that the sublime turn on "ideas" of pain and danger). I therefore do not see how Kant's example of the God-fearing man could be
considered as a guide to the experience of the Dynamically Sublime; it is
simply a commonsense illustration of how it is possible to fear without
being (actually) afraid.[8]

Comparing the Dynamically Sublime with the Mathematically Sublime
at this point, one could say that, just as in the latter we judge natural
magnitude *as if* it were infinite or absolute, though it is not, in actuality,
infinite, in the former we judge natural power *as if* it were an actual threat
to us, even if it is not in fact. Thus there is a certain measure of symmetry or
parallelism between the two types of sublimity, with regard to their "as if"
status. But the "as if" in the Dynamically Sublime requires an added level
of reflection that was not required in the Mathematically Sublime; for to
perceive a nonactual threat as if it were an actual threat involves a virtual
projection, a "thinking of a case." This is no doubt what prompted Kant to
remark that his explanation of the Dynamically Sublime may appear "far-
fetched and subtle" (CPJ, 5:262), a qualification that Kant did not feel was

---

[7] Crowther, *The Kantian Sublime*, 109.
[8] Moreover, it would be nonsensical to maintain that God has no dominion over us, as if we could
    resist God's power in the manner we resist the power of nature.

necessary in the relatively more straightforward presentation of the Mathematically Sublime.

Kant explicitly rejects Burke's example of release from danger, which Burke uses to illustrate the operation of mixed pleasure:[9]

> Someone who is afraid can no more judge about the sublime in nature than someone who is in the grip of inclination and appetite can judge about the beautiful. The former flees from the sight of an object that instills alarm in him, and it is impossible to find satisfaction in a terror that is seriously intended. Hence the cessation of something troublesome is *joyfulness*. But this joyfulness on the account of liberation from a danger is accompanied with the proviso that one never again be exposed to that danger; indeed one may well be reluctant to think back on that sensation, let alone seek out the opportunity for it. (CPJ, 5:261)[10]

For Kant, the joy upon the release from pain, though it may indeed involve a kind of mixed pleasure, nevertheless has nothing to do with the feeling of the sublime, for the negativity of the experience – pain – predominates (in other words, not all instances of mixed pleasure are sublime, though all instances of the sublime involve mixed pleasure). It is more akin to simple trauma, as opposed to the uplifting, exalting experience of sublimity, which ultimately involves satisfaction (and, presumably, a desire for a repetition of the experience). One would not accept to undergo torture to experience the "joy" of being delivered from it.

The final stage of Kant's basic presentation of the Dynamically Sublime addresses the seeming paradox of a "resistance to that which cannot be resisted": the aesthetic consideration of a natural object to which *physical* resistance would be futile gives us pause to consider our own fortitude, our ability as rational and not merely physical beings to *morally/spiritually* resist, that is, to act in contradiction to our natural instinct of self-preservation (presumably for some moral cause, but stipulating a particular end would take us out of the realm of aesthetic judgment).[11] The paradox

---

[9] As I argued in Chapter 6, the "removal of pain" in the narrow escape from danger is not a description of the sublime in Burke's account.

[10] In the *Anthropology*, Kant articulates a view that is closer to that of Burke – but only with respect to emotions excited by sympathetic identification: "This is why people run with great desire, as to a theater play, to watch a criminal being taken to the gallows and executed. For the emotions and feelings which are expressed on his face and in his bearings have a sympathetic effect on the spectators and, after the anxiety the spectators suffer through the power of the imagination ... the emotions and feelings leave the spectators with a mild but nevertheless genuine feeling of relaxation, which makes their subsequent enjoyment of life all the more tangible" (APP, 7:238–9).

[11] Nevertheless, it would seem that an evil person can also display great courage and transcend the limits of his or her sensuous existence.

is resolved in the separation of our physical from our moral being and of two corresponding concepts of self-preservation:

> The irresistibility of [the] power [of nature] certainly makes us, considered as natural beings, recognize our physical powerlessness, but at the same time it reveals a capacity for judging ourselves as independent of it and a superiority over nature on which is grounded a self-preservation of quite another kind than that which can be threatened and endangered by nature outside us, whereby the humanity in our person remains undemeaned even though the human being must submit to that dominion. (CPJ, 5:262–3)

The aesthetic encounter with powerful nature shows that our *dignity* ("the humanity in our person remains undemeaned") as beings that are not subject to our animal nature is measured by the gap that separates our "physical powerlessness" from our *moral powerfulness*. We see our superiority to nature within ourselves, our self-mastery, as extending to nature outside of us: for by *virtually* conquering our natural inclinations we show ourselves to be (morally/spiritually) stronger than the nature that threatens us. The Dynamically Sublime demonstrates, makes "palpable" (CPJ, 5:262), to use Kant's term, the *transcendence* of our sensuous self by our moral self (our freedom to resist), and therefore the "humanity in our person" is not only "undemeaned" but is also *exalted* in this virtual conquest of nature. Thus the dual structure of sublimity as dominating-exalting corresponds to the dual nature of the sensual-moral self (that is to say, the moral transcendence of sensible limitations in terms of our capacity to resist or overcome).

Although both the Mathematically and the Dynamically Sublime reveal our *superiority* to nature, the Dynamically Sublime additionally reveals our *independence from* nature (within and without), that is, our *autonomy*, and for this reason is more directly connected with morality. It will be recalled that in the rational demand for totality (in the Mathematically Sublime) we discover in ourselves a "non-sensible standard" (CPJ, 5:261) for judging, but this in and of itself does not show us to be *independent* from nature; that is, it does not concern the will and its freedom. In the *Groundwork*, Kant appears to anticipate the Dynamically Sublime, asserting that "it is just in this independence of maxims from all such incentives that their *sublimity* consists, and the worthiness of every rational subject to be a lawgiving member in the kingdom of ends; for otherwise he would have to be represented only as subject to the natural law of his needs" (G, 4:439, my emphasis). In Kant's account of morality, we must submit to the moral law, but this "submission" is qualified by the fact that we *willingly* do so, because it is a law we give ourselves.[12] Interestingly, Kant invokes the sublime while making this very point in the *Groundwork*: "For there is indeed no sublimity in him insofar as he is *subject* to the moral law, but there certainly is insofar as he is at the same time *lawgiving* with respect to it and only for that reason subordinated to it" (G, 4:440, original emphasis). Only the moral law has dominion over our entire being (thus effectively replacing divine authority). In realizing the rational demand for autonomy we discover our volitional independence from nature in the realization of a higher form of self-preservation, namely the self-preservation of the rational-moral self that overrides or overcomes the natural instinct of self-preservation of our sensual being. Resistance to the power of nature is, in effect, resistance to our own physical instincts and inclinations; the most threatening nature cannot make us do anything against our will; our resistance, our will is absolute.

Thus in demonstrating our freedom and autonomy vis-à-vis nature, the Dynamically Sublime shows how we "measure ourselves against the apparent all-powerfulness of nature" (5:261).[13] We see our own power of resistance, our refusal to "bow" (CPJ, 5:262) to overwhelming nature, mirrored, as it were, in nature's might, insofar as the former is proportional to the latter. Kant in fact explicitly describes the experience as the collision of two powers, our power versus the power of nature, or *Kraft* versus *Macht* (both rendered as "power" in English): "[Overwhelming nature] calls forth our power [*Kraft*] (which is not part of nature) . . . to regard its power [*Macht*] . . . as not having . . . dominion" (CPJ, 5:262).[14] The encounter with natural might "calls forth" our own power, revealing our freedom *in a case where it is most threatened*. Insofar as *Macht* is associated with authority, that is, with the sense of something having power over us, as opposed to *Kraft*, the power or capacity to do something, Kant can be read as surreptitiously advocating for a kind of Enlightenment anti-authoritarianism in his Dynamically Sublime.[15]

---

[12] But this does not mean that we *create* the moral law, like a Nietzschean will to power. Allen Wood points out that, for Kant, the moral law is in fact a natural law; that is, it objectively exists in the nature of things. Thus, "although we can *consider* our will as the author of the law, it is *not* (properly speaking) the author of the law" (Wood, *Kantian Ethics*, 113, emphasis in the original). That is, we see ourselves as if we had authored the law, when in fact we only *give* it to ourselves.

[13] Kant remarks similarly in the *Anthropology*: "The *sublime* is awe-inspiring *greatness* (*magnitudo reverenda*) in extent or degree which invites approach (in order to measure our powers against it)" (APP, 7:243, original emphasis).

[14] I give the full quotation below.

[15] As expressed in his famous 1784 essay "Beantwortung der Frage: Was ist Aufklärung?" ("Answering the Question: What is Enlightenment?" contained in Kant, *Practical Philosophy*, 11–22).

This idea of overcoming moral adversity is in fact the very definition of Kant's idea of "moral worth," one of the key concepts of his moral theory. Allen Wood observes that moral esteem "is reserved only for those who find themselves in a situation of adversity, one in which their natural inclinations do not make it easy to conform to moral principles. The action with authentic moral worth is the one where the agent faced with adversity rises to the occasion and does the dutiful thing *in spite of* the adverse circumstances."[16] In other words, what is essential to morality does not show itself in situations where it is easy to do the right thing, but rather in those in which we are *challenged*. Wood in fact employs the word "sublime" in describing Kant's concept of moral worth: "The sublimity of a hard-won victory over ourselves is more to be esteemed than the ingenuous charm of a good nature that faces no such opposition."[17] In this sense, one could say that Kant's concept of morality is also defined by a heroic subjectivity.

11.2   Virtual heroism

We have yet to discuss how Kant specifically characterizes the Dynamically Sublime in such terms, although the ideas of facing fear and of resisting a great threat are highly suggestive. Kant often resorts to heroic language, as in the following paragraph:

> As long as we find ourselves in safety . . . we gladly call these objects sublime because they elevate the strength of our soul above its usual level, and allow us to discover within ourselves a capacity for resistance of quite another kind, which gives us the courage to measure ourselves against the apparent all-powerfulness of nature. (CPJ, 5:261)

Words such as "strength," "courage," "resistance," as well as the idea that our "soul" is elevated "above its usual level" all connote a heroic disposition. Although this heroic-aesthetic feeling is available in principle to everyone, Kant will later say that only those with the proper cultivation, for instance, the bourgeois, are in fact able to attain it. Through the Dynamically Sublime, the bourgeois esthete, enveloped "in safety," comes to an aesthetic realization of his or her nobility of soul. The Dynamically Sublime thus effectively appropriates for the bourgeois the cast of mind that previously attached to a specific social caste as its natural essence, namely the aristocracy. As in his moral philosophy, Kant divorces

---

[16] Wood, *Kantian Ethics*, 29, my emphasis.   [17] Wood, *Kantian Ethics*, 30.

the idea of nobility of soul or mind from social hierarchy, thereby transforming it into a universal concept of human dignity. Although this democratizing aspect of the aesthetics of sublimity may be seen as a function of Kant's overall emphasis on universal rationality, the specifically figurative or symbolic importance of the sublime in this effort should not be understated.

The precise relation of Kant's theory of sublimity to his moral theory is a matter of vigorous debate, even if all agree that aesthetic feeling, no matter how proximate to moral feeling, is not identical to it. Nevertheless, Kant's descriptions of the Dynamically Sublime often seem to blur the line between aesthetics and morality,[18] as in the following passage:

> In our aesthetic judgment nature is judged as sublime not insofar as it arouses fear, but rather because it calls forth our power [*Kraft*] (which is not part of nature) to regard those things about which we are concerned (goods, health and life) as trivial, and hence to regard its power [*Macht*] (to which we are, to be sure, subjected in regard to these things) as not having the sort of dominion over ourselves and our authority to which we would have to bow if it came down to our highest principles and their affirmation or abandonment. (CPJ, 5:262)

The invocation of "our highest principles" in this passage would appear to bring morality directly into the equation. However, it is really a kind of virtual projection ("to which we would have to bow *if* it came down to ..."). In other words, the Dynamically Sublime offers only aesthetic support to the notion that human beings would not be capable of sacrificing their lives for ideals such as honor or (political) freedom if they were captive to their physical nature and its immutable law of self-preservation.[19] The Dynamically Sublime demonstrates our self-mastery: that our duty to the moral law cannot be constrained by our physical nature insofar as it is a matter of determining the will (that is, one may be in actuality too physically weak to rush into battle, but the *will* to do so remains untouched by such weakness). Nevertheless, the merely aesthetic judgment does not actually determine the will; it only suggests the feeling that the will *could be so determined*.

We should note that the potential moral situation the Dynamically Sublime dramatizes is not a matter of everyday morality, but of an

---

[18] We observed this in Chapter 8, with regard to the second *Critique*.

[19] Although Kant does not talk about suicide in this context, one would have to assume that it would not be an example of elevation of mind if it involved simply an escape from fear or the pain of excessive grief; for in that case we would not be rising above our sensuous nature, but rather submitting to it.

exceptional, heroic form, that is, morality under extreme, life or death conditions (moral adversity, as discussed above). Thus: "Nature is here called sublime merely because it raises the imagination to the point of presenting *those cases* in which the mind can make palpable to itself the sublimity of its own vocation even over nature" (CPJ, 5:262, my emphasis). These "cases" are the *virtual projection* of ourselves into situations of absolute resistance suggested by the encounter with overwhelming natural power. We therefore discover ourselves to be (virtually) *fearless* in the Dynamically Sublime – the very opposite of Burke's conception of sublime terror. Nevertheless, this does not contradict the requirement that "nature must be represented as arousing fear," since the concept of fearlessness has meaning only in regards to a threat.

We have yet to adequately describe how the heroic mindset of the Dynamically Sublime can be consistent with the safety condition in Kant's account – namely the requirement that we must be in a "safe place" (APP, 7:243) to judge powerful nature aesthetically – which, though it was implied in the stipulation that we do not experience actual fear while perceiving something as threatening, was nevertheless not addressed directly. Kant is well aware of this issue, noting that "this self-esteem [the feeling of elevation] is not diminished by the fact that we must see ourselves as safe in order to be sensible of this inspiring satisfaction, in which case (it might seem), because the danger is not serious, the sublimity of our spiritual capacity is also not to be taken seriously" (CPJ, 5:262). In other words, the "safety condition" might make the Dynamically Sublime seem like a sort of "armchair" heroics, a false heroism. Nevertheless, while the sublime might not involve "emotion from real danger" (CPJ, 5:253), it still involves emotion.[20] Kant must thus walk a fine line between actuality and illusion: "The satisfaction here concerns only the *vocation* of our capacity as it is revealed to us in such a case, just as the predisposition to it lies in our nature; while the development and exercise of it is left to us and remains our responsibility" (CPJ, 5:262, original emphasis). That is to say, the heroic disposition realized aesthetically does not imply an actual capacity for heroic action, only the supersensible "vocation" – our predisposition for transcendence – that makes such action possible. Thus, Kant concedes, "if he takes his reflection this far, [he] may be conscious of his *present actual powerlessness*" (CPJ, 5:262, my emphasis).

---

[20] This might appear to involve what Paul Guyer calls "emotions at play" versus "emotions at work" (developed in his *A History of Modern Aesthetics*, vol. 1) but, as I argued in Chapter 6, I find the notion of virtuality to be more apt.

Nevertheless, the experience is not an illusion. The heroic feeling experienced in the Dynamically Sublime is real, but it concerns only the idea of ourselves as beings capable of absolute resistance due to our natural predisposition for rational ideas. Henry Allison comments:

> The key point is that what we become conscious of aesthetically, that is, feel approvingly, in the experience of the dynamically sublime, is only the "vocation" [*Bestimmung*] of our faculty insofar as the predisposition [*Anlage*] to it lies in our nature. This is equivalent to our moral autonomy or self-legislative capacity, which is to be distinguished from the *actual* strength of will or autocracy required to fulfill the demands of this self-legislation.[21]

By using the word "actual," Allison seemingly subscribes to a notion of virtuality (a word he does not use) in regards to the Dynamically Sublime. Feeling *as if* one could do heroic deeds is not tantamount to (actually) having the strength of will to (actually) do so. Bourgeois esthetes can lay claim to a heroic nature without ever being in a position to actually test themselves. Nevertheless, we must keep in mind that since the sublime involves a spiritual feeling (*Geistesgefühl*) or high-minded disposition (*Gemütsstimmung*, etymologically related to the word for "vocation," *Bestimmung*) the feeling of the Dynamically Sublime should be considered as being intrinsically linked to a self capable of heroic action.[22] If our aesthetically realized supersensible vocation were completely divorced from practical rationality, Kant's arguments regarding the integration of the three *Critiques* would be greatly weakened. This manner of linking the world of sense to the world of spirit (*Geist*) through the Dynamically Sublime thus affirms our freedom vis-à-vis nature in a way that is much more socially and politically relevant than the parallel operation of the Mathematically Sublime.[23]

While one could certainly act in a cowardly manner after experiencing the Dynamically Sublime, the reverse is not true: for the Dynamically Sublime *is*, structurally speaking, a description of the mental disposition of the hero (the true hero manifests a superior strength in the face of great obstacles), as Kant will in fact show in some of his examples (such as the warrior). The difference is that, unlike morality, aesthetic experience does not determine the will (and even morality does not determine the *strength*

---

[21] Allison, *Kant's Theory of Taste*, 330, my emphasis.

[22] For example, religious enthusiasm, which Kant will in fact discuss in relation to the sublime, often inspires us to do things that we would not normally do or be capable of doing (for moral or immoral ends).

[23] One could also mention in this context Kant's discussion of genius in §49, in which he asserts that *Geist* is the "animating principle in the mind" (CPJ, 5:313).

of the will). The heroic mindset that is occasioned aesthetically must be considered as being indeterminate with regard to the activity of the will, though the same mental state obtains in both virtual-aesthetic and actual-moral manifestations of heroic subjectivity.[24]

11.3   The sublimity of war

The difficult-to-grasp element of nonactuality or virtuality in the Dynamically Sublime leads Kant to note that "to be sure, this principle [of nonactuality] seems far-fetched [or 'high-flown,' *überschwenglich*] and subtle, hence excessive for an aesthetic judgment" (CPJ, 5:262). To make his point more concretely, Kant resorts to images taken from the "common judgment":

> The observation of human beings shows the opposite, that it can be the principle for the most common judgings even though one is not always conscious of it. For what is it that is the object of the highest admiration even to the savage? Someone who is not frightened, who has no fear, thus does not shrink before danger but energetically sets to work with full deliberation. And even in the most civilized circumstances this exceptionally high esteem for the warrior remains, only now it is demanded that he at the same time display all the virtues of peace, gentleness, compassion and even proper care for his own person, precisely because in this way the incoercibility of his mind by danger can be recognized. (CPJ, 5:262)

The example is noteworthy in that it involves the use of a figure to illustrate the mental state of the Dynamically Sublime,[25] thereby uniting aesthetic and social-cultural reflection. For in the example of the warrior's nobility of mind, Kant draws attention to the nexus between a mental state and a social or class concept (the warrior aristocracy). In addition, Kant would also seem to be making a historical point about the transition from a feudal to a modern mercantile society, that is, from a society in which one's heroic nobility of mind is defined by the practice of war to one in which such a disposition is tempered by civil society and the "virtues of peace." Kant evinces a seeming nostalgia for the heroic age; for he remarks that "even" in "civilized" societies an "exceptionally high esteem for the warrior remains": civilization values that which in some sense negates its values.

---

[24] This was discussed in Chapter 8.
[25] Allison (in *Kant's Theory of Taste*, 331) sees the fact that Kant is using an example from the human-cultural sphere as a "minor problem," since sublimity is of the mind: "The true locus of the sublime . . . is the self." We observed something similar in regards to the architectural examples employed in the Mathematically Sublime.

Kant transforms this nostalgia into a critique of modern society, in his assertion that "war is sublime":

> Hence however much debate there may be about whether it is the statesman or the general who deserves the greater respect in comparison to the other, aesthetic judgment decides in favor of the latter. Even war, *if it is conducted with order and reverence for the rights of civilians*, has something sublime about it, and at the same time makes the *mentality* of the people who conduct it in this way all the more sublime, the more dangers it has been exposed to and before which it has been able to assert its courage; whereas a long peace causes *the spirit of mere commerce* to predominate, along with base selfishness, cowardice, and weakness, and usually debases the *mentality* of a populace. (CPJ, 5:263, my emphasis)

The question here is whether war and the warrior spirit that Kant describes are simply *images* of sublimity; that is, they concern *only* aesthetic judgment, or whether Kant means to say that the *mentality* of a people conditioned by the noble requirements of waging war (self-sacrifice) is superior to a mercantile, bourgeois society oriented toward self-interest, in which case it would also be a kind of collective ethical judgment or cultural critique. In fact, the passage can be read as averring both. Kant first stipulates that it is "aesthetic judgment" (and thus not moral judgment) that decides in favor of the general over the statesman, with regard to who deserves the "greater respect." But in the second part of the passage, focusing on the phenomenon of war itself, Kant clearly indulges in cultural criticism, counterpoising the "spirit of commerce," with its "base selfishness, cowardice, and weakness," to the sublimity and courageousness of earlier warrior societies. Thus Kant employs the sublime to denounce certain aspects of "civilization," while extolling the heroic virtues of "primitive," or premodern societies, virtues he believes his contemporaries might do well to emulate. In effect, Kant is complicating the Enlightenment narrative of social progress by invoking the *topos* of the "decline of civilization" – a *topos* that, as we have seen, is also present in Burke's and Longinus's theories of sublimity.[26]

As the historian David Bell has observed, this type of sentiment was not at all unusual for the period; it was actually a feature of Enlightenment thought:

---

[26] Kant's passage echoes Longinus's discourse on the decline of Roman society: the lack of greatness of spirit as a consequence of an all-consuming desire for wealth and pleasure. As we saw in Chapter 6, the anxiety toward the development of bourgeois society away from heroic values also animated Burke's assertion that the feeling of sublimity is rooted in the instinct of self-preservation, an instinct that is rarely aroused in a society oriented toward luxury and pleasure.

From within the Enlightenment itself, critiques of the new theories of peace were taking shape, grounded in the belief that the progress of commercial civilization represented anything but an unalloyed benefit. "Primitive" societies ... [had] a vital fire and a passion that the civilizing process was steadily leeching away, leaving humanity lethargic, soft, and decadent, incapable of great deeds or great beauty. Civilization resembled a degenerative disease, but war could provide a vaccine.[27]

In this vein, the philosopher and linguist Wilhelm von Humboldt (1767–1835, founder of the Humboldt University in Berlin) wrote that "war is one of the healthiest phenomena for the cultivation of the human race.... It is the admittedly fearful extreme, through which active courage in the face of danger, labor, and fortitude are tested and steeled."[28] Viewed in context, Kant's remarks express a widely shared sentiment. What is important for this study is the way in which such a sentiment is linked to the theory of sublimity, effectively wedding aesthetic reflection to cultural critique. As suggested above, Kant's assertion that "a long peace" and the concomitant development of a commercial spirit "usually debase the mentality of a populace" clearly goes beyond merely aesthetic reflection.

Allison, however, dismisses the idea that Kant might be making a moral judgment or cultural critique in this passage:

> The major interest of the passage lies however, in its apparent glorification or, perhaps better, "sublimification" of war.... For the understanding of the sublime, the essential point is that it is an *aesthetic judgment* that prefers the general to the statesman or, more generally, that admires the warrior for his courage. Since an aesthetic judgment is *not* a moral evaluation, it does not suggest a favorable moral verdict on war or those who wage it. What it does suggest is, rather, that an uninvolved spectator would feel that there is something uplifting or inspiring in the resolution with which a soldier faces death because it represents something that is essential to morality, namely the valuation of something as higher than physical existence, even though the particular valuation in question may not be made on moral grounds or even concern a morally permissible end.[29]

Allison's assertion is correct, as far as it goes. But he is wrong to collapse the specific point about the preference for the general over the statesman (which, I concur, concerns an aesthetic rather than a moral judgment) into the more general point about war, which, as argued above, involves the question of cultural development more broadly and is not a merely aesthetic judgment. If

---

[27] David Bell, *The First Total War: Napoleon's Europe and the Birth of Warfare as We Know It*, 78.
[28] Quoted in Bell, *The First Total War*, 82.
[29] Allison, *Kant's Theory of Taste*, 331, original emphasis.

Kant were making a merely aesthetic point he would not have added the caveat: "If [war] is conducted with order and reverence for the rights of civilians," an assertion that certainly concerns "a morally permissible end."

As was observed in the chapter on Burke, Kant too uses the concept of the sublime in this section to resurrect and appropriate for the ascendant bourgeoisie the values that had been associated with the noble or warrior class at an earlier stage of European history. The idea that the bourgeois (in other words, a cultivated person) can attain sublimity of mind means that he or she can, in a dispositional sense, be "noble" in realizing aesthetically that quality of mind that had for centuries defined, and in some sense legitimated, the existence of the upper social strata.

11.4   The sublimity of God

Near the end of the section on the Dynamically Sublime, Kant returns to a discussion of God, a subject on which he had briefly touched in the idea of the God-fearing man. As a thinker genuinely concerned with religion,[30] Kant is keenly aware of the religious implications of the sublime, which are, somewhat counterintuitively, seen in his account as attaching only to the Dynamically Sublime rather than to the Mathematically Sublime. Given the traditional association of God with infinity, one might have thought that the Mathematically Sublime would have been the more natural place for such reflections (as in Burnet's *The Sacred Theory of the Earth*). However, as we have seen in previous chapters, the association of God with power and terror was a conventional theme of the discourse of sublimity, particularly in Burke, and Kant no doubt felt obliged to address it.

The model for thinking the nexus between sublimity and religion is John Dennis, for whom God's wrath is the very embodiment of sublime terror. After offering a list of sublime objects, including "Torrents, Earthquakes, Volcanoes . . . ," Dennis writes that "of all these ideas none are so terrible as those which shew the Wrath and Vengeance of an angry God . . . because . . . He may deliver us from all other Terrors, but nothing can save and defend us from him" (CW I, 361–2). This is why, according to Dennis, "Religious Ideas" are the principal source of the sublime.[31]

---

[30] Wood notes that "Kant is fundamentally a *religious* thinker. For his highest hopes for human history are pinned on religious values and religious institutions" (*Kant's Ethical Thought*, 318, original emphasis).

[31] Kant too can be said to have conceived of something similar. John Zammito observes, with respect to Kant's doctrine of "Aesthetic Ideas," that "for Kant art could not simply be *mimetic*. Its primary purpose was to *express* the supersensible. Art was the vehicle for the expression of religious and rational ideas" (*The Genesis of Kant's* Critique of Judgment, 289).

Although Kant will raise similar images – "we usually represent God as exhibiting himself in anger but at the same time in his sublimity in thunder, storm, earthquake, etc." (CPJ, 5:263) – he evinces a more secular attitude toward the relation between natural power and the divine.

Dennis's influence is most apparent in Burke's section on "Power" (E, Part II: v), where Burke observes that of all the attributes of God, including his vastness and infinity, we are most struck by his power; we "shrink into the minuteness of our own nature, and are in a manner *annihilated before him*" (E, 63, my emphasis). Kant is clearly responding to this passage in his remarks on God's might. The problem for Kant is distinguishing proper from improper relations to the divinity as they relate to his theory of sublimity. For to incorporate the idea of God as a "force which nothing can withstand" into the theory of the Dynamically Sublime, which involves a successful (moral) resistance to an overwhelming power, would mean that we can heroically resist God – a proposition that is ethically and religiously absurd (it in fact corresponds to the description of Satan).

On the other hand, the submission or slavishness that characterizes a certain ("primitive" or archaic) religious attitude toward the deity is anathema to Kant's concept of sublimity as self-exaltation and as an index of human autonomy (and to Kant's rational conception of religion more generally):[32]

> Here it seems to be not a feeling of the sublimity of our own nature but rather submission, dejection, and a feeling of complete powerlessness that is the appropriate disposition of the mind to the appearance of such an object [God], and which is also usually associated with the idea of it in the case of natural occurrences of this sort [thunder, storm, earthquake]. In religion in general submission, adoration with bowed head, and remorseful and anxious gestures and voice, seem to be the only appropriate conduct in the presence of the Deity, and so to have been adopted and still observed by most people. But this disposition of the mind is far from being intrinsically and necessarily connected with the idea of the *sublimity* of religion and its object. (CPJ, 5:263, original emphasis)

Remarkably, Kant here seeks to define the authentic religious attitude via the aesthetic concept of sublimity – hence Kant's use of the terms "intrinsically" and "necessarily" in this passage, which underscore the proximity, almost to the point of identity, between a sublime state of mind and a

---

[32] See Kant's 1793 *Religion within the Boundaries of Mere Reason* (in Kant, *Religion and Rational Theology*) and Allen Wood's two books: *Kant's Rational Theology* and *Kant's Moral Religion*.

genuinely religious one. Kant will therefore dismiss as a form of "super-stition" (CPJ, 5:264) natural might considered as the expression of divine might, concluding that a person who believes in the personification of natural power and fears it as a manifestation of divine justice "does not find himself in the right frame of mind to marvel at the greatness of God, for which a mood of calm contemplation and an entirely free judgment is requisite" (CPJ, 5:263).[33] The authentic religious attitude requires the same conditions as aesthetic judgment! The mental disposition one finds in the experience of sublimity is not only conducive to morality but, even more directly, to the proper attitude toward God and religion:

> Only when if he is conscious of his upright, God-pleasing disposition do these effects of power serve to awaken in him the idea of the sublimity of this being, insofar as he recognizes in himself a sublimity of disposition suitable to God's will, and is thereby raised above the fear of such effects of nature, which he does not regard as outbursts of God's wrath. (CPJ, 5:263)

In other words, one gains insight into the sublimity of God through the sublimity of mind occasioned by the virtual resistance to natural might. The rational transcendence of sensual attachment in the Dynamically Sublime demonstrates how the human will can be harmonized with the divine will. In this sense, the Dynamically Sublime implies a kind of demystification, an enlightened state of religious understanding. The result is a fully secularized view of nature (vaguely reminiscent of the displace-ment of paganism by Christianity).

The demystification of nature mirrors the demystification of sublimity itself as a term that should not apply to nature, but only to the human or the divine mind:

> Thus sublimity is not contained in anything in nature, but only in our mind, insofar as we become conscious of being superior to nature within us and thus also to nature outside us (insofar as it influences us). Everything that arouses this feeling in us, which includes the *power* [*Macht*] of nature that calls forth our own powers [*Kräfte*], is thus (although improperly) called sublime; and only under the presupposition of this idea in us and in relation to it are we capable of arriving at the idea of the sublimity of that being who produces inner respect in us. (CPJ, 5:264)

Whereas it is improper to call any object of nature "sublime" (elevated, *erhaben*), it is appropriate to speak of the sublimity of God. However, it is not the sublimity of God that produces the awareness of our own

---

[33] However, at CPJ, 5:258 Kant had used the phrase "calm contemplation" to define the judgment of the beautiful in contradistinction to that of the sublime.

sublimity, but the other way around. Thus Paul Guyer observes: "God's creation is humbled before our own free reason and even the sublimity of God himself can be appreciated through the image of our own autonomy."[34] One can trace this idea back to Longinus, who observes that "sublimity raises us toward the spiritual greatness of god" (36.1), meaning that our mental elevation puts us in touch with that element in ourselves that most approaches or approximates the divine.

One can certainly read Kant's digression on religion in the Dynamically Sublime in terms of a desire to reconcile the secularizing tendencies of Enlightenment thought with Christian Pietism, a desire evident in all of his three *Critiques* and emblematized in his famous pronouncement: "Thus I had to deny *knowledge* in order to make room for *faith*" (CPuR, B xxx, original emphasis). What one could call Kant's soft Lutheranism not only allows, but also prefigures such a reconciliation. For, in Martin Luther's contention that the authentic Christian-religious attitude lay not in bowing to the "sublimity" of the religious authorities in Rome but in every individual's capacity to discover the divine spark within, in the sublimity of mind attained through personal and unmediated reflection on the sacred texts, is Luther not the grandfather of the Enlightenment and the progenitor of modern individualism? If Luther's and Kant's anti-authoritarianism and revolutionary call for human autonomy set the stage for a secularization of culture and the decline of faith, this result certainly ran counter to their intentions.

***

This chapter has argued that Kant's description of the aesthetic encounter with powerful nature is in fact a description of a heroic subjectivity, an idea that has not only a specifically moral meaning, in the idea of "moral adversity," but also important sociocultural implications, namely in the contrast between the heroic spirit of the warrior and the "spirit of commerce" of the bourgeois, and in the confrontation between the primitive personification of the "wrath of God" and the Christian-Protestant idea of the "sublimity of God."

Considering the Mathematically and the Dynamically Sublime together, we can now make the following observation. The idea that the sublime involves an irreducible *conflict* with nature, whereas the beautiful involves *harmony* with nature, underlines Kant's attempt in his third *Critique* to reconceive the *meaning* of nature: on the one hand, as

---

[34] Guyer, *Kant and the Experience of Freedom*, 259.

mechanistic, sensual, simply contrapurposive (ugly or simply threatening), nature is antagonistic to human freedom; on the other, as hospitable and purposive (the aesthetic judgment of the beautiful), but also as overwhelming (contrapurposive) and purposive (for the whole vocation of the mind, the judgment of the sublime), or as exhibiting systematicity (scientifically purposive, teleological judgment), nature can be seen as supportive of human freedom. As these two chapters have argued, Kant clearly finds in the aesthetics of sublimity a more effective or direct way to resolve the tension between nature and freedom (and thus morality).

CHAPTER 12

Sublimity and culture in Kant

As noted in previous chapters, most commentators see Kant as privileging nature in his account of aesthetic experience.[1] Indeed, the principal aim of the *Critique of the Power of Judgment* is not to elucidate aesthetic experience per se but to bridge the divide between nature and freedom, the phenomenal and the noumenal, in the Critical Philosophy. Thus Kant discusses beauty, sublimity, and fine art in this work, not simply because he believes they are intrinsically interesting and in need of philosophical attention but because they can demonstrate how a certain experience of nature, namely one involving a (noncognitive) judgment of pleasure or pain, is also an experience of freedom and thus of a mental state reflective of or conducive to morality. If, due to the exigencies of the Critical Philosophy, Kant is unable to focus on the question of the sublimity in artifacts, this does not thereby mean that he thought the topic unworthy of study – he had, after all, written about it at length in his *Observations*, and, as I noted in the Introduction, Kant's lifelong passion for Milton's *Paradise Lost* is certainly an indication of his sensitivity to sublimity in poetry.[2] On the other hand, it would be a mistake to think that Kant conceives of the aesthetic experience of nature as if culture were irrelevant to that experience. Even if Kant privileges *the perspective of nature*, rather than that of art or culture, art nevertheless provides the model for the noncognitive experience of nature, insofar as nature is judged *as if* it were art, that is, according to the notion of a "Technik der Natur" (technique of nature): "The concept of

[1] An exception is Paul Guyer: "It would be a mistake to think that such judgments [of nature] should be the norm for all aesthetic judgments; rather Kant begins with them because they are the *simplest* cases of aesthetic judgment" (*Kant*, 312, original emphasis). Most scholars would probably agree with Uygar Abaci's assessment that "the most we can get from the [third] *Critique* is impure, restricted, and still problematic cases of artistic sublimity, but by no means a coherent theory" ("Kant's Justified Dismissal of Artistic Sublimity," 237).

[2] Sanford Budick even goes so far as to assert that it was Kant's "experience of the sublime, especially in Milton's poetry," in the 1780s that "made possible ... 'the grand disclosure' of freedom and moral feeling" (*Kant and Milton*, 2 [embedded quotations are from Kant, CPaR, 5:94]).

nature as art" (CPJ, 5:246).[3] Conversely, fine art, insofar as it is an art of genius, is an expression of nature (within us), even if we are aware that it is also a product of human intentionality: "*Genius* is the inborn predisposition of the mind (*ingenium*) *through which* nature gives the rule to art (CPJ, 5:307, original emphasis). Thus nature and culture clearly work in tandem in Kant's aesthetic thought.

The first section of this chapter studies §29 of the third *Critique*, in particular Kant's seemingly contradictory stipulation that a judgment of sublimity requires a certain degree of culture (*Kultur*) and moral preparation, even if such judgments, like all aesthetic judgments, make a claim to universality (that is, they are *necessary*, as opposed to being empirical and contingent). The second section discusses the General Remark following §29, namely what Kant calls the "aesthetically sublime" – affects and mental states – including how these relate to literary examples and genres. The final section focuses on the vexed question of how sublimity is possible in artistic representation and in artifacts more generally, if art must always be subject to the dictates of taste. I attempt to resolve this dilemma by considering the proximity between Kant's notions of ugliness and sublimity and by coordinating passages from the *Anthropology* with Kant's theory of fine art and genius in the third *Critique*.

12.1 Culture, morality, and necessity

If one excludes the General Remark appended to it, §29 is the shortest section among those devoted to the sublime. It is also perhaps the densest and most difficult to interpret; for it proposes to treat in just a few short paragraphs such fundamental concepts as culture and morality and their relation to aesthetic judgment. Entitled "On the modality of the judgment of the sublime in nature," §29 ostensibly deals with the question of the "presumed necessity" (CPJ, 5:266) of judgments of sublimity, an investigation that involves two distinct points: (1) the rationale for the universal validity of judgments of the sublime; (2) the rationale for the different mental requirements of judgments of beauty and sublimity respectively. Since the second point appears to conflict with the first (it denies universality), this is where Kant begins his discussion.

---

[3] In the First Introduction to the third *Critique*, Kant writes: "We shall in the future also use the expression 'technique' [*Technik*] where objects of nature are sometimes merely *judged as if* their possibility were grounded in art, in which case the judgments are neither theoretical nor practical" (FI, 20: 200–1, original emphasis). I discussed this passage in Chapter 9. See also CPJ, 5:233.

As the two introductions to the third *Critique* make clear, all aesthetic judgments, by virtue of being grounded in reflective judgment (subjective purposiveness), are universal; that is, they *claim* universal assent and possess normative force. But Kant also seeks to account for the *fact* that aesthetic judgments may not agree; that is, they may be deficient in *actual experience*, and, further, the judgments of the beautiful and the sublime may differ with regard to the level of agreement one can actually or ideally expect. Thus Kant writes that "just as we reproach someone who is indifferent in judging an object in nature that we find beautiful with a lack of *taste*, so we say of someone who remains unmoved by that which we judge to be sublime that he has no *feeling*. We demand both however of every human being" (CPJ, 5:265, original emphasis).[4] In other words, the universal claim to validity presupposes a judging capacity that is *common* to – though not necessarily *fully developed* in – all.

Significantly, Kant sees the judgment of the sublime as less widely shared in fact than that of the beautiful, though, logically speaking, each has an equal *claim* to universality. The difference lies in the degree of "culture" (*Kultur*) required for each type of judgment:

> We cannot promise ourselves that our judgment concerning the sublime in nature will so readily find acceptance by others. For a far greater *culture*, not merely of the aesthetic power of judgment, but also of the cognitive faculties on which that is based, seems to be requisite in order to be able to make a judgment about this excellence of the objects of nature. (CPJ, 5:264, my emphasis)

Kant takes pains to point out that the sublime "is not therefore first generated by culture and so to speak introduced into society merely as a matter of convention; rather it has its foundation in human nature" (CPJ, 5:265). That is to say, sublimity is not cultural in the sense of being empirical and relative; it is transcendentally grounded in our rational nature. However, what Kant exactly means by *Kultur* in this passage is unclear. Does he mean the general "improvement" of our faculties, that is, of their functionality? Or is he referring to the exposure to the higher intellectual arts or the attainment of a certain level of sociality, as when he writes: "Everyone who has any culture" (wenn er einige Kultur hat) (CPJ, 5:266)? The idea of being *in possession* of culture would seem to imply the

---

[4] Kant had made a similar remark in the *Observations*: "Of whichever sort these finer feelings that we have thus far treated might be, whether sublime or beautiful, they have in common the fate of always seeming perverse and absurd in the judgment of those who have no feeling attuned to them" (O, 2:224).

acquisition of cultural content and not merely the better functioning of the faculties, though these may be exercised and thereby improved in the acquisition of culture. While these different senses of "culture" are certainly interrelated, it is nevertheless difficult to discern, without some distinctions, what kind of cultural training specifically prepares us for sublimity – for instance, reading epic poetry, attending philosophy lectures or religious sermons, frequenting elegant salons, and so on – except to say, rather broadly, that "the disposition of the mind to the feeling of the sublime requires receptivity to ideas" (CPJ, 5:265).[5] Kant would thus seem to imply that "culture" encourages "receptivity to ideas."

As Kant suggests, the receptivity to ideas encouraged by culture involves practical rather than pure reason. This would appear to privilege the Dynamically Sublime (the practical-rational idea of autonomy) over the Mathematically Sublime (the pure-rational idea of totality). Indeed, the example Kant provides in this section involves power:

> Without the development of moral ideas, that which we, prepared by culture, call sublime will appear merely repellent to the unrefined person. He will see in the proofs of the dominion of nature given by its destructiveness and in the enormous measure of it power, against which his own vanishes to nothing, only the distress, danger, and need that would surround the person who was banished thereto. (CPJ, 5:265).

Similar to what we earlier observed with regard to general pronouncements on sublimity that seemed to apply only to the Mathematically Sublime, here the Dynamically Sublime is cited to support arguments concerning the modality of the sublime in general. Nevertheless, the point that Kant endeavors to make is that the judgment of sublimity "can be required of everyone and demanded of him along with healthy understanding, namely in the predisposition of the feeling for (practical) ideas, that is, to that which is moral" (CPJ, 5:265). This raises the question of the relative priority of culture and morality with respect to sublimity. In the above passage Kant insists that culture is a mediating influence between morality and sublimity; that is, morality is conducive to sublimity *by means of culture*.[6] Speaking about the beautiful in art (in §52: On the combination of the beautiful in one and the same product), Kant makes a similar observation:

---

[5] Kant does insist that the "agreeable" does not contribute to culture, since it is "simply a matter of enjoyment" (CPJ, 5:266).

[6] Guyer sees this as a sign of the inherent *impurity* of judgments of sublimity, because culture involves "intellectual content." See Guyer, *Values of Beauty*, 156–161.

> Yet in all beautiful art what is essential consists in the form, which is purposive for observation and judging, where the pleasure is at the same time culture [*Kultur*] and disposes the spirit [*Geist*] to ideas, hence makes it receptive to several sorts of pleasure and entertainment – not in the manner of sensation (the charm or the emotion), where it is aimed merely at enjoyment [*Unterhaltung*], which leaves behind it nothing in the idea, and makes the spirit dull, the object by and by loathsome [*anekelnd*], and the mind, because it is aware that its disposition is contrapurposive in the judgment of reason, dissatisfied with itself and moody. If the beautiful arts are not combined, whether closely or at a distance, with moral ideas, which alone carry with them a self-sufficient satisfaction, then the latter is their ultimate fate. (CPJ, 5:326)

This passage makes the same basic argument from the perspective of the beautiful and with the same ambiguity: if the experience of beauty and sublimity is already culture, how then can culture be an independent factor in that experience? Moreover, as suggested in the previous passage (and in CPJ, 5:292), if it is moral development that allows one to appreciate the sublime (and fine art), and if moral development is sufficient, then why invoke culture rather than morality as an essential factor in preparing us for sublimity?

To further complicate matters, Kant sometimes suggests that sublimity is a preparation for morality, rather than the other way around: "In fact a feeling for the sublime in nature cannot even be conceived without connecting it to a disposition of the mind that is similar to the moral disposition" (CPJ, 5:268). Thus Henry Allison, for example, speaks of the sublime as "moral facilitator."[7] But if Kant holds that culture and morality are mutually implicit, how to explain the case of the highly cultured but wicked person, unless such a possibility is definitionally impossible according to Kant – that is, that a "cultivated" person is ipso facto a moral person and the reverse.

To address fully the general relation between culture and morality in Kant's thought would take us too far afield. Let us therefore focus only on Kant's purpose for bringing up morality in §29, namely as a proof of the necessity of judgments of sublimity: "We require it under a subjective presupposition (which, however, we believe ourselves justified in demanding of everyone), namely that of a moral feeling in the human being, and so

---

[7] "The sublime puts us in touch (albeit merely aesthetically) with our 'higher self'; and, as such, it may help to clear the ground, as it were, for genuine moral feeling and therefore, like the sensitivity to natural beauty, though in a very different way, function as a moral facilitator" (Allison, *Kant's Theory of Taste*, 342).

we also ascribe necessity to this judgment" (CPJ, 5:266). In other words, the universality of judgments of sublimity is grounded in our natural predisposition toward morality. It is because we are moral beings that we can experience sublimity; those who are maleficent and have little or no moral feeling would not be able to attain the high-mindedness required in the judgment of sublimity. In this presupposition of a mental disposition that is at once aesthetic and morally informed, Kant reveals himself to be much closer to Longinus's notion of "nobility of mind" (*megalophrosynê*) than to Burke's sensationalism.

In §39 ("On the communicability of a sensation"), Kant speaks about the "moral foundation" of sublimity due to its proximity to the supersensible:

> The pleasure in the sublime in nature, as a pleasure of contemplation involving subtle reasoning [*der vernünftelnden Kontemplation*], also lays claim to universal participation, yet already presupposes another feeling, namely that of its supersensible vocation, which, no matter how obscure it might be, has a moral foundation. But that other human beings will take regard of it and find a satisfaction in the consideration of the brute magnitude of nature (which cannot be truthfully ascribed to the sight of it, which is rather terrifying) is not something that I am justified in simply presupposing. Nevertheless, in consideration of what should be taken into account of in those moral predispositions on every appropriate occasion, I can still require even that satisfaction of everyone, but only by means of the moral law, which for its part is in turn grounded on concepts of reason. (CPJ, 5:292)

Kant appears somewhat dubious that many people will be able to perform the kind of "contemplation involving *subtle* reasoning" that would allow them to convert "the consideration of the brute magnitude of nature," the sight of which is "terrifying" (in other words, the Dynamically Sublime, even if it is produced by sheer magnitude), into a morally purposeful disposition, thereby taking satisfaction in the experience. It is no doubt culture that favors the development of this *subtle* reasoning or contemplation in the sublime. Thus the beautiful, since it does not require such "subtle reasoning," is more universal *in fact*: "By contrast, the pleasure in the beautiful is neither a pleasure of enjoyment, nor of lawful activity, and not even of a contemplation involving subtle reasoning in accordance with ideas [*der vernünftelnden Kontemplation nach Ideen*], but of mere reflection" (CPJ, 5:292). At the very least, then, it is the closer proximity of sublimity to morality that makes the sublime more difficult to attain than the beautiful; for, just as it is difficult, in a situation of adversity, to transcend one's

sensible inclination and follow the stern command of the moral law, it is
similarly difficult to face the overwhelming power of nature and realize one's
supersensible vocation (sublimity of mind).

12.2   The aesthetically sublime: affects and mental states

The long General Remark appended to §29, on Kant's discussion of affects
as they relate to states of mind (*Gemütszustand*),[8] is an important but often
neglected part of Kant's theory of sublimity. Paul Crowther sees it as a
"subcategory of dynamic sublimity,"[9] while Allison goes so far as to call it
"a new form of the sublime," which "does not seem to fall into either of the
two species distinguished in the Analytic."[10] Kant himself uses the term
"aesthetically sublime," to describe the type of sublimity discussed in this
section, and I follow his lead in this chapter. It may appear odd to
distinguish a category of the "aesthetically sublime," since, for Kant, all
judgments of sublimity are by definition "aesthetic" judgments (even if
they are not judgments of taste). But here "aesthetically sublime" refers to
an *external* perspective on a state of mind rather than to a subjective
experience considered from the inside, as it were (as in the
Mathematically and the Dynamically Sublime). Thus by "aesthetically
sublime" Kant means illustrative *images* of sublimity or pseudo-sublimity,
drawn from life or artistic examples.

This section thus harks back to his early *Observations*, but also to many
of the examples used in the second *Critique*, as if Kant were attempting to
reconcile his early aesthetic thought and his moral philosophy with his
newfound transcendental outlook on aesthetics. In the second *Critique*, for
example, Kant remarks that "actions of others that are done with great
sacrifice and for the sake of duty alone may indeed be praised by calling
them *noble* and *sublime* deeds" (CPaR, 5:85, original emphasis). Is this an
aesthetic or a moral judgment? As I argued in Chapter 8, such judgments
are neither purely moral nor purely aesthetic; they are a kind of mixed
judgment. Similarly, in the General Remark Kant observes that the "good,
judged aesthetically [*ästhetisch beurteilt*], must not be represented [*vorges-
tellt*] so much as beautiful but rather as sublime" (CPJ, 5:271).[11] As earlier
noted, Robert Clewis sees this statement as justifying the category of the

---

[8] "This state of mind [*Gemütszustand*] [that is, enthusiasm] seems to be sublime" (CPJ, 5:272).
[9] Crowther, *The Kantian Sublime*, 116.   [10] Allison, *Kant's Theory of Taste*, 306.
[11] This statement would appear to suggest a way of articulating a concept of sublimity in artistic
representation. See the last part of this chapter.

"moral sublime," a category he invents.[12] I, however, contend that Kant's own category of the aesthetically sublime is both more appropriate and less fraught with interpretative problems.

The principal focus of the General Remark is the idea of "enthusiasm" (*Enthusiasm* in German, deriving from the Greek *enthousiasmos*, "possession by a god"),[13] a term that Kant uses throughout his corpus, from his *Observations* of 1674 to his 1798 work *The Conflict of the Faculties*. Here he defines *Enthusiasm* as (1) "a stretching of the powers through ideas, which give the mind a momentum that acts far more powerfully and persistently than the impetus given by sensory representations" (CPJ, 5:272); and (2) as "the idea of the good with affect" (CPJ, 5:272). The latter emphasizes the mixture of morality and aesthetics we observed in our discussion of the *Critique of Practical Reason*, in which Kant had defined "moral enthusiasm" as "an overstepping of the bounds of human reason undertaken on principles" (CPaR, 5:85), as contrasted with "a sober but wise moral discipline" (CPaR, 5:86). Moral enthusiasm is thus an impure and potentially dangerous form of morally directed reflection, since it threatens to go beyond rational restraint. In the third *Critique*, Kant observes that the mental state (*Gemütszustand*) of enthusiasm "seems to be sublime, so much that it is commonly maintained that without it nothing great can be accomplished" (CPJ, 5:272).[14] However, because this state of mind is produced by (or mixed with) affect and, according to Kant, because affects are "blind" (that is, they can lead one astray),[15] enthusiasm "cannot in any way merit a satisfaction of reason" and thus cannot be considered authentically sublime (a mental disposition that immanently reveals our rational/ moral vocation). In short, enthusiasm is a mental state that is *deficient* in regards to the sublimity of mind that is the crux of Kant's theory. "Nevertheless, enthusiasm is aesthetically sublime" (CPJ, 5:272), as Kant writes. The "nevertheless" is important, particularly when interpreted in light of the "seems" in the above passage, for it indicates that Kant aims to make a clean break between the two principal forms of sublimity of mind, the Mathematically and the Dynamically Sublime,

---

[12] See Robert Clewis, *The Kantian Sublime and the Revelation of Freedom*, 88. I argued in Chapter 8 that Clewis's category was problematic at best.

[13] See Chapter 1 for a discussion of this term.

[14] Clewis notes (*The Kantian Sublime and the Revelation of Freedom*, 40) that Kant had expressed this idea in his *Essay on the Maladies of the Mind* (1764) (in Kant, *Anthropology, History, and Education*).

[15] Even if a (practical) end is first given by reason, Kant says that affect renders it blind in its "implementation" (CPJ, 5:272).

and the concept of the "aesthetically sublime" discussed in this section.[16]

The key to understanding enthusiasm, a term that, as noted above, recurs rather frequently in the Kantian corpus, is the concept of *affect*. In a footnote, Kant distinguishes affect [*Affeckt*] from passion [*Leidenschaft*]:

> *Affects* [*Affeken*] are specifically different from *passions* [*Leidenschaften*]. The former are related merely to feeling [*Gefühl*]; the latter belong to the faculty of desire, and are inclinations that make all determinability of the faculty of choice by means of principles difficult or impossible. The former are tumultuous and unpremeditated, the latter sustained and considered; thus indignation, as anger, is an affect, but as hatred (vindictiveness), it is a passion. The latter can never, in any circumstances, be called sublime [*erhaben*], because while in the case of an affect the freedom of the mind is certainly *hampered*, in the case of passion it is removed. (CPJ, 5:272, original emphasis)

Kant's point here is simply to show how enthusiasm, because it is based on affect rather than passion (*Leidenschaft*), can be considered aesthetically sublime. Affect involves an *intensity* of feeling that is spontaneous and momentary. Since it impedes mental freedom only temporarily, the "determinability" of the moral will is still *possible* (though *qua* aesthetic judgment it will never be actual). As an "inclination," on the other hand, *Leidenschaft* is completely incompatible with the freedom condition of sublimity and thus with morality; moreover, it does not possess the temporal intensity of affect that, since Longinus, has been the hallmark of the sublime.[17]

Clewis makes a good point, however, when he notes that if enthusiasm conduces only to the aesthetically sublime and not to the sublime proper, on account of its dependence on affect, then how are we to understand those passages in which Kant explicitly associates the feeling of the sublime (proper) with affect? For example: "The astonishment bordering on terror, the horror and the awesome shudder which grip the spectator in viewing mountain ranges towering to the heavens, deep ravines and the raging torrents in them, deeply shadowed wastelands inducing melancholy reflection, etc." (CPJ, 5:269). Although Kant generally prefers to describe the feeling of sublimity in terms of "admiration or respect" (CPJ, 5:245), he

---

[16] Clewis, however, seeks to show "how enthusiasm can be an aesthetic feeling of the sublime, and not simply elicit aesthetic experience in spectators or observers" (*The Kantian Sublime and the Revelation of Freedom*, 184). It is unclear in this instance whether Clewis aims to redefine Kant's concept of the aesthetically sublime to make it cohere with the sublime proper or to redefine the sublime proper to make it cohere with the concept of the aesthetically sublime. Either way he is arguing against Kant's manifest position on the subject.

[17] See Chapter 1. Interestingly, Kant does not mention the term *Rührung* (emotion) in this context, a term he uses elsewhere to characterize the effect produced by the sublime.

also notes in the Remark that admiration is a kind of astonishment, which Kant defines as an affect. Kant observes that a "noble" state of mind

> arouses not so much *astonishment* [*Verwunderung*] (an affect in the repre-
> sentation of novelty that exceeds expectation) as *admiration* [*Bewunderung*]
> (an astonishment [*Verwunderung*] that does not cease once the novelty is
> lost), which happens when ideas in their presentation unintentionally and
> without artifice agree with aesthetic satisfaction. (CPJ, 5:272, original
> emphasis)[18]

Admiration, which is here defined as *a kind of astonishment*, is thus closer to a moral feeling such as respect than to a *mere affect* such as astonishment.[19] Tellingly, this passage is actually an implicit critique of Burke,[20] whose empirical account of sublimity privileges pure affect (sensationalism). It will be recalled that Burke had stipulated that "astonishment" and "amaze-ment" are the effect of the sublime in the "highest degree"; whereas "admiration, reverence, and respect" are "inferior effects" (E, 53). Kant reverses this hierarchy, thereby putting his theory of sublimity at the furthest remove from a sensationalist aesthetics.

Kant describes enthusiasm more positively a bit later in the General Remark, citing the sublimity of the First Commandment ("Thou shall not make unto thyself any graven image . . .")[21] as the source of "the enthusiasm that the Jewish people felt in its civilized period for its religion when it compared itself with other peoples" (CPJ, 5:274). Kant suggests that the very idea of prohibiting sensible representation of the divine reveals a state of mind attuned to sublimity. Kant's observation that "perhaps there is no more sublime passage in the Jewish Book of the Law" recalls the Longinian idea of sublimity (*hypsos*) in the verbal arts; for "sublime passage" refers both to the content (the thought) and the expression (form) of the utterance. But Kant's main purpose in citing this example is to illustrate the idea of "negative" or "abstract" presentation:

---

[18] Kant makes a similar distinction in Part Two of the third *Critique*, the Critique of the Teleological Power of Judgment: "Astonishment [*Verwunderung*] is a mental shock at the incompatibility of a representation and the rule that is given through it with the principles already in the mind, which thus produces a doubt as to whether one has seen or judged correctly; but admiration [*Bewunderung*] is an astonishment that continually recurs despite the disappearance of this doubt" (CPJ, 5:365).

[19] Paul de Man sees the close etymological relationship between *Verwunderung* and *Bewunderung* as determining Kant's idea: "Is not the persuasiveness of the entire passage on the recovery of the imagination's tranquility after the shock of sublime surprise based, not so much on the little play acted out by the senses, but on the proximity between the German words for surprise and admiration *Verwunderung* and *Bewunderung*?" (*Aesthetic Ideology*, 89). But as I note above, the passage is in fact a commentary on Burke (E, 53), where no such linguistic proximity inheres.

[20] See Chapter 8.   [21] Exodus 20:4.

> There need be no anxiety that the feeling of the sublime will lose anything through such an abstract presentation, which becomes entirely negative in regard to the sensible; for the imagination, although it certainly finds nothing beyond the sensible to which it can attach itself, nevertheless feels itself to be unbounded precisely because of this elimination of the limits of sensibility; and that separation is thus a presentation of the infinite, which for that very reason can never be anything other than a merely negative presentation, which nevertheless expands the soul. (CPJ, 5:274).

More than any other, this passage has given rise to the so-called postmodern interpretation of Kant in recent discussions of cultural studies and critical theory, in that it seemingly describes how to think the limits of representation (the presentation of what cannot be presented), an idea that has had particular resonance in debates about the representation of the Holocaust and the condition of abstract art.[22] However, the passage is primarily about the *experience of unboundedness* that reveals our (natural) vocation for the infinite and the divine, not a meditation on the idea of the limits of representation.[23] The contemporary interpretations or uses of Kant's theory invariably neglect or deemphasize the idea of the "expansion of the soul," the sense of *sublimity of mind* that accompanies such a negative presentation, according to Kant.[24]

One detects in the idea of negative presentation the influence of Kant's Lutheran Pietism: the preference for a simple and unadorned décor in places of worship, in contrast to elaborate images and sculptural renderings of religious subjects, such as one finds in Catholic churches. In Kant's view, the direct presentation of the plastic arts can be an impediment to the attainment of a state of mind conducive to an authentically religious attitude (and thus to the sublime).[25] The fact that Kant mentions only Judaism and "Mohamedanism" in this context perhaps reflects a reluctance to bring up the sort of religious questions that had violently divided Europe and Germany itself for centuries.

Kant's motivation for discussing the idea of negative presentation also concerns morality: how can/should the moral law be represented? Applying the idea of negative presentation to the moral law, which is "deprived of everything that the senses can recommend it" (CPJ, 5:274),

---

[22] See Jean-François Lyotard, *The Differend* and *The Inhuman: Reflections on Time.*

[23] This said, I do not mean to imply that there is anything inherently wrong with using this passage to develop a theory of representation, as Lyotard does. Here it is a matter of understanding sublimity in the context of Kant's thought.

[24] However, Derrida's notion of "superelevation" appears to capture it well. See Chapter 10.

[25] See the last section of Chapter 11.

Kant asserts that when the idea of morality is laid bare (that is, without sensible support), one must take care to "moderate the momentum" of the imagination "so as not to let it reach the point of enthusiasm" (CPJ, 5:274). Nevertheless, we should still not "fear ... the powerfulness of these ideas, to look for assistance for them in images and childish devices" (CPJ, 5:274), which would appear to be an anti-Catholic statement.

Somewhat unexpectedly, Kant turns to the political implications of negative presentation and the use of images:

> That is why even governments have gladly allowed religion to be richly equipped with such supplements and thus sought to relieve the subject of the bother but at the same time also of the capacity to extend the powers of his soul beyond the limits that are arbitrarily set for him and by means of which, as merely passive, he is easily dealt with. (CPJ, 5:274–5)

The State has an interest in curbing the mental expansion induced by sublimity and enthusiasm: the maintenance of social order. By encouraging the use of images ("supplements"), the State thereby forestalls the negative presentation of the sublime and the (excessive) enthusiasm it engenders. Enthusiasm can thus be said to define the revolutionary state of mind: a combination of a blind affect with the idea of the good – or, more concretely, a mixture of idealism and violence. Although in this passage Kant appears to take a position against State authority, an authority that suppresses the free mental development of its citizens, Kant also implicitly cautions that enthusiasm can be used in a politically volatile way, such as during the French Revolution, the event that forms the historical backdrop to the writing of the third *Critique*.[26] Revolutions are the expression of an uncontainable and unstable enthusiasm. This is as close as Kant ever comes to detailing the political implications of sublimity in the third *Critique*, though he does make reference to the French Revolution in a late work, *The Conflict of the Faculties* (1798), arguing that, while "*enthusiasm* as such deserves censure" (CF, 7:86, original emphasis), presumably insofar as it leads to "misery and atrocities" (CF, 7:85), "genuine enthusiasm moves only toward what is ideal and, indeed, to what is purely moral, such as the concept of right, and it cannot be grafted onto self-interest. Monetary rewards will not *elevate* the adversaries of the revolution to the zeal and *grandeur of soul* which the pure concept of right produced in them" (CF, 7:86, my emphasis). In other words, enthusiasm

---

[26] Or in our own time: the mass crowds assembled before Hitler or Mussolini were certainly gripped by "enthusiasm" – toward the most morally reprehensible ends.

for certain ideals, namely the concept of right, is sublime and morally praiseworthy, even if some of the concrete effects of enthusiasm, such as the Terror of 1793, for example, are negative.

Finally, Kant addresses the seeming proximity between enthusiasm (*Enthusiasm*) and irrationality or madness, which he calls *Schwärmerei*. Kant asserts that the "pure, elevating [*seelenerhebende*], merely negative presentation of morality, by contrast [to political enthusiasm] carries no risk of *visionary rapture* [*Schwärmerei*], which is *a delusion of being able to see something beyond all the bounds of sensibility*" and thus a "delusion of mind [*Wahnwitz*]" (CPJ, 5:275, original emphasis). Kant sees this "delusion of mind" (which he contrasts with enthusiasm as a "delusion of sense [*Wahnsinn*]"), as "least of all compatible with the sublime, since it is brooding and absurd" (CPJ, 5:275). Thus not all "negative presentation" is sublime or refers to ideas of reason (or engenders mental expansion): "To rave [*rasen*] with reason" is anathema to Kant's Enlightenment view of religion (and of artistic genius, for that matter).[27] Given that *Schwärmerei* can also be translated in English as "enthusiasm," Kant should thus be read as distinguishing between enthusiasm and fanaticism,[28] the one motivated by *affect* and the other by *passion* (recalling CPJ, 5:272): "In enthusiasm, as an affect, the imagination is unreigned; in visionary rapture (*Schwärmerei*), as a deep-rooted, oppressive passion, it is unruled. The former is a passing accident, which occasionally affects the healthiest understanding; the latter is a disease that destroys it" (CPJ, 5:275).

Kant's sharp, condemnatory language in this section on *Schwärmerei* must be understood within its larger historical and intellectual context.[29] David Hume had written that "a gloomy, hare-brained enthusiast, after his death, may have a place in the calendar; but will scarcely ever be admitted, when alive, into intimacy and society, except by those who are as delirious

---

[27] This critique of *Schwärmerei* recalls Kant's denunciation of superstition/fanaticism in the Dynamically Sublime, where it concerned seeing threatening nature as the expression of God's wrath.

[28] Kant writes in the *Anthropology*: "Fanaticism must always be distinguished from *enthusiasm*. The former believes itself to feel an immediate and extraordinary communion with a higher nature, the latter signifies the state of mind which is inflamed beyond the appropriate degree by some principle, whether it be by the maxim of patriotic virtue, or of friendship, or of religion, without involving the illusion of a supernatural communion" (APP, 2:252, note).

[29] Charles Taylor notes that "much of the historical practice of Christianity ran afoul of the new ethic of purely immanent human good: all striving for something beyond this, be it monasticism, or the life of contemplation . . . everything which took us out of the path of ordinary human enjoyments and productive activity, seemed a threat to the good life, and was condemned under the name of 'fanaticism' or 'enthusiasm'" (Taylor, *A Secular Age*, 263).

and dismal as himself."³⁰ Already in the 1760s Kant had remarked that "the enthusiast [*Schwärmer*] comes to believe that he can find all his phantoms [*Hirngespinsten*], and every particular sect its dogmas, in the Bible. It is not that they learn these things in the Bible so much as they read them into it."³¹ In the 1770s, Kant found himself opposing the counter-Enlightenment and proto-Romantic *Sturm und Drang* movement, whose ideological patrons were Kant's former student Johann Georg Hamann and his philosophical rival Johann Gottfried Herder.³² Kant thus seeks to carefully calibrate his own views on concepts such as enthusiasm and ecstasy (from the Greek *ekstasis*),³³ as evidenced in one of his unpublished lecture courses on anthropology (*Anthropology Friedländer* of 1775–1776):

> The state of mind in which one is beside oneself and, with regard to the passions, no longer has control over oneself, greatly transforms the clarity of our representations into obscurity. Thus through great joy or pain, the individual comes to be beside himself, and this is ecstasy, which signifies that state of mind in which the individual is beside himself and is incapable of realizing his actual state, since he has been carried away by the intensity of the inner representations, [and] where the intensity of the inner representa-tion brings him to the point that it dispels the intensity of the outer representation. The taste for the world of spirits is a part of this, where someone claims to have been sensible of the community of spirits. Such fanaticisms provide occasion for ecstasy. Whoever wanders about in his thoughts, without being conscious of the actual world, is dreaming, which is natural. However, whoever is beside himself, is a dreamer while awake, which is as harmful as sleepwalking. (LA, 25:509)

The sublime thus represents for Kant a *secularizing* concept, one that allows him to separate fanatical ecstasy from authentic transcendence, archaic from enlightened religion. In view of the risk of irrationality that the sublime and associated affects posed, Kant's challenge was to contain, within a rational outlook, "the inscrutability of the idea of reason" that "entirely precludes any positive presentation" (CPJ, 5:275).³⁴

In addition to "enthusiasm," the other major concept discussed in the General Remark is that of the "noble," which Kant initially describes as a

---

³⁰ Hume, *An Enquiry Concerning the Principles of Morals* (1751) (http://www.gutenberg.org/files/4320/4320-h/4320-h.htm, accessed February 8, 2015).
³¹ *Reflection* 313, quoted in Zammito, *The Genesis of Kant's* Critique of Judgment, 33.
³² Herder does in fact discuss the sublime. See Rachel Zuckert, "Awe or Envy: Herder contra Kant on the Sublime."
³³ I discussed this concept in detail in Chapter 1.
³⁴ This "challenge" is of course what has made the Kantian sublime fertile ground for poststructuralist theory.

mental state *without* affect: "Even *affectlessness* (*apatheia, phegma in sig-nificatu bono* [apathetic, phlegmatic in a positive sense]), in a mind that emphatically pursues its own inalterable principles is sublime, and indeed in a far superior way, because it also has the satisfaction of pure reason on its side. Only such a mentality is called *noble*" (CPJ, 5:272, original empha-sis). Interestingly, Kant does not qualify this noble state of mind as "aesthe-tically sublime" but as sublime *tout court*. This makes sense, given that it matches the mental disposition of the Dynamically Sublime. Only when it is suggested by artificial objects or literary works – "e.g., buildings, costume, a literary style, a bodily posture" (CPJ, 5:272, original emphasis) – does the idea of the noble give rise to a judgment of the aesthetically sublime.

Kant further develops his conception of the noble by comparing strong and weak affects. Nobility of mind is associated with the vigorous or spirited disposition, that is, with *heroic* qualities:

> Every affect of the *courageous sort* (that is, which arouses the consciousness of our powers to overcome any resistance (*animus strenui*)) is *aesthetically sublime*, e.g., anger, even despair (that is *enraged*, not the *despondent* kind). Affect of the *yielding* kind, however (which makes the effort at resistance itself into an object of displeasure (*animum languidum*)), has nothing noble in it, although it can be counted as belonging to beauty of the sensory kind. (CPJ, 5:272, original emphasis)

The terms "resistance" and "courage" certainly recall the Dynamically Sublime (particularly the image of the warrior). Like Burke (in his opposition between labor and languor), Kant associates weakness with the beautiful and strength with nobility and sublimity: "We have *brave* [sublime] and *tender* [beautiful] emotions ... a tenderhearted but at the same time weak soul ... reveals a beautiful side" (CPJ, 5:273, original emphasis). Kant also applies this judgment to specific literary genres. High literature, such as epic and tragedy, appeals to our elevated or noble disposition and is a privileged source of the representation of affects of the courageous sort; low art corresponds to the lower emotions (the languid emotions): "Novels, sentimental plays, shallow moral precepts, which make play with (falsely) so-called noble dispositions, but in fact enervate the heart, and make it unreceptive to the rigorous precept of duty and incapable of all respect for the dignity of humanity in our own person and the right of human beings" (CPJ, 5:273).[35] This statement echos

---

[35] In the *Anthropology*, Kant asks why the young prefer tragedy while older people prefer comedy: "The reason for the former is in part exactly the same as the one that moves children to risk danger: presumably, by an instinct to test their powers" (APP, 7:263). It will be recalled that Kant had remarked in the *Observations*: "*Tragedy* is distinguished from *comedy*, primarily in the fact that in the former it is the feeling for the *sublime* while in the latter it is the feeling for the *beautiful* that is touched" (O, 2:212, original emphasis).

the fusion of literature and morality in the 1764 *Observations*. The replacement of the epic by the novel and of tragedy by sentimental plays is, for the late eighteenth-century Kant, a sign of cultural degeneration – echoing the Longinian association of cultural decline with a lack of sublimity. Kant thus implicitly advocates for the restoration or reinvigoration of the sublime genres as the antidote to *petit bourgeois* literature.[36]

12.3 The artificial sublime: fine art, aesthetic ideas, and indirect presentation

The question of how Kant treats sublimity in artifacts divides into two aspects: (1) the question of sublimity in fine art, the arts of genius; (2) the question of sublimity in manmade structures that cannot be considered to be products of a genius-creator, such as the Pyramids, as we saw in the Mathematically Sublime. Both involve the problem of the "impurity" of a judgment of taste, since in the artificial object, whether an example of fine art or not, "both the form and the magnitude are determined by a human purpose" (CPJ, 5:252–3). In this section I treat principally the question of sublimity in fine art, although many of Kant's formulations about fine art also apply to manmade objects. (The question of sublimity in architecture was addressed in Chapter 10.)

The fact that the Kant of the *Critique of the Power of Judgment* rarely discusses how the sublime relates to fine art has been the source of much conjecture – and consternation – among commentators. Some have attempted to fill this lacuna by drawing on Kant's theory of genius and aesthetic ideas,[37] whereas others agree with Paul Guyer's assessment that "the experience of the sublime . . . does seem to be exclusively an experience of nature rather than of art."[38] Still others prefer a "minimalist" view.[39]

---

[36] In actuality, as Erich Auerbach has shown in his *Mimesis*, it is the realist novel of the nineteenth century that will bridge the gap between lofty and tragic seriousness and the representation of the everyday. See Robert Doran, "Literary History and the Sublime in Erich Auerbach's *Mimesis*."

[37] See the last chapter of Crowther's *The Kantian Sublime*, entitled "Sublimity, Art, and Beyond" and Budick's *Kant and Milton*, esp. 269–274.

[38] Guyer, *Kant*, 312. Similarly, Frances Ferguson observes: "Thus, although he can, with Burke, include both natural and artificial objects in the category of the beautiful, [Kant] restricts the sublime to human pleasure in nature" (*Solitude and the Sublime*, 4).

[39] "Kant does not deny a place to the sublime in fine art, though, in contrast to most contemporaries and, indeed, the whole tradition stemming from Longinus, he certainly tends to minimize it" (Allison, *Kant's Critique of Taste*, 337). Clewis cites Allison's view approvingly in *The Kantian Sublime and the Revelation of Freedom*, 116–125 (esp. 118). Few commentators make the kind of robust, positive argument that one finds in Crowther (*The Kantian Sublime*) and Budick (*Kant and Milton*).

While there are certainly obstacles to speaking about sublimity in art from the perspective of Kant's third *Critique*, it is fairly clear from his scattered statements on the topic, both in this work and in the *Anthropology from a Pragmatic Point of View*, that Kant did envision such a possibility, even if he does not theorize it in any sustained manner.

The main impediment to conceiving of sublimity in art from a Kantian perspective, it would seem, is formal: fine or beautiful art (*schöne Kunste*) is by definition *beautiful* art; it exhibits *purposive form* and is an object of taste; the sublime, on the other hand, at least in its Mathematical and Dynamical modes, involves a *contrapurposive* presentation (nonpurposiveness form or formlessness), that is, one of boundlessness or powerfulness respectively, and is thus not a proper object of taste (a judgment of simple pleasure). In the *Anthropology*, Kant claims that this "problem" is actually the solution:

> *Beauty* alone belongs to taste; it is true that the *sublime* belongs to aesthetic judgment, but not to taste. However, the *representation* of the sublime can and should nevertheless be beautiful in itself; otherwise it is coarse, barbaric, and contrary to good taste. Even the *presentation* of the evil or ugly (for example, the figure of personified death in Milton) can and must be beautiful whenever an object is to be represented aesthetically, and this is true even if the object is a *Thersites*. Otherwise the presentation produces either distaste or disgust, both of which include the endeavor to push a representation that is offered for enjoyment. (APP, 7:241, original emphasis)

The first sentence follows the basic theory of aesthetics outlined in the third *Critique*. But then Kant makes a rather startling volte-face by seemingly contradicting his initial statement, by setting up a strict dichotomy between the concept of sublimity in art (representation) and the concept of sublimity *tout court* (in nature): whereas in the aesthetics of nature the sublime is necessarily *opposed to taste*, producing complex rather than a simple pleasure (due to a contrapurposiveness for the imagination that is, by this very fact, purposive for reason), an apprehension of the sublime in art would have to *cohere with taste*, that is, with the pleasure taken in beautiful form. This thought is also echoed in the third *Critique*: "The presentation of the sublime, so far as it belongs to beautiful art, can be united with beauty in a *verse tragedy* a *didactic poem*, an *oratorio*" (CPJ, 5:325, original emphasis). Thus there would appear to be little or no daylight between the *Anthropology* and the third *Critique* on this question. However, if sublimity is "beautiful in itself," thereby nullifying the oppositional presentation of beauty and sublimity set out in §23 of the third *Critique* (emotional excitement versus calm contemplation, form versus formlessness, purposiveness versus contrapurposiveness), then how can this *sublimity-within-beauty* produce complex pleasure, since the presentation is no longer contrapurposive for the imagination? And if it does not produce complex pleasure, how can it be a matter of the sublime? Or should sublimity in art be considered a pseudo-sublimity, a pale reflection of the real thing? At the very least, it would seem that Kant is here proposing an exception to the oppositional relation between the beautiful and the sublime that Burke had codified in his *Enquiry*.

One possible way forward is to interpret sublimity-within-beauty as a relation between content and form.[40] On this reading, Kant appears to imply a kind of two-layered structure: on one level, the artwork, whether beautiful or sublime, exhibits purposive form and is judged according to taste; but within purposive form, the sublime content (and perhaps even sublime expression) nevertheless shows itself to be a kind of *redeemed* contrapurposiveness – contrapurposiveness redeemed by purposive form – without thereby losing the force that in nature allows the contrapurposiveness to produce the feeling of the sublime. The obvious awkwardness of conceiving such a coincidence of sublimity and beauty within the limitations of the Kantian-Critical perspective has led many commentators to turn to Kant's doctrine of "aesthetic ideas" for assistance, a possibility I will shortly consider.

Another way to proceed is to emphasize the analogy, in the above-quoted passage from the *Anthropology*, between sublimity and ugliness, a relation that was explored earlier in this study.[41] As a special kind of contrapurposiveness – that is, as a special kind of ugliness – sublimity, like ugliness, is rendered beautiful by its representation. In fact, the concept of mimetic art as transformative of a negative (contrapurposive) reality through representation boasts a long history in aesthetic thought.[42] Aristotle had written in the *Poetics* that "we enjoy contemplating the most precise images [*eikônes*] of things whose actual sight is painful to us, such as the forms of the vilest animals and of corpses" (1448b).[43] In the third *Critique* Kant observes in a similar vein:

---

[40] Indeed, as Crowther observes, "Kant has a tendency, when expressing himself in terms that point to a link between art and sublimity, to emphasize sublimity as a feature of content rather than sublimity of expression" (*The Kantian Sublime*, 160).

[41] In Chapter 9, I wrote: "Ugly objects divide into the simply contrapurposive and the purposively contrapurposive: that is, those that are simply ugly and those that are, by virtue of their specific contrapurposiveness (boundless limitlessness or threatening power), suitable to a 'purposive use' for our rational supersensible vocation (a judgment of sublimity)."

[42] See Robert Doran, "Mimesis and Aesthetic Redemption."

[43] For Aristotle, this transformation of the object occurs through the *technê* of mimesis and its cognitive value (recognition of relations of likeness). See Stephen Halliwell, *The Aesthetics of Mimesis*, 177–206.

> Beautiful [fine] art displays its excellence precisely by describing beautifully things that in nature would be ugly or displeasing. The furies, diseases, devastations of war, and the like can, as harmful things, be very beautifully described, indeed even represented in painting. (CPJ, 5:312)

The "furies" and "devastations of war" can be seen as ugly objects that might elicit the feeling of sublimity, all while being presented in an artistically successful or pleasing manner (that is, as conforming to a judgment of beauty/taste). Unlike Burke, who, as we saw in Chapter 6, thought that mimetic art "revealed its power" only when representing mundane realities, Kant contends, like Aristotle, that "art displays its excellence" precisely in those representations that transform the horrors of the world; for this is where art is tested, as it were, where its beautifying capacity is stretched to the limit. Whereas Aristotle had used visual mimesis (images, *eikônes*) as his paradigm for the assertion of mimesis's transformative effect, Kant is less sanguine about the capacity of the visual arts to bring about the necessary transformation of the (ugly) object. The qualifier "indeed even" with regard to painting indicates a certain mistrust of the visual. That Kant does not see verbal and visual mimesis in the same light is immediately confirmed when Kant asserts that an unredeemed ugliness arouses only "disgust/loathing (*Ekel*)" (CPJ, 5:312):[44]

> For since in this strange sensation, resting on sheer imagination, the object is represented as if it were imposing the enjoyment which we are nevertheless forcibly resisting, the artistic representation of the object is no longer distinguished in our sensation itself from the nature of object itself, and then it becomes impossible for the former to be taken as beautiful. The art of sculpture, since in its products art is almost confused with nature, has also excluded the representation of ugly objects from its images, and thus permits, e.g., death (in a beautiful genius) or the spirit of war (in the person of Mars) to be represented through an allegory or attributes that look pleasing, hence only indirectly by means of an interpretation of reason, and not for the aesthetic power of judgment alone. (CPJ, 5:312)[45]

Insofar as it asks us to enjoy the horrible object itself, rather than the (tasteful) representation, visual art is particularly prone to arousing disgust or loathing. This assertion echoes the above-cited passage from the

---

[44] For an exhaustive study of the relation between aesthetics and disgust, see Winfried Menninghaus, *Disgust: Theory and History of a Strong Sensation*, esp. 103–120 on Kant.

[45] The editor (Paul Guyer) notes that "here Kant appears to allude to the argument of Lessing's *Laokoon* (1766), which holds that pain or other forms of ugliness can be described in poetry but not represented directly in painting or sculpture, because beauty is the first law of the visual arts (see chapter 2 in *Laokoon*)" (Kant, *Critique of the Power of Judgment*, 382, n. 41).

Anthropology: "Otherwise the presentation produces either distaste or disgust, both of which include the endeavor to push a representation that is offered for enjoyment." But in that passage Kant also implied that, if not handled properly, *verbal* representation could arouse disgust as well. The proximity of the visual arts to nature, in particular sculpture, *necessitates* the use of allegory to present ugly or painful things *indirectly*. Since "aesthetic judgment alone" is not capable of grasping allegorical significance, such indirect presentation necessarily involves an "interpretation of reason," thereby demonstrating its proximity to the sublime. With regard to its transformative potential, indirect presentation thus appears to be more decisive for Kant than the "excellence" of artistic mimesis. Kant's preference for poetry is no doubt rooted in its penchant for indirect presentation (or what Burke called "obscure" images)[46] and concomitant stimulation of reason.

Thus the view that sublimity is *impossible* in visual art from a Kantian perspective is, I think, deeply flawed. As Arthur Danto expresses this view (in an article on the twentieth-century painter Barnett Newman):

> Since Kant was constrained to think of art in terms of pictures as mimetic representations, there was no way in which painting could be sublime. It could only consist in pictures of sublime natural things, like waterfalls or volcanoes. While these might indeed be sublime, pictures of them could at most be beautiful.[47]

But Kant's point is that while artistic representation *must* be beautiful, it *can at the same time* be sublime, though visual art, because of its (excessive) likeness to what it represents, must especially use indirect presentation. This suggests that sublimity in visual art may indeed have to be nonmimetic or at least paramimetic (to the extent that allegory resembles something),[48] thereby opening up a consideration of the possibility of sublimity in abstract art from a Kantian standpoint (as Lyotard has done).[49]

---

[46] "When painters have attempted to give us clear representations of these very fanciful and terrible ideas, they have I think almost always failed" (E, 64).

[47] Arthur C. Danto, "Barnett Newman and the Heroic Sublime," *The Nation*, June 17, 2002 (http://www.thenation.com/article/barnett-newman-and-heroic-sublime, accessed August 9, 2013).

[48] John Zammito holds that "for Kant art could not simply be *mimetic*. Its primary purpose was to *express* the supersensible" (*The Genesis of Kant's* Critique of Judgment, 289).

[49] "The current of 'abstract' painting has its source, from 1912, in this requirement for indirect and all but ungraspable allusion to the invisible in the visible. The sublime, and not the beautiful, is the sentiment called forth by these works" (Jean-François Lyotard, *The Inhuman*, 126). But sublimity is not tantamount to transcendence or artistic greatness in Lyotard's schema; it becomes instead a generic marker.

If there seem to be two conditions of sublimity-within-beauty, namely formal beauty (mimesis) and indirect presentation, we might well ask: if mere "indirect" representation is sufficient to transform the contrapurposiveness of the ugly object (or object conducive to sublimity), then why is formal beauty cited as the principal criterion for converting contrapurposiveness into purposiveness? Kant appears to see it as a case of either/or, given the phrase "allegory *or* attributes that look pleasing"; that is, indirect presentation or purposive form can redeem/transform the ugly/sublime contrapurposiveness of the object. With respect to the sublime, however, Kant would appear to suggest that, given its proximity to reason, indirect presentation is an *additional necessary condition* (that is to say, the artistic rendition of nonsublime ugliness requires only purposive form). The idea of indirect presentation can, with some caveats, be assimilated to Kant's idea of "negative presentation" (as described in the General Remark after §29), which, as we saw above, Kant defines as "abstract presentation" or the "presentation of the infinite" (CPJ, 5:274). One could perhaps stipulate that indirect presentation can be beautiful or sublime, whereas negative presentation is exclusively sublime, insofar as it involves a feeling of transcendence (the dual overwhelming-exalting structure of experience) connected to the sacred or morality. Negative presentation can thus be thought of as a subset or species of indirect presentation.

Indirect presentation is essentially Kant's doctrine of aesthetic ideas, which is discussed in the section following the above-quoted passage (§49). Kant defines the "aesthetic idea" as

> that representation of the imagination that occasions much thinking though without it being possible for any determinate thought, i.e., *concept*, to be adequate to it, which, consequently, no language fully attains or can make intelligible. – One readily sees that it is the counterpart (pendant) of an *idea of reason*, which is, conversely, a concept to which no *intuition* (representation of the imagination) can be adequate. (CPJ, 5:314)

This initial definition offers little support for the idea of sublimity in artworks. Sublimity pertains to the ideas of reason, but the aesthetic idea seems to concern only the inadequacy of concepts for a presentation of the imagination – that is, the indeterminate concepts of reflective judgment, which could be a matter of beauty or sublimity. Indeed, Kant states that "beauty (whether it be beauty of nature or of art) can in general be called the *expression* of aesthetic ideas" (CPJ, 5:320, original emphasis). Thus the doctrine of aesthetic ideas does not pertain exclusively to art (as some assume), even if it appears to be more helpful in or appropriate to discussions of art (especially poetry).

Kant then muddies the waters by describing a much more intimate relation between aesthetic and rational ideas:

> One can call such representations *ideas*: on the one hand because they at least strive toward something lying beyond the bounds of experience, and thus seek to approximate a presentation of concepts of reason (of intellectual ideas), which gives them the appearance of objective reality.... The poet ventures to make sensible rational ideas of invisible beings, the kingdom of the blessed, the kingdom of hell, eternity, creation, etc., as well as to make that of which there are examples in experience, e.g., death, envy, and all sorts of vices, as well as love, fame, etc., sensible beyond the limits of experience, with a completeness that goes beyond anything of which there is an example in nature, by means of an imagination that emulates the precedent of reason in attaining to a maximum; and it is really the art of poetry in which the faculty of aesthetic ideas can reveal itself in its full measure. (CPJ, 5:314, original emphasis)

There is a great deal in this passage that connotes sublimity: the striving "toward something lying beyond the bounds of experience"; the idea of imagination emulating reason's drive to "attain to a maximum";[50] the nexus between rational or supersensible ideas (the source of sublimity) and poetry (which Kant considered the greatest of the fine arts and thus the art with the greatest capacity for sublimity);[51] the allusions to Milton's *Paradise Lost* ("the kingdom of the blessed, the kingdom of hell"),[52] which Kant considered a model of sublimity itself.[53] In short, the aesthetic idea is the aesthetic presentation of an idea of reason, an idea that is "beyond experience," both in the sense of not being part of the natural-phenomenal world ("invisible beings," and so on, essentially what John Dennis had called "Religious Ideas," referring paradigmatically, like Kant, to *Paradise*

---

[50] See Chapter 10.

[51] Indeed, Kant's description of poetry resembles in many respects his description of the sublime: "The art of poetry (which owes its origin almost entirely to genius, and will be guided least by precept or example) claims the highest rank of all. It *expands the mind* by setting the imagination free and presenting, within the limits of a given concept and among the *unbounded* manifold of forms possibly agreeing with it, the one that connects its presentation with a fullness of thought to which *no linguistic expression is fully adequate*, and thus *elevates* itself aesthetically to the *realm of ideas*" (CPJ, 5:326, my emphasis).

[52] In the *Observations* Kant had spoken of the sublimity of "the description of the kingdom of hell by Milton" (O, 2:208). One wonders, in fact, just how much Kant's views on sublimity in poetry really changed from 1764 to 1790, despite all the revolutions in his thought.

[53] Budick observes that "in §49 Kant builds on the unique status of Milton's poetry in contemporary German culture" and that "for Kant Milton is the exemplary modern original genius of the sublime" (*Kant and Milton*, 255, 257).

Lost)[54] and in the sense of having a "completeness" that goes beyond nature. The passage would thus seem to support the view that sublime poetry allows us to experience the supersensible in an analogous manner to the sublime in nature: for just as sublimity in nature was based on a finite presentation of infinity,[55] sublimity in art (exemplarily in poetry) is based on a (sensible) image of a (nonsensible) rational idea, that is, a poetic *figure* (an indirect presentation). Moreover, the fact that an aesthetic idea (as expressed in art) is both beautiful (purposive form, taste) and relates to rational ideas (the sublime) would seem to comport with – and perhaps even account for – the notion of sublimity-within-beauty. In other words, the aesthetic idea can be a matter of the beautiful *tout court* or of sublimity-within-beauty, depending on whether, or the extent to which, it "seek[s] to approximate a presentation of concepts of reason." Poetry has more of a capacity for sublimity, then, since it is "the art of poetry in which the faculty of aesthetic ideas can reveal itself *in its full measure*" (my emphasis).

Allison, however, feels that many interpreters, in wishing to assimilate the doctrine of aesthetic ideas to the sublime, have ignored "the deep differences between the actual operation of the imagination in the two cases." According to Allison, the imagination "in the case of the beautiful and its expression of aesthetic ideas . . . points to the supersensible in virtue of its being, as it were, too rich for the understanding"; in this case, the imagination is "overly purposive," which contrasts with the sublime proper (the Mathematically and Dynamically Sublime), where it is a matter of the "contrapurposiveness of the imagination, its *inability* to realize the demands of reason, that accounts for the manner in which it points to the supersensible."[56] We should note first that Allison, in this instance, does not consider Kant's idea of poetic sublimity (Milton), as articulated in the *Anthropology* (7:241) as well as in the third *Critique* (CPJ, 5:314, 325). With regard to Allison's specific point, that one must distinguish the "overly purposive" from the "contrapurposive," Allison assumes that one judges sublimity in nature in the same manner as sublimity in art. However, if sublimity in art is conditioned by beauty, the idea of the "contrapurposiveness of the imagination" is not a relevant criterion. One can, of course, ask if the experience of sublimity in art is somehow deficient or secondary vis-à-vis sublimity in nature,[57] but this is no

---

[54] See Chapter 5.   [55] See Chapter 10.
[56] Allison, *Kant's Theory of Taste*, 341, original emphasis.
[57] Clewis makes a good point when he writes that "it would be inconsistent for Kant to hold that the sublime in general can reveal human freedom but that the sublime in art cannot" (*The Kantian Sublime and the Revelation of Freedom*, 118).

more problematic than the question of the relation between natural and artistic beauty (namely, the question of the "purity" of aesthetic judgment, adherent versus free beauty, and so on).

To better understand how the doctrine of aesthetic ideas might be applied to a specific case, let us turn to the most clear-cut example of sublimity in the verbal arts in the *Critique of the Power of Judgment*:

> Perhaps nothing more sublime has ever been said, or any thought more sublimely expressed, than in the inscription over the temple of *Isis* (*Mother Nature*): "I am all that is, that was and that will be, and my veil no mortal has removed." *Segner* made use of this idea by means of a vignette, *rich in sense*, placed at the beginning of his theory of nature, in order at the outset to fill his pupil, whom he was ready to ready to lead into this temple, with the holy fear that should dispose the mind to solemn attentiveness. (CPJ, 5:316, footnote, original emphasis)

This example, which comes closest to expressing a specifically Longinian perspective on sublimity,[58] would appear to militate against the idea that sublimity merely resides in the content of artworks, in the "what," rather than in the form ("sublimely expressed"). For just as Longinus establishes the primacy of the natural over the technical sources of sublimity, while nevertheless preserving the importance of expression, Kant too insists principally on what Longinus calls "grandeur of conception," namely Kant's aesthetic idea, to which the phrase "rich in sense" (Allison's "overly purposive") can be said to approximate (Longinus writes: "Real sublimity contains much food for reflection" [7.2]).[59] Finally, the idea of "holy fear" suggests a role for the Dynamically Sublime, with its mixture of religious and aesthetic aspects, in the judgment of sublimity in the verbal arts.

To sum up, then, it would appear that Kant conceives of sublimity-within-beauty as contrapurposive content redeemed by both purposive form and by an "interpretation of reason" provoked by indirect presentation (via visual or verbal tropes or figures). This conclusion would appear to be supported by a passage from the *Anthropology* that discusses the

---

[58] Indeed, Allison observes that "Kant is here, at least in part, appealing to the traditional rhetorical conception of the sublime as consisting essentially in an 'elevated tone' or 'high style,' that is, a sublimity in the manner of artistic depiction, rather than in the object depicted" (*Kant's Theory of Taste*, 338). Part I of this study has, of course, contested the idea of the "traditional rhetorical conception of the sublime."

[59] As Rodolphe Gasché writes: "Kant's definition of aesthetic ideas as representations that occasion much thought echoes Longinus's claim that true sublimity either touches the spirit of a well-read man 'with a sense of grandeur or leave[s] more food for reflection in his mind than the mere words convey'" (*The Idea of Form*, 236–237).

evocation of sublimity by *description* as opposed to direct perception, as in nature:

> The *sublime* is the counterweight [*Gegengewicht*] but not the opposite [*Widerspiel*] of the beautiful; because the effort and attempt to raise ourselves to a grasp (*apprehensio*) of the object awakens in us a feeling of our own greatness and power; but the representation in thought [*Gedankenvorstellung*] of the sublime by *description* or presentation can and must always be beautiful. For otherwise the astonishment becomes a *deterrent*, which is very different from *admiration*, a judgment in which we do not grow weary of being astonished. (APP, 7:243, original emphasis)

The first sentence seeks to attenuate the oppositional relation between sublimity and beauty *in general*, to make the idea of sublimity in art appear more palpable. But the main interest of the passage lies in the notion of sublimity-by-description (a formulation that indicates the verbal and the visual arts, the *representational* arts), which seems to reinforce the idea of beautiful form redeeming sublime/ugly content. In addition, the use of the term *Gedankenvorstellung* (representation in thought), insofar as it can be identified with an "interpretation of reason," would appear to confirm the reading offered above concerning indirect presentation. Discussing religious sermons and tragedy in the third *Critique*, Kant writes that "the sublime must always have a relation to the *manner of thinking*, that is, to maxims for making the intellectual and the ideas of reason superior to sensibility" (CPJ, 5:274, original emphasis). Thus, to the extent that *both* natural perception and artistic representation concern "ideas of reason" that conduce to sublimity (CPJ, 5:245), the effect of Milton's poetry, in terms of the sublimity of mind it elicits, and the actual perception of "the dark and raging sea" (CPJ, 5:256) would be equally powerful.[60] Indeed, while sublimity-by-description might imply that art is at one remove from sublimity proper, Kant also notes that sublimity-within-beauty produces the same *overall effect* as the sublime in nature, namely "admiration" – the term used in the third *Critique* along with "respect" (CPJ, 5:245) to denote the experience of sublimity. From this perspective, then, sublimity-within-beauty could not be considered qualitatively inferior to sublimity in nature, even if no specific mention is made of complex pleasure in the passage from the *Anthropology* (although, as I pointed out in Chapter 9, admiration, in Kant's usage, does imply an element of negativity). However, for his account

---

[60] In the *Observations*, Kant had similarly remarked: "The *sight* of a mountain whose snow-covered peak arises above the clouds, the description of a raging storm, or the *description* of the kingdom of hell by Milton, arouses satisfaction, but with dread" (O, 2:208, my emphasis). See Chapter 7.

of sublimity-within-beauty to be truly convincing, Kant would still need to address the question of complex pleasure in art.

***

This chapter has argued that the cultural perspective is an integral part of Kant's theory of the sublime, even if there are points of tension with his account of sublimity in nature. To this end, I have endeavored to make the following four points: (1) there is no unmediated experience of nature for Kant; that is, despite his philosophical preference for experiences of natural objects at the furthest remove from human intentionality, culture provides the basis for the experience of nature, especially in the sublime, but also in the beautiful; (2) Kant's theory of affects as states of mind judged aesthetically, that is, from an observer position, offers the possibility of judging sublimity in artworks as well as in cultural examples; (3) the idea of negative presentation reveals the cultural dimension of moral ideas, exemplarily, the role of the sublime in understanding the First Commandment and in the *representation* of the moral law – with the concomitant secular-religious ambiguity; (4) culture in the form of artworks, particularly exalted poetry, is a powerful stimulation to ideas; thus sublime art, sublimity-within-beauty, is more closely related to reason and to philosophical reflection than those artworks merely judged beautiful, as in Aristotle's famous dictum: "Poetry is more philosophical and more elevated [*spoudaioteron*] than history, since poetry relates more of the universal" (*Poetics*, 1451b).[61]

---

[61] The translator, Stephen Halliwell, notes that "*spoudaios* . . . denotes ethical distinction and gravity of tone" (*Aristotle* Poetics, *Longinus* On the Sublime, *Demetrius* On Style, 47, note f).

Conclusion

I have undertaken this exploration of the major and key theories of sublimity during the period of its initial flourishing (1674–1790), with a view toward understanding how and why this concept came to exert such a powerful and fascinating influence over modern thought. My effort to address this question led me to posit a certain unity of the discourse of sublimity, a unity based on the identification of a transcendence-structure: the paradoxical experience of being at once overwhelmed and exalted, humbled and elevated, an experience that recalls, and to some extent reconfigures, the religious or mystical experience of transcendence. I have thus sought to answer a historical question by elucidating a transhistorical structure – a sort of *longue durée* of the sublime.

The transcendence-structure is not, however, merely one aspect of sublimity, but rather its defining feature during the period of its emergence as a critical concept.[1] If I have chosen to concentrate on structural features, that is, on continuities and commonalities, rather than on ruptures and differences, it is because I wish to understand how the sublime held appeal in radically divergent contexts – in ancient rhetoric, neoclassical and baroque literary criticism, empirical-sensationalist psychology, and transcendental philosophy – without fundamentally changing its meaning, namely by maintaining its connotation of transcendence. My answer is that, by displacing religious experience into art and the aesthetic experience of nature, the sublime represents a form of resistance to the secularizing tendencies of modern culture, an effort that blurs the category distinction between the religious and the secular, the sacred and the profane, resulting in a kind of "religion without religion."[2]

---

[1] Just as for Erich Auerbach, the structure of the "mixture of styles" (the sublime in the humble – *sublimitas* and *humilitas*) is the defining feature of realistic representation as expounded in his *Mimesis: The Representation of Reality in Western Literature*. See Robert Doran, "Literary History and the Sublime in Erich Auerbach's *Mimesis*."

[2] See Jacques Derrida, *The Gift of Death*.

Indeed, one could observe certain parallels between my interpretation of sublimity as a secular version of religious transcendence and recent discussions of the "postsecular."[3] However, rather than a *return* of the (repressed) religious or sacred that the "postsecular" appears to indicate,[4] the sublime in the modern era instead represents an attempt to *reconcile* a quasi-religious notion of transcendence with secularizing tendencies: an accommodation expressed, for example, in Boileau's use of *fiat lux* and Dennis's use of *Paradise Lost* to assert a continuity between secular and sacred text through the sublime; in the idea of sublime terror in Dennis and Burke as a kind of sacred fear that indicates a relation to the transcendent in secular – poetic and natural – contexts; and in Burke's and Kant's use of the sublime to distinguish an enlightened from an archaic religious attitude (namely, a loving/benevolent versus a wrathful/vengeful God). In short, modern interpreters of sublimity sought to emphasize how art and nature can offer an *analogous* experience to that found in the authentically religious or mystical realm – with all of the conceptual ambiguity and equivocation that such a relation suggests.

By offering a unified and structural – but historically conditioned – conception of the discourse of sublimity from Longinus to Kant, I have sought to overcome the dichotomy between what are generally considered to be two distinct and opposed traditions of sublimity, the "rhetorical" and "aesthetic" – a dichotomy that has, in my view, obscured the significance of the sublime for modern thought. I have thus endeavored to show how the dual transcendence-structure traverses the domains of art and nature, the literary-rhetorical and the aesthetic-philosophical: specifically, how the "rhetorical" perspective on sublimity (in Longinus, Boileau, and Dennis) reveals itself to be a protoaesthetics and how the "aesthetic" view (in Burke and Kant – which was developed before the term "aesthetic" had any definite meaning) is deeply informed by exalted poetry (Milton) and by literary and rhetorical theory.

This structural approach has also allowed me to emphasize the constitutive role of the sublime in the development of modern subjectivity.

---

[3] See Jürgen Habermas, "Notes on a Post-Secular Society," 2008 (http://www.signandsight.com/features/1714.html, accessed December 16, 2013). See also Dominick LaCapra's recent (2013) book *History, Literature, and Critical Theory*.

[4] As defined by LaCapra: "The postsecular is neither the secular nor the religious or sacred but somehow both – or betwixt and between. It comes into its own in the attempt to re-enchant the world, even to evoke a sense of the uncanny, the epiphanous, the extraordinariness of the ordinary, indeed the miraculous endowed with grace, charisma, the gift of grace. The postsecular has a very labile, often rather confused relations with the aesthetic, notably in the enshrined 'trinity' of the performative, the uncanny, and the sublime" (*History, Literature, and Critical Theory*, 136).

For the most important corollary of the dual transcendence-structure is the relation of sublimity to the powers of the mind, in particular the idea of aesthetic high-mindedness (nobility of soul), which has its origin in Longinus's notion of *megalophrosynê*. This idea is clearly the source of both the moral meaning of sublimity and a related sociohistorical dimension. Hence my exploration of the role of the sublime in shaping attitudes toward the major social revolution of modernity: the decline of the aristocracy (the warrior-nobility) and the concomitant emergence of the bourgeoisie as the dominant social class. The modern sublime becomes, in the manner of the Hegelian *Aufhebung*, the site of a bourgeois appropriation of the heroic ethos of the old nobility, negating it on the level of class while preserving and affirming it on the affective-dispositional level. Moreover, this moral and democratizing aspect constitutes a cultural-critical perspective on modernity, a nexus inspired by Longinus's critique of cultural decline in the last chapter of his *On the Sublime*. Thus one cannot separate Boileau's use of the protobourgeois figure of the *honnête homme* (a few years after the Fronde) from his invocation of Corneille's *Qu'il mourût* (Die!) and the heroic death of (Cassius) Longinus; or separate Dennis's observation that the sublime, through "Religious Ideas," "ennobles those [emotions] which are commonly base and dejected" (CW I, 230) from his critique of the poetry of his time as "miserably fall'n" (CW I, 328); or separate Burke's description of sublimity as based on the instinct of self-preservation from his effort to define the ambitious bourgeois as a heroic, self-made man who elevates himself through arduous *labor*; or separate Kant's description of the Dynamically Sublime as a feeling of absolute moral resistance to a superior power (self-sacrifice in the face of death) from his critical contrast between the bourgeois "spirit of commerce" and the heroic fearlessness of the warrior.[5] In all of these instances, the idea of sublimity of mind grounded in the transcendence-structure is connected to cultural critique.

Another corollary of the transcendence-structure explored herein is the anthropological concept of human *telos*: the purpose of human life as a striving to go beyond limits or toward the divine.[6] Longinus remarks that sublimity reveals "what we were born for" (35.1). The *vocation for*

---

[5] However, as I suggest in Chapter 10, the Mathematically Sublime also contains an element of the heroic: the subject is raised to feel its *superiority* in its mental expansiveness, that is, "a feeling of our own greatness and power" (APP, 7:243).

[6] "Something higher than human is sought in literature" (Longinus, *On the Sublime*, 36.3). By this, Longinus means that sublimity divinizes the human, not that sublimity is somehow nonhuman, as Thomas Weiskel would have it (*The Romantic Sublime*, 3).

transcendence is thus revealed to be a natural human desire to outstrip oneself (what Barnett Newman calls "man's natural desire for the exalted")[7] – with all the attendant egalitarian-democratic and mercantilist--economic meanings that accrue to this concept during the modern period (as in Burke's notion of sublime *ambition*). Our common destiny as beings naturally oriented toward infinity, toward the transcendence of limits, finds its fulfillment in the social emancipation of the modern subject.[8] Hence Kant's notion of the "higher purposiveness" of sublimity: by asserting our subjective superiority in the face of overwhelming nature (the threat to sensibility both in terms of our imaginative capacity, the Mathematically Sublime, and of our instinct of self-preservation, the Dynamically Sublime), thereby affirming our vocation for the supersensible (the rational overcoming of sensibility),[9] Kant articulates a concept of secular transcendence – *immanent* transcendence – that is at once opposed and structurally identical to the religious variety. In short, the modern subject achieves autonomy *through* transcendence.

***

The multivalent significance of the transcendence-structure I have endeavored to elucidate in these pages has, I hope, revealed new meanings and connections by opening up the study of the sublime to an enlarged perspective, one in which the historical, religious, sociological, psychological, political, moral, semantic, and anthropological aspects of this concept are understood as fundamentally interrelated. Through this combination of structural unity and expanded perspective, I have thus sought to achieve a deeper understanding of how the sublime became a key concept in modern critical thought and of why it continues to fascinate, inspire, and perplex.

---

[7] Newman, "The Sublime Is Now" (1948), in: *Barnett Newman: Selected Writings and Interviews*, 173.
[8] In our own time, technology would appear to be the privileged figure of human self-transcendence: putting a man on the moon, and so on – but also the image of an apocalyptic self-destruction (nuclear war).
[9] Paul Crowther speaks of "an *experiential* idea of reason" in the Kantian sublime (*Critical Aesthetics and Postmodernism*, 136, original emphasis).

Bibliography of works cited

Abaci, Uygar. "Kant's Justified Dismissal of Artistic Sublimity." *Journal of Aesthetics and Art Criticism* 66, no. 3 (2008): 237–51.

Abrams, M. H. *The Mirror and the Lamp: Romantic Theory and the Critical Tradition.* Oxford: Oxford University Press, 1953.

Addison, Joseph. *Critical Essays from the Spectator.* Ed. Donald Bond. New York: Oxford University Press, 1970.

  Remarks on Several Parts of Italy: In the Years 1701, 1702, 1703. London: J. and R. Tonson and S. Draper, 1753.

Adorno, Theodor. *Aesthetic Theory.* Minneapolis: University of Minnesota Press, 1997.

Allison, Henry E. *Kant's Theory of Taste: A Reading of the* Critique of Aesthetic Judgment. Cambridge: Cambridge University Press, 2001.

Ankersmit, F. R. *Sublime Historical Experience.* Stanford, CA: Stanford University Press, 2005.

Ashfield, Andrew, and Peter de Bolla, Eds. *The Sublime: A Reader in British Eighteenth-Century Aesthetic Theory.* Cambridge: Cambridge University Press, 1996.

Aristotle. *The Metaphysics.* Trans. John H. McMahon. New York: Prometheus Books, 1991.

  On Rhetoric. Trans., notes, and appendices, George A. Kennedy. Oxford: Oxford University Press, 1991.

  Poetics. Trans. Stephen Halliwell. In: *Aristotle* Poetics, *Longinus* On the Sublime, *Demetrius* On Style (Loeb Classical Library). Cambridge, MA: Harvard University Press, 1995.

Auerbach, Erich. *Literary Language and Its Public in Late Latin Antiquity and in the Middle Ages.* Princeton, NJ: Princeton University, 1993.

  Mimesis: The Representation of Reality in Western Literature. Trans. Willard R. Trask. Princeton, NJ: Princeton University Press, 1953.

Axelsson, Karl. *The Sublime: Precursors and British Eighteenth-Century Conception.* New York: Peter Lang, 2007.

Baillie, John. *An Essay on the Sublime.* London: 1747. http://www.earthworks.org/sublime/Baillie/index.html.

Bäumler, Alfred. *Das Irrationalitätsproblem in der Ästhetik und Logik des 18. Jahrhunderts bis zur Kritik der Urteilskraft.* Halle an der Saale: 1923.

Le problème de l'irrationalité dans l'esthétique et la logique du XVIIIe siècle. Trans. Olivier Cossé. Strasbourg: Presses Universitaire de Strasbourg, 1999.

Barnouw, Jeffrey. "The Morality of the Sublime: Kant and Schiller." *Studies in Romanticism* 19 (1980): 497–514.

"The Morality of the Sublime: To John Dennis." *Comparative Literature* 35, no. 1 (1983): 21–42.

Beardsley, Monroe C. *Aesthetics from Classical Greece to the Present: A Short History*. New York: Macmillan, 1966.

Beck, Lewis White. *A Commentary on Kant's* Critique of Practical Reason. Chicago: University of Chicago Press, 1960.

Early German Philosophy: Kant and His Predecessors. Cambridge, MA: Belknap Press of Harvard University Press, 1969.

Bell, David. *The First Total War: Napoleon's Europe and the Birth of Warfare as We Know It*. New York: Mariner Books, 2007.

Bessière, Jean. *La littérature et sa rhétorique: La banalité dans le littéraire au XXe siècle*. Paris: Presses Universitaires de France, 1999.

"Le Sublime aujourd'hui: d'un discours sur le pouvoir de l'art et de la littérature, et de sa possible réécriture." In: *La littérature et le sublime*. Ed. Patrick Marot. Toulouse: Presses Universitaires du Mirail, 2007: 419–58.

Bloom, Harold. *The Anxiety of Influence: A Theory of Poetry*. Oxford: Oxford University Press, 1973.

"Poetry, Revisionism, Repression." In: *Critical Theory Since 1965*. Ed. Hazard Adams and Leroy Searle. Tallahassee: University of Florida Press, 1986: 331–44.

Bohrer, Karl Heinz. *Suddenness: On the Moment of Aesthetic Appearance*. Trans. Ruth Crowley. New York: Columbia University Press, 1994.

"Instants of Diminishing Representation: The Problem of Temporal Modalities." In: *The Moment: Time and Rupture in Modern Thought*. Ed. Heidrun Freise. Liverpool: Liverpool University Press, 2001: 113–34.

Boileau, Nicolas (Despréaux). *Oeuvres complètes*. Ed. Françoise Escal. Bibliothèque de la Pléiade. Paris: Gallimard, 1966.

Art poétique. Paris: Flammarion, 1969.

"Preface." Longinus. *Traité du sublime*. Trans. Boileau. Ed. and intro. Francis Goyet. Paris: Le Livre de Poche, 1995.

Bouhours, Dominique. *Les Entretiens d'Ariste et d'Eugène* (1671). Ed. Bernard Beugnot and Gilles Declercq. Paris: Champion, 2003.

La Manière de bien penser dans les ouvrages d'esprit. Paris: Sébastien Mabre-Cramoisy, 1687.

Brady, Emily. *The Sublime in Modern Philosophy: Aesthetics, Ethics, and Nature*. Cambridge: Cambridge University Press, 2013.

Brody, Jules. *Boileau and Longinus*. Geneva: Droz, 1958.

Budick, Sanford. *Kant and Milton*. Cambridge, MA: Harvard University Press, 2010.

Bullard, Paddy. *Edmund Burke and the Art of Rhetoric*. Cambridge: Cambridge University Press, 2011.

"Burke's Aesthetic Psychology." In: *The Cambridge Companion to Edmund Burke*. Eds. David Dwan and Christopher Insole. Cambridge: Cambridge University Press, 2012: 53–66.

Bullough, Edward. "'Psychical Distance' as a Factor in Art and as an Aesthetic Principle." *British Journal of Psychology* 5 (1912): 87–117.

Bundy, Murray Wright. *The Theory of the Imagination in Classical and Medieval Thought*. Urbana: University of Illinois Press, 1927.

Burke, Edmund. *A Philosophical Enquiry into the Origin of Our Ideas of the Sublime and the Beautiful* (1757/1759). Ed. Adam Phillips. Oxford: Oxford University Press, 1990.

A Philosophical Enquiry into the Origin of Our Ideas of the Sublime and the Beautiful (1757/1759). Ed., intro. and notes, J. T. Boulton. New York: Routledge, 1958/2008.

"An Appeal from the New to the Old Whigs" (1791). In: Edmund Burke, *Selected Writings and Speeches*. Ed. and intro. Peter J. Stanlis. Washington, DC: Regnery Publishing, 1963: 623–57.

Burnet, Thomas. *The Sacred Theory of the Earth* (1681/1684). Ed. Basil Willey. London: Centaur Press Limited, 1965.

Cherchi, Paolo. "Marino and the *Meraviglia*." In: *Culture and Authority in the Baroque*. Ed. Massimo Ciavolella and Patrick Coleman. Toronto: University of Toronto Press, 2005: 63–72.

Clery, Emma J. "The Pleasure of Terror: Paradox in Edmund Burke's Theory of the Sublime." In: *Pleasure in the Eighteenth Century*. Eds. Roy Porter and Marie Roberts. New York: New York University Press, 1996: 164–81.

Clewis, Robert R. *The Kantian Sublime and the Revelation of Freedom*. Cambridge: Cambridge University Press, 2009.

Costa, Gustavo. "Longinus' Treatment of the Sublime in the Age of Arcadia." *Nouvelles de la République des Lettres* 1 (1981): 65–86.

Costelloe, Timothy M., Ed. *The Sublime: From Antiquity to the Present*. Cambridge: Cambridge University Press, 2012.

Courtine, Jean-François, Michel Deguy, Eliane Escoubas, Philippe Lacoue-Labarthe, Jean-François Lyotard, Louis Marin, Jean-Luc Nancy, and Jacob Rogozinski. *Du Sublime*. Paris: Belin, 1988.

Of the Sublime: Presence in Question. Trans. Jeffrey S. Librett. Albany: SUNY Press, 1993.

Crimp, Douglas. "The End of Painting." *October* 16 (1981): 69–86.

Cronk, Nicholas. *The Classical Sublime: French Neoclassicism and the Language of Literature*. Charlottesville, VA: Rockwood Press, 2003.

Crowther, Paul. *The Kantian Sublime: From Morality to Art*. New York: Oxford University Press, 1989.

"Authentic Moral Commitment: Kant's Phenomenology of Respect." *Filozofski Vestnik* 13, no. 2 (1993): 43–57.

Critical Aesthetics and Postmodernism. Oxford: Oxford University Press, 1993.

The Kantian Aesthetic: From Knowledge to the Avant-Garde. New York: Oxford University Press, 2010.

Curtius, Ernst Robert. *European Literature in the Latin Middle Ages.* Trans. Willard R. Trask. Princeton, NJ: Princeton University Press, 1983.

Danto, Arthur. "Narrative Sentences." *History and Theory* 2, no. 2 (1962): 146–79.

"Barnett Newman and the Heroic Sublime." *The Nation*, June 17, 2002. http://www.thenation.com/article/barnett-newmanand-heroic-sublime, accessed August 9, 2013.

Darwall, Stephen. "Two Kinds of Respect." *Ethics* 88, no. 1 (1977): 36–49.

"Kant on Respect, Dignity, and the Duty of Respect." In: *Kant's Ethics of Virtue.* Ed. Monika Betzler. Berlin and New York: Walter de Gruyter, 2008: 175–200.

De Bolla, Peter. *The Discourse of the Sublime: Readings in History, Aesthetics and the Subject.* New York: Basil Blackwell, 1989.

Declercq, Gilles. "Boileau-Huet: la Querelle du *Fiat lux*." *Biblio 17* 83 (1994): 237–62. (Actes du Colloque de Caen Pierre-Daniel Huet [1630–1721]).

Delehanty, Ann T. "Mapping the Aesthetic Mind: John Dennis and Nicolas Boileau." *Journal of the History of Ideas* 68, no. 2 (2007): 233–53.

De Man, Paul. *Aesthetic Ideology.* Ed. and intro. Andrzej Warminski. Minneapolis: University of Minnesota Press, 1996.

Demetrius. *On Style.* Trans. Trans. Doreen C. Innes and W. Rhys Roberts. In: *Aristotle* Poetics, *Longinus* On the Sublime, *Demetrius* On Style (Loeb Classical Library). Cambridge, MA: Harvard University Press, 1995.

Dennis, John. *The Critical Works of John Dennis.* 2 vols. Ed. Edward Niles Hooker. Baltimore: Johns Hopkins University Press, 1943.

Derrida, Jacques. *La vérité en peinture.* Paris: Flammarion, 1978.

"Economimesis." *Diacritics* 11, no. 2 (1981): 2–25.

The Truth in Painting. Trans. Geoff Bennington and Ian McLeod. Chicago: University of Chicago Press, 1987.

The Gift of Death. Trans. David Wills. Chicago: University of Chicago Press, 1995.

Descartes, René. *Les passions de l'âme* (1649). Paris: Flammarion, 1996.

Dewar-Watson, Sarah. "Shakespeare and Aristotle." *Literature Compass* 1, no. 1 (January 2003–December 2004). http://onlinelibrary.wiley.com/doi/10.1111/j.1741-4113.2004.87.x/abstract, accessed, February 12, 2015.

Dickie, George. *The Century of Taste: The Philosophical Odyssey of Taste in the Eighteenth Century.* Oxford: Oxford University Press, 1996.

Dionysius of Halicarnassus. *The Three Literary Letters.* Ed. W. Rhys Roberts. Cambridge: Cambridge University Press, 1901.

Dionysius of Halicarnassus On Literary Composition. Edited with introduction, translation, notes, glossary, and appendices, by W. Rhys Roberts. London: Macmillan, 1910.

Doncieux, George. *Le Père Bouhours: Un jésuite homme de lettres* (1886). Geneva: Slatkine Reprints, 1970.

Doran, Robert. "Literary History and the Sublime in Erich Auerbach's *Mimesis*," *New Literary History* 38, no. 2 (2007): 353–69.

"Mimesis and Aesthetic Redemption." In: *Rethinking Mimesis: Concepts and Practices of Literary Representation.* Eds. S. Isomaa, S. Kivistö, P. Lyytikäinen, S. Nyqvist, M. Polvinen, and R. Rossi. Newcastle upon Tyne: Cambridge Scholars Publishing, 2012: 201–25.

"Imitation and Originality: Creative Mimesis in Longinus, Kant, and Girard." In: *René Girard and Creative Mimesis*, ed. Vern Neufeld Redekop and Thomas Ryba. Plymouth: Lexington Books, 2014: 111–22.

Dubos, Jean Baptiste (Abbé). *Réflexions critiques sur la poésie et la peinture* (1719). Paris: Ecole Nationale Superièure des Beaux-Arts, 1993.

Critical Reflections on Poetry, Painting and Music. With an Inquiry into the Rise and Progress of the Theatrical Entertainments of the Ancients. London: J. Nourse, 1748.

Duro, Paul. "Observations on the Burkean sublime." *Word & Image: A Journal of Verbal/Visual Enquiry* 29, no. 1 (2013): 40–58.

Egan, James. "Rhetoric and Poetic in Milton's Polemics of 1659–60." *Rhetorica: A Journal of the History of Rhetoric* 31, no. 1 (2013): 73–110.

Elias, Norbert. *The Civilizing Process:* Vol. 1: *The History of Manners*. Oxford: Blackwell, 1969; Vol. 2: *Power and Civility*. Oxford: Blackwell, 1982.

Ferguson, Frances. *Solitude and the Sublime: Romanticism and the Aesthetics of Individuation*. New York: Routledge, 1992.

Flory, Dan. "Stoic Psychology, Classical Rhetoric, and Theories of Imagination in Western Philosophy." *Philosophy and Rhetoric* 29, no. 2 (1996): 147–67.

Forsey, Jane. "Is a Theory of the Sublime Possible?" *The Journal of Aesthetics and Art Criticism* 65, no. 4 (2007): 381–9.

Fry, Paul. *The Reach of Criticism: Method and Perception in Literary Theory*. New Haven, CT: Yale University Press, 1983.

Fumaroli, Marc. *L'Âge de l'éloquence: rhétorique et "res literaria" de la Renaissance au seuil de l'époque classique*. Geneva: Droz, 1980.

Furniss, Tom. *Edmund Burke's Aesthetic Ideology: Language, Gender and Political Economy in Revolution*. Cambridge: Cambridge University Press, 1993.

Gadamer, Hans-Georg. *Truth and Method*. Trans. Joel Weinsheimer and Donald G. Marshall. New York: Continuum, 1989.

Gasché, Rodolphe. *The Idea of Form: Rethinking Kant's Aesthetics*. Stanford, CA: Stanford University Press, 2003.

". . . And the Beautiful? Revisiting Edmund Burke's 'Double Aesthetics.'" In: *The Sublime: From Antiquity to the Present*. Ed. Timothy M. Costelloe. Cambridge: Cambridge University Press, 2012: 24–36.

Gauchet, Marcel. *Le désenchantement du monde: une histoire politique de la religion*. Paris: Gallimard, 1985.

The Disenchantment of the World: A Political History of Religion. Trans. Oscar Burge. Fwd. Charles Taylor. Princeton, NJ: Princeton University Press, 1997.

La révolution moderne: L'avènement de la démocratie I. Paris: Gallimard, 2007.

Gerard, Alexander. *An Essay on Genius* (1774). https://archive.org/details/essayongeniusoogera.

Giacomini, Lorenzo. *Discorso del furor poetico* (1587). In: *Trattati di poetica e retorica del Cinquecento*, vol. 3. Ed. Bernard Weinberg. Bari: G. Laterza, 1972.

Gibbon, Edward. *The Decline and Fall of the Roman Empire*. Hertfordshire: Wordsworth Editions, 1998.

Gilby, Emma. *Sublime Worlds: Early Modern French Literature*. London: Legenda, 2007.

Girard, René. *Mensonge romantique et vérité romanesque*. Paris: Hachette, 1961.

Deceit, Desire, and the Novel: Self and Other in Literary Structure. Trans. Yvonne Freccero. Baltimore: Johns Hopkins University Press, 1965.

Mimesis and Theory: Essays on Literature and Criticism, 1953–2005. Ed. Robert Doran. Stanford, CA: Stanford University Press, 2008.

Goldthwait, John. Introduction. *Observations on the Beautiful and Sublime* (1764). Trans. John T. Goldthwait. Berkeley: University of California Press, 1960: 1–38.

Gould, Thomas. *The Ancient Quarrel between Poetry and Philosophy*. Princeton, NJ: Princeton University Press, 1990.

Goyet, Francis. "Le Pseudo-Sublime de Longin." *Etudes Littéraires* 24, no. 3 (1992): 105–20.

Le sublime du "lieu commun": L'invention rhétorique dans l'Antiquité et à la Renaissance. Paris: Champion, 1993.

"Introduction." *Longin, Traité du Sublime*. Ed. Francis Goyet. Paris: Le Livre de Poche, 1995.

"Longin, le sublime et la guerre." *Studi di letteratura francese* 22 (1997): 105–18.

"Raison et sublime dans le premier livre de l'*Art poétique* de Boileau." In: *La littérature et le sublime*. Ed. Partick Marot. Toulouse: Presses Universitaires du Mirail, 2007: 137–60.

Graziani, Françoise. "Le miracle de l'art: Le Tasse et la poétique de la *meravigla*." *Revue des Etudes Italiennes* 42, no. 1–2 (1996): 117–39.

Grube, G. M. A. "Notes on the *Peri hypsous*." *American Journal of Philology* 78 (1957): 355–74.

The Greek and Roman Critics. Indianapolis, IN: Hackett, 1965.

"Introduction." Longinus. *On Great Writing*. Trans. G. M. A. Grube. Indianapolis: Hackett, 1991: vii–xxi.

Guerlac, Suzanne. "Longinus and the Subject of the Sublime." *New Literary History* 16, no. 2 (1985): 275–89.

The Impersonal Sublime: Hugo, Baudelaire, Lautreamont. Stanford, CA: Stanford University Press, 1990.

Guyer, Paul. *Kant and the Claims of Taste*. Cambridge, MA: Harvard University Press, 1979.

Kant and the Experience of Freedom. Cambridge: Cambridge University Press, 1993.

Values of Beauty: Historical Essays in Aesthetics. Cambridge: Cambridge University Press, 2005.

Kant. New York: Routledge, 2006.

"Translator's Introduction." In: Immanuel Kant, *Anthropology, History, and Education*. Cambridge: Cambridge University Press, 2007: 18–22.

"The German Sublime after Kant." In: *The Sublime: From Antiquity to the Present*. Ed. Timothy M. Costelloe. Cambridge: Cambridge University Press, 2012: 102–17.

A History of Modern Aesthetics. 3 vols. Cambridge: Cambridge University Press, 2014.

Halliwell, Stephen. *The Aesthetics of Mimesis: Ancient Texts and Modern Problems*. Princeton, NJ: Princeton University Press, 2002.
  Between Ecstasy and Truth: Interpretations of Greek Poetics from Homer to Longinus. Oxford: Oxford University Press, 2012.
Hartmann, Pierre. *Du Sublime: Boileau à Schiller*. Strasbourg: Presses Universitaire de Strasbourg, 1997.
Hasselquist, D. Fredrik. *Reise nach Palästina in den Jaren 1749–1752*. Johann Christian Koppe, 1762.
Heath, Malcolm. "Longinus, *On Sublimity*." *Proceedings of the Cambridge Philological Society* 45 (1999): 43–74.
  "Longinus, *On Sublimity* 35 no. 1." *The Classical Quarterly* 50, no. 1 (2000): 320–3.
  "Longinus and the Ancient Sublime." In: *The Sublime: From Antiquity to the Present*. Ed. Timothy M. Costelloe. Cambridge: Cambridge University Press, 2012: 11–23.
  Ancient Philosophical Poetics. Cambridge: Cambridge University Press, 2013.
Heidegger, Martin. "*What is Metaphysics?*" (1929). http://www.stephenhicks.org/wp-content/uploads/2013/03/heideggerm-what-is-metaphysics.pdf.
  Being and Time: A Translation of Sein und Zeit. Trans. Joan Stambaugh. Albany: SUNY Press, 2010.
Henn, T. R. *Longinus and English Criticism*. Cambridge: Cambridge University Press, 1934.
Herrick, Marvin T. *The Fusion of Horatian and Aristotelian Literary Criticism, 1531–1555*. Urbana: University of Illinois Press, 1946.
Hesiod, *Works and Days*. Trans. Hugh G. Evelyn-White. http://www.sacred-texts.com/cla/hesiod/works.htm, accessed January 17, 2013.
Hipple, Walter John. *The Beautiful, the Sublime, & the Picturesque in Eighteenth-Century British Aesthetic Theory*. Carbondale: Southern Illinois University Press, 1957.
Hoffmann, Roald, and Iain Boyd Whyte. *Beyond the Finite: The Sublime in Art and Science*. Oxford: Oxford University Press, 2011.
Horace. *Art of Poetry*. http://www.gutenberg.org/cache/epub/9175/pg9175-images.html, accessed April 4, 2015.
Huet, Pierre-Daniel. *Demonstratio evangelica* (1672). http://books.google.com/books?id=Y68WAAAAQAAJ&printsec=frontcover&source=gbs_ge_summary_r&cad=0#v=onepage&q&f=false, accessed April 18, 2013.
  "Lettre de M. Huet à M. Le Duc de Montausier" (1683). In: *Mémoires de Daniel Huet*. Trans. Charles Nisard. Paris: Hachette, 1853: 275–91.
Hughes, Fiona. *Kant's Critique of Aesthetic Judgment: A Reader's Guide*. New York: Continuum, 2009.
Hugo, Victor. *Les Misérables*, vols. I–III. Paris: Le Livre de Poche, 1985.
Hume, David. *An Enquiry Concerning the Principles of Morals* (1751). http://www.gutenberg.org/files/4320/4320-h/4320-h.htm.
  "Of the Standard of Taste" (1757). http://www.bartleby.com/27/15.html.
Innes, Doreen. "Longinus: Structure and Unity." In: J. G. Abbenes et al. *Greek Literary Theory after Aristotle*. Amsterdam: Amsterdam University Press, 1995.

"Longinus, Sublimity, and the Low Emotions." In: *Ethics and Rhetoric: Critical Essays for Donald Russell on His Seventy-Fifth Birthday*, Ed. Doreen Innes, Harry Hine, and Christopher Pelling. Oxford: Clarendon Press, 1995: 323–33.

"Longinus and Caecilius: Models of the Sublime." *Mnemosyne* 55, no. 3 (2002): 259–84.

Kant, Immanuel. *Kritik der Urteilskraft*. Frankfurt am Main: Suhrkamp, 1968.

Anthropology from a Pragmatic Point of View. Trans. Victor Lyle Dowdell. Ed. Hans H. Rudnick. Carbondale: Southern Illinois University Press, 1978.

Critique of Judgment. Trans. Werner Pluhar. Indianapolis, IN: Hackett, 1987.

Religion and Rational Theology. Trans. Allen Wood and George de Giovanni. Cambridge: Cambridge University Press, 1996.

Critique of Pure Reason. Trans. Paul Guyer and Allen Wood. Cambridge: Cambridge University Press, 1998.

Practical Philosophy. Ed. and trans. Mary Gregor. Cambridge: Cambridge University Press, 1999.

Critique of the Power of Judgment. Ed. and trans. Paul Guyer and Eric Matthews, Cambridge: Cambridge University Press, 2000.

Anthropology, History, Education. Ed. Gunter Zoller and Robert B. Louden. Cambridge: Cambridge University Press, 2007.

Lectures on Anthropology. Ed. Robert B. Louden and Allen W. Wood. Cambridge: Cambridge University Press, 2012.

Kemal, Salim. *Kant and Fine Art: An Essay on Kant and the Philosophy of Fine Art and Culture*. Oxford: Clarendon Press, 1986.

Kennedy, George A. *A New History of Classical Rhetoric*. Princeton, NJ: Princeton University Press, 1994.

Kinneavy, James. "*Kairos* in Classical and Modern Rhetoric." In: *Rhetoric and Kairos: Essays in History, Theory, and Praxis*. Ed. Phillip Sipora and James S. Baumlin. Albany: SUNY Press, 2002: 58–76.

Kirwan, James. *The Aesthetic in Kant*. London: Continuum, 2004.

Sublimity: The Non-Rational and the Rational in the History of Aesthetics. New York: Routledge, 2005.

Kramnick, Issac. *The Rage of Edmund Burke: Portrait of an Ambivalent Conservative*. New York: Basic Books, 1977.

Kuehn, Manfred. *Kant: A Biography*. Cambridge: Cambridge University Press, 2002.

LaCapra, Dominick. *History, Literature, and Critical Theory*. Ithaca, NY: Cornell University Press, 2013.

Lessing, Gotthold Ephraim. *Laocoön: An Essay on the Limits of Painting and Poetry* (1766). Trans. Edward Allen McCormick. Baltimore: Johns Hopkins University Press, 1962.

Levine, Joseph M. *Between the Ancients and Moderns: Baroque Culture in Restoration England*. New Haven, CT: Yale University Press, 1999.

Litman, Théodore. *Le Sublime en France: 1660–1714*. Paris: A. G. Nizet, 1971.

Locke, John. *An Essay Concerning Human Understanding* (1689). London: Everyman, 1947/1993.

Lollini, Massimo. *Le muse, le maschere e il sublime: G. B. Vico e la poesia nell'età della "Ragione Spiegata."* Naples: Guida, 1994.

Longinus. *Dionysii Longini rhetoris praestantissimi liber de grandi sive sublimi orationis genere.* Ed. F. Robortello. Basel, 1554.

Dionysii Longini De sublimi genere dicendi. Ed. P. Manutius. Venice, 1555.

Dionysii Longini De grandi sive sublimi genere orationis. Ed. F. Porto. Geneva, 1569.

Dionysii Longini de Sublimi dicendi genere liber a Petro Pagano latinitate donatus. Ed. P. Pagano. Venice, 1572.

Dionysii Longini. . . De grandi sive sublimi genere orationis. Ed. G. de Petra. Geneva, 1612.

Dionysiou Longinou rhētoros Peri hypsous logou biblion: Dionysii Longini rhetoris præstantissimi liber De grandi loquentia sive sublimi dicendi genere Latine redditus hypothesesi synoptikais et ad oram notationibus aliquot illustrates. Ed. G. Langbaine. Oxford, 1636/1638.

Dell'altezza del dire. Ed. Niccolò Pinelli. Padua: G. Crivellari, 1639.

Peri hypsous, or, Dionysius Longinus of the height of eloquence. Rendered out of the original by J. H. Esq. Ed. and trans. John Hall. London: Daniel, 1652.

Dionysii Longini philosophi et rhetoris Peri Hypsous libellus, cum notis, emendationibus et praefatione. Ed. T. Faber. Salmurii, 1663.

Dionysii Longini De Sublimitate commentarius ceteraque quae reperiri potuere. J. Tollius. Utrecht, 1694. (First reprint of Robortello's Latin marginalia.)

Dionysius Longinus on the Sublime. Ed. and trans. William Smith. London, 1739.

Dionysius Longin vom Erhabenen: Griechisch und Teutsch; Nebst dessen Leben, einer Nachricht von seinen Schrifften, und einer Untersuchung, was Longin durch das Erhabene verstehte. Trans. Karl Heinrich von Heinecken. Dresden, 1737/1742.

Dionysii Longini De sublimitate. Ed. Benjamin Weiske. Leipzig: Weigel, 1809.

Longinus On the Sublime. Trans. H. L. Havell. London: Macmillan, 1890. http://www.gutenberg.org/files/17957/17957-h/17957-h.htm.

On the Sublime (1899). Ed., notes, trans., W. Rhys Roberts. Second ed. Cambridge: Cambridge University Press, 1907.

"Longinus" on the Sublime. Ed. D. A. Russell. Oxford: Oxford University Press, 1964.

On Sublimity. Trans. D. A. Russell. In: *Ancient Literary Criticism: The Principal Texts in New Translations.* Eds. D. A. Russell and M. Winterbottom. Oxford: Oxford University Press, 1972.

On the Sublime. Trans. with commentary by James Arieti and John M. Crossett. New York: Edwin Mellen Press, 1985.

On Great Writing (On the Sublime). Trans. G. M. A. Grube. Indianapolis: Hackett, 1991.

Traité du sublime (1674/1683/1701). Trans. Boileau. Ed. and intro. Francis Goyet. Paris: Le Livre de Poche, 1995.

Aristotle Poetics, *Longinus* On the Sublime, *Demetrius* On Style (Loeb Classical Library). Trans. Stephen Halliwell (Aristotle), Trans. W. Hamilton Fyfe and Ed. D. A. Russell (Longinus), Trans. Doreen C. Innes and W. Rhys Roberts (Demetrius). Cambridge, MA: Harvard University Press, 1995.

Dionisio Longino, Del sublime. Ed. C. M. Mazzucchi. Milan: Vita E Pensiero, 2010.

Longuenesse, Beatrice. *Kant and the Capacity to Judge: Sensibility and Discursivity in the Transcendental Analytic of the* Critique of Pure Reason. Princeton, NJ: Princeton University Press, 1998.

Lucretius. *De rerum natura.* http://www.gutenberg.org/files/785/785-h/785-h.htm.

Lyotard, Jean-François. *Le différend.* Paris: Éditions de Minuit, 1983.

The Differend: Phrases in Dispute. Trans. Georges Van Den Abbeele. Minneapolis: University of Minnosota Press, 1988.

The Inhuman: Reflections on Time. Trans. Geoffrey Bennington and Rachel Bowlby. Stanford, CA: Stanford University Press, 1991.

Leçons sur l'Analytique du sublime. Paris: Galilée, 1991.

Lessons on the Analytic of the Sublime. Trans. Elizabeth Rottenberg. Stanford, CA: Stanford University Press, 1994.

Macksey, Richard. "Longinus Reconsidered." *MLN* 108 (1993): 913–34.

Malm, Mats. "On the Technique of the Sublime." *Comparative Literature* 52, no. 1 (2000): 1–10.

Marin, Louis. "Le sublime dans les années 1670." *Papers on French XVIIth-century Literature* 25 (1986): 185–201.

"1674: On the Sublime, Infinity, Je ne sais quoi." In: *A New History of French Literature.* Ed. Denis Hollier. Cambridge, MA: Harvard University Press, 1989/1994: 340–45.

Marshall, David. *The Surprising Effects of Sympathy: Marivaux, Rousseau, Diderot, and Mary Shelley.* Chicago: University of Chicago Press, 1988.

Marshall, David L. *Vico and the Transformation of Rhetoric in Early Modern Europe.* New York: Cambridge University Press, 2010.

Martin, Eva Madeleine. "The 'Prehistory' of the Sublime in Early Modern France: An Interdisciplinary Perspective." In: *The Sublime: From Antiquity to the Present.* Ed. Timothy M. Costelloe. Cambridge: Cambridge University Press, 2012: 77–101.

McCall, Marsh. *Ancient Rhetorical Theories of Simile and Comparison.* Cambridge, MA: Harvard University Press, 1969.

McCloskey, Mary A. *Kant's Aesthetic.* London: MacMillan Press, 1987.

Meerbote, Ralf. Ed. *Kant's Aesthetics.* Atascadero, CA: Ridgeview, 1991.

"The Unknowability of Things in Themselves." *Proceedings of the 3rd International Kant Congress.* Ed. Lewis White Beck. Dordrecht: Reidel, 1972: 415–23.

Meier, Georg Friedrich. *Betrachtungen über den ersten Grundsatz aller schönen Künste und Wissenschaften.* Halle: Carl Hermann Hemmerde, 1757.

Mendelssohn, Moses. *Philosophical Writings.* Cambridge: Cambridge University Press, 1997.

Menninghaus, Winfried. *Disgust: Theory and History of a Strong Sensation.* Trans. Howard Eiland and Joel Golb. Albany: SUNY Press, 2003.

Merritt, Melissa McBay. "The Moral Source of the Kantian Sublime." In: *The Sublime: From Antiquity to the Present.* Ed. Timothy M. Costelloe. Cambridge: Cambridge University Press, 2012: 37–49.

Milton, John. *Paradise Lost* (1667/1674). http://www.gutenberg.org/cache/epub/20/pg20.html.

Mitchell, W. J. T. *Iconology: Image, Text, Ideology.* Chicago: University of Chicago Press, 1986.

Monk, Samuel H. *The Sublime: A Study of Critical Theories in XVIII-Century England.* Ann Arbor: University of Michigan Press, 1935.

Morris, David B. *The Religious Sublime: Christian Poetry and the Critical Tradition.* Lexington: University Press of Kentucky, 1972.

"Gothic Sublimity." *New Literary History* 16, no. 2 (1985): 299–319.

Murry, Penelope. "Poetic Inspiration in Early Greece." *Journal of Hellenistic Studies* 101 (1981): 87–100.

Nahm, M. C. "'Sublimity' and the 'Moral Law' in Kant's Philosophy." *Kant-Studien* 48 (1957): 502–24.

Nehamas, Alexander. *Virtues of Authenticity: Essays on Plato and Socrates.* Princeton, NJ: Princeton University Press, 1998.

Neuhouser, Frederick. *Rousseau's Theodicy of Self-Love: Evil, Rationality, and the Drive for Recognition.* Oxford: Oxford University Press, 2008.

Newman, Barnett. "The Sublime Is Now." In: *Barnett Newman: Selected Writings and Interviews.* Berkeley and Los Angeles: University of California Press, 1990: 170–3.

Nicolson, Marjorie Hope. *Mountain Gloom and Mountain Glory: The Development of the Aesthetics of the Infinite* (1959). Ithaca, NY: Cornell University Press, 1997.

Nietzsche, Friedrich. "Homer on Competition." In: *On the Genealogy of Morality.* Trans. Carol Diethe, ed. Keith Ansell-Pearson. Cambridge: Cambridge University Press, 1994: 187–94.

Norman, Larry F. *The Shock of the Ancient: Literature and History in Early Modern France.* Chicago: University of Chicago Press, 2011.

Parret, Herman. "From the *Enquiry* (1757) to the Fourth *Kritisches Wäldchen* (1769): Burke and Herder on the Division of the Senses." In: *The Science of Sensibility: Reading Burke's Philosophical Enquiry.* Ed. Koen Vermeir and Michael Funk Decard. New York: Springer, 2012: 91–106.

Partridge, E. *Origins: An Etymological Dictionary of Modern English.* New York: Macmillan, 1958.

Patrizi, Francesco. *Della Poetica* (1586). Ed. Danilo Aguzzi Barbagli. Florence: Istituto Nazionale di Studi sul Rinascimento, 1969–71.

Paul, H. G. *John Dennis: His Life and Criticism.* New York: Columbia University Press, 1911.

Pender, Elizabeth. "Spiritual Pregnancy in Plato's *Symposium*." *Classical Quarterly* 42 (1992): 72–86.

Perrault, Charles. *Parallèle des Anciens et des Modernes en ce qui regarde les Arts et la Science.* Paris: Jean Baptiste Coignard, 1688.

Peyrache-Leborgne, Dominique. *La poétique du sublime de la fin des Lumières au Romantisme.* Paris: Honoré Champion, 1997.

Phillips, Adam. "Introduction." Edmund Burke, *A Philosophical Enquiry into the Origin of Our Ideas of the Sublime and the Beautiful.* Ed. Adam Phillips. Oxford: Oxford University Press, 1990.

Pillow, Kirk. *Sublime Understanding: Aesthetic Reflection in Kant and Hegel.* Cambridge, MA: MIT Press, 2000.

Pinkard, Terry. *German Philosophy 1760–1860: The Legacy of Idealism.* Cambridge: Cambridge University Press, 2002.

Plato. *Complete Works.* Ed. John M. Cooper. Indianapolis, IN: Hackett Publishing Company, 1997.

Platt, Peter G. "'Not Before either Known or Dreamt of': Francesco Patrizi and the Power of Wonder in Renaissance Poetics." *Review of English Studies* 43 (1992): 387–94.

Pocock, Gordon. *Boileau and the Nature of Neo-Classicism.* Cambridge: Cambridge University Press, 1980.

Pope, Alexander. "Essay on Criticism" (1709). http://poetry.eserver.org/essay-on-criticism.html.

Pope, Alexander, John Gay, and John Arbuthnot. *Three Hours after Marriage* (1717). http://www.gutenberg.org/files/37667/37667-h/37667-h.htm.

Porter, James. *The Sublime in Antiquity,* Cambridge: Cambridge University Press, forthcoming.

Quint, David. *Epic and Empire.* Princeton, NJ: Princeton University Press, 1993.
Cervantes's Novel of Modern Times: A New Reading of Don Quijote. Princeton, NJ: Princeton, 2003.

Quintilian. *Institutio Oratoria.* Cambridge, MA: Harvard University Press, 1998.

Race, W. H. "The Word *Kairos* in Greek Drama." *Transactions of the American Philological Association* 111 (1981): 197–213.

Rancière, Jacques. *Aisthesis: Scènes du régime esthétique de l'art.* Paris: Galilée, 2011.
Aisthesis: Scenes from the Aesthetic Regime of Art. Trans. Zakir Paul. London: Verso, 2013.

Rapin, René. *Les Réflexions sur la poétique de ce temps et sur les ouvrages des poètes anciens et modernes* (1674/1675). Ed. E.T. Dubois. Geneva: Droz, 1970.

Refini, Eugenio. "Longinus and Poetic Imagination in Late Renaissance Literary Theory." In: *Translations of the Sublime: The Early Modern Reception and Dissemination of Longinus' Peri Hupsous in Rhetoric, the Visual Arts, Architecture and the Theatre.* Eds. Caroline van Eck, Stijn Bussels, Maarten Delbeke, and Jürgen Pieters. Leiden: Brill, 2012: 33–53.

Riado, Benjamin. *Le Je-ne-sais-quoi: Aux sources d'une théorie esthétique au XVIIe siècle.* Paris: L'Harmattan, 2012.

Roberts, Rhys. "The Literary Circle of Dionysius of Halicarnassus," *The Classical Review* 14, no. 9 (1900), 439–42.

Robortello, Francesco. *In Aristotelis poeticam explicationes.* Florence, 1548/1555.

Rorty, Richard. *Take Care of Freedom and Truth Will Take Care of Itself: Interviews with Richard Rorty.* Ed. Eduardo Mendicta. Stanford, CA: Stanford University Press, 2006.

Rousseau, Jean-Jacques. *Discours sur l'origine et les fondements de l'inégalité parmi les hommes* (1755). Paris: Flammarion, 2011.

Russell, D. A. "De Imitatione." In: *Imitation and Latin Literature.* Ed. David West, Tony Woodman, and Anthony John Woodman. Cambridge: Cambridge University Press, 1979: 1–16.

"Longinus" On the Sublime. Ed., intro., and commentary D. A. Russell. Oxford: Oxford University Press, 1964.

Ryan, Cressida. "Burke's Classical Heritage: Playing Games with Longinus." In: *The Science of Sensibility: Reading Burke's Philosophical Enquiry.* Ed. Koen Vermeir and Michael Funk Decard. New York: Springer 2012: 225–45.

Saint Girons, Baldine. *Fiat lux: Une philosophie du sublime.* Paris: Quai Voltaire, 1993.

Le sublime de l'antiquité à nos jours. Paris: Desjonquères, 2005.

Savary, Nicholas. *Lettres sur l'Egypte où l'on offre le parallèle des mœurs anciennes et modernes et de ses habitants,* Paris: 1786.

Schulte-Sasse, Jochen. "Herder's Concept of the Sublime." In: *Herder Today: Contributions from the International Herder Conference.* Ed. Kurt Mueller-Vollmer. Berlin: Walter de Gruyter, 1990.

Screech, M. A. *Ecstasy and the Praise of Folly.* London: Duckworth, 1980.

Shaftesbury, Anthony Ashley Cooper, Third Earl of. *Sensus Communis, an Essay on the Freedom of Wit and Humour* (1709). http://ebooks.cambridge.org/chapter.jsf?bid=CBO9780511803284&cid=CBO9780511803284A014.

Shapshay, Sandra. "Schopenhauer's Transformation of the Kantian Sublime." *Kantian Review* 17 no. 3 (2012): 479–511.

Shaw, Philip. *The Sublime.* New York: Routledge (The New Critical Idiom), 2005.

Shell, Susan. "Kant as Spectator: Notes on *Observations on the Feeling of the Beautiful and the Sublime.*" In: *New Essays on the Precritical Kant.* Ed. Tom Rockmore. Amherst, NY: Humanity Books 2001: 66–85.

"Kant as Propagator: Reflections on *Observations on the Feeling of the Beautiful and Sublime.*" *Eighteenth-Century Studies* 35, no. 3 (2002): 455–68.

Shiner, Whitney. *Proclaiming the Gospel: First-Century Performance of Mark.* Harrisburg, PA: Trinity Press International, 2003.

Shuger, Debora K. "The Grand Style and the *genera dicendi* in Ancient Rhetoric." *Traditio* 40 (1984): 1–42.

Sikes, E. E., *The Greek View of Poetry.* London: Methuen, 1931.

Sircello, Guy. "How Is a Theory of the Sublime Possible?" *The Journal of Aesthetics and Art Criticism* 51, no. 4 (1993): 541–50.

Smith, Adam. *Theory of Moral Sentiments* (1759). New York: Prometheus Books, 2000.

Spinoza, Baruch. *Theologico-Political Treatise* (1670). http://ebooks.adelaide.edu.au/s/spinoza/benedict/treatise/chapter7.html.

Spencer, T. J. B. "Longinus in English Criticism: Influences before Milton." *The Review of English Studies* 8, no. 30 (1957): 137–43.

Stendhal. *Le Rouge et le Noir* (1830). http://www.gutenberg.org/files/798/798-h/798-h.htm.

Stone, Lawrence. *The Crisis of the Aristocracy, 1558–1641.* Oxford: Clarendon Press, 1965.

Struever, Nancy S. "Alltäglichkeit, Timefulness, in the Heideggerian Program." *Heidegger and Rhetoric.* Eds. Daniel M. Gross and Ansgar Kemmann. Albany: State University of New York Press, 2005: 105–30.

Tasso, Torquato. *Discourses on the Heroic Poem.* Trans. Marialla Cavalchini and Irene Samuel. Oxford: Oxford University Press, 1985.

Taylor, Charles. *A Secular Age.* Cambridge, MA: Harvard University Press, 2007.

Till, Dietmar. *Das doppelte Erhabene.* Tübingen: De Gruyter, 2006.

"The Sublime and the Bible: Longinus, Protestant Dogmatics, and the 'Sublime Style.'" In: *Translations of the Sublime: The Early Modern Reception and Dissemination of Longinus' Peri Hupsous in Rhetoric, the Visual Arts, Architecture and the Theatre.* Ed. Caroline van Eck, Stijn Bussels, Maarten Delbeke, and Jürgen Pieters. Leiden: Brill, 2012: 55–64.

Trédé, Monique. *Kairos: L'à-propos et l'occasion (le mot et la notion, d'Homère à la fin du IVe siècle avant J.-C.).* Paris: Editions Klincsieck, 1992.

Walker, Jeffrey. *Rhetoric and Poetics in Antiquity.* Oxford: Oxford University Press, 2000.

Walsh, George B. "Sublime Method: Longinus on Language and Imitation." *Classical Antiquity* 7, no. 2 (1988): 252–69.

Watson, Gerard. *Phantasia in Classical Thought.* Galway: Galway University Press, 1988.

Weber, Samuel. *Benjamin's –abilities.* Cambridge, MA: Harvard University Press, 2008.

Weinberg, Bernard. "Translations and Commentaries of Longinus, *On the Sublime,* to 1600: A Bibliography." *Modern Philology* 47, no. 3 (1950): 145–51.

A History of Literary Criticism in the Italian Renaissance. Chicago: Chicago University Press, 1961.

"Une Traduction Française du 'Sublime' de Longin Vers 1645." *Modern Philology* 59, no. 3 (1962): 159–201.

Weiskel, Thomas. *The Romantic Sublime: Studies in the Structure and Psychology of Transcendence.* Baltimore: Johns Hopkins University Press, 1976.

West, David, Tony Woodman, and Anthony John Woodman, eds. *Creative Imitation and Latin Literature.* Cambridge: Cambridge University Press, 1979.

White, Hayden. *The Content of the Form: Narrative Discourse and Historical Representation.* Baltimore: Johns Hopkins University Press, 1987.

White, Luke, and Claire Pajaczkowska. *The Sublime Now.* Newcastle upon Tyne: Cambridge Scholars Publishing, 2009.

Wood, Allen. *Kant's Moral Religion*. Ithaca, NY: Cornell University Press, 1970/
2009.
   Kant's Rational Theology. Ithaca, NY: Cornell University Press, 1978/2009.
   Kant's Ethical Thought. Cambridge: Cambridge University Press, 1999.
   Kantian Ethics. Cambridge: Cambridge University Press, 2008.
Vardoulakis, Dimitrios. "The Play of *Logos* and *Pathos*: Longinus' Philosophical
   Presuppositions." In: *Greek Research in Australia: Proceedings of the Fourth
   Biennial Conference of Greek Studies*. Ed. E. Close, M. Tsianikas, and
   G. Frazis. Adelaide: Flinders University Press, 2003: 47–62.
Vasalou, Sophia. *Schopenhauer and the Aesthetic Standpoint: Philosophy as a Practice
   of the Sublime*. Cambridge: Cambridge University Press, 2013.
Verene, Donald Phillip. *Vico's Science of the Imagination*. Ithaca, NY: Cornell
   University Press, 1981.
Vermeir, Koen, and Michael Funk Deckard, Eds. *The Science of Sensibility:
   Reading Burke's Philosophical Enquiry*. New York: Springer, 2012.
Vico, Giambattista. "On the Heroic Mind" (1732). In: *Vico and Contemporary
   Thought*. Eds. Giorgio Tagliacozzo, Michael Mooney, and Donald
   Phillip Verene. Atlantic Highlands, NJ: Humanities, 1976.
   "De mente heroica" (1732). http://www.ispfab.cnr.it/article/Testi_Ed_Critica_De
   MenteHeroicaDef_Rev.
   The New Science of Giambattista Vico. Trans. Thomas Goddard Bergin and Max
   Harold Fisch. Ithaca, NY: Cornell University Press, 1968.
   La scienza nuova (1725/1744). Ed. Paolo Rossi. Milan: Biblioteca Universale
   Rizzoli, 1977.
Young, Edward. *Conjectures on Original Composition*. London: A. Millar and R.
   and J. Dodsley, 1759.
Zammito, John H. *The Genesis of Kant's* Critique of Judgment. Chicago: Chicago
   University Press, 1992.
Zuckert, Rachel. "Awe or Envy: Herder contra Kant on the Sublime." *Journal of
   Aesthetics and Art Criticism* 61, no. 3 (2003), 217–32.

Index

Astonishment, 1, 9, 12
  in Longinus, 10, 17, 28, 40–6, 71, 74, 130–1
  in Burke, 145–6, 164
  in Kant, 13, 195, 222, 239, 268–9, 284
Atticism, 30, 32, 83, 112
Auerbach, Erich
  Literary Language and Its Public, 36, 194
  Mimesis, 78, 113, 275, 286
Aufhebung, 288
autonomy
  of art, 16
  as subjective freedom, 17, 22, 190, 201,
    208, 289
  in the Dynamically Sublime, 211, 221, 246–7,
    251, 256, 258, 263
awe, 1, 8–10, 12–14
  in Longinus, 10, 17–18, 28, 41, 44–5, 84–6
  in Boileau, 103–4
  in Burke, 145–6, 148–50, 164, 167–8
  in Kant, 193, 222, 227, 239, 247, 268–9, 274
  see also thaumasion

Baillie, John, 7, 142
  An Essay on the Sublime, 33, 110, 145, 167
Baumgarten, Alexander Gottlieb, 7, 16, 143,
  175, 203
Bäumler, Alfred, 107
Barnouw, Jeffrey, 13–14, 18, 102, 124, 127, 136
Beardsley, Monroe C., 40
beauty (the beautiful), 1, 2, 4, 8, 10, 38, 41, 65, 79,
    84, 139
  Boileau's concept of, 116–17, 119
  Burke's concept of, 21, 143–4, 147, 150–1,
    154–5, 162
  Kant's concept of, 17, 23, 60, 175, 177, 179–84,
    195, 197–9, 202–4, 202–20, 221–4, 228, 233,
    235, 238, 240, 245, 254, 257, 258–9, 260–6,
    274, 275–85
Beck, Lewis White, 7, 175–8, 189, 194, 204, 205
Bell, David, 253–4
Berkeley, George, 185
Bessière, Jean, 3, 17–18, 22
Bible, the, 31, 132, 164, 226, 273
  and the debate with Huet, 13, 113, 115–20
Bloom, Harold, 3, 66–7
Bohrer, Karl Heinz, 47–48
Boileau, Nicolas (Despréaux), 2, 6–8, 13, 20–1, 30,
    31, 36, 41, 66, 97–123, 124, 128, 129–31,
    139–40, 175, 182–3
  debate with Huet, 13, 98, 109, 115–20, 134–5,
    157
  honnête homme (concept of), 20, 97, 108–10,
    114, 122–3, 142, 162, 288
  and *fiat lux* (Let there be light), 98, 109, 115–23,
    129, 140, 287

translation of Longinus, 4, 8, 11, 15, 20, 23,
    29–30, 34, 42, 61, 87, 100–2, 117
  Réflexions critiques, 48, 107, 114, 119, 121
  Preface to Longinus translation, 9–11, 102–22,
    142, 162
bourgeois, bourgeoisie, 12, 20–2, 288
  in Boileau, 97, 110, 122–3
  in Burke, 142, 159–64, 169
  in Kant, 241, 248, 251, 253, 255, 258, 275
Bouhours, Dominique, 7, 99, 106–7, 175
boundlessness, 86, 88, 94, 211–12, 216, 228, 276
Brady, Emily, 5, 6–7, 8
Brody, Jules, 3, 29, 102
Budick, Sanford, 5, 19, 65, 180, 260, 275, 281
Bullard, Paddy, 141, 143, 144, 154, 164
Bullough, Edward, 151
Bundy, Murray Wright, 69
Burke, Edmund, 2–23, 141–69, 287–9
  and Longinus, 43, 45, 55, 74, 88, 94
  and Boileau, 101, 110, 118, 123
  and Dennis, 124–5, 133–6, 139–40
  and Kant's *Observations*, 175–6, 178–83
  and Kant's *Critique of Practical Reason*, 192, 195
  and Kant's *Critique of Judgment*, 204, 213, 215,
    227–8, 233, 240–5, 250, 253, 255–6, 265, 269,
    274, 277–9
Burnet, Thomas
  The Sacred Theory of the Earth, 18–19, 86–8,
    126–7, 144, 146, 222, 229, 255

Caecilius of Calacte, 31, 32–3, 64, 72, 83
Catholic, 162, 270–1
Cato (the Younger), 99, 110–11, 122, 183
charm, 105
  in Longinus, 40–1, 47
  in Kant, 180, 183, 197, 198, 248, 264
Cherchi, Paolo, 104
Christ, 44, 78, 110, 113
Christian,Christianity, 12, 14, 43–4, 78, 87
  in Boileau, 98, 103, 113, 115–20
  in Dennis, 124, 127, 129, 136, 138, 140
  in Burke, 166–9
  in Kant, 191, 241, 257–8, 272
Cicero, 14, 30, 31, 47
civilization, 137, 159, 252–4
classic, classical, 32, 49, 54, 65, 93, 100
Clery, Emma J., 21, 142, 161–4
Clewis, Robert R., 3, 5, 186, 196–7, 266–8,
    275, 282
cognition, 71, 166, 175, 177, 185, 187, 203–5,
    208–9, 211, 217, 223
colossal, the, 222, 237–9
comedy, 36, 77, 133, 182, 274
communicability, 81, 209, 265
competition, 64, 66–8, 84–6, 93, 227